LOST CAUSES

CONFLICTING WORLDS
NEW DIMENSIONS OF THE AMERICAN CIVIL WAR

T. Michael Parrish, Series Editor

LOST CAUSES

CONFEDERATE DEMOBILIZATION & THE MAKING OF VETERAN IDENTITY

BRADLEY R. CLAMPITT

LOUISIANA STATE UNIVERSITY PRESS

BATON ROUGE

Published by Louisiana State University Press
lsupress.org

DESIGNER: Michelle A. Neustrom
TYPEFACE: Minion Pro

The author's research for this book was supported in part by the East Central University
Foundation. The author particularly thanks Gerald Williamson and Phyllis Danley.

JACKET PHOTOGRAPH: Civil War ruins in Hampton, Virginia. Photo courtesy of Prints and
Photographs Division, Library of Congress.

LIBRARY OF CONGRESS CATALOGING-IN-PUBLICATION DATA
Names: Clampitt, Bradley R., 1975– author.
Title: Lost causes : Confederate demobilization and the making of veteran
   identity / Bradley R. Clampitt.
Other titles: Confederate demobilization and the making of veteran identity
Description: Baton Rouge : Louisiana State University Press, [2022] | Series: Conflicting worlds:
   new dimensions of the American Civil War | Includes bibliographical references and index.
Identifiers: LCCN 2021046942 (print) | LCCN 2021046943 (ebook) | ISBN 978-0-8071-7716-7
   (cloth) | ISBN 978-0-8071-7765-5 (pdf) | ISBN 978-0-8071-7766-2 (epub)
Subjects: LCSH: Confederate States of America. Army—Demobilization. | Veterans—Confederate
   States of America—History. | United States—History—Civil War, 1861–1865—Veterans. | United
   States—History—Civil War, 1861–1865—Social aspects. | Veterans—United States—History—
   19th century. | United States—History—Civil War, 1861–1865—Psychological aspects. | Southern
   States—Social conditions—History—19th century. | Reconstruction (U.S. history, 1865–1877)
Classification: LCC E545 .C53 2022 (print) | LCC E545 (ebook) | DDC 973.7/4—dc23/
   eng/20211013
LC record available at https://lccn.loc.gov/2021046942
LC ebook record available at https://lccn.loc.gov/2021046943

CONTENTS

LOST CAUSES

INTRODUCTION

During the historic summer of 1865, after four years of service in the American Civil War, a young Confederate infantry private journeyed from a military prison in Maryland to his home in South Carolina. He arrived to an empty house and presumed, apparently correctly, that all residents had gone to church. Predictably and with enthusiasm, the weary wanderer continued his trek toward reunion. After all, the house of worship stood only about another mile away, an easy jaunt for such a hardened veteran and experienced traveler. "I expected them all to rush to me with glad and welcome exclamations but no, they stood aghast," he recalled. "Not a soul spoke. Why, they acted as if they were seeing a ghost, and in a way they were." According to that soldier's account, he had arrived at his own funeral. After a few moments, shock and tears turned to joy and laughter. The Palmetto State infantryman eventually enjoyed his long-sought homecoming.[1]

Could this really have happened? Perhaps some version of these events transpired. Although it strains credulity to believe that the young soldier actually stumbled upon his own funeral, many soldiers' families indeed presumed them dead, only to reunite with their loved one weeks later. This infantryman found himself a prisoner of war, unbeknownst to his comrades, who assumed that he had been killed in action and reportedly spread the news of his demise. He later wrote to his relatives from prison, but when he remained there weeks after the surrenders, the family purportedly assumed the worst. His service record indicates that he enlisted in 1861 at age eighteen, though census records suggest that his enlistment occurred closer to sixteen. His service record further documents one wound, at least one hospitalization, and two captures by Federal forces before his official parole in 1865.[2]

That South Carolinian's account bears some of the hallmarks of what might be deemed the traditional or popular interpretation of Confederate demobilization. The popular image of the homeward journey of Johnny Reb, advanced by soldiers at the time and in many accounts since, essentially reads something like this: Upon the conclusion of the war thousands of courageous Confederate veterans, penniless and starving, found themselves hundreds of miles from home. Through wit, tenacity, and camaraderie, with enthusiastic assistance from proud southern civilians, and without the benefit of a structured demobilization process enjoyed by their Federal counterparts, the soldiers scattered in all directions, typically on foot. Defeated but undaunted, Rebels then embarked upon journeys of epic proportions to reach their loved ones and experienced iconic homecoming moments with families and, in some accounts, loyal freedpeople who celebrated the return of the warriors in gray. Devastated by the failure of their cause, they nonetheless reappeared as conquering heroes of sorts for having resisted insurmountable odds and having bravely contested what would immediately be termed the greatest of lost causes. Indeed, a central tenet of Lost Cause ideology held that whatever else had been lost in the war, southern honor remained unsoiled.[3]

For some southern fighting men that description largely rings true. Thousands of Confederate veterans traversed scores and even hundreds of miles across a war-torn landscape with little assistance. They survived harrowing odysseys that most present-day readers could likely only imagine. However, Union and Confederate officers worked together to formulate and implement a system of Confederate demobilization that eventually imposed a modicum of structure onto the madness. This book examines the mindset of those soldiers as they began their journeys home, chronicles the creation and implementation of the system, details the logistics of the homeward journeys, documents and explains the chaos and lawlessness that swept so much of the immediate postwar South in the summer of 1865, and finally, scrutinizes the actual homecoming moment and the soldiers' thoughts and actions in the immediate aftermath of defeat. Ultimately, the demobilization experience reinforced existing bonds forged between Confederate soldiers in wartime and in the immediate aftermath of the conflict helped to establish the ideological underpinnings of the Lost Cause.

The men chronicled here, of course, survived the war, but perhaps only just. They remained in service until the bitter end, but had the conflict continued, these combatants might well have perished like hundreds of thousands of others. They would not have made those famous journeys home and would not have undergone the transformations discussed in the chapters that follow. That fact informs the wartime and postwar accounts of many of the soldiers under consideration.

This book presents a portrait of a specific group of people in a particular moment in time, and it examines Confederate soldiers during a brief period of transition, fundamentally important to their identities. Historian Eric J. Leed's classic study of World War I soldiers examines those combatants in part through the interpretive lens of liminality, the notion that men at war endured a transitory period in which they experienced certain rights of passage. What Leed describes as liminal rites for fighting men essentially placed soldiers in a temporary status between states, places, and conditions. In effect, soldiers in the Great War existed between classifications beyond the bounds of civilian law and society. Confederate soldiers-turned-veterans examined here occupied a similar liminal zone as they transitioned from war to peace.[4] Civil War historians have built a voluminous catalog of common soldier studies and a burgeoning literature on veterans.[5] This study examines the interlude between soldier and veteran and reveals how defeat and demobilization reinforced Confederate identity, and how Confederate veterans refused to submit to external forces that sought to redefine fundamental concepts of southern manhood.

Rank and file southern soldiers and officers of the highest order often voiced the popular, traditional interpretation of Confederate demobilization with colorful language and the occasional flair for the dramatic. A former private in a Mississippi infantry regiment recalled that the "soldiers were paroled as fast as possible and turned loose to get home the best they could. We had known nothing but war for four years, but the home-journey was the tug of war. No transportation, no rations, no money, ragged and heart-sick, with miles and miles between us and our home 'away down south in Dixie.' . . ." More famously, none other than that Rebel-turned-Republican, Lieutenant General James Longstreet, wrote that three days after the iconic surrender at Appomattox Court House, Virginia, the soldiers "stacked their arms, folded their colors, and walked empty-handed to find their distant, blighted homes."[6]

Although the modern reader might be tempted to dismiss such accounts as Lost Cause mawkishness or the ramblings of embittered, defeated Rebels, a close reading of these and other sources cited throughout this book reveals a far more nuanced story. Both of the above accounts derive from men who surrendered with the Army of Northern Virginia at Appomattox. As discussed later, the demobilization experiences of certain soldiers of that famed army most closely approximate the traditional, popular imagery of the ragged, penniless Rebel who traversed hundreds of miles with precious little assistance. To be fair, leaders at Appomattox began to consider the challenges of Confederate demobilization. However, the Army of Northern Virginia surrendered and started for home before Union and Confederate officers could implement a bona fide system, complete with rations and transportation passes for travel by water and rail. In other words, for certain segments of the Confederate military, particularly Robert E. Lee's famed legions, the Lost Cause version of demobilization stands essentially correct.

Other firsthand soldier accounts highlight the need for further consideration of every aspect of demobilization. One Texas private journeyed more than eight hundred miles from Georgia to his home in the Lone Star State. His story proves common enough, except that the twenty-one-year-old claimed to have completed most of that trek on crutches. He gratefully acknowledged aid offered by civilians along the way, admitted to the use of the railroad for part of the trip, and completed the final portion of the journey on the back of a borrowed mule. Still, the young cavalryman implied that he hobbled much of that distance on crutches. Perhaps he did exactly that, but the other elements of his account read quite like so many other typical narratives. Civilians provided material and financial support, he rode trains for at least some portion of the journey, and a beast of burden performed the remainder of the heavy lifting.[7]

Meanwhile, a former Tennessee infantryman recalled that he covered the distance of approximately ninety miles from Atlanta to Dalton in north Georgia on crutches, before the "Yankees then gave transportation home." That matter-of-fact description perfectly illustrates a common experience for thousands of individuals but also highlights the system that assisted most demobilized soldiers. As explained in chapter two, the system of Confederate demobilization that developed included substantial transportation assistance for thousands of southern veterans in the form of passes that permitted free travel on railroad cars and vessels on rivers or along the coasts. Civil War historians already know that Confederate soldiers availed themselves of rail and water transport whenever possible, but a common misperception holds that the war had left the southern rail lines in such shambles that the cars provided little meaningful assistance to demobilized veterans.[8]

In reality, as chapters two and three demonstrate, numerous railroads operated in the region, if intermittently, and carried thousands of Confederates for significant portions of their journeys. Rail travel often proved unsafe, to be sure, but it remained widely available. Moreover, many prisoners of war traveled hundreds of miles by rail across the North and portions of the South during their homeward journeys. One such soldier, a Virginia private who spent time in the infantry and the cavalry, ended the war imprisoned in Maryland. He covered most of the distance to his home by rail and saw no need to walk the remainder of the journey. "I then went to Winchester, but found no conveyance up the Valley. I determined, however, not to walk, and would sit by the roadside waiting for some one to come along in a buggy or wagon, so I could ride with them as far as they went." This strategy carried the resourceful young veteran the final sixty-eight miles to his parents' home.[9]

Such tales make for fascinating reading but collectively also provide opportunities for careful analysis. Although no obvious reason exists to *assume* dishonesty in any of the accounts cited above or throughout this book, perhaps certain instances, in particular the gallant Texan's odyssey on crutches, could be considered cases of embellishment by omission. Another veteran quoted from that frequently cited contemporary poem for Confederate soldiers, "Our Heroic Dead," written by a Rebel officer and destined to become a veritable Lost Cause eulogy for martyred southern combatants. The former Virginia cavalryman quoted, among other lines, those which read, "Yes, they grow 'taller' as the years go by, / And the world learns how they could do and die." The passage clearly reads as a call for enduring tribute to fallen Confederates as the years pass, though the modern reader with a sardonic but playful bent could be forgiven the impulse to interpret the line differently. Perhaps the verse could also be applied to the potential for embellishment by those who regaled readers with autobiographical war stories. One might think of individuals whose alleged juvenile athletic achievements grow greater with each passing decade.[10]

However, rather than dismiss postwar sources as worthless or hopelessly flawed, this study embraces the opportunity to employ both postwar and wartime accounts and, whenever, possible, compare the two. An iconic study of British soldiers' experiences in the First World War emphatically warns readers to consider the context of first-person accounts written from memory and concludes that "the memoir is a kind of fiction." The author of course referred not to literal fiction, but rather, the concept that memoirs represent the war experience as that individual recalled, or perhaps, chose to remember. What that study described as the "ritual of military memory" held that "Everyone who remembers a war first-hand knows that its images remain in the memory with special vividness." Here again, the issue remains not necessarily whether the veteran recalled each experience correctly, but rather that certain incidents—moments of gaiety and pleasure or acts of cowardice and cruelty—conjured more powerful mental images than others and thus might be more or less likely to grace the pages of the memoir. Thus Civil War memoirs and regimental histories cited throughout this study themselves constitute historical artifacts and teach us as much about the soldiers' self-image as they do about the actual conflict.[11]

Civil War historians virtually never confront the challenge of a dearth of sources. In this case, however, postwar writings that addressed relevant aspects of demobilization provided an essential boost to the sample size. After all, this analysis examines not Civil War or even Confederate soldiers overall, but Confederates still under arms at the end of the war who wrote about the issues under consideration. Thus a challenge became an interpretive opportunity through the inclusion of postwar accounts.

At times the book highlights and explains consistencies and discrepancies between wartime sources such as diaries and letters and postwar accounts found in memoirs, regimental histories, and veteran questionnaires. To cite just one example, postwar authors generally did not appear more patriotic and determined to continue the fight amid rumors of overall defeat but almost always proved more verbose and frequently more philosophical about the meaning of the war. Postwar writers had the time to compose as much as they pleased, the benefit of years to reflect on their service, and potentially the desire to manipulate posterity's perception of them. Such accounts naturally drew inspiration in part from experiences with Reconstruction or conceivably later by a spirit of reconciliation. Wartime accounts in general reveal equal Rebel dedication but tended to be less effusive or philosophical, and more focused on immediate, real-world concerns such as survival and daily life after defeat. Circumstances of necessity dictated such differences. Prisoners of war had time on their hands and their lengthy narratives often reflect that fact. However, other wartime writers might have scribbled a brief diary entry in a crowded train depot or under a tree while waiting out the rain.

Regardless of the date of composition, firsthand soldier accounts must be examined with a careful eye, on a case-by-case basis, and analyzed to create a collective portrait. Careful, critical reading differs from skeptical or cynical dismissal of the sources as sentimental, self-serving tripe. Even in instances when the source reads as exactly that, the historian must still consider that account and determine its place in the story of demobilized Confederate soldiers. (For further discussion of sources and methodology see the Appendix.)

One of the most surreal historic moments in American history provides the context for Confederate soldiers' demobilization, homeward journeys, and return to civilian life. The examination of Confederate demobilization commences within the period of several weeks during which the country simply drifted along during the final days of its most traumatic and transformative event. Certain Confederate armies had surrendered, yet others remained in the field. Abraham Lincoln had been assassinated. Though practically over, the war officially still raged. The United States government had enacted no official plan for Reconstruction, and thousands of square miles of territory in the South witnessed utter lawlessness. In many areas no authority existed at all. The Confederate government had been effectively destroyed, its president and cabinet were in flight from the fallen capital, certain state governments had collapsed, and many military units had disintegrated or had degenerated into armed mobs. That dangerous chaos awaited demobilized southern soldiers.

Confederates who marched home in the spring and summer of 1865 had survived severe trauma—combat, camp life, privations, homesickness, death of comrades, destruction of homelands—and all in defeat. They had endured the crucible of war and now confronted the unknown. That uncertain future that threatened Confederate soldiers, suddenly civilians again, weighed heavy on their minds throughout the entire period covered in this study.

The story of Confederate demobilization logically begins with the mental state of the individuals in question. Chapter one analyzes the combatants' mind-set at the time of capitulation and examines consistencies and discrepancies between wartime and postwar accounts. When did they admit overall defeat and did that vary by army or region? For those who insisted on continued resistance, how did they propose to prolong the war effort? Predictably, many of these men remained angry and determined to continue resistance. After all, these men held the line, under arms, prepared to fight. So until a string of historic events in April and May 1865, of course most of them still believed in and supported the Confederate States of America to some degree. Though not the average southerner in this regard by that late in the conflict, they certainly typified the average Rebels who remained in the ranks.

Once Johnny Rebs accepted the failure of the Confederate cause, soldiers expressed shock and devastation, though a relative few claimed to have anticipated the demise of the southern republic. Others evinced anger, humiliation, and even relief, though the outward manifestation of relief could prove problematic in the presence of comrades, and created a sense of guilt even among those who kept such sentiments to themselves. Some inevitably pondered whether the horrific death toll and widespread destruction had been in vain. Most of those examined here, however, denied the futility of their service. Rather, expressions of pride and defiance proved common, reinforced by adamant declarations that Confederate soldiers and the South in general had served a noble cause. Moreover, individual Confederates at the end of the war and years later often insisted on informing readers that they had remained under arms until the bitter end and thus had performed their duty. In other words, they not only did their duty, they wanted credit for having done so. Once the certainty of defeat surpassed all reasonable doubt, and with his spirits uplifted by that realization, the typical Confederate veteran's thoughts turned to the well-being of family, and he finally, mercifully, marched toward home. Husbands and fathers among the veterans rushed home as rapidly as possible to resume the masculine role of provider for those they cherished most.

An excellent recent study of the emotional worlds of southern men, written by James J. Broomall, posits that Confederate soldiers created emotional communities to provide comfort and support. Their words thus depicted the wide range of sentiments produced by the conflict that destabilized the confidence and self-assuredness of white southern men. During Reconstruction, veterans resuscitated those wartime emotional communities in an attempt to restore the white supremacist social order disrupted by war and emancipation, and contributed to southern lore that explained Confederate defeat in honorable terms.[12] The conclusions of the present study largely support Broomall's findings but illustrate that such developments began immediately with demobilization. Moreover, the sentiments of those men under consideration here demonstrate that Confederate veterans never saw the need to restore the old social order because they never considered it entirely overturned but merely temporarily disrupted. Defeat and emancipation shook the foundations of white southern society but failed to destroy the structure entirely. Similarly, Confederate veterans sought to redefine, not to recover, their masculine ethos because they never surrendered the definition of manhood to external forces.

How to get home presented the next great obstacle, but fortunately for the common Confederate soldier, what began as little better than "every man for himself" rather quickly evolved into an efficient system created and implemented by officers in blue and gray. Cooperation between erstwhile enemies made possible the impressive achievement of Confederate demobilization. The considerable effort expended by Federal officials to facilitate the homeward journeys of Confederate veterans is understandable. Humanitarianism and practicality merged to expedite the process. After all, the last thing that northern officers and officials wanted was thousands of hungry and bitter former soldiers roaming the countryside.

Chapter two examines that system and includes an explanation of the parole process, the provision of rations and transportation for Confederate troops by Union authorities, and both Union and Confederate implementation efforts. The chapter further scrutinizes tensions between Confederate soldiers who served until the surrenders and deserters who reappeared to secure paroles; explores interactions between Johnny Reb and Billy Yank, and Confederates' intense frustrations with regard to the role of African American Union troops in demobilization; examines the myriad ways in which the system sometimes broke down; and illustrates the most common travel routes. Finally, although the demobilization and travel experiences for southern soldiers varied by individual, certain general trends emerged based upon theater of service and destination.

The demobilization system created for former Rebel soldiers addressed only certain aspects of the discharge process typical in later conflicts. Confederate demobilization centered primarily upon issues of personnel management, transportation logistics in particular. At the conclusion of twentieth-century conflicts, demobilization also dealt with postwar employment and personal health concerns for individual soldiers and considered continued, perpetually evolving postwar international responsibilities for armies overall. The Confederacy and its armies ceased to exist, and the typical southern veteran faced postwar survival on his own. Temporary sustenance and transportation assistance formed the essential elements of Confederate demobilization.[13]

Regardless of the support provided by northern and southern authorities, ultimately it was individual Confederate veterans who faced the logistical challenge of the actual journey home. Years of service and drudgery had prepared hardscrabble soldiers for the unprecedented trial that confronted them. "They had been schooled in toils and hardships until they could walk like horses, endure like oxen, and sleep anywhere that alligators could." Those words attributed to a Confederate soldier perfectly describe the circumstances encountered by

Rebels upon discharge. Thousands of war-weary veterans faced arduous journeys home but, as the statement implies, years of strenuous service in camp, battle, and on the march had, perhaps ironically, prepared them for that final mission. According to that same account, soldiers who trekked toward home "regarded the long tramp with less aversion than one would at first imagine."[14]

Water and rail transportation facilitated the journey for thousands, but many soldiers failed to avail themselves of those advantages, and at any rate, river traffic and railroads did not serve certain regions. Chapter three therefore traces those treks and uncovers several prominent recurring themes. Soldiers tended to travel in small groups, numerous enough to provide security but few enough to facilitate the gathering of adequate provisions from farms along the way. Southern civilians in towns, cities, and in the countryside typically provided food and shelter, but also offered assistance in other forms. Occasionally civilians refused to assist traveling soldiers or demanded compensation. Interestingly, soldiers strenuously objected to requests for remuneration in certain situations but not in cases where the product or service requested pertained to the livelihood of the civilian. A fascinating barter system emerged that revealed the resourcefulness of soldier and civilian alike. Predictably, communities around the South received soldiers in a variety of ways—usually with warm welcome, occasionally with caution or even disdain, and sometimes with silence. Finally, although most Johnny Rebs rushed home to their loved ones as quickly as possible, some traveled at a leisurely pace, took frequent detours for myriad reasons, delayed their travel, or in a relative few cases, never went home.

Unfortunately, during the spring and summer of 1865 throughout much of the South, "No right acknowledged now except might, no property safe which is not defended with pistol and rifle," in the words of one officer.[15] Because citizens sometimes refused to assist soldiers, and because the amount and quality of aid received from Federal authorities varied, many soldiers resorted to whatever means necessary to obtain food and transportation. The resultant chaos and soldiers' justifications for their actions form the basis of the next chapter. Combatants and civilians looted government warehouses in cities all around the South, and often the bedlam spread to residential neighborhoods and private property. The countryside became a no-man's-land populated by lawbreakers of all sorts. Certain areas, the trans-Mississippi region in particular, fell victim to widespread lawlessness because of the complete absence of authority. Occasionally Confederate soldiers victimized the very people whom they had defended for years.

A clear pattern emerged to explain the chaos. Two factors—the timing of demobilized Confederates passing through a region and the presence or absence of Federal troops—almost always determined the timing and extent of disorder. The spread of anarchy generally followed the east-west chronological pattern of Confederate surrenders. Richmond, Virginia, became the symbolic and literal starting point, while the North Carolina–South Carolina–Georgia corridor suffered the worst mayhem east of the Mississippi River. The trans-Mississippi region endured the most widespread chaos, and within that theater the eastern half of Texas set the unenviable standard for lawlessness, without question. All across the South, residents of communities and homesteads along major travel routes suffered terribly, though seemingly isolated rural areas experienced similar bouts of plunder. Sources examined in chapter four reveal that civilians actually came to *expect* passing soldiers to steal.

How did Confederate veterans justify their chicken-stealing and fence-post-burning along the way? Wartime and postwar sources collectively provide interesting and nuanced answers. Of course some ne'er do wells, solider and civilian, simply took advantage of the chaos to prey upon more vulnerable individuals. Others took food and supplies out of material necessity to facilitate homeward journeys. Some stole private and public property, though many soldiers insisted that they restricted their plunder to the property of the former Confederacy. Soldiers often had been unpaid for weeks or even months, the Confederacy had ceased to exist, and diehard Rebels recoiled in disgust at the thought of Yankees claiming the property. A common sentiment quickly took hold that soldiers, though not civilians, deserved the property for the reasons already stated but also because of their immense sacrifice. Moreover, soldiers and observers at the time further reasoned that the amount of food and other materials stored in government warehouses revealed inhumane hoarding amidst the suffering and privation endured by Confederate service men. Rebel officers acknowledged that leftover military property would be turned over to Union officials.[16] But what about other materials? With regard to the plundered Confederate government property, southerners raised the perplexing question of whether the rioters' actions even constituted theft. After all, who exactly owned the property of the failed republic? Chapter four also places the chaos of Confederate demobilization in the context of other problematic demobilizations, including those in the twentieth century.

Those chaotic scenes witnessed and often exacerbated by soldiers during their arduous journeys home afforded the first glimpse of what was to be the postwar South, and provide the setting for chapter five. The first half of the chapter scrutinizes the culmination of demobilization and the homeward journeys—the actual homecoming moment. On the surface, modern readers might dismiss homecoming accounts as sentimental Lost Cause apologia. Such a short-sighted assumption overlooks an opportunity to examine wartime and postwar accounts that chronicle an iconic moment in American history. Several recurring themes emerge in those narratives, and a careful reading reveals that, although most were joyful family reunions that treated defeated Rebels as conquering heroes, other homecomings only intensified extant melancholy brought on by defeat, concern for family, and anxiety over the worrisome future. In the heartrending words of an officer from a Virginia infantry regiment, "I arrived home on the 15th, to find my wife on the verge of the grave. My little children did not know me."[17]

Images of intense material shortages and the devastation of war conditioned the minds of soldiers-turned-veterans as they coped with defeat and confronted a revolutionized society. Three themes dominated the thoughts of Confederate veterans upon homecoming—immediate economic survival, a radically altered relationship with freedpeople, and life under Yankee rule—all against the backdrop of fearful uncertainty. Studies have documented Union and Confederate veterans' long-term struggles toward postwar readjustment.[18] Still, the men examined here at least began the transition to civilian life with remarkable rapidity and with a powerful sense of purpose. Analyses of that rapid and conscious effort to seize control of their postwar fates and to reestablish dominance of southern social, legal, and political conditions continue the recent trend of historians to challenge the thesis of hibernation, that Civil War veterans distanced themselves from their wartime experiences and identity for a period of approximately fifteen years.[19]

Although disappointed by the failure of their cause, Confederate veterans confronted their new existence with vigor. Many went to work on a new crop or sought employment immediately after they arrived home. Far from broken souls, these individuals evinced a resolve to meet the new challenges of the postwar world. Regrettably, some channeled their remaining energies into organized resistance against the advancement of African American civil rights and the onset of Congressional Reconstruction. Fearful of confiscation, humiliation, and revenge, Confederate veterans acted swiftly to seize the initiative and to control the development of the postwar South. In certain cases, their actions foreshadowed the formation of organizations such as the Ku Klux Klan, but the vast majority of southern veterans resisted northern rule through other means, including veterans' organization and political mobilization. As early as the summer of 1865 these men expressed concerns over military occupation, and chafed especially at the presence of African American soldiers. They fumed at what they considered humiliation intentionally inflicted upon them by Federal officers in the wake of defeat. Confederate veterans who had fought to the bitter end to create a southern republic shifted their focus toward the establishment of a postwar South that preserved the values of that fallen nation, sans slavery, and restored white southern control over their collective lives.

One influential study of Civil War memory has argued persuasively that veterans on both sides remained steadfast in the righteousness of their respective causes well into the twentieth century. Thus reunion differed fundamentally from reconciliation. That book offered a corrective to the widespread interpretation that touted a mutual belief in white supremacy as a unifying force that brought together northern and southern whites during postwar generations. Moreover, Caroline Janney's *Remembering the Civil War* argued that white supremacist ideology had long existed on both sides and proved common even among northern proponents of emancipation. Therefore white supremacy ultimately acted as a deterrent to true reconciliation because it served as a unifying force for racial solidarity among white southerners. Janney's fine study traces such developments from the immediate postwar period to the early twentieth century.[20] In contrast, this book demonstrates that such sentiments reigned immediately upon surrender and that demobilization and the fear of an uncertain future further reinforced those attitudes. Confederate veterans have been correctly described as "custodians" of Civil War memory, and that service began immediately at the conclusion of the war.[21]

As part of the continued identification with the Confederacy, veterans immediately and effectively resisted external efforts to force upon them an altered definition of southern manhood. Outside forces may alter an individual's masculinity only if that man concedes. No man truly mindful of his masculinity consciously permits another, particularly an enemy, to define his manhood. Rather, the man will, consciously or subconsciously, reshape the standards to fit his needs. Confederate veterans therefore defined themselves as men based upon courage and loyalty exhibited in battle, dutiful military service to country until end of the conflict, and the resumption of their roles as family men—

husbands, fathers, providers, brothers, and sons. The men examined through-out these pages proved themselves in those matters, but their fight continued after capitulation on the battlefield. Even in a radically transformed postwar South, Confederate veterans defined their own identities. In the end they con-trolled the broader narrative of southern history and culture through the rec-lamation of political dominance, the rise of veterans' organizations, and the prevailing and unifying influence of the Lost Cause. Any assessment of mas-culinity, particularly among recently demobilized fighting men, must consider the potent entity of testosterone-driven individual pride and the conscious or subconscious—but determined—pursuit of alpha male status. In effect, that natural drive within each man reflects an individualized manifestation of what historians have frequently called mastery, a fundamental pillar of masculinity, discussed in multiple chapters below.

Ultimately, the war itself solidified the common principles of Confeder-ate soldiers and rendered them perpetual Rebels. Defeat and demobilization reinforced that identity and hardened the recalcitrant, unapologetic attitudes of southern veterans. The men under scrutiny here surrendered only when soundly beaten by the mighty Yankee war machine, they served to the end de-spite signs of impending defeat, and they demanded credit for that dedication. After having survived the war, these men frequently endured a final trial to reach home and loved ones, sometimes only to encounter further devastation in the form of lost or suffering family members and dilapidated homesteads. Con-federate veterans typically blamed such misery on the overreaching arm of Fed-eral authority. All of this collectively fortified an identity forged in war, based upon shared suffering and sacrifice, a pervasive commitment to white suprem-acy, and an aversion to Federal rule and all things northern. Unnerved further by a powerful sense of uncertainty for the future, Confederate soldiers-turned-veterans looked to each other for solidarity and thus never left behind the Rebel identity. Southern veterans therefore remained Confederates despite permanent demobilization and the demise of the Confederate States of America.

I often think, my dear mamma,
That he'd come back to me
If he only knew how very glad

His little boy would be.
I wonder if papa is out
In all this cold and rain!
What makes you cry, my mother dear?
When will he come again?

She pressed her little one close to her heart,
As if to still its pain,
While the rain rushed by with a sullen roar,
And the pelting hail beat more and more
Against the window pane;
And said, in a voice more sad than before,
"Hush, son, when the war is o'er,
Papa will come again."[22]

1

REBELS
RESOLUTE

THE MIND OF JOHNNY REB
UPON SURRENDER

When the final guns fell silent at Appomattox Court House, Virginia, at least one Confederate soldier believed that he and his comrades in the Army of Northern Virginia had claimed yet another triumph over their Federal foes. Under the impression that Rebel forces had disabled their opponents' guns, a Virginia infantry sergeant confided to his diary that "All the men were jubilant as we concluded we had whipped the enemy." The road to escape from Federal clutches appeared clear, but rather than advance to the front, the men received orders to countermarch and stack arms. When the soldiers prepared to dig breastworks, officers announced that such precaution would not be necessary. Unsure of what to think, the soldiers began to hear whispers of General Robert E. Lee's surrender to Lieutenant General Ulysses S. Grant. Unlike many of his comrades who now faced lengthy journeys across multiple states to reach their homes and families, the twenty-four-year-old Virginia sergeant would soon trek only one hundred miles. Similar to innumerable brothers-in-arms, however, the demise of Lee's legendary army and the practical end of the Confederate experiment left him "thunderstruck."[1]

Myriad scholarly studies document the predictably astonished pronouncements of soldiers and civilians around the South. Despite obvious signs of the weakening of Lee's army—obvious at least in hindsight—Rebels in and out of the ranks expressed shock and dismay at the failure of the Confederate States of

America and the downfall of its greatest army. Although a relative few antici-pated defeat, many could not or would not believe the news. Indeed, they often vehemently denied the reports.[2] Building upon extant literature, analysis of the reactions of soldiers still in the ranks around the Confederacy at the end of the war reveals that the dismay proved as near-universal as historians have gener-ally believed, but what patterns do the sources reveal with regard to region of service? Did soldier accounts written during the tumultuous closing scenes of the war differ from those penned by veterans years later? Moreover, did the sur-render of the Army of Northern Virginia necessarily signal the end of the war? If not, what proved necessary to crush the hopes of the most diehard Rebels? Finally, and most importantly, what does all of this indicate about the mindset of thousands of war-weary, battle-hardened men who journeyed home in 1865 to a world radically transformed?

Within the Army of Northern Virginia certain units remained so convinced of the fallacy of surrender reports that they prepared to shoot those who fled the scene or even spoke of capitulation. Others not only denied the reports but dismissed such talk as unrealistic, yet another in the series of ridiculous rumors that swept through the South by 1865. Still, as the day wore on and the reality of defeat confronted the grizzled veterans, men wept and wandered about unsure of the meaning of it all and uncertain of what to do next. One officer, prescient of the sentiments that would pervade all Rebel armies during the coming weeks, decried that "all was lost save honor." Meanwhile, a member of the rearguard remembered the typical shock and tears at hearing the news, though with the advantage of years of hindsight, and suggested that by that point the men had recognized the inevitability of defeat.[3]

Elsewhere in Virginia astonishment ruled the day. To the west in the Shenan-doah Valley, one observer compared soldiers to statues on horses when they heard the reports, while a group of soldiers who fled Lee's army—in an attempt to reach the Army of Tennessee to the south—encountered still others who re-fused to believe the news. Most significantly, when the first demobilized soldier returned to his small hometown in West Virginia, locals not only dismissed his account of Lee's surrender but allegedly arrested him on charges of desertion. Only the arrival of other soldiers during subsequent days secured his release. The treatment of the suspected deserter upon his return contrasts sharply with the typically warm receptions received by Confederates who returned home only after official surrender and parole, discussed in chapters three and five.[4]

Soldiers with General Joseph E. Johnston's Army of Tennessee—and other western troops scattered around the Carolinas, Georgia, Florida, Tennessee, Alabama, and Mississippi—exhibited similar surprise. In mid-April one diarist in Tennessee dismissed the news as mere propaganda reported in Yankee newspapers, while an officer on a recruiting trip in Georgia scoffed at the story: "It seemed unbelievable, and I denied the report." Not to be outdone, an officer with a flair for the dramatic declared, "Great God! can it be true? I have never for a moment doubted the ultimate success of our cause. I cannot believe it." A veteran who served in North Carolina at the time later recalled that he deemed the news absurd and had initially condemned demobilized soldiers who passed through as deserters.[5] Trans-Mississippi Confederates received the dramatic news in similar fashion.[6]

One other category of Rebel combatants echoed the sentiments of shock and dismay but typically persisted longer in their incredulity. Southern men wasting away in northern prisons of course encountered different circumstances from those faced by their brothers-in-arms who surrendered in the field. Still in the service of their country yet unable to affect the war's outcome, prisoners lived with feelings of helplessness, denied even the grim satisfaction to go down fighting. Chronic boredom, homesickness, and a listless existence subjected such men to daily rumors that suggested impending release. Most, however, eventually knew better than to believe rumors, even those that ultimately proved true. In one such case, a Georgia infantryman imprisoned at Fort Delaware, responded to premature reports of Lee's capitulation penned a sarcastic diary entry: "*believed it of course.*" Some prisoners refused to accept as true the failure of Lee's army even as late as May, and offered the perfectly reasonable argument that if the war had actually ended they would have been released from prison. For some only the sights and sounds of Yankee celebrations, the firing of salutes, and the parole and release of fellow prisoners-of-war convinced them of the demise of Lee's army and eventually the death of the Confederacy.[7]

That raises a reasonable question—what did it take for diehard Rebels to believe that the Army of Northern Virginia had surrendered? Time after time in diaries, letters, and memoirs, southerners pointed to the sight of Lee's disheveled veterans on their homeward trek. Soldiers in other armies routinely dismissed the reports until the reality of defeat marched passed them in the form of bedraggled comrades. In particular, the men of the Confederacy's other potent force, the Army of Tennessee, generally dismissed the reports as mere rumor, until southbound trains carried their defeated comrades into North Carolina.

Elsewhere, a soldier's diary entry illustrated perfectly the common perspective. In early April in Lynchburg, Virginia, a Kentucky cavalry officer denied the reports of the final days of Lee's army as the unreliable tales of stragglers and deserters. The Kentuckian refused to place stock in the words of such characters until the numbers increased during the ensuing days to such an extent that even the most intransigent Rebel could no longer deny reality.[8]

Some southerners of course did not need to see beaten warriors returning home in order to confront the certainty of defeat. A relative few believed the reports easily and others had even anticipated overall Confederate failure. At times such expressions doubtless reflect genuine sentiments, at other times closer analysis of the sources reveals wild swings in emotions during short periods. The Virginia infantryman who had presumed Rebel victory at Appomattox, for example, personifies the highs and lows experienced by Confederates during those momentous days in the spring and summer of 1865. On April 1, the twenty-four-year-old hoped for overall victory by prolonging the war and forcing Union leadership to tire of the conflict. He mocked what he believed to be northern dependence on foreign troops to replenish Grant's ranks. The following day, however, amid swirling reports about the fate of Petersburg and Richmond, the young man worried: "I am afraid Grant will destroy this army if we have to fall back far. He has fresh cavalry, good horses—we have walking skeletons. I trust he will not follow too closely—but any soldier would have sense enough to do that." The defeat of Lee's army would end the war, in the mind of this soldier, but he hoped for another chance to fight. Insisting that he would never surrender, he speculated that he would never again see a "calm moon." On April 3 he managed to express confidence and pessimism within the course of a single day. Petersburg and Richmond had indeed been evacuated, and he admitted that a massive explosion had frightened him. He made up his mind to resist the "invaders" to the last ditch but acknowledged that he may never see that opportunity. As his comrades speculated on the impending campaign, most expected a prolonged struggle, but he did not. Rather, he admitted that the war was essentially over. The emotional swings continued throughout the day and for more than a week. That soldier's experience reminds the modern reader not to rely too heavily on a single diary entry, and to consider multiple factors that shaped sentiments.[9]

Clearly some combatants believed the news of Lee's capitulation and fully understood its larger ramifications. One Richmond native who witnessed the burning and evacuation of his city acknowledged that he and many other soldiers chose not to wait for the end. He learned of Lee's surrender while on the run to avoid capture and to reach a physician relative in Lynchburg to seek treatment for his wounded arm. Similarly, days earlier a cavalryman in Mississippi anticipated overall Confederate defeat even before Lee's surrender. He wrote to his wife that the loss of Mobile, Alabama, had struck a severe blow to the southern cause. He wondered where the Yankees would strike next and lamented that they could attack wherever they chose. Most telling, although he knew that Confederate cavalry in the area led by Nathan Bedford Forrest would go after Federal forces, he admitted that the hungry, grumbling southerners simply were no longer up to the task. Weeks later, a Princeton-educated Confederate in Demopolis, Alabama, learned of Lee's surrender only in late April. Although he had typically evinced strong morale, he admitted that no one doubted the news of Lee's surrender, and that Johnston's army now faced desperate circumstances. That Rebel grasped the reality of defeat and readied himself to move on. "This is the bluest place I have seen," he lamented, "and I shall be glad to get away from it today." [10]

Those individuals recorded or recalled logical responses to the historic events that surrounded them, yet they claimed no wisdom or foresight beyond that of their comrades and neighbors. Others, however, with the advantage of hindsight, later insisted that they had long since anticipated the demise of the southern republic. One aged Confederate veteran, writing in 1913, dated the death of the Confederacy as early as the fall of Vicksburg, Mississippi, in 1863, or at least the removal of Joseph E. Johnston from command of the Army of Tennessee during the Atlanta campaign in the summer of 1864. A fellow western Rebel emphasized the devastation of that army at the battle of Franklin in late 1864. Indeed, multiple veterans pointed to that final winter of the conflict. As one less-than-charitable memoirist remarked, from that point the inevitability of Confederate defeat was obvious to "all intelligent" people. That veteran, who somehow insisted that he and his comrades never lost faith in the administration in Richmond, bemoaned the government's failure to secure a peace settlement by February 1865. He deemed all loss of life after that point unnecessary and recalled the difficulty that he and his comrades had encountered in exposing themselves to danger, with the knowledge that such risk was pointless. A comrade from Kentucky, meanwhile, insisted that after that winter, the "entire fabric was broken." [11]

These purportedly prophetic comrades all wrote years after the war, not only with the advantage of hindsight but with the ability, and perhaps the desire, to shape history's perception of them. In most cases the authors likely wrote truthfully, though such accounts permitted the veteran to claim that he had re- mained steadfast to the end but had recognized the severity of challenges that faced the Confederacy. Such an individual would appear worthy of the man- tle of proud, masculine Confederate veteran, yet not delusional enough (years later) to have expected overall victory by late spring 1865. Another veteran who wrote during the postwar period illustrated the potential nuance of some recol- lections. Although the former Tennessee infantryman claimed to have seen the end coming, he acknowledged that defeat shocked most of his comrades, who had not even considered surrender. Though impressed with their bravery and dedication to the Confederate cause, the Tennessean insisted that his brothers- in-arms were too intelligent not to recognize the untenable state of affairs.[12]

Other Rebel soldiers, writing during the war's closing scenes, described the opposite circumstances. They remained steadfast despite the submission of their comrades. One such soldier from Louisiana urged his mother to ignore unfa- vorable reports from the East and assured her that "As long as our army remains firm in their dedication to have our freedom, we have nothing to fear." Others had yielded, he continued, but "I am willing to shoulder my gun as long as there is an armed yankee on the land." Although he may have consciously sought to prop up his mother's spirits, a subsequent letter to another correspondent re- iterates his resolve.[13]

The letters of Private Benjamin Glover provide an example of a soldier who remained steadfast despite his recognition of impending defeat and also illus- trate the ability of Confederate soldiers to reassure loved ones while confront- ing reality. An Alabama native who had moved to Florida two years before the war, Glover enlisted in an infantry regiment in his new home state. Thirty-three years of age at the end of the war, he wrote frequently to his wife, Mary Eliza- beth, whom he affectionately referred to as Betty. Though identified as a farmer in the census, he descended from a line of prominent planters and possessed a personal estate valued at almost $40,000. Writing from North Carolina in early April, he urged Betty not to make herself uneasy and somehow pledged to her that he would be home by June. He had no reason to expect a leave of absence at that period of the war, so the assurance of his impending return could be interpreted as a sign that he expected the war to end soon. This becomes per- fectly clear in light of his other advice, which included a warning not to accept Confederate money and not to pay any taxes or tithes. Though he admitted that the presence of Yankee forces in the region made him nervous for her safety, he clearly sought to establish a sense of normality. "Kiss the baby for me. Tell the negroes howdy."[14]

Obviously most of Glover's comrades recognized that the destruction of the Army of Northern Virginia heralded the downfall of the Confederacy. It remains equally evident, as illustrated by multiple historians, that a significant number of Rebels refused to concede defeat in response to the events at Appomattox. Many soldiers insisted on continued resistance and even offered various strategies to secure independence. Although it remains difficult to conjure a scenario that portends a Confederate victory without the Army of Northern Virginia at full strength, the notion of continued resistance should not be dismissed as wildly unrealistic. More importantly, although most modern readers recognize that the fateful meeting between Grant and Lee represented the beginning of the end, such a conclusion was by no means apparent to *every* Rebel *at the time.* Numerous Johnny Rebs examined throughout the remainder of this chapter insisted on continued resistance after Appomattox and some even acknowledged overall defeat in response to other, subsequent events.[15]

To be sure, those who continued to breathe fire and demand a fight to the last ditch even after Appomattox could not be considered representative of all Confederate soldiers in the ranks and certainly not indicative of the general sentiment of southern people. However, such individuals existed in meaningful numbers and persisted adamantly in their beliefs, or at least assertive in their claims, that victory remained within reach. A relative few who represented the extreme even among the fire-breathing diehards placed the blame squarely on the shoulders of the iconic Rebel commander. Lee had sold the Confederacy, one soldier fumed to his wife, while a Richmond government official lamented that Jefferson Davis would never forgive the general for the decision to capitulate. A Texan's wrath exceeded that of even those compatriots. Although he remained hopeful for victory, he lamented the shameful conduct and demoralization of troops all around him, all of which he traced to Lee's surrender. If that capitulation doomed the Confederacy, he wondered, should the general be hanged?[16]

More often, Rebel soldiers remained supportive of Lee and steadfast in their dedication to the Confederate cause. But how did these individuals intend to defeat the powerful Federal war machine without the Army of Northern Virginia as an organized fighting unit, particularly in light of their failure to secure victory even with Lee and his army in the field? Some diehards offered no idea how to secure victory; their language clearly indicates that they did not consider the war concluded. Others offered no specific strategy but demanded continued resistance in some form. *Fight on,* they shouted. Still others pointed to three specific strategies: unite Confederate forces under Johnston; take to the mountains and/or resort to guerrilla warfare; or make a stand in the Trans-Mississippi theater, usually in Texas.

Certain Rebels acknowledged that Appomattox represented a severe blow to the Confederate cause, but their diaries, letters, and memoirs make it evident that they expected the war to continue. According to one intransigent Rebel, while in prison he and certain comrades reminded the conquered majority that Lee himself was not the cause and that other armies remained in the field. In mid-April an army doctor in North Carolina admitted that it was the darkest hour in the short history of the Confederacy, yet he and his comrades remained hopeful for independence as he speculated on future troop movements. Similarly, two weeks later a Texan wrote in a letter home that, despite gloomy prospects, he expected to be sent to Tennessee. Other enlisted men and officers around the South penned similar mundane entries. The commonplace character of such statements reinforces the point that these individuals simply expected the conflict to continue.[17]

More fire-breathing comrades, however, demanded the chance to fight. Where and how to fight, or why they should expect success, they never bothered to share. As one diehard Confederate boasted from eastern Mississippi to his wife in mid-April, the Yankees could never triumph as long as one Rebel remained with forty rounds of ammunition. If a soldier could conceivably surpass the boastful arrogance of that combatant, that honor belongs to a remarkably obstinate Texan. Encamped on an arid stretch of land near Brownsville in South Texas, he wrote to his sister in early May. Lee had surrendered only a small force, he reasoned, while Johnston maintained a larger army. The Union would need a standing army of one million to subdue the South permanently, while as many as 200,000 proud southern men stood poised to resist and ready to choose slavery over subjugation at the hands of Yankees. "If I can't have a Confederacy I don't want anything else." One would be hard pressed to find a more fire-breathing Rebel by May 1865. Perhaps his isolated location, distant from major campaigns, influenced his determination to fight on. What cannot be doubted is the determination in his language and the implication that even the cessation of organized combat need not necessarily end southern resistance to northern rule.[18]

Numerous comrades shared that Texan's inclination toward guerrilla warfare. Historians have chronicled this phenomenon and have meticulously analyzed the strategic prudence of such an endeavor. That concept received en-
dorsements from soldiers and officers, in all theaters of conflict, in wartime and
postwar writing. Moreover, even those who opposed the measure—as too dras-
tic or somehow immoral or less noble than organized combat—often insisted
that it could have been successful. One emotional Louisiana soldier in early
May 1865 considered continuation of the war a calamity but preferable to subjugation, and partisan warfare presented the most judicious strategy to avoid life
under Yankee domination. Despite a degree of support for the guerrilla option,
a wide disparity existed with regard to its implementation. The most common
proposals involved the concentration of forces in mountainous regions. Other
officers proposed to arm the men individually but send them home in order to
resist Federal rule *after* a negotiated peace.[19]

A less dramatic and romanticized option appealed to many Confederates,
including Jefferson Davis and certain cabinet officials and generals, in the aftermath of Appomattox. The chief executive, in flight along with the remains of the
Confederate government, linked up with Joseph E. Johnston and his Army of
Tennessee in North Carolina. Although Davis had implied support for the guerrilla option in the immediate aftermath of the fall of Richmond, one week later
he endorsed a vague plan to concentrate Confederate forces in North Carolina.
Then, in a series of meetings with generals and cabinet officials over the course
of multiple days, the president's plans evolved to include a massive recruiting
effort and ultimately an ill-defined attempt to continue resistance somewhere
farther west, despite pleas from Johnston and other officers to secure the best
possible terms of surrender. Although Davis's exact plans remain unclear, he adamantly refused to submit after Appomattox, even after authorizing Johnston to
discuss surrender terms with Major General William T. Sherman.[20]

Soldiers and officers who shared their president's determination but rejected the guerrilla option placed great faith in Johnston. Enlisted men and officers in the Army of Tennessee who favored continued resistance after Appomattox opted to remain under Johnston's leadership. Others who managed to
escape Lee's downfall traveled south to unite with their western brothers-in-
arms rather than disband and journey home. One Virginia native who fled his
home state to join up with Johnston's army described a roadside littered with
discarded guns, cartridge boxes, and other accoutrements, a clear sign that most
of his comrades had resolved to fight no more. The son of an Irish immigrant,

the determined Virginia native had left behind his study of the law to join the Confederate war effort. Combatants who trudged south in order to continue the fight against a powerful enemy clearly constituted the minority, but the submission of others hardly dissuaded such men.[21]

Johnston's capitulation rendered the defiance of those men futile, though a final resolution remained in the minds of the most unwavering Rebels. A minority of officers, enlisted men, and government officials advocated a mass westward migration designed to stage a desperate stand for southern independence in the Trans-Mississippi Confederacy. Though numerous individuals advocated the move west of the river, two revealing themes emerge throughout these accounts. First, even those who wrote during the chaotic closing weeks of the war recognized the plan as a last-ditch strategy born of desperation, but some unwavering Rebels embraced it anyway, because it presented at least an opportunity to go down fighting. Confederate officer and later staunch advocate of the Lost Cause, Jubal Early, predictably articulated the mindset better than most. Early advocated a concentration of forces in the Trans-Mississippi theater "with the hope of at least meeting an honorable death while fighting under the flag of my country." Second, some soldiers and officers, in wartime and postwar accounts, legitimately believed that the desperate course of action could conceivably succeed if carried out with vigor and resolve. In early May, a soldier wrote to his father from Shreveport, Louisiana, to describe the desperate situation. He doubted the resolve of soldiers and civilians in the region but acknowledged legitimate potential in the proposal if single-minded Rebels concentrated specifically in Texas.[22]

Certain Trans-Mississippi comrades of that soldier evinced more confidence in themselves and their brothers-in-arms. They, too, recognized the finality of the scheme, and more than matched the aggressive rhetoric of their comrades from the Eastern and Western theaters. The most aggressive and boastful Trans-Mississippi Rebels readied to protect "every inch of soil to the Rio Grande" from the hated invaders, and were prepared to stand alone against the vandal hordes if necessary. Organized, intact units combined with distance from immediate enemy threat to bolster their chances for success, according to one officer. The struggle could continue for years in the vast empire of Texas, if only the people would unite.[23]

Whether a general pledge to continue the struggle, a resort to guerrilla warfare, a scheme to concentrate forces in North Carolina, or a plan to make a gallant stand in Texas, all such accounts, wartime and postwar, shared a central message—a minority of Rebel soldiers still in the ranks remained steadfast in support of the Confederate cause even after the death of its most powerful army. Though defense of soldier honor and legacy remained typically implicit in the accounts, some explicitly absolved the soldiers of any culpability in the downfall of the southern republic. One veteran even reminded readers that their "beloved general," not the soldiers, had made a deal that fateful Sunday in Virginia. Generations ago, an educated, insightful, and unusually droll Civil War general recorded a shrewd observation on the nature of veterans' postwar claims. In his classic memoir, Richard Taylor wryly noted that many soldiers insisted that they would have died in the last ditch but the generals' willingness to surrender prevented such a denouement. Nineteenth-century Americans dared not question such bold statements because the public had proclaimed their veracity and had anointed the men national heroes. The former general sardonically concluded that one must never question the court of public opinion.[24]

Certainly the soldiers who insisted upon those varied strategies of continued resistance represented a minority even among the diehards who fought to the bitter end. That begs the question, when did Confederate soldiers who remained in service at the war's end actually acknowledge defeat? The fall of Richmond signaled the end for a relative few, while obviously the surrender of the Army of Northern Virginia ended the hopes of more Rebels than any other event. As one aged veteran remembered, when the defeated Lee returned to the fallen capital and entered his Richmond residence, he closed the door on the Confederate States of America. Still, others clung to faint hopes until the capitulation of the Army of Tennessee. A veteran recalled his regiment's march through a small town, greeted by the waves and cheers of the occupants of a female academy. The beaten combatants barely responded, however, because they considered themselves "part of the funeral procession going home from the burial of the dead Confederacy." Others, less specific and without the melodramatic imagery, understandably acquiesced in response to the accumulation of calamitous news.[25] Careful examination of numerous accounts by Rebel soldiers from points around the Confederacy provides insight into the mind of the defeated Johnny Reb and reveals a remarkable consistency between wartime and postwar perceptions.

The Federal capture of the Rebel capital signified the doom of the Confederate experiment for certain Rebels. Whether in response to the symbolic power of the fall of Richmond or the logistical nightmare created by the loss of the administrative center, some combatants saw no reason to await the demise of the armies to pronounce death upon their beloved southern republic. None other than George Pickett of Gettysburg fame wrote to his wife hours before Lee's surrender and pointed explicitly to the fall of Richmond as the source of the greatest gloom to settle over his command. That development crushed the cause at that point, he admitted, but at least that also meant an end to the fighting, suffering, and dying. Whether to comfort his wife, himself, or perhaps both, Pickett concluded, "Peace is born." Years later a Virginia cavalryman echoed the general's assessment. In dramatic prose that would have been the envy of any Lost Cause champion, the veteran proclaimed that the southern people had reached the limits of human endurance and that even Rebel gallantry could not overcome such starvation and nakedness. As he remembered it, the Confederate cause died when the hated Yankees captured Richmond.[26]

Predictably, more than any other event, Lee's submission the following week at Appomattox crushed the aspirations of many diehard Rebels. Moreover, more Confederates explicitly pointed to that iconic moment than to any other incident. A closer analysis of the sources indicates the prevalence of that sentiment across the Confederacy and illustrates a remarkable similarity between postwar and wartime accounts across every region of the South. Veterans who wrote after the war spilled gallons of ink in discussions of Appomattox in memoirs and regimental histories. Comparable sentiments abound regardless of the theater in which the veteran served. Many individuals who fought in Virginia at the time of Lee's surrender doubtless shared the memories of a soldier who recalled "We left the famous field of Appomattox, which sounded the death knell to our hopes of independence of which we had dreamed. . . . But we must not be cast down. Were we not still Lee's veterans, and had he not prayed that God would extend His blessing and protection? Human virtue should equal human calamity; and we rose to the occasion."[27] Rebels who served in the Western theater at the end of the war also frequently remembered Appomattox as the end of the Confederacy. A twenty-one-year-old Arkansas private, for example, proved typical of many western Confederates when, upon hearing the news of Lee's surrender, he espoused continued faith in Johnston but acknowledged the senselessness of further bloodshed.[28] Veterans who served farther west, isolated in the trans-Mississippi region, at war's end also frequently recalled Appomattox as the death of the Confederate cause.[29]

A Virginia staff officer who wrote years after the war recalled that he and his comrades did not initially understand that Lee's surrender signified overall Confederate defeat but only later recognized that fact.[30] Although others doubtless shared that perspective, that written account is an anomaly among the individuals sampled here. In fact, analysis of wartime sources yields results virtually identical to those of veteran accounts and demonstrates that postwar writers did not simply benefit from hindsight and accept conventional wisdom with regard to the perceived significance of Appomattox. That soldiers in the Army of Northern Virginia and elsewhere in the state considered Lee's surrender tantamount to catastrophe probably appears so obvious that it needs no reinforcement here. However, the actions of one group of Lee's legions exemplified that position. According to the April 22, 1865, diary entry of one former infantry sergeant, while multiple Rebel armies remained in the field, the men in his county had already begun the formation of a Confederate veterans' association.[31] Although only a single example, the establishment of that local organization years before the generally recognized emergence of Confederate veterans' associations indicates that at least some Rebels anticipated the memory wars later to be waged by North and South. The United Confederate Veterans officially organized in 1889, but this example from a Virginia county clearly indicates that some southern fighting men, even if *unconsciously,* intended to shape the public perception of their collective service before the actual end of hostilities. As later chapters reveal, ex-Confederates *consciously* focused on retaining their Rebel identity, resistance to Reconstruction, and immediate financial recovery, all as part as a collective strategy to determine the course of the postwar South and to resist outside influences on individual and collective southern identities.[32]

Confederate combatants elsewhere also grasped the significance of the events at Appomattox. A number of western and Trans-Mississippi soldiers also acknowledged overall defeat upon the surrender of their eastern brothers-in-arms. As one Louisiana diarist lamented, Lee's surrender meant the return to Yankee rule and resumption of life under the people whom he and his countrymen held in "horror."[33]

Rebels who recorded their observations from Federal prisoner-of-war camps during the war's closing scenes frequently echoed the acceptance of overall defeat upon the demise of the Army of Northern Virginia, though the preponderance of time on their hands sometimes permitted more verbose and philosophical lamentations on the subject. One prisoner confined at Fort Delaware perceived a change not only among his comrades after Appomattox but also in the treatment of prisoners by guards and officials. Before Lee's surrender, he surmised, "we were a power able to enforce treatment by retaliation. Now we are nothing but rebels. Then we were Rebel soldiers." To be sure, as discussed above, other prisoners held out hope somewhat longer but most typically differed from their comrades in the field in no meaningful way on the question of what event forced their acknowledgement of the failure of the Confederate cause.[34]

A significant portion of Rebels who remained in the ranks or in prison that final spring considered the surrender of Johnston and the Army of Tennessee the death knell of Confederate hopes. Whether they shared powerful sentiments in diaries and letters written in the heat of the moment or recorded their observations years later in memoirs or regimental histories, some breathed fire and insisted upon a fight to victory or to the bitter end. For others less dramatic if not less determined, their words and actions simply indicate that in their minds the war continued until the loss of Johnston's western boys. This sentiment proved especially common among soldiers from that army and elsewhere in the western or Trans-Mississippi theaters. Despite the greater fame and glory attributed to their eastern brothers-in-arms, western troops exhibited immense pride in themselves and comrades, and tremendous confidence in Johnston as commander. Moreover, western soldiers in many cases quite literally defended their homes and families. Probably no greater motivation exists for a soldier. The men of the Army of Tennessee, after all, constituted the army of the western Confederacy. Some of these men insisted that the surrender of the Army of Northern Virginia inflicted a terrible, but not fatal, blow upon the Confederate cause. Interestingly, as accounts discussed earlier in this chapter demonstrate, some prisoners-of-war—and, more important, even certain members of the Army of Northern Virginia—shared their western comrades' dogged determination and support for continued resistance under the command of Johnston.[35]

A relative handful of Confederate soldiers and officers acknowledged overall defeat in response to two other specific developments, both of which carried potentially powerful psychological value. First, the capture of Jefferson Davis by Union cavalry crushed the waning hopes of a small number of southern soldiers who still held out hope in early May 1865. Clearly, the imagery of the Confederate chief executive in Federal custody was symbolic of the termination of dreams of southern independence. Moreover, many southerners recognized the president's unyielding resolve to continue resistance and carry the war west of the great river. Whatever his flaws, no Rebel in any capacity exceeded Davis in dedication to the concept of an independent southern republic. Thus, the capture of arguably the most diehard Rebel of all crushed the spirits of some who held out to the bitter end.[36] Second, a few dedicated southern men acknowledged defeat only upon the disintegration and surrender of the Confederate Trans-Mississippi Army. Although overall victory by that point appears wildly unrealistic, the demise of the last remaining official and somewhat organized Confederate army ended dreams of grandeur among even the most resolute Rebels.[37]

A significant number of other Confederate fighting men pointed to nothing specific but made it clear through their words and actions that the war continued despite the surrenders of the two most powerful southern armies. Such men avoided dramatic, fiery language about a fight to the last ditch but simply discussed the next troop movements, where they expected to be sent, or the prospects of future campaigns. Multiple soldiers from all three theaters wrote of gloomy prospects throughout April and even well into May 1865, but clearly had not acknowledged general defeat. For example, one Rebel, either exceedingly determined or shockingly oblivious, wrote to an officer on May 5, 1865, from Lexington, Virginia, to demand a hearing with regard to his property rights. He insisted upon a board of two or three Confederate officers to consider his case. Despite the mundane language and subject matter of the letter, the missive indicates that the man either believed that the Confederacy still existed or that it would again. Meanwhile, a twenty-two-year-old Georgia cavalry officer admitted that the surrender of Lee's army inflicted a devastating toll on the Confederacy and that reports of the impending capitulation of Johnston's army caused great consternation and uncertainty among western troops. Indeed, he acknowledged that those events clearly ended the hopes of many of his comrades. He, however, continued to discuss the future war effort until late April. That Georgian remained among those who at one point claimed that they would continue the fight elsewhere even if their army surrendered. Most significant, he and a meaningful number of others only gradually grasped the failure of their cause, and they never pointed to a specific event to signify defeat. A select few comrades who wrote in later years echoed that wartime outlook.[38]

One veteran who put pen to paper a decade after the war neatly summarized the sentiments expressed above but also, probably unintentionally, hinted at a somewhat more specific explanation. "It is impossible to say precisely when the conviction became general in the South that we were beaten. I cannot even decide at what time I myself began to think the cause a hopeless one, and I have never yet found one of my fellow-Confederates, though I have questioned many of them, who could tell me with any degree of certainty the history of his change from confidence to despondency." The verbose veteran's subsequent description of the closing scenes of conflict provides a slightly more detailed portrait of the collapse of Confederate aspirations. He sincerely denied that a particular event dashed his hopes. However, though never explicitly stated, the implicit message in the remainder of his memoir remains clear. Like a number of comrades, the accumulation of setbacks eventually wore him down and forced him to face reality. The fall of Richmond, the surrenders of Lee and Johnston, the capture of Davis, and the subsequent capitulation of other, smaller forces collectively weighed heavy on the minds of dedicated Rebels. In some cases, particularly in isolated areas of the Trans-Mississippi theater such as Indian Territory, individuals received reports of major events in rapid succession, which almost certainly compounded the perceived consequence of the reversals.[39]

Once such grizzled veterans admitted the harsh reality of defeat, they could not be persuaded to sacrifice further. The acquiescence of the true diehard Rebels, the men most dedicated to the pursuit of southern independence, represented more than merely a sign of the finality of the conflict. Under normal circumstances those still in the ranks at the end were those most likely to respond to impassioned pleas to fight on. In camps and prisons throughout the Eastern and Western theaters, however, speeches and rallies no longer moved the spirit of Johnny Reb. As long as Confederate victory remained attainable, such speeches often improved morale to some extent. After the admission of defeat, soldiers generally ignored and occasionally mocked the entreaties. According to the diary of a young Alabama infantry captain then in North Carolina, one politician's passionate appeal for continued resistance through guerrilla warfare met with the approval of a single drunken soldier. Weeks later in a Federal prison camp, a soldier lamented that expressions of defiance "are now coming to a rather begging tone."[40]

Although speeches and rallies that urged soldiers to fight on largely failed all around the Confederacy after Appomattox, the Trans-Mississippi theater provides the clearest example of the concept and its most vociferous rejections of the continued entreaties to fight on. West of the great river, soldiers typically received the devastating news of the capitulation of the Army of Northern Virginia and the Army of Tennessee, as well as the submission of other forces east of the Mississippi River in quick succession. Thus, Trans-Mississippi Rebels understood that should they continue the war they would face the mighty Yankee war machine essentially alone. In the face of certain defeat, Confederates west of the great river chose capitulation in order to preserve their own lives and to protect their homes and families from pointless destruction. The government that they had served had disintegrated, and the nation that they had endeavored to create had ceased to exist except in the imaginations of a select few. Moreover, if the largest and most powerful Confederate armies could not defeat the powerful blue legions, how could the scattered fragments of the Trans-Mississippi Army accomplish that task? Although civilians and officials continued to call for resistance, soldiers outwardly rejected such petitions at Shreveport, Houston, Galveston, and numerous smaller communities, especially in Texas. One intuitive Rebel from East Texas captured the sentiment perfectly when he succinctly but brilliantly surmised that, "there is no use in men a-going in and getting killed without any hopes of success."[41]

Whether a specific setback or an accumulation of events signified the downfall of the Confederacy in the mind of each soldier, acquiescence to ultimate defeat led to a somewhat predictable range of emotions. Numerous diaries, letters, memoirs, and regimental histories featured unsurprising expressions of sadness and even seemingly utter devastation. Many also included lamentations of almost unbearable humiliation, manifestations of intense anger or disgust, declarations that the author had done his duty, and ultimately, among the soldiers examined here, poignant and understandable expressions of relief. Careful scrutiny of soldier reactions to overall Confederate defeat provides the opportunity to compare wartime and postwar accounts and also to establish the mindset of Johnny Rebs as they prepared to make their way home. An understanding of the outlook of returning veterans proves particularly important in light of the violent struggles of the Reconstruction era.[42]

One study of the emotional history of southern men before, during, and after the war briefly examines the reactions of Confederates to defeat. James J. Broomall found a range of emotions that included individual attempts to balance the sadness of defeat with the joy of returning home and, collectively, a range from moderation to defiance. The findings presented below echo and expand upon those findings to reveal additional reactions. Broomall argued that soldiers created emotional communities to provide collective support and to help them recover mastery of their "private and public worlds." The conclusions discussed below support that compelling thesis by demonstrating that those developments began immediately during demobilization. Moreover, Broomall's conclusions and those in the present study place demobilized soldiers in a middle ground of sorts, recalling Eric J. Leed's application of liminality to the study of World War I soldiers. The transitory period of demobilization thus informed the mindsets of ex-Rebels by reinforcing their collective Confederate identity and providing the ideological underpinnings for what became the Lost Cause.[43]

Countless firsthand accounts depict soldiers who faced predictable sadness, general emotional fragility, or genuine devastation. Man after man referenced dejection, thoughts of subjugation, and the sight of hardened veterans who wept like children. All that they had fought for had collapsed around them amidst crushing failure. Such men had experienced suffering, fighting, and killing on a scale unprecedented for the American people, only to endure shocking defeat. Modern readers must keep in mind that such men represented the diehards who were defiantly still in the ranks in 1865, and their distressed reactions to the death of the Confederate experiment for which they had fought so long remain perfectly believable. In fact, no compelling reason exists to assume that the hard-bitten veteran soldiers who expressed such powerful emotions were merely posturing for posterity. Moreover, despite years of warfare and waning Confederate prospects, the ultimate downfall of the southern republic struck the remaining troops essentially all at once. As one soldier-poet lamented only one year after the war, "My life is like the blighted oak. . . ." Such dramatic quotations from wartime and postwar sources could fill pages, but in mid-April 1865 one Louisiana Rebel summarized the widespread anguish experienced by so many men in the face of surrender: "I leave this sad and humiliating subject sobbing."[44]

That soldier expressed the sentiments of more comrades than he probably realized. As his lament suggests, he and countless others experienced a more specific and intense reaction than mere temporary outbursts of grief. Indeed, during the immediate aftermath of overall Confederate defeat, countless soldiers-turned-veterans endured a mutually reinforcing combination of humiliation and anger. Some men immediately worried that Confederate failure had brought shame not only upon the soldiers but on their families as well. In fact, that Louisianan quoted above bewailed that he had hoped not to be so soon reunited with his wife in humiliation. Others found the greatest embarrassment in having lost to Yankees, or as one diarist noted, the "worthless fellows" whose backs the Rebel warriors had so frequently seen. That summer another Rebel balked at the prospect of swearing loyalty to the flag "I had seen so often trail in the dust." In a similar, martial vein, a Virginia infantry sergeant who surrendered at Appomattox decried the shame of capitulation and wondered in his diary what the fallen southern icons Stonewall Jackson and Jeb Stuart would have said. Others turned their concerns to the ranks of common soldiers and reflected on fallen comrades. One Virginian, for example, decried his sad heart, empty stomach, and the loss of the cause: "But they, our dead comrades, were spared the terrible humiliation of defeat and so were blessed compared with us who remain."[45]

No mere melodramatic tripe born of frustration, such sentiments proved common among Civil War soldiers who faced the humiliation of defeat. Death in combat while rendering the ultimate service to their country provided the ultimate measure of masculinity. Scholars have demonstrated that in the minds of many soldiers, an honorable death effectively established forever the masculine trait of a fighting man's legacy.[46] In light of this, the mere fact that a Confederate soldier served to the end of the conflict, thus risking death even toward the bitter end, represents an especially powerful indicator of manhood. Moreover, survivors who returned to homes and loved ones amid the shame of defeat were, ironically, denied an honorable death. Instead, many demanded recognition for their dutiful service to the war's ultimate conclusion, as discussed below.

Such powerful feelings of dishonor further intensified the anger that raged within thousands of men who had fought to the bitter end. They directed their fury at leadership, men who remained at home, those who had abandoned the cause, and occasionally even toward those who had served until the end but disbanded their units sooner than the diehards deemed honorable. Essentially, thousands of exhausted, beaten, and humiliated men sought someone to blame. As more than one veteran noted, after so much fighting and dying, surrender and total defeat proved difficult to bear.

For a small number of Rebels, the manifestation of their anger focused on the specific concern that it had all been in vain. In addition to the anguish suffered at the thought of dreams dashed and tears shed in memory of fallen comrades buried on killing fields throughout the South, Confederate soldiers who served to the end faced the maddening apprehension that it had all been pointless. Long absences from families, destruction of the landscape, unprecedented loss of life, and all for what, some wondered. One soldier pointed specifically to the loss of slavery, dissolution of the Confederacy, and an unthinkable return to the Union. For what had they struggled so mightily? Widespread feelings of anger and devastation at having lost the war contributed to the conclusion that the entire war effort may have been senseless. And that realization—of having potentially sacrificed so much for nothing—intensified their bitter feelings of anger and devastation.

Frustration in particular fueled such assertions, as evidenced by the rapidly changing emotions displayed by the soldiers under consideration here. One particularly hardcore Rebel deemed the entire war effort pointless, and became so frustrated that he proclaimed the war proof that the American people overall remained simply incapable of governing themselves. A comrade, who spent the war's final days in a Federal military prison, opined dramatically: "To think that all the blood and treasure, which the South has so unsparingly poured on the altar of our country, should have been shed in vain. Oh! How many unhappy mothers are now mourning throughout the South for the useless slaughter of their sons." Only weeks later, however, he reasoned that it had not all been in vain because the southern people would emerge all the better for having suffered the trials and tribulations of the conflict.[47]

Overall, concerns that Confederate efforts and sacrifices had been wasted proved genuine and intense, but not particularly prevalent. Moreover, careful reading of the sources illuminates that such concerns were short-lived, heat-of-the-moment reactions to catastrophe. Veterans who wrote after years of reflection typically did not evince such apprehension. Most authors of memoirs and regimental histories of course remained dyed-in-the-wool Rebels, proud of their wartime exploits and dedicated to the notion of whatever they believed the Confederacy embodied. Typical veterans were unlikely to cast aspersions on the sacrifices of their comrades and countrymen. Therefore, the dearth of postwar epistles on the allegedly needless effusion of blood makes sense.

A North Carolina private offered sentiments far more compelling and representative when he concluded of fallen comrades, "the cause for which they gave their lives is lost, but they positively did not give their lives in vain. They gave it for a most righteous cause, even if the Cause was lost." Besides the denial that the struggle had been in vain, that enlisted man's commentary illustrates two other important points. First, to recognize defeat differed from accepting that the fight had been pointless. Second, and more important, numerous defeated Rebels insisted on the justness of their cause. This occurred not merely in Lost Cause–inspired ramblings of aged veterans. Rather, it was also prevalent among soldiers in the spring and summer of 1865. That same private, for example, concluded his diary with the assertion that "I still say our Cause was just, nor do I regret one thing I have done to cripple the North."[48]

The young North Carolina infantryman's confidence and persistence mirrored that of many comrades who adamantly insisted upon the righteousness of their actions, individually and collectively. Thousands of dedicated Rebels left the ranks in 1865 unyielding in their belief in the principles for which they had enlisted and fought. In an evocative display of masculine obstinacy, one artillery private and Virginia native expressed in May 1865, "This day four years ago I left home for the army. It has been four years of blood, hardship, sickness and danger and its end finds me a prisoner of war at this horrid prison den, and my country desolated, pillaged, plundered and conquered by these vile Yankees. Yet I believe we Rebs are going to be proud of these four years of war. . . . And we have no excuses to make for our actions."[49]

Beyond the predictable pride and obstinacy of grizzled veterans of arduous campaigns, such defiant attitudes accurately framed the mindset and spirit of men recently defeated after immense sacrifice, but now expected to return to civilian life and resume their existence as loyal and productive citizens. Meanwhile, their erstwhile enemies occupied their homelands and enforced a new reality that ripped asunder certain fundamental aspects of southern society. Numerous soldiers under consideration here returned home feeling weary and overpowered but unapologetic and steadfast in pro-Confederate spirit. As the violent struggles of Reconstruction loomed, many such men remained every bit the Rebels that they had been four years earlier. As one unrepentant veteran insisted, he and his comrades could proudly "transmit as a heritage to their children their acts and deeds under the Stars and Bars."[50] (See chapter five of this study for more on the postwar persistence of Confederate identity.)

Within the broad concept of soldiers' persistence that they had acted correctly and in defense of principle, more specifically, many soldiers vehemently maintained that they had done their individual duty. As one Rebel wrote from Indian Territory during the summer of 1865, though he left the war with nothing and received the thanks of no one, he remained satisfied because "having done my duty is my reward." Such claims, of course, obviously reflected a powerful concern for, and careful defense of, honor and reputation. In effect, Johnny Reb insisted not only that he had done his duty but also that the world needed to know that he had done his duty. He stayed to the bitter end, and he wanted credit for having stayed to the bitter end. At times the desire for recognition was implicit, while at other times soldiers openly demanded credit. One soldier, still in a northern prison in May 1865, repeatedly insisted that he had honored his commitment and wrote to his wife, "I sacrificed everything but life, and hazarded that, many times & in many ways, in behalf of my country. I have not the slightest fear that any man can ever point at me a finger of scorn and say 'you done it.'" Although the outcome had been determined in the minds of all but the most delusional, the war officially continued, and duty dictated that a soldier remain in the ranks until surrender and parole.[51]

Confederate soldiers' insistence upon credit for faithful service to the bitter end exemplifies a cornerstone of nineteenth-century southern masculinity—courage. Northern and southern fighting men of course valued that important and demonstrable trait, but nineteenth-century southern men in particular, before and during the war, rooted masculine identity in that volatile notion of personal and family honor. In the Civil War, the mere act of enlistment and service to one's cause demonstrated a degree of manhood through bravery, but without question, combat provided the ultimate test of masculinity. As multiple historians have argued, in effect, during the great crisis fighting was the responsibility of every man, and to avoid that sacrifice meant branding oneself as less than a man. Soldiers protected individual and family honor through public demonstration of courage, manifested most obviously in the crucible of battle. Combat offered the ultimate test of courage and therefore the ultimate gauge of manhood.[52] Southern women understood that Confederate veterans desired recognition of their honorable service. Wives and mothers promised fighting men that their brave and dutiful service had preserved individual and family honor. One proud and sympathetic mother assured her anguished Rebel son that he had done everything possible to serve his cause. "You have almost laid down your life for the Confederacy."[53]

Rebels' dogged demands for acknowledgement of dutiful service through to the final death throes of their failed southern republic and their unapologetic insistence upon the justness of their failed cause further highlight Confederate veterans' adaptability and determination to self-define individual and collective manhood. Defeat need not deny manhood nor even dilute the virility of masculine identity, particularly when Lost Cause adherents insisted that victory had always remained unrealistic anyway. Rather, Confederate veterans simply redirected the defining characteristic of manhood from defeat at the hands of the mighty Yankee war machine to the powerful notion that true diehard Rebels had fought to the bitter end for a cause that remained imminently worthy and correct despite its failure. In other words, although they capitulated on the battlefield, Johnny Rebs never surrendered to another group's definition of manhood, particularly when that victorious and vastly more numerous belligerent "should" have triumphed anyway.

Obviously, Confederate veterans in 1865 never consciously interpreted these developments in terms of gender and masculinity. However, obstinate Johnny Rebs certainly recognized attempts to revolutionize their society and to remake the South in the image of the North. Moreover, southern veterans resented the fact that the attempted imposition of a new identity came at the hands of their recent opponents, whom they blamed for so much destruction and suffering. Confederate veterans deliberately acted individually and collectively to contrast their image from that of their northern rivals during the immediate postwar period. As discussed in chapter five, determined efforts toward economic recovery and resistance to Federal Reconstruction efforts and the advancement of civil rights for former slaves served to fortify the bonds forged between Confederate fighting men during the war itself. The demobilization experience kept alive the brotherly bonds forged in combat, reminded southern veterans of their shared sacrifice and common enemy, and therefore contributed to the foundations of the Lost Cause creed.

Such conscious, organized, and aggressive activity toward the protection of a collective identity on the part of Confederate veterans continues recent historians' challenges to the once-prominent interpretive concept of "hibernation" among veterans: the notion that, upon returning from war, ex-soldiers immediately turned their minds away from the conflict and its myriad problems in favor of a recovery period of approximately fifteen years, during which they suppressed the excruciating memories of service. Recent scholarship on Union veterans disputes this thesis through the careful study of those combatants' immediate postwar activities, including the formation of organizations and the publication of a staggering number of firsthand accounts of individual and unit service.[54] Although the creation of larger veterans' organizations and the movement to build monuments accelerated during subsequent decades, veterans' actions on both sides during the immediate postwar years undermine the notion of hibernation. The analysis of Confederate veterans under examination here supports the findings of scholars of Union veterans with regard to the lack of a hibernation period. Collectively that scholarship and the present study help to reopen for investigation that period immediately after the war, sometimes lost between the military events of the war and the study of veterans' later activities. Specifically, during the period in question, Confederate veterans acted swiftly to plant the seeds of Lost Cause ideology and to secure control of the Civil War narrative through insistence upon the righteousness of their cause and dogged resistance to external attempts to redefine southern identity.

One such southern cavalryman—writing decades after the war in reference to the end of the conflict—typified many of his defiant comrades when he insisted that, *if asked,* he and his unit would have crossed the Mississippi River westward to continue the fight, even after they realized the futility of further resistance. Instead, they accepted their fate and surrendered in Alabama only once it was clear that they had done everything humanly possible to secure Confederate victory. Thus, he covered all his bases: brave enough and dedicated enough to fight even after crushing defeat was certain; intelligent enough to recognize defeat and avoid crossing the line between gallantry and stupidity; and honorable enough to acquiesce peacefully to the terms of surrender. Ultimately, he faithfully carried out his duty in pursuit of a virtuous cause.[55]

A second narrative thread emerges from the frequent allusions to faithful service through to the end of the war. Soldiers obviously sought defense of their actions, preservation of individual and family honor, and the shaping of individual postwar reputations. Such writings that emphasize dedication to duty also help to explain why so many men remained in the ranks even after defeat appeared increasingly certain. Moreover, insistence upon dutiful service to the very end, even from men who desperately wanted to return to their homes and loved ones, proved common in all Confederate armies and theaters of the war. One homesick Texan who pined for his wife and baby wanted his mate to know that he sought nothing more than to return to her that moment but that he refused to leave before final surrender because he would do nothing to dishonor his family. Another prideful Texan wrote similarly to his wife from Mississippi in the closing days of April 1865. "I would like much to be with you again but do not know whether I ever shall be or not. I have escaped well so far, for which I thank God. But I hope I may be spared to get home again honorably. Some of the boys are going home without papers, but unless my notion changes. . . . I will never run away." The preservation of family honor as much as individual reputation motivated and shaped the masculine ethos of many diehard Confederate soldiers.[56]

As discussed earlier, numerous soldiers expressed genuine belief in prospects for victory until very late in the war. More important and more specific, whether authentic assurance or manufactured daring for the sake of appearance, such men by the late spring of 1865 must not be considered representative of the southern people overall, Confederate soldiers in general, or even those dedicated men who remained under arms after Appomattox. Accounts discussed in this chapter demonstrate that individuals acknowledged defeat at different times and in reaction to diverse developments. Whether the fall of Richmond, the surrender of the Army of Northern Virginia or the Army of Tennessee, the capture of Jefferson Davis, or the collective depressive effects of those developments crushed an individual Confederate soldier's hopes for victory, from a broad historical perspective, all of those events occurred within a relatively short period. Regardless of the exact moment of the acceptance of defeat, almost everyone recognized that the cause had failed by some point in April, or May for the true diehards. To be sure, belief in legitimate prospects for Confederate victory kept men in the ranks into the spring of 1865. But when defeat became certain in the minds of virtually all reasonable participants, dedication to dutiful service—and therefore the importance of individual and family honor—kept many Rebels in the ranks until formal surrender.

One resolute Rebel stated this unambiguously in a letter to his mother in late April 1865 from Petersburg, Virginia. Though Lee had surrendered at Appomattox, he and his comrades yet resisted Federal overtures for formal capitulation. "We are now surrounded on all sides by Yankees but continue to hold our own more from a sense of honor and duty however than from any hope that it will do any good." As that message makes clear, Confederate soldiers who remained in the field to the end out of a sense of honor and duty knew exactly why they stayed. Perhaps a droll Missouri infantry captain illustrated this most explicitly when on May 12, 1865, he quipped: "There is honor in being the last to desert the ship and we are almost alone in the sinking wreck." In sum, thousands of southern soldiers remained in the ranks to the bitter end and after victory proved impossible, because of genuine dedication to honor and duty, but equally importantly, because they wanted recognition for that commitment and because they refused to yield to a redefined definition of manhood forced upon them by external entities.[57]

That common insistence upon credit for faithful, dutiful service sheds light on the nuances of the final common reaction to overall Confederate defeat—relief. Many soldiers, even some of the most dedicated Rebels under consideration in this study, acknowledged relief at the end of the conflict. Even those most devastated by the failure of the cause found solace in the resumption of peace and the return of something that resembled normality. Expression of relief in no way undermined each soldier's commitment to his cause. Rather, each man conveyed predictable and understandable human emotions shared by countless survivors of war. Numerous individuals sampled here evinced relief

without overt explanation or even acknowledgment.[58] Some explicitly acknowledged the lifting of the burden, though thousands of others shared the sentiment without having left a written account that confessed as much.

Multiple factors explain why some men never expressed relief. First, as with
any concept, some men simply never mentioned it in their diaries, letters, or
memoirs. Such an omission in no way confirms the absence of said sentiments.
Second, and herein lies the connection to duty and the importance of recognition of service, some individuals simply confessed shame at the notion of an
admission of relief. Because courage in the face of combat exemplified the masculine ideal, an expression of relief might be perceived as cowardice or fear of
facing further trials. As one Tennessee infantry captain recalled, sadness and
gloom pervaded, "but with all our sorrow there was a feeling of relief that the
war was at last over, that we were at liberty to go home, once more. I am afraid
if the truth were known that we were not as sorry as we should have been. The
feeling of relief was so great that for a time all else was forgotten in the satisfaction that gave." Meanwhile, a dedicated Rebel who wrote from Florida in May
1865 stood less tolerant of his relieved comrades and reinforced the taboo on
open expression of relief. "Everything looks quiet and gloomy here," he opined,
"but there are some who show in their faces that they would like to be jubilant
if they dared." Finally, other soldiers acknowledged not only trepidation toward
the expression of happiness that the war had ended, but shame at even *feeling* relieved. One veteran recalled years later that as a nineteen-year-old South Carolina private he was ashamed of himself for his sense of relief. Initially upon hearing the news of surrender he cried along with countless comrades. But when he
"remembered that the cruel war was over and we were free to go home to the
family and remain, no more starving, freezing, fatigue and danger of death and
capture, I laughed out loud. Then remembering past glory of Lee was gone, what
surrender involved, I was ashamed of my mirth and cried again."[59]

Johnny Reb hesitated to express relief openly for fear that comrades might
question his courage and dedication to the cause, and he confronted intense inner shame at even private feelings of relief because painful questions might arise
from within. As a group of South Carolinians began their homeward trek from
Appomattox, the bounce in their collective step revealed a mounting joy and
recognizable sense of liberation. Despite conflicted emotions and occasional
jokes that were met with restrained, insincere laughter, one relieved soldier
dared to sing the opening stanzas of the popular tune, "The Girl I Left Behind

Me." An unsympathetic comrade swiftly halted the impromptu expression of unmentionable gaiety. After spitting upon his presumably indiscreet comrade, the offended party made clear his offense. "We ain't heroes anymore. We're just a bunch of whipped dogs goin' home with our tails between our legs."[60]

The proscribed character of expressions or even thoughts of relief remains evident, but no more so than the *prevalence* of such statements among Confederate soldiers. So, what exactly explains why so many dedicated, fire-eating Rebel fighting men proved so joyful amidst the greatest calamity most could conjure? First, why overlook the obvious? These men had endured, in most cases, years of combat, myriad battles and multiple campaigns, and the hardships and diseases inherent in camp life; and any such veteran had suffered or even witnessed the deaths of treasured comrades. Therefore, some doubtless rejoiced not simply because they had survived, but because they realized that all of those dangers loomed to the very end. Comrades of one Georgia infantryman grasped that potential all too well. He suffered a mortal wound in the defense of Petersburg, Virginia, on April 2, 1865. Had he avoided that fatal shot, he would have reunited with his young wife only days later. Instead, strangers soon informed her of his death. Although she probably had already learned of her loss, a comrade wrote to the widow in June to notify her of her mate's passing and to describe his final moments. With his dying breath he sang a hymn and declared his wish to have seen his beloved again. The compassionate comrade, still recovering from a wound himself, described the loving care provided her husband by nurses, who also oversaw his burial.[61]

Survivors naturally recognized their good fortune to have avoided such a heartrending demise only days before a return to civilian life. That knowledge points to a second explanation for expressions of relief among even diehard Rebels—capitulation ended the excruciating suspense. Despite the devastating and humiliating reality of defeat, at least soldiers knew their collective and individual fates. Additionally, the cumulative effect of all this created daily living conditions so difficult and stressful that almost anything else seemed preferable. Individual soldiers' relief, of course, could be explained by any of these factors. Some men, however, actually experienced the entire array. A soldier encamped in East Texas at war's end wrote letters to family in which he conveyed virtually all of the above sentiments, and one other, within a span of two weeks.[62]

That Texan pointed to the single most powerful and easily the most commonly expressed explanation for relief in defeat—the return to family. Despite

what Confederate soldiers considered a catastrophic cessation, peace meant reunion with those they held most dear. The burning desire to return to family, a
fundamental human emotion indeed, dominated the thoughts of countless soldiers by the closing weeks of the war. One western soldier betrayed his anguish
over his family in multiple consecutive letters to his wife in early April 1865. His
every thought focused on her and their son, he assured his wife. One letter con-
tained a rather thinly veiled reference to his absence at least preventing an additional pregnancy. He even parented from afar, as he sent kisses to his son and
urged his wife not to scold the boy. Let him have his fun in these difficult times,
the young father reasoned, because the lad naturally missed his papa. What that
soldier obviously suffered, another expressed explicitly only two weeks later. A
Tennessee captain admitted in his diary that "a general Joy seems to beam from
almost every face at the prospect of peace and the thoughts of home to and
meeting loved ones from whom they have long been seperated."[63]

Beyond the fundamental human emotion of longing for family, soldiers,
particularly husbands and fathers, expressed concern for the physical safety
and general material well-being of loved ones at home without them. As chaos
reigned throughout much of the former Confederacy, soldiers justifiably ago-
nized over families at the mercy of roving bands of ne'er do wells, intent on un-
told nefarious deeds. In the words of one Rebel still in a Federal prison camp, "I
cannot but think that the women & children in North Ala must be in a terrible
condition no protectors. Negroes & worse Tories having entire possession of
the Country God protect them for they can receive no assistance from us." To
put it another way, Johnny Reb needed to get home primarily because he was
needed at home.[64]

Husbands and fathers among Confederate soldiers in particular endured
that emotional trauma. Historians have increasingly and persuasively argued
for the necessity of a broader and more flexible definition of manhood among
Civil War soldiers that considers the deeper, emotional worlds of the combatants. Moreover, no single definition of manhood perfectly encompasses every
fighting man. Nineteenth-century men themselves of course complicated such
analyses further because they often neglected to, or perhaps consciously chose
not to, commit such emotions to paper for future historians' examination.[65]

Civil War soldier-fathers on both sides suffered immense emotional trauma
as a result of extended separation from their children. Here, too, historians
now recognize that the concept of fatherhood embraced far more than simple

domestic or biological circumstances. In contrast to the stereotype of the unin-volved patriarch, fathers who served during the war actually longed for active roles in child rearing. In fact, studies demonstrate that more than simply reveal-ing pre-existing conditions, the desperate circumstances of the war, including extended periods of separation, compelled men to maintain increasingly in-tense emotional bonds with loved ones. Fathers especially struggled with feel-ings of isolation and helplessness during a time when their families might con-front emergencies. This heavy burden and powerful need to provide for and protect wives and children formed a fundamental aspect of all married Civil War soldiers' masculine identity by any definition.[66]

Naturally those same veterans confronted the challenge of returning to marriages sometimes inescapably altered by the events and sufferings of the pre-vious few years. Spouses learned how to reestablish lives together, a task often made more difficult amidst dire postwar economic circumstances. Many wives understood and even shared veterans' fears that children might forget their fa-thers. Countless women also intuitively sensed the oppressive fear among fight-ing men that life at home had gone on without them and that the defeated Rebel veterans now confronted the appalling prospect of life under the rule of their hated vanquishers. All such emotional concepts formed fundamental, if less ob-vious, components of manhood among Civil War soldiers in general and among the Confederates examined here in particular.[67]

Thus, predictably, thousands of individuals on both sides throughout the war at some point decided that the lure of home exceeded their dedication to their respective causes. For some, this led to desertion. Equally evident, a great many Confederates acquiesced to the temptation of home only after they had conceded overall defeat. After all, in the minds of most Civil War soldiers on both sides, desertion signified cowardice and disloyalty and violated the fun-damental masculine values of honor and courage, at least until victory proved beyond reach.[68] At that point, once a soldier in the field had honorably met his obligations, there really remained no legitimate reason to prolong the absence from his loved ones. Once almost-certain defeat became official, virtually any sensible husband and father considered his return to his family the responsible and honorable thing to do. Why prolong the privation and potential danger faced by those who depended upon him when the war could no longer be won? A thirty-four-year-old Arkansas infantry captain expressed it best when he de-scribed an encounter with Federal officers in Nashville, Tennessee, during his homeward journey. The Union officers rejected the paroles issued to the Confederates upon surrender and demanded that the defeated men swear an oath of allegiance to the United States in order to secure satisfactory paroles. When the Federals threatened to send the men to northern prisons for failure to comply, the Arkansas captain noted that "with one exception we thought it prudent, and even patriotic, to comply with the terms rather than be stubborn, which would only have prolonged our suffering and been equivalent to divorcing ourselves from our wives and making orphans of our helpless children."[69]

For men held captive, the decision to abandon resistance and to take the steps necessary to return to home and family proved virtually identical. The choice became simpler still upon the capitulation of the respective armies that they had served. Their units no longer existed, and after a certain point neither did the country that they had fought to establish. There remained no rational reason to struggle with the decision. Many of course had long refused to sign an oath of allegiance to the United States in exchange for release from prison, instead holding out for the more honorable release on parole once the war had officially concluded. This show of defiance mirrored that of the soldier in the field who remained in the ranks, long after his recognition of defeat, until official surrender and parole. The dreaded oath remained unpalatable, but it meant a return to family. In the words of one Virginian, written to his wife, "I expect to meet you soon, not crowned with the laurels of victory but with the oath crammed down my throat, a quiescent citizen of the United States."[70]

Therefore, despite the different environment, the basic thought process and evolution of sentiments for prisoners mirrored that of their comrades in the field. They accepted the oath of allegiance and walked out of prison only once they had concluded that the Confederacy ceased to exist, that they were satisfied that they had done everything reasonably possible, and that their dedication to duty could never be questioned.

One anguished Alabamian, in the span of less than one month, managed to progress through the entire range of concerns expressed individually and collectively by many comrades in an effort to justify taking the oath. The futility of further resistance, the crushing desire to reunite with his family, the treatment of prisoners, responsibilities at home, and the complex question of honor all weighed heavy on the tormented husband and father. Although he second-guessed his decision to take the oath, his most compelling justification—through weeks of diary entries—could not be more apparent. From his confines at Fort

Delaware, he reasoned that honor had kept him there and honor would send him home. Articulate in his own way and with powerful reason he concluded, "Honor, to Keep me here in Safety & comparative comfort. when it may be that Wife Children Mother Sister are suffering insult oppression want all of which I might by my presence avert from them. Methinks, that Honor would bid me go to them." Although the transition might have been subconscious, the Alabaman's masculine ethos had helped to keep him in his country's service. Now, in the face of certain defeat and with his family's safety foremost in his thoughts, the masculine need to protect and provide compelled him to go home.[71]

Because dreams of home and family haunted the minds of Confederate fighting men, many soldiers' thoughts logically turned to preparations to begin their lives anew. Here we refer not to long-term visions or even to immediate postwar adjustment after arrival at home, to be discussed later. Rather, here we consider how soldiers pondered the immediate needs for themselves and families before actual demobilization. Could he still make something of the harvest? How much had been done in his absence? How much food and other provisions had his loved ones stored? Would he need to seek employment elsewhere? Interestingly, soldiers frequently pondered such questions within days of surrender or even before capitulation. Already their minds focused on the return to civilian life, and for some the thought itself was therapeutic. As the men conversed among themselves, attempted to move past the humiliation and devastation of defeat, and began to question what to do next, one Virginian recalled: "The discussion of the question brought relief from the horrid feeling of vacuity which oppressed the soldier and introduced him to the new sensations of liberty of choice, freedom of action—full responsibility. For capital he had a clear conscience, a brave heart, health, strength, and a good record. With these he sought his home." Thoughts of family and moving on with life not only help to explain the initial expressions of relief among many Confederate combatants, but the continued discussion of the subjects further strengthened that sense of inner peace and permitted each soldier solace in the knowledge that he could return to his family having satisfied any reasonable standard of duty or masculinity.[72]

That philosophical Virginian wrote with the comfort and perspective of nearly three decades of postwar experience. For other veterans, of course, more practical matters took precedence in their thoughts of moving on. One such Rebel, an Arkansas infantry officer then in Texas, wrote to his wife in late May 1865 amid the chaotic disintegration of Confederate Trans-Mississippi forces. He arranged for relatives—who would return home before he could get there—to check in on his family. More telling, he instructed his wife: "Tel Walker to try to save as much wheat as possible, & to work like a little man." Census records indicate that the young man in question was the officer's teenaged nephew who resided in the family household. That a soldier, farmer, husband, father, and provider would shift his thinking to the postwar fate of his family seems hardly surprising, even during the intense closing scenes of the conflict. A responsible man understood that despite the demise of the would-be nation that he had cherished and struggled to establish, a family, a farm, and an uncertain future awaited his return.[73]

Here again, Johnny Reb surrendered his cause but refused to yield to another's definition of his manhood. Confederate veterans' masculine ethos suffered under the strain of defeat, emancipation, financial difficulties, and in some cases, lingering physical effects of war. However, ex-Confederate fighting men confronted the reality of the postwar South but steadfastly resisted the notion that Yankee armies or anyone else could destroy their manhood. Confederate veterans sought instant financial recovery not merely for obvious practical reasons but also to demonstrate for all observers that they would resume the mantle of provider. In the words of a historian who examined the postwar experiences of veterans in Virginia, "In the end, although Southern white masculinity was threatened, it eventually recovered some of its antebellum strength." Among the men examined here, that recovery began instantly and with fierce resolve. That determination to recuperate his financial world represented Johnny Reb's practical need to restart his life, his continued defiance of northern rule, and resistance to the attempts of outside forces to undermine his masculine identity.[74]

That Arkansas soldier who made arrangements for his family in his absence personified the sense of relief and the desire to move on with life expressed by so many Confederates. Other soldiers discussed in this chapter shared those sentiments but also voiced shock, anguish, humiliation, and concern for the safety and well-being of their loved ones. Each man processed defeat differently, of course, but some soldiers progressed rather quickly through a wide range of emotions. One soldier recalled that he and a comrade discussed their fate for several hours "and laughed and cried alternately like two hysterical women." A Confederate general struck a far more serious chord in his memoirs, though he articulated essentially the same point. The former officer acknowledged a harsh reality that faced at least some of his men. "They knew that burnt homes and

fenceless farms, poverty and ashes, would greet them on their return from war."
Still, the officer emphasized the many advantages that the South offered its veterans and urged his men to embrace his optimistic outlook. Often the very men
who had been so devastated in defeat began their journeys home with something of a bounce in their step.[75]

That certainly proved true of young Evan Shelby Jefferies of the Sixteenth
Mississippi Infantry. In many ways Jefferies personifies the typical Rebel who remained under arms until the final surrenders. In a letter written in April 1865, he
admitted to his wife that he had no idea how long it would be before he could return to her, but that he intended to resign in order to form a cavalry unit to operate entirely within his home state. Reality set in rapidly, however, as revealed in
an addendum to the letter after his initial closing and signature. He would leave
tomorrow and should arrive home within a few days. A dedicated Confederate
capable of matching the fiery rhetoric of the most determined Rebel, Jefferies
remained in service so late in the war explicitly, at least in part, because he refused to bring shame upon himself or his relatives. His sense of manhood simply would not countenance the threat of dishonor to his family. Moreover, similar to numerous comrades, in his role of masculine protector he expressed grave
concern for his young wife's safety in his absence, even urging her to stay at his
father's home as much as possible. "The Yanks are treating our ladies worse now
than ever they savage every woman they can get their hands on."[76]

Jefferies's focus on his wife and child after a prolonged absence also typified
the mental state of Johnny Reb. For this particular soldier, however, the torment
of war produced at least a brief burst of introspection and forced the Mississippian to reevaluate himself as a man and husband. A mere twenty-two years old,
he pined for his wife Katie, herself but twenty, and sent well-wishes to his young
son. "May he ever be gentle & kind & never cause your dear heart one moment
trouble O may he be to you as I will be if God in his mercy sees fit to spare my
worthless life as long as your life lasts." The protracted absence from his young
family and the uncertainty of a reunion or even his survival forced Jefferies to
seek his mate's forgiveness and to commit himself to a better tomorrow should
he make it back to her. "Katie I am unworthy of you I know it & feel it more &
more every day I have not been the husband that I should have been for kind
loving words I have returned angry oaths & looks." The outpouring of regret and
pledge of greater devotion and compassion continue for numerous excruciating
sentences before Jefferies's thoughts return again to his child. "Kiss my little boy
a thousand times for me & don't let him forget his Papa!"[77]

Scholars have identified expressions of grave concern among civilians North and South, particularly relatives of returning veterans, that the war years had corrupted the morals of Civil War soldiers. Excessive drinking, gambling, and the violation of established sexual mores especially concerned those who awaited the return of their beloved combatant. Jefferies of course chose not to explain his feeling of unworthiness to his bride. Perhaps he suffered immense guilt for his unidentified actions while away from home, or possibly he simply endured crushing sadness and guilt for being away from his young wife and child.[78]

Though very much the typical Johnny Reb with regard to his mindset at war's end, in other ways Jefferies differed from most of his comrades and thus presents an intriguing case study that illustrates the challenges inherent in group portraits. The son of an exceedingly wealthy planter whose personal property and real estate value exceeded $150,000 in 1860, the young Mississippian came of age on a plantation and thus his upbringing could hardly be described as typical. In this regard he shared more in common with his wife, herself the daughter of a prosperous attorney, than with most of his comrades. Despite his determined support of the Confederacy, Jefferies joined the army in spring 1862, placing him in the ranks of soldiers who have been termed "late enlisters." An excellent study of late enlisters has demonstrated convincingly that myriad reasons prevented these men from joining up immediately after the Fort Sumter crisis. Though typically less ideological than their comrades who signed up during the chaotic days of 1861, late enlisters collectively served as efficiently as any other segment of the soldiery.[79]

The youthful, fiery, and ideologically inclined Jefferies, then, defies simple categorization, and his actual military service only muddies the waters further. Captured and paroled within his first year, Private Jefferies served until late 1863, at which time he received his discharge, having hired a substitute. The poor soul who replaced him later fell in combat in 1864, presumed killed in action. Although his service record ends with his 1863 discharge, Jefferies obviously returned to the field at some point, in some capacity. The Confederate Congress abolished the practice of substitution in December 1863 and in January 1864 decreed that conscription again applied to principals who had hired substitutes. Although sources offer no clear indication, perhaps the change in legislation explains Jeffries's return to the ranks. His marriage and the birth of his son occurred during the period after the conclusion of his service record and thus almost certainly during his time away from the army. Despite the absence of such notation in his service record, the Mississippi private remained present for duty at the end of the war and outwardly projected the attitude and determination of an obstinate Rebel.[80]

Such determined fighting men throughout the Confederacy expressed genuine shock and dismay at the news of Appomattox. Many even aggressively denied the reports until they witnessed Lee's legions marching homeward. Although those predictable reactions reflect sentiments expressed in wartime and postwar accounts, the relative few who claimed the foresight to expect overall Confederate defeat by spring 1865 were somewhat more likely to have made such claims during the postwar years. To be sure, most postwar writers said nothing of the sort, but individuals who claimed to foresee overall Confederate failure were likely to have written those statements in later years.

Most Confederate soldiers who remained in the ranks at war's end recognized that Appomattox effectively ended the conflict. Although hardly universal, that reality appears obvious in wartime and postwar accounts, in massive quantities, in all theaters of the war, despite a determined and vocal minority that insisted upon continued resistance. Other Rebel soldiers acknowledged defeat only in response to other events. A few pointed to the fall of Richmond, but that historic event looms larger in postwar sources as a factor in the admission of defeat. Others acquiesced only in response to the accumulation of Confederate setbacks that spring and summer. Far more common, however, the capitulation of the Army of Tennessee ended the hopes of most southern soldiers who persisted after Appomattox. Here again, comparisons of wartime and postwar accounts yields no definitive difference, but a distinct and probably predictable regional pattern emerges. Western and Trans-Mississippi theater soldiers proved far more likely to lose faith only after the demise of the Army of Tennessee. Eastern theater units had already surrendered, and thus only a relative handful retained hope based upon the presence of the Confederacy's primary western army. More important, Johnston's surrender dashed the hopes of many western Rebels as it marked the death of their army, the one that they had served and that had defended their homes and families. Trans-Mississippi soldiers, of course, recognized that the demise of the Army of Tennessee left only Confederate forces west of the Mississippi River to stand against the entire Federal war machine.

Once Johnny Reb had admitted defeat, he expressed a range of emotions that included grief, humiliation, and anger, as well as concerns for the potential futility of so much sacrifice, a defense of the righteousness of his cause, an insistence upon credit for having served to the end, relief, and thoughts of moving on with life. All such reactions appear in wartime and postwar accounts and from soldiers in all theaters, though a few slight variations emerge. For example, expressions of humiliation in the aftermath of surrender emerge more commonly in postwar accounts, while analysis of adamant defenses of the Confederate cause reveals a subtler trend. When soldiers wrote in defense of the cause in wartime diaries and letters, they typically referenced both individual and collective service. In other words, *I* did right, and *we* did right. Postwar writers expressed the same general ideas but far more often wrote about the collective—*we* did right, and *we* make no apologies. Perhaps the timing makes this trend predictable because most such tracts appeared in print during the volatile days of Reconstruction and the proliferation of Lost Cause ideology, and because of the more general urge to defend one's respective side during the years that followed a controversial and devastating conflict.

Numerous Confederate soldiers admitted to a powerful sense of relief upon the conclusion of the conflict. Many also turned their attention to their immediate postwar lives. In both cases, wartime and postwar accounts coincide. Moreover, a somewhat surprising absence of a pattern can be found in the accounts of men whose thoughts turned to moving on with their lives. Surprisingly, married men did not express such concerns more often than their single comrades. Certainly, married men understandably turned their energies to the sustenance of their families during the summer of 1865. From a different perspective, however, many young, single veterans directed their remaining youthful exuberance toward the next stage of their lives.

Before that phase could begin, the demobilized Confederate soldier would have to find his way home. Despite the demise of the would-be nation and the chaos that enveloped most of the South during the spring and summer of 1865, Rebel and Yankee officers worked together to create a system of Confederate demobilization that eventually facilitated the homeward trek of thousands of soldiers-turned-veterans. The development of that system and the logistical obstacles confronted by authorities on both sides constitute the next chapter for Johnny Reb.

2

YANKEES & REBELS

THE SYSTEM OF CONFEDERATE DEMOBILIZATION

Once Union victory and Confederate defeat became reality, the minds of officers on both sides turned to terms of capitulation. The respective conferences between erstwhile belligerents of course resulted in various well-known surrender ceremonies but, more relevant here, those meetings also led to the creation of an actual, organized system of Confederate demobilization. Analysis of that system in this chapter highlights the development and importance of the parole process and the provision for substantial rations and transportation made for Confederate soldiers by Union authorities. Upon the establishment of the scheme, emphasis turns next to the interplay between northern and southern men, successes and breakdowns of the system, Confederate implementation of the plan, and finally, analysis of basic logistics such as method, distance, and routes of travel.

Conditions of surrender for all Confederate forces generally mirrored those famously generous terms offered by Ulysses S. Grant to Robert E. Lee at Appomattox Court House, Virginia, April 9, 1865. However, during subsequent negotiations, Union and Confederate officers drafted additional stipulations that directly affected individual soldiers and dramatically altered their journeys home. Thus despite an initial lack of a discernible Confederate demobilization system, a basic concept began to emerge at Appomattox, and a full-scale system took shape during the capitulation of the Army of Tennessee in North Carolina in late April 1865. Among the provisions agreed upon at the various surrender conferences, the most significant stipulations that directly affected individual demobilized Confederates included parole requirements that permitted Rebels the use of government and private transportation sources, rations distributed by Federal officials, and the limited retention of arms for safer travel and for the security of the countryside.[1]

As had been the case throughout most of the conflict, a parole identified a soldier as a prisoner of war and represented a signed pledge that he would not fight again until exchanged. Although the surrenders meant the end of the war in any practical sense, the respective generals lacked the authority to bring an official close to the struggle. Thus, while everyone soon recognized the war's conclusion, the defeated Rebels remained technically prisoners. That status helps to explain Lee's insistence upon such signed documents as some form of protection from harassment for his homebound legions. The parole documented that the traveling soldier came under terms agreed upon at the respective surrender. So powerful and widespread was this interpretation that in the minds of many southerners the documents symbolized a veritable certificate of immunity against any future legal actions taken by Federal authorities.[2]

The process for the distribution of paroles varied by location and circumstance, though most adhered to one of the following arrangements. In some instances, authorities sent infantry and cavalry to different sites to expedite the process. Men released from northern military prisons of course received the document before they left the facility. For units that remained organized and present for an official surrender, the men typically received paroles from their officers either on site or after they had traveled together some distance toward their home state, a strategy designed to encourage orderly behavior. Although most units disbanded long before they reached their states of residence, many traveled some portion of the journey together to a designated place, whereupon officers distributed paroles and divided resources, and comrades parted ways one last time.[3]

The story of one such unit from the Army of Tennessee is typical. The South Carolinians marched together more than one hundred miles from the general vicinity of Greensboro, North Carolina, to a small village in their home state. During the seven-day trek, the men dispersed during the daytime to secure food and reassembled each night, in part for their collective security. On May 8, 1865, the comrades distributed resources by lottery drawing, received their paroles, bid their final goodbyes, and marched toward their respective homes.[4]

In cases of individual soldiers or units scattered about the countryside in isolated commands or for various reasons separate from any organized unit, the men were instructed to go to one of the many sites established by Union authorities to collect their paroles. This proved especially common in the Trans-Mississippi theater, where, in the absence of a meaningful Federal presence, the Rebel army essentially disintegrated before formal surrender. Even troops who returned home from other theaters availed themselves of those parole locations. For example, a group of more than one hundred soldiers, many of them Texans, left their command in North Carolina without paroles but secured the documents from Federal authorities in Louisiana. Because of the chaotic overall conditions in that region in May–June 1865, the location of entire units remains difficult to pinpoint. (See chapter four for more on the turmoil west of the Mississippi River during the closing scenes of the war.)[5]

Although especially common in the far west, men from all regions of the South followed the same procedure when not present for one of the major surrenders. One Alabama cavalryman, home on furlough with an illness at the time of the surrenders, traveled to Montgomery for parole. Meanwhile, in the Shenandoah Valley of Virginia, a group of Kentuckians learned of the demise of Lee's army from passing soldiers and questioned what that development meant for them. Uncertain of what to do, some insisted upon a trek south to link up with other Confederate units that remained in the field. Even officers were unsure of the proper course of action and thus simply advised the men to fend for themselves. Eventually a group of approximately twenty traveled together to Charleston, West Virginia, to secure paroles and transportation passes and soon afterward parted ways.[6]

Regardless of the procedure followed at various points around the South, the distribution of paroles highlighted an embarrassing issue for Confederate leaders. At the sites of major surrenders, particularly Appomattox, the quantity of paroles issued to Confederate soldiers exceeded the number of men actually present for duty at the time of capitulation. Certainly stragglers, wounded men, and those detailed to non-combat duties explained a small part of the discrepancy. Equally obvious, however, thousands of deserters thronged to parole centers to secure the valuable paperwork. So many unattached individuals from the Army of Northern Virginia and the Army of Tennessee poured into Greensboro, North Carolina, for paroles that the Federal supervisor of the process there reopened his office.[7]

That embarrassment for the Confederate high command became a controversy of a different sort among average southern soldiers. Those who had served faithfully to the end—exercising admirable patience by delaying longed-for homeward treks while they waited for paroles—understandably fumed at the sight of thousands of deserters who obtained the same documentation that the diehards received. Those who completed their service honorably, at immense risk to their own lives, expressed intense bitterness toward those who had failed to match their commitment. Moreover, Johnny Reb quite reasonably wanted credit for his actions. No true blue Rebel genuinely wanted to sign a Yankee parole until he accepted either overall Confederate defeat or at least the official capitulation of his unit, at which point he very much wanted that important paper. In later years many men would claim meritorious service but he who had remained true to the colors and secured a parole often believed that such a document provided at least some tangible evidence of his rightful claim to the honor of diehard Rebel. It thus proved difficult, even excruciating, to watch deserters stroll in to secure the same valued certificate. Worse yet, one Georgia infantry captain recorded in his diary that many men who had abandoned their commands not only showed up for paroles but afterward actually marched with their former comrades to the depot to secure rail transport.[8]

Confederate officers of course understood the bitterness directed toward deserters in general and especially in the direction those who secured paroles. In Meridian, Mississippi, Lieutenant General Richard Taylor directed the distribution of paroles and even briefly supervised Federal officers and soldiers who assisted with the process. So many deserters showed up that Confederates who had served to the end faced delays of several days. Very much aware and respectful of the veterans' perspective and cognizant of the nonsensical concept that faithful soldiers should wait for deserters, Taylor eventually intervened and halted the distribution of paroles to deserters, at least until all faithful combatants had been issued their papers.[9]

Rebel officers at Meridian also ignored the abuse soldiers inflicted upon the undesirables who straggled into camp for paroles. Predictably, Union officers and enlisted men on the scene typically overlooked the abuse as well. Clearly sympathetic to the sacrifices of fellow combatants, the northern men empathized with the animosity that their erstwhile enemies directed toward deserters. A twenty-four-year-old infantryman and musician from Louisiana described the scene. After the Rebels stacked arms and prepared to endure the tedious interval to procure paroles and permission to head for home, "Many men who had never seen service and some who had quit on the change of commanders at Atlanta, were also at Meridian to receive paroles. Some of them were handled roughly by our soldiers, much to the amusement of the Federals who were guarding us."[10]

A nineteen-year-old artilleryman who arrived in Meridian for surrender and parole from the evacuation of Mobile, Alabama, recalled a similar but more explicit version of the episode. Incensed by the presence of those who had left their "hiding places," soldiers took matters into their own hands to torment the known deserters, to the delight of the men in blue. "Some were beaten, some ridden on rails, some had their heads and beards shaved—one side only, etc.," the veteran remembered with satisfaction. "Our friends the enemy looked on and enjoyed it as much as we did and never interfered. Brave men always feel the same about such things. Much of this took place in the middle of the town where everybody could see. I see one picture now—a big fellow astride a rail held high up by a number of hands, yells of derision and contempt all about him. Absurd yet humiliating."[11]

Interestingly, beyond concerns about deserters and the parole process, Confederate soldiers at this late stage of the war said relatively little about desertion. Perhaps they deemed it an unfortunate aspect of the war to which they had become numb by that point, or perhaps by spring and summer 1865 many concluded that it simply no longer mattered. Soldiers condemned deserters to be sure and the bitterness remained widespread even late in the conflict. Many pointed to the honor of having served to the end, and even the least philosophically inclined fighting man understood that desertion while victory remained remotely attainable violated the most basic expectations of manhood. Moreover, predictably, soldiers applied sundry unflattering labels to those who had abandoned the cause. In fact, even the mere word "deserter" became an epithet after the war, as in the case of the Virginia infantryman who won election as mayor of his hometown during the summer of 1865, despite the efforts of a conglomeration of opponents whom he termed bushwhackers, union men, and deserters. As that account illustrates, deserters frequently bore the blame for any number of crimes and misdeeds that they might or might not have actually committed.[12]

Despite the obvious bitterness that soldiers directed toward those former comrades who failed to complete their terms of service, the collapse of the Confederacy, surrenders, parole process, and the desire to go home all combined to create a gray area surrounding one aspect of desertion. Thousands of men from all three theaters left the armies without paroles during the days immediately before the surrenders and thus, technically, they deserted. Although soldiers typically denounced such behavior, and indeed some firebrands continued to condemn anything that might be considered desertion under any definition, many clearly considered this different from the actions of those who had abandoned their country and comrades while victory remained attainable. Therefore, those soldiers who left at the end, in effect with only hours remaining in the life of the respective army, generally escaped the wrath of their fellow fighting men. Those men who served until the bitter end met the threshold of diehard Rebel but simply went home without a piece of paper. Furthermore, in some cases the enlisted men merely followed the orders or examples of their officers.

Two accounts are representative of the nuanced evolution of Confederate perspectives on desertion once the reality of defeat had taken root. As one prominent veteran recalled of the dying days of one army, "Officers as high as colonels, not only countenanced, but participated in the shameful conduct." But another veteran who recalled a similar scene elsewhere captured the larger point, and expressed the general sentiment shared with countless soldiers under consideration in this study, when he wrote that "desertions were now becoming numerous among those who considered further contention useless, but who, I believe, to a man, would have kept true to the last, and fought against desperate odds, as long as there was the slightest hope of success." Clearly, then, the timing with regard to the theoretical possibility of victory established the threshold of what constituted desertion in the minds of Confederates at this late stage of the conflict.[13]

The controversial and sought-after paroles also entitled traveling Johnny Rebs to rations distributed by the Federals at numerous locations around the South and even beyond. Grant, of course, fed the famished Rebels at Appomattox, primarily with confiscated Confederate supplies. General Johnston and Major General John M. Schofield, William T. Sherman's subordinate, formulated a plan that brought approximately one quarter-million rations by rail to the men of the Army of Tennessee. Part humanitarian and part pragmatist, Federal commanders acted out of genuine concern for the well-being of their respected former enemies but also hoped to limit chaos and lawlessness that could result from thousands of starved men gathered together under desperate circumstances.[14]

More important than the substantial provisions delivered at the time of surrender, paroles entitled Confederate soldiers to rations provided by Federal forces at various points *during* their travel. More than any aspect of the surrender agreements other than transportation allowances, the organized distribution of rations to traveling demobilized soldiers reveals the development of a system of Confederate demobilization. Typically, after Federal forces occupied a particular community, demobilized Rebels who passed through showed their paroles, usually at the provost marshal office, and secured rations and transportation. For example, in early May, Johnston identified the three best depots in Georgia to supply soldiers as Augusta, Washington, and Griffin, a much-traveled route that eventually led countless men into Atlanta. That important city hosted thousands of men from both of the two great Rebel armies during demobilization.[15]

Countless other locales also functioned as veritable oases for weary veterans as they traversed the countryside. Provost marshal offices in small towns and larger cities served in that same capacity. Although sources identify far too many sites to mention, certain communities on popular travel routes housed rations for literally thousands of demobilized Confederates. In Tennessee, countless soldiers visited Chattanooga, Nashville, and Memphis, while farther south, Montgomery, Jackson, and Vicksburg hosted the many Rebels who traversed that common westerly route. As coastal cities, Mobile and New Orleans accommodated numerous Rebels, while soldiers who departed from the Crescent City within their home state often secured provisions in Baton Rouge, Alexandria, and Shreveport, Louisiana. Men released from prison camps frequently found sustenance in Cincinnati, Ohio; Louisville, Kentucky; Baltimore, Maryland; Richmond, Virginia; and even New York City, depending on route and mode of transport.[16]

The coveted and controversial paroles related directly to another term of surrender agreed upon by Union and Confederate officers that directly affected the return journeys of demobilized Rebels and focused on various agreements related to transportation. At Appomattox, Lee famously requested that Confederate officers retain their horses for transportation and future use, and Grant obliged. In fact, the official agreement finalized at Appomattox the day after the iconic meeting permitted officers as well as cavalrymen and artillerists who provided their own mounts to retain possession of the valued animals. Further, the stipulations allowed officers to employ Confederate government property to transport private belongings home but required its return to United States officials upon arrival at the respective veteran's final destination. Although subordinate officers finalized such details, in Special Orders No. 73 Grant personally made clear that paroles entitled soldiers from the Army of Northern Virginia to the use of United States government-operated transports and railroads free of charge during their homeward journeys. During the ensuing several weeks the presence of soldiers on trains became so prevalent that, though not explicitly stated in the terms of surrender, even privately operated railroads transported southern veterans to their homes, often even without a pass.[17]

Weeks after Appomattox, the surrender agreement of the Army of Tennessee in North Carolina expanded upon transportation-related arrangements. Johnston and Sherman benefited from the experiences of Lee and Grant and provided more far-reaching terms that assisted veterans' travel. After reaching a general settlement fundamentally similar to that agreed upon in Virginia, Johnston worked with Sherman's subordinate Schofield to draft supplemental terms that permitted Confederates to make use of government field transportation, including artillery horses, for their travel home and for "subsequent use in their industrial pursuits." On the surface that provision appeared only a slight difference of semantics from the Appomattox convention. In reality, however, Johnston's insistence upon the inclusion of that stipulation actually led to the distribution of countless horses and mules among Confederates, facilitated homeward travel, provided invaluable stock for farms all across the South, and set the precedent followed by other officers in subsequent surrenders. (This and other public property distribution by western and Trans-Mississippi Confederates is further discussed below.) Finally, Johnston and Schofield arranged water transportation via New Orleans and Mobile for individuals bound for Arkansas and Texas.[18]

The final supplementary term of consequence agreed upon by Johnston and Schofield did not draw intense criticism from civil officials in Washington, shockingly, and proved imminently necessary for the safe travel of former Confederate soldiers. The agreement allowed one-seventh of each unit that traveled together to retain firearms to assist with the preservation of law and order in the countryside and to protect the veterans as they traversed what turned out to be a veritable lawless no-man's-land in many cases.[19]

Thus an actual organized system took shape remarkably quickly under the leadership of Johnston, more than anyone else, working closely initially with Sherman but more so with Schofield. Those officers learned from the initial experience of Lee and Grant, who, along with various subordinate officers, performed well under the circumstances at Appomattox despite a reasonable lack of preparation for the challenge of how to return thousands of demobilized soldiers to their distant homes during the chaotic closing scenes of war. Circumstances changed dramatically during the few weeks between the surrenders at Appomattox and Durham Station. Johnston and his Federal counterparts witnessed the passage of many of Lee's veterans and thus endeavored successfully to manage the next stage of demobilization more efficiently and to establish a more systematic process. The capitulation of the Army of Tennessee, not that of the Army of Northern Virginia, then, set the standard for subsequent Confederate surrenders as a result of cooperation between Rebel and Yankee commanders.

Federal efforts to assist with the creation of a Confederate demobilization process originated in part from basic benevolent considerations, but Union leaders also worked diligently to get southern soldiers home as quickly as possible in order to limit bands of men roaming the countryside. As Schofield noted with more than a hint of derision, he assisted Johnston's men with "two hundred and fifty thousand rations, with wagons to haul them, to prevent the troops from robbing their own people."[20] After all, from the perspective of Union authorities, demobilized Confederate soldiers constituted scores of thousands of trained and battle-scarred military veterans, many of whom were angry and bitter, penniless and desperate, and hundreds of miles from home. Northern officers needed Johnny Reb to go home.

Some northern observers initially considered the terms of surrender too lenient, particularly the release of so many Confederate soldiers to return home unmolested based simply on a parole. However, informed participants recognized the value of a speedy demobilization to overall public safety, and understood that holding defeated Rebels in camps and prisons any longer really served no purpose whatever and might have been deemed unnecessarily retributive.[21]

Certainly Federal officers on the scene who daily dealt with transitory soldiers recognized the need to keep them moving. One commander in Knoxville, Tennessee, for example, unsure of his authority over soldiers passing through from Lee's army, inquired of a superior whether he could issue them rations and load them onto trains to "get rid of them." Those individuals, he reasoned, were "penniless and without food, and must live by begging or stealing." The officer further hoped to load other "obnoxious and troublesome characters" to be removed from Knoxville along with the soldiers.[22] A few weeks later another Union officer in Tennessee requested and received the services of gunboats to assist with the transport of an entire Confederate brigade. Apparently the concentration of so many Rebels, "a thousand strong," made the officer nervous.[23]

Meanwhile the handling of another situation further highlights the practical motives of Federal authorities. During a short-lived controversy that resulted in the temporary suspension of paroles of Confederate soldiers from Kentucky and Missouri, one northern officer contacted Secretary of War Edwin Stanton to request permission to process a group of parolees scheduled to arrive at his location within days. The War Department struggled to decide exactly how to handle men from those two states that never seceded but obviously supplied significant numbers of recruits to the Confederacy. A senior officer who directed affairs in Alabama also sought Stanton's permission to send Missourians and Kentuckians home because "If they are obliged to remain here it will cause much embarrassment to us as well as to the people in this region."[24]

Stanton referred the matter to that most pragmatic officer, Grant, who predictably sorted through the bureaucratic nonsense to reveal the bigger picture. If Rebel soldiers endeavored to reach their homes and had been properly included in an official surrender, the general surmised, "they should by all means be allowed to go." Grant further revealed his impatience with the entire matter. "For my part I do not see half the objection to whipped rebels, bound by a solemn oath to observe the laws prevailing where they may be, and to do no act against the Government, going into loyal communities, than I do to retaining in those communities disloyal men, as we are doing, who are bound by no oath, and who have suffered nothing from the war." In other words, honor the paroles, which included a sworn oath not to take up arms against the United States until released from that obligation, and send the men home.[25]

The practical and benevolent motives that dictated official policy sometimes also influenced the actions of individual officers and enlisted men in blue. In a few cases after the surrender at Appomattox, Union officers actually provided cavalry escorts for the first leg of the journey of Confederate units. The war officially continued at that point, thus the Federal cavalry escorted their paroled adversaries through Union lines but also provided security because of the unstable conditions throughout the countryside. Northern officers sometimes also made special arrangements for their southern counterparts that exceeded the provisions offered to enlisted men. One Confederate recalled that a Federal instructed him to take possession of an ambulance and four good mules "and go home in style." A second Union officer increased the offer until the Confederate ultimately left with an ambulance, one horse, and four mules, one of which he gave to his father-in-law upon his arrival at home. Such special arrangements between officers proved quite common, especially with regard to transportation.[26]

Johnny Reb and Billy Yank interacted regularly during demobilization as part of the process of the distribution of paroles and rations and the arrangement of transportation. However, individual Union soldiers and units sometimes provided direct assistance to traveling Confederates, of their own volition. One Mississippi infantry private who traveled across multiple states after a stint in a northern prison fondly recalled one such experience. On his way home he and some comrades passed through a small town in Pennsylvania where the civilians refused to feed or otherwise assist the hungry Rebels. Outside of town, however, the weary travelers encountered a group of approximately twenty Federal soldiers. The northern men called the southerners to their camp, fed them heartily, and the next morning filled their haversacks and "started us on our journey with a better opinion of our fellow man than we had entertained in some time."[27]

As that account illustrates, the former adversaries frequently encountered each other during Johnny Reb's homeward travel outside of Billy Yank's procedural role, and the typically good-natured interactions often left lasting impressions on the southern men. After all, soldiers on both sides at this point often shared a mutual respect and shared relief that the war had ended and that they would soon return to their homes and families. Confederate soldiers frequently commented on the courteous treatment afforded them by their erstwhile opponents during and after the various surrenders.[28]

Even amidst the famously magnanimous spirit that pervaded the atmosphere at Appomattox, acknowledged by countless men in blue and gray, palpable tension weighed heavy enough that officers on both sides took careful measures to limit the likelihood of violent confrontations. Acceptance of defeat obviously did not mean admission of guilt or the renunciation of the cause on the part of Rebel soldiers. Thus the relatively peaceful interactions between former adversaries could be at least partially attributed to conscious efforts on the part of officers who recognized that the conclusion of the war scarcely meant the end of differences.[29]

Certainly the rapid development of a demobilization system could not guarantee such humane or even civil treatment afforded to the southerners by northern soldiers. However, outside of garrisoned towns, Federal troops typically allowed traveling Confederates to pass unmolested, sometimes without even an acknowledgement of their presence. Indeed, the generally respectful, or at least uneventful, interactions proved so commonplace that the exceptions, discussed below, are conspicuous. A Missouri infantryman who passed through Natchitoches, Louisiana, on his way home offered a typical observation when he noted that the Federals who garrisoned the post were not "overbearing" toward the passing Rebels.[30]

Demobilized Confederates who availed themselves of river or rail transportation provided by the government sometimes traveled alongside Union soldiers. Such trips proved typically unremarkable, though memorable episodes occurred on occasion. An Alabama infantryman who traveled by rail across part of Georgia in June 1865 claimed in a postwar account that Federal troops amused themselves by shooting animals from the train. Allegedly the reckless soldiers even targeted an ox harnessed to a plow used by a woman at that moment. The Rebel and his frustrated comrades knew that they could do nothing to stop the irresponsible behavior. Although one might reasonably suspect distortion fueled by more than a tinge of postwar bitterness in that account, another soldier who traveled with Federal troops by river in Louisiana noted that the northern men amused themselves by shooting alligators from the vessel.[31]

At the opposite end of the spectrum, a group of southern men who traveled with northerners on the Mississippi River en route to St. Louis formed a brief bond with their counterparts. Johnny Reb and Billy Yank initially avoided each other during the trip but eventually the men in blue gathered around the southerners who had begun to sing popular songs of the day. After the tension eased, the men became friendly and continued their musical celebration throughout the night. One southerner, only nineteen at the time, remembered the episode fondly and with a sentimental flair. He recalled that "a chord had been struck which vibrated in all hearts, and knew no North, no South. There we were, Rebs serenading Yankees. They kept us singing far into the night and when we wound up with 'Home Sweet Home,' the ice was broken completely, and we were on terms of easiest fellowship for the rest of the trip. What creatures we are! What bundles of contradictions!"[32]

Predictably, such camaraderie proved more elusive between demobilized Confederate soldiers and northern civilians. Often northern citizens, who had not endured the shared sacrifice of the battlefield, turned a cold shoulder to demobilized Rebel soldiers in need. On occasion, however, northern noncombatants assisted southern men with food and shelter as an act of simple compassion. Other times the soldiers learned that the host was actually a native southerner or Confederate sympathizer. This proved particularly common among riverboat pilots and train conductors.[33]

One veteran recalled remarkable hospitality from residents in Philadelphia, Pennsylvania, on his way home from a stint in a Federal prisoner-of-war camp. As he and hundreds of other former prisoners passed through the City of Brotherly Love in mid-July 1865, children and others brought them lemonade and baskets of food. A particularly attractive young woman who dispensed cold beverages from a window made a lasting impression on the youthful soldier, then only seventeen years of age. "It was lucky for me when her supply gave out for I was near the breaking point. That was the nearest I had been to a girl in a year."[34]

The generally friendly or unremarkable interactions between Johnny Reb and Billy Yank, and the occasional generosity of northern civilians, illustrates an interesting and all-too-brief friendly interlude between the death and destruction of the Civil War and the continued intense sectional animosity of Reconstruction. Moreover, the immense logistical support provided to paroled Confederate soldiers by Federal authorities points to a major departure from the popular image of the bedraggled Rebel who traveled home hundreds of miles unassisted. Certainly many Confederate veterans endured brutal journeys that match that description. However, Union and Confederate authorities worked together to create a system that assisted, to various degrees, the majority of southern soldiers with their homeward journeys.

Inevitably, the system often broke down for any number of reasons. In some cases, officers and enlisted men simply refused to cooperate. For example, Confederate officers ordered to retain unit organization until they reached their respective home states before the distribution of paroles typically ignored or modified those directives, thus turning men loose into the countryside, left to their own devices. Northern authorities occasionally suspended travel in certain regions amid ongoing tensions, an action that left some demobilized Confederates at least temporarily without the promised free transportation. Sometimes plain bad luck and poor timing caused the system to fail an individual soldier. In some cases, various factors delayed veterans' homeward journeys until late summer, by which time Union authorities generally considered the free pass system complete and typically no longer required train and riverboat operators to honor paroles.[35]

At other times, individuals plausibly misunderstood the procedures or remained so distrustful of the Federals that they refused to participate. Thus disbanded Confederates sometimes avoided the parole process because they feared that willful acceptance assured them a sentence in a northern prison. Still others remained uncertain whether the paroles restricted them to their homes. Sometimes Johnny Reb's sense of honor worked against him and undermined the system designed for his benefit. Upon acknowledgement of overall defeat, many soldiers refused to remain in camp long enough to secure a parole. In some of these cases, the soldier chafed at the pledge not to take up arms against the United States. Others who refused to await paroles rejected the entire concept and considered a parole unnecessary. Unquestionably, some never bothered to analyze the situation so closely, and simply wanted a head start on the journey home.[36]

Whatever the motives for those soldiers who left without paroles, the potential downside of their actions immediately became clear. Individuals and even entire units who headed for home without the valued papers denied themselves rations, transportation assistance, and unimpeded passage through Union lines. One such soldier, a Texas cavalryman who left North Carolina without a parole, eventually saw the error of his ways. After making his own way from North Carolina to Alabama, the Texan used a copy of another soldier's parole to secure transportation. Now cognizant of the merits of the system, he abandoned the notion of an arduous overland trek to the Lone Star State in favor of river transport from Selma to Mobile on the Gulf Coast, then secured passage aboard a steamer to New Orleans and eventually to Galveston.[37]

Dilapidated railroads, freak accidents, or unfortunate human error explain other system breakdowns. Rail travel brought together all of those factors and affected a significant number of soldiers, including demobilized Union soldiers. Southerners in all theaters of the war availed themselves of free rail transportation, typically to their tremendous benefit. However, multiple soldiers complained of drunken conductors, and train wrecks occurred with alarming frequency, often with fatalities. One veteran recalled a trip from Virginia through North Carolina and into South Carolina. Many soldiers had crowded onto the roofs of cars, with predictable consequences. When the roof collapsed on one car, dropping soldiers onto their comrades below, that individual and his travel party eschewed the precarious convenience of the railroad and elected to walk the remainder of their journey, a distance of almost one hundred miles.[38]

Another veteran recalled a harrowing tale of a train ride in Tennessee with a more unfortunate conclusion. The riders, Rebels and Yankees alike, again crowded into and onto the cars and placed their lives in the hands of an intoxicated engineer. As the train crossed a bridge seventy-five feet above a creek bed, a number of cars separated from the others. The veteran who remembered the story and other fortunate souls escaped onto the bridge, but such good fortune evaded others. Years later he remembered the disturbing details and the tragic irony. "The wreck was a fearful sight. After gathering up the wounded and dead we found thirteen who had gone through the war, and who a little while ago were full of hope and joy at the prospects of once again crossing their own threshold, and pressing to their hearts the loved ones they had left at home."[39]

The experience of an Arkansas infantryman perfectly encapsulates the dangers of rail travel and the potential breakdowns of the overall demobilization system. After he and comrades marched from North Carolina to East Tennessee, they boarded a train bound for Little Rock. Once again a visibly drunken conductor piloted the men toward disaster. When the wreck occurred, the Arkansan found himself pinned under a train car. After his rescue from the wreckage, Federal officials transported him to a hospital in Knoxville with serious injuries to his hips and shoulders. Weeks later, in mid-July he headed west by rail to Nashville, where he obtained his parole but was informed that he would receive no further rations and no additional free rail transport. Federal officers did permit him to board a government vessel on the Cumberland River. From there the twenty-one-year-old former private made his way to the Ohio River and meandered along to Cairo, Illinois. There he and some comrades found a southbound riverboat loaded with other paroled Confederates and piloted by a southerner. They boarded that vessel and traveled down the Mississippi River to Memphis, where the young Arkansan disembarked and eventually made his way home overland.[40]

Though typically safer than rail transport, river travel could also prove perilous for homebound Confederate soldiers. Although nothing occurred on the scale of the infamous wreck of the *Sultana* that claimed the lives of at least 1,700 Union soldiers, one incident prematurely ended the homeward journeys of an unknown number of unfortunate southern soldiers and claimed the lives of other passengers as well. Initial reports indicated that in early June 1865 the steamer *Kentucky*—laden with approximately 1,200 paroled Confederates—sank in the Red River, south of Shreveport, Louisiana. The vessel descended rapidly into the muddy river and, as initially reported, claimed the lives of as many as two hundred people. Days later a survivor insisted that the loss of life had been exaggerated, and that no more than twenty white people and approximately fifty Black people, most of the latter women and children, had perished.[41]

Subsequent reports presented a clearer picture of the tragic affair. In total probably nine hundred, rather than twelve hundred, persons had been aboard, primarily paroled soldiers from Missouri, Arkansas, and Louisiana. Some 250 horses on board also perished. The *Kentucky* departed Shreveport on the evening of June 9 en route to New Orleans, struck a snag and began to take on water. The damaged vessel traveled several miles farther and passed the steamer *Chapin*, which had tied up for the night. By the time the crew realized the extent of the damage and attempted to reach the bank, the *Kentucky* sank almost instantly in twenty feet of water. Many unfortunate souls trapped below deck, including an undetermined number of children, drowned.[42]

The captain of the *Chapin* blamed the disaster entirely on human error. His vessel left Shreveport within one hour after the departure of the *Kentucky* and others. He presumed that the boats would all travel the Red River within relative distance of each other and that all would tie up for the night. After the captain had moored his vessel for the evening he witnessed the *Kentucky* pass him at considerable speed. Soon notified of the accident by witnesses on shore, he steamed the *Chapin* toward the scene to render aid. The intrepid officer and his crew rescued as many souls as possible, but afterward he fumed, "If I had the power, I would hang the captain and pilots to the first tree that I could find."[43]

A Missouri soldier who survived the wreck described the terrible scene in his diary. At the sound of the alarm people rushed to the decks in their night clothes and were thrown "wildly into the angry waves." He scrambled about clinging to one part of the vessel, then another, as the rear of the boat settled to the bottom, the stern above the waterline. Sensing his opportunity, he seized a door and swam for safety, noting that "I felt a measure of relief when I had the open river before me." Although far from the riverbank, he "had the advantage of being alone, and I reached the shore without great difficulty with all my clothes on." Others suffered worse fates during the grim disaster. "Many a poor fellow . . . was dragged down by others in their dying struggles." Instantly aware of the context of the calamity, he concluded that "The scene was painful in the extreme. It seemed especially hard that this sad thing should happen just when we were on our way home."[44]

Other logistical challenges encountered by Confederate soldiers despite the development of the demobilization system ranged from broken down trains and dangerous river crossings to fatal explosions and uncomfortable encounters with wildlife. In Louisiana a large group of returning Rebels piloted a steamer themselves when no crew was readily available, though the vessel broke down before the intended destination. In Tennessee, between Chattanooga and Nashville, men allegedly pushed a train up a hill when it proved no longer up to the task. Another travel party considered themselves fortunate to sleep on the floor of a hotel in Salisbury, North Carolina, only to be terrorized by rats throughout the night. Meanwhile, a group of Rebels in Virginia who had just begun their homeward trek slept under a house and shared the meager accommodations with what appears to have been a mother canine of some sort and her litter of puppies "who kept up an infernal yelling nearly all night, besides filling us with fear."[45]

As those wildlife encounters illustrate, environmental factors sometimes confronted the determined travelers. One such soldier who floated down the Mississippi River quite reasonably bemoaned harassment by "that very sociable little bird, so prevalent on the Father of Waters and familiarly known as the mosquito, became so intimate with my hands and face last night that I could not sleep for his caressing." The next day he and two comrades entered the mouth of the White River and struggled through the snake-infested swamps of eastern Arkansas. The danger and difficulty of the trek only increased because the trio lacked the requisite skills to row and navigate through such a treacherous environment. The thirty-four-year-old infantry captain admitted that "we found the labor fatiguing and soon had blistered hands because we were ignorant of the mode of operating the oars. It was difficult to pull through briars, cane, and saplings, the more so since there was no certainty that we were traversing the road."[46]

That soldier's humility provides the most unusual aspect of his description of his harrowing journey. He actually admitted his lack of knowledge of the area and dearth of expertise with his chosen mode of travel. Elsewhere an officer insisted that he traveled good roads with clearly marked intersections and thus found his way easily. Nevertheless, in light of so many challenges and the great distances traveled by demobilized Confederate soldiers, despite the admirable work performed by officers on both sides to establish a systematic process, remarkably few demobilized Confederates lost their way. Or perhaps extraordinarily few admitted to getting lost. Earlier in his journey that modest Arkansas captain admitted to having taken the wrong road, an error that led him twelve miles out of the way. Whether directionally challenged or merely more forthright than others, that Confederate proved the exception. Only a few soldiers studied here admitted to getting lost, taking a wrong road, or even to asking for directions.[47]

Of course, as the above accounts of wrecked trains and sunken vessels demonstrate, certain obstacles seriously impeded veterans' homeward travel.

Some individuals faced the ultimate in tragic irony—they survived the war but perished on the way home. Such men escaped countless Yankee bullets or survived dreaded prisons, only to die in a railroad accident or drown in a river. However, the enemy factored into one final obstruction in the demobilization system. Although nothing of consequence transpired during most interactions between Johnny Reb and Billy Yank, not all interactions between the former belligerents passed without incident. Perceptive Confederate soldiers understood at least the uncertainty of exchanges with Federals, and the risk of the unknown sometimes dictated those returning Rebels' actions. Such was the case for a soldier who avoided the shortest route to his home because Union gunboats patrolled the nearest river crossing and he questioned how he might be received. In a similar but more significant example, a Texan sent word to his wife that he could not come home to his family until he learned how the Federals there would treat former Confederate soldiers. In the meantime, he assured her that he would make arrangements for her and the children.[48]

Unpleasant interactions between Confederates and Federals took numerous forms. Fist fights erupted between paroled Confederates and German Union troops in Richmond, worsened by tensions in the immediate aftermath of Abraham Lincoln's assassination. Farther south, many Confederates paroled after the surrender of the Army of Tennessee encountered an aggressive mounted force with ambiguous loyalties under the leadership of George Kirk, in the area of Asheville, North Carolina. From the perspective of many Army of Tennessee veterans, during demobilization Kirk and his men amounted to little more than bushwhackers in uniform. More often, unpleasant encounters consisted of random meetings between drunken men or misunderstandings about parole policy. Other times a disdainful northern officer unnecessarily poured salt in the proverbial wound with a verbal jab or two. In one such case a Confederate officer ignored the anti-southern tirade of his northern counterparts and graciously insisted that such actions were not representative of the Union men whom he had encountered.[49]

Beyond those random clashes, three common themes emerged among the hostile interactions between blue- and gray-clad soldiers during Confederate demobilization. First, Confederate veterans who fumed with intense anger, even years later, sometimes wrote of encounters that emphasized or reminded them of defeat and their newfound, albeit temporary, powerlessness against Yankee rule. A sickly soldier who traveled home aboard a Federal vessel complained when a sailor swept his shoes overboard into the sea. He dared not complain, however, because "I might have followed the shoes." More revealing is the case of a Rebel soldier who seethed years afterward about the time that a Union soldier took his hat but immediately returned it essentially because he deemed the headpiece unfit to steal. The Mississippian, who had actually had another hat taken by a Union officer just days earlier, recalled: "Nothing in all my life ever before or since, I think, made me so angry, and if I had but had a weapon, I believe in spite of consequences I would have killed him, at least I felt that way at the time." Most revealing, he described his sentiments in that moment as "helpless anger." Such insulting reminders of literal helplessness temporarily challenged the masculinity of even the most hardened fighting man. More important, the seeds of anger nurtured by such displays further motivated Confederate veterans to resist northern rule during the postwar years.[50]

Meanwhile a former musician and infantryman grasped the potentially far-reaching consequences of such ongoing hostility. He described tensions between blue and gray in Mobile, Alabama, where in at least one instance Union soldiers insisted that Rebel veterans should be hanged. The southerners dared not respond. With the benefit of hindsight and knowledge of the tenor of postwar Reconstruction, the veteran noted with resignation but also ominous determination: "At that time quiet submission was the only thing that could be done. Duty had called us to arms, and now duty called us home, and when there, we could take a survey of the situation and shape our course." That diehard Confederate veteran never surrendered to his opponents' definition of manhood. Rather, like so many of his comrades, he simply adjusted his mindset to formulate a strategy for future continued resistance.[51]

The second controversy common to hostile interactions between demobilizing Confederates and Union soldiers centered upon the assassination of Abraham Lincoln. More specifically, Confederates often feared retaliation in the form of unrestrained violence against demobilized veterans or some unknown severe treatment in the case of those still in Federal custody. A recent study of northern reaction to the assassination illustrates that the southern soldiers' fears were perfectly realistic as the nation mourned the tragic and unnecessary demise of its leader. Ex-Confederates, whether they wrote at the time or later, typically lamented Lincoln's death. In some cases, the southern men simply denounced the barbarous act for its savage cruelty, while others with foresight immediately worried about the implications for Reconstruction under the control of the United States Congress or President Andrew Johnson, Lincoln's successor, who was considered a traitor to the South by many Confederates at the time.[52]

Not every Rebel regretted the demise of the great Union leader. Some admitted to mixed feelings on the subject. Such individuals lamented the manner of death but acknowledged that they could muster no sympathy for the fallen president. One Texan admitted a twinge of guilt for finding at least a bit of satisfaction in the news, "Though it does not show a spirit of Christianity to rejoice at such wickedness." A Georgia comrade wrote home that he rejoiced that Lincoln did not survive to witness the death of the Confederacy. Meanwhile, a verbose Virginian best expressed the range and evolution of sentiments. Though he eventually concluded that "time taught us that Lincoln was a man of marvelous humanity," he initially mustered no such magnanimity. "For four years we had been fighting. In that struggle, all we loved had been lost. Lincoln incarnated to us the idea of oppression and conquest. We had seen his face over the coffins of our brothers and relatives and friends, in the flames of Richmond, in the disaster at Appomattox. In blood and flame and torture the temples of our lives were tumbling about our heads. We were desperate and vindictive, and whosoever denies it forgets or is false. We greeted his death is a spirit of reckless hate."[53]

Because of a lack of discretion or restraint, some Rebels openly expressed their pleasure with Lincoln's death. Unsurprisingly, this contributed to tension that temporarily undermined the usually uneventful interactions between the blue and gray during Confederate demobilization. Federal soldiers seethed with anger upon hearing of their leader's death and understandably resented what they deemed improper reactions from their defeated foes. Union troops at countless locations as well as those who served as prison guards warned Rebels to keep quiet on the subject. Demobilized Confederates, and especially those still in Federal custody at various prisons around the North, quite reasonably feared retaliation. Disbanded Confederates suffered indignities and feared violence and the disruption of the system that provided them with rations and transportation, though because they remained on the move those fears typically proved temporary. Some Rebels worried that the South in general might suffer severe repercussions at the hands of Federal forces and government officials. Prisoners of war remained particularly vulnerable and frequently noted that their privileges diminished dramatically and that their relationships with prison guards suffered immediately upon Lincoln's death. Prisoners perceived intense anger specifically among African American Union soldiers, especially prison guards.[54]

Predictably, then, the third theme that characterized unfriendly interactions between Union and Confederate soldiers during demobilization centered on encounters with northern troops who were Black. Southern soldiers obviously chafed at the notion of African American soldiers in general. More importantly, Rebels sometimes considered the employment of Black soldiers as guards of demobilizing Confederates and prisoners of war as intentionally disrespectful. Taunts from African American guards irritated Confederate soldiers and prisoners more than those hurled by their white northern counterparts, in part because such behavior might have been perceived as an indication of what could be expected in the postwar South. One particularly exasperated veteran blamed northern officials more so than soldiers when he fumed that "Victory is not enough—there must be some punishment for the survivors of the defeated armies. They must be humiliated. They must be made to see their former slaves placed in authority over them."[55]

As that veteran's words illustrate, the presence of African American troops at prisons and on duty around the South simply fueled a rage that seethed beneath the surface for countless diehard Rebels. Defeat had changed nothing with regard to what the average southern soldier considered the proper racial hierarchy. One such group of demobilized Confederates who had waited in line for hours for rations complained that Black soldiers moved to the front of the line upon arrival. Another diarist fumed that he and others were awakened in the middle of the night and expelled from a shelter to make room for a contingent of Black troops. A veteran who passed through New Orleans summarized the situation and the Confederate soldiers' attitudes perfectly. As he and his comrades marched to their temporary quarters in a vacant warehouse, they took offense to the identity of their guards. "The entrance to the place was, on this special occasion, guarded by sentinels of the African persuasion: Augustus Ceazar Cuffy on the right, and Washington Rastus Cuffy on the left. . . . [T]his incident was only an index to the hearts of our successful enemies, and a foretaste of what was in store for us."[56]

The above accounts of hostile encounters between Union and Confederate soldiers at various locales around the South generally stand out as atypical. However, one region became notoriously difficult for passing southern soldiers. Tennessee brought together several factors that undermined the generally positive interactions witnessed elsewhere. Particularly in East Tennessee, the large presence of Unionist civilians and African American troops combined to create a less-than-hospitable environment for returning Rebels. Moreover, southern veterans who returned to Tennessee or passed through cities in the Volunteer State often encountered occupation troops rather than those they had recently fought against. One Confederate veteran later recalled that conditions in East Tennessee were so wretched and dangerous for passing Rebels that "we thought that our chances would be better with the Comanche Indians as neighbors on the frontier of Texas, than near the home of our childhood."[57]

In East Tennessee two major issues arose between Confederate soldiers and Federal forces. First, officers at various locations in the region misunderstood, questioned, or disputed various conditions of the Rebels' paroles. In late April, for example, Union officers temporarily refused to permit demobilized southern soldiers from Tennessee to remain in their home state because a parole did not entitle them to enter a "loyal" state. Merely another manifestation of the Kentucky–Missouri controversy, and this situation further illustrates that despite the surrenders the war continued. In each case, however, a simple if unappetizing remedy emerged for the southerners. Paroled Confederates from the Volunteer State who swore an oath of allegiance to the United States were permitted to stay.[58]

Another controversy that arose in East Tennessee and vicinity centered upon paroled veterans' possession of horses. Although stipulations of surrender explicitly stated that southern men could retain their own mounts and animals that had been Confederate army property, officers in East Tennessee divested many demobilized Rebels of their mounts as they passed through the region. Federal officers elsewhere also questioned the procedure, but East Tennessee witnessed large-scale confiscation of horses, particularly at Chattanooga and Strawberry Plains near Knoxville. Decades later the United States government compensated Confederate veterans or their families for the appropriated animals.[59]

The second significant problem between Confederate and Union forces in East Tennessee centered on frequent and intense encounters with African American Union soldiers. Without question the most significant such activity occurred in Greeneville, a frequently used point of entry onto the railroad for westbound Confederate soldiers. There northern officers required demobilized Confederates to march between rows of United States Colored Troops (USCT) in what the southern men judged, probably correctly in this instance, an act deliberately designed to humiliate them. Multiple Rebels told essentially the same story, focused on Union officers' refusal to prevent angry African American troops from hurling epithets, taunts, and threats at the southern men. The men in blue shouted at the Rebels to remember Fort Pillow, site of the massacre of Black and white Union troops, and the battle of Nashville, which featured significant contributions from African American regiments. One unapologetic Confederate veteran reasoned that the Black soldiers blamed the southerners for the death of their "temporal savior" Abraham Lincoln and claimed: "We believed then that the plan had been laid to have these infuriated negroes murder us all, and twenty-seven years has not changed our opinion."[60]

Similar to confrontations with white Federal troops elsewhere, during the tumultuous days in Greeneville, Confederate soldiers typically knew better than to resist. Instead, they endured the entire spectacle "with clenched fists and gnashing teeth." Another Rebel veteran recalled: "Our boys were smart—they kept their heads up, eyes to the front, did not return a word, and walked in the middle of the road. The writer walked near the Federal lieutenant who had come out to meet and escort us in. He rode with his pistol in hand and didn't say a word, and his face was a pale as the paper we are writing this on. He evidently appreciated the perilous situation we were in." Once again, those Rebels never entertained the possibility of surrendering to another group's definition of manhood. Rather, they endured the insults, bided their time, and redirected their masculine impulses to plans for postwar resistance.[61]

It could be argued that the mere sight of armed African American men, particularly freedmen, in the uniform of the enemy presented an obvious challenge to the concept of mastery, a cornerstone of masculine identity among nineteenth century southern white males. Military service obviously undermined the traditional stereotype of Black men as intellectually childlike, incapable of such important and arduous service, and therefore inferior to the white southern masculine ideal.[62] However, for many Confederate veterans the presence of African American troops struck a different chord. Rather than fuel introspective contemplation about fundamental traits of manhood, confrontations with Black soldiers intensified anger toward Federal foes because of the widespread belief that northern officers intentionally sought to humiliate demobilized Confederates. After all, by this point in the war the presence of USCT units was hardly a novelty, and significant numbers of Rebel fighting men had even expressed support for the notion of arming freedmen for Confederate service.[63] Thus demobilized Rebels may have perceived a threat to their masculine ideals through encounters with African American soldiers, but once again, rather than surren-

der to the threat, demobilizing Confederates simply redefined southern masculinity with an increasing determination to shape the future of the postwar
South on their own terms. As one Rebel quoted earlier noted, quiet submission
was the only course until the veterans could return to their homes to mobilize
again, this time to battle their collective foes in a different arena for political
control of the South.

In Chattanooga, Confederates also noted a significant number of African
American soldiers but, with the occasional exception, those encounters proved
generally uneventful. Though usually less provocative than the scenes in Greeneville, marching under the guard of Black troops "was humiliating," one Rebel
diarist opined, "but 'might makes right,' and we had to submit without a mur-
mur." Instead, Confederates who passed through Chattanooga focused their
complaints on the local provost marshal, who detained parolees for several days,
considerably longer than officers in most other occupied cities. After five days'
confinement, one group of paroled Rebels marched to the railroad depot but
waited in the sun for hours. "God will avenge," one infantry captain vowed.[64]

Despite the unusual delays, in Chattanooga many western Rebels secured
railroad passes and boarded trains bound for Nashville. In that Middle Tennessee city, southern soldiers again occasionally clashed with African American
troops, and again sometimes quarreled with officers who quibbled over parole
technicalities. Nashville officers in particular insisted on new paroles and sworn
oaths of allegiance from Missouri and Kentucky soldiers before General Grant's
pragmatic solution resolved that matter. One "little upstart of a sergeant" at the
provost marshal's office even refused further transportation passes to a group of
Kentucky cavalrymen, because, he reasoned, they were close enough to home.
"Whoop! but how I wanted to wring his neck! But he had a lot of soldiers, with
sharp pointed guns around him." The Kentuckians then secured passage on a
river steamer at their own expense for the final leg of their journey.[65]

Most demobilized Rebels who passed through Nashville, however, encountered an entirely different set of circumstances. In Tennessee's capital city, Federal authorities typically did not imprison passing Confederates. Rather, after
temporary detainment, the soldiers secured various types of accommodations
about the town, including shelters established for soldiers and refugees. Perhaps the city's wartime reputation for debauchery motivated Federal officials
there to move demobilized southerners through the city as rapidly as possible; policing local conditions presented severe enough challenges. One soldier

described the town as dirty and "squally," while another took grim delight in a comrade's assault on Jewish lemonade vendors, to the delight of onlooking northern soldiers.[66]

Clearly, Federal implementation of Confederate demobilization varied by location, but, other than in East Tennessee, a relatively systematic pattern emerged. When the time arrived for Confederate officers and soldiers to implement the system, the first challenge to arise was the distribution of money and resources. Upon the surrender of the Army of Tennessee, officers received funds from the Confederate treasury, on its flight from Richmond, typically in the form of silver, and distributed the coffers to the men before they left for home. More than $37,000 in silver passed into the hands of demobilized soldiers. Sources indicate different individual amounts received, though most fell within the range from $1.17 to $2.50, with $1.25 by far the most common estimate. Official orders mandated an equal distribution of funds to each infantry corps, artillery and cavalry unit, headquarters staff, and hospital personnel. However, many individuals received a larger share because the number of men actually present for duty had dwindled during the surrender negotiations. Soldiers from the Army of Tennessee also received other goods of value and, in certain cases without approval, civilians in the region also obtained goods. One officer even requested permission to sell pontoon bridges and leftover wagons for the benefit of the men in his brigade.[67]

Most men spent the money, or a portion of it, to facilitate their homeward journeys. The valuable silver—combined with rations and, dependent on the route of travel, transportation provided by the Federals—eased at least part of the trek for many veterans of the Army of Tennessee. One twenty-six-year-old Georgia infantry captain even quipped that he considered himself rich upon receiving the silver and no longer cared "which way the wind blows." Others had a different idea in mind for their silver, or indeed for that of their comrades. One veteran later claimed to have received a share of $26, saved it all, and had it made into spoons. A less fortunate young comrade who actually served in the Army of Northern Virginia but was paroled in North Carolina, carved his initials into the lone coin he received, only to have it stolen the next day.[68]

When possible, officers at subsequent Confederate surrenders followed the example of the Army of Tennessee and dispersed resources to soldiers as part of demobilization, though without the benefit of the treasury silver. Officers frequently promised an equal allocation of goods as a scheme to keep men in camp or to preserve the peace in a particular city or community amidst the confusion of the war's closing scenes. This proved an especially common tactic throughout the chaotic Trans-Mississippi theater in the absence of any semblance of actual authority. Without benefit of the systematic procedures of the Army of Tennessee, officers farther west generally improvised.[69]

Confederate officers faced a far greater challenge and dramatically more consternation from soldiers with the distribution of transportation resources such as horses, mules, and wagons. In fact, the allocation of money and material goods proved a comparatively uncomplicated process. Of course not every man could receive a horse, and this produced significant disturbances in camps. Not every soldier sought the animals, preferring instead to avail themselves of rail or water transportation provided by the Federals. Many others, however, desperately sought horses and mules not merely to facilitate travel but for farm work or simply as something of value with which they could jumpstart their postwar lives. Although Army of Tennessee officers eventually settled on a specific allocation and issued explicit orders to direct the process, those actions could not preclude the confusion and tension that had already swept through the camps. A series of vague, ever-changing, and countermanded orders had created considerable uncertainty among not only enlisted men but even among senior officers. As Lieutenant General Alexander P. Stewart warned, if the specifics could not be sorted out quickly, "a good deal of trouble is anticipated."[70]

Stewart could not have been more prescient. Frequently officers kept men on duty only with the promise of a horse or mule, though with each passing day even that approach increasingly failed. Predictably, fighting and theft escalated dramatically. Each man looked out for himself during this frenzied period, though the tensions were not entirely random or motivated exclusively by individual concerns. As Stewart had indicated, enlisted men collectively expressed concern that officers might receive a disproportionate share of transportation resources. Lieutenant General Stephen D. Lee sought clarification through the muddle of conflicting orders with regard to whether officers would receive additional wagons to transport their personal baggage. Although he claimed that he would accept whatever decision was rendered, he acknowledged that "I would prefer, of course, to get along comfortably, if possible." Though clearly expecting privileges beyond those extended to his men, to his credit Lee recognized the soldiers' frustrations and the potential volatility of the situation. "There is considerable feeling among the troops on this point," he wrote another officer.

"They now lay claim to everything, and it is my belief that they will strip most of the generals of their wagons on starting."[71]

For those units within the Army of Tennessee who remained together for the initial stage of their journey home, the officers and men actually carried out an organized and systematic distribution of animals and wagons at chosen locations, whereupon brothers-in-arms bid final goodbyes, comrades went their separate ways, and veteran units dissolved into history with a degree of honor. In at least one case, a regiment that disbanded outside a small village in South Carolina employed a simple lottery to allocate the resources. For many other units in the Army of Tennessee, disorder prevailed and no such organized scenes played out. Instead, general confusion reigned, and similar scenes played out across the crumbling Confederacy.[72]

While Confederate officers and enlisted men resolved the problem of money and transportation resources allocation, the determination of travel routes presented the other major logistical challenge. For the Army of Tennessee, officers identified three specific routes of travel for those units that remained organized, but even those plans addressed only the initial portion of the trip. The army split into three columns as they ventured out of North Carolina. One followed a westerly course through Morganton, North Carolina, and into the mountains bound for East Tennessee. A second column pursued a more southwesterly course through Spartanburg and Abbeville, South Carolina, while the third followed a roughly parallel track just farther south via Chester and Newberry, South Carolina. The careful planning for those initial miles of the homeward journeys reflects the continued theme of Joseph E. Johnston's concern for the well-being of his veterans, an attempt to impose some order, and an effort to limit the chaos that soon befell much of the South. Even for those who followed orders and marched as intact units in those three columns, the organization typically lasted only a matter of days before officers distributed paroles, money, and transportation resources, and the soldiers went their separate ways whether individually or in small groups. At that point, travel became not necessarily every man for himself, but certainly each group for itself.[73]

Most soldiers of course acted largely on their own or in concert with close comrades to choose their direction. Although several major routes, to be discussed below, ultimately became the norm for thousands of demobilized Confederates, individuals charted their course based on a number of considerations. Usually the soldier and his travel companions simply selected what they expected to be the fastest route. However, in some cases alternate routes promised a better chance to secure food and shelter. Others chose different, even very indirect paths in order to avoid bushwhackers or Union forces. Some men took detours to visit friends or family or for other personal reasons, while others took significantly longer routes via rail or water in order to avoid travel by foot, horseback, or wagon. In the words of a Rebel surgeon who trekked home with his family and endured unpleasant conditions aboard a small vessel on the Ouachita River in Arkansas, "I slept indifferently, the accommodations are poor, and the fare coarse, but it is preferable to an overland trip in a wagon." Similarly, a Texan who traveled home from Camp Douglas in Illinois avoided overland travel due west from Vicksburg to Shreveport in favor of moving south on the Mississippi River to connect to the Red River, which he took to the northwest toward Shreveport. As a result, his homeward journey was considerably longer than it would appear on a map had he taken a direct route.[74]

For most demobilized Rebels, destination rather than army affiliation ultimately determined the most likely route. Because all three major Confederate armies, the Army of Northern Virginia, the Army of Tennessee, and the Trans-Mississippi Army, included men from multiple regions across the South, there existed no such thing as the typical route of travel for a soldier from a particular army. Moreover, some men received their paroles in or very near their home states or even their actual homes. A Virginian who capitulated at Appomattox, a North Carolinian surrendered by Johnston in the Tar Heel State, or a Texan who departed his unit within the Lone Star State during the breakup of the Trans-Mississippi Army typically simply took the fastest or easiest route home. He might have walked a number of miles, hopped a train for the next leg of the journey, hitched a ride on a wagon for some distance, and then walked the final few miles.

Therefore the more fruitful line of inquiry is to consider the routes of those soldiers whose experiences more closely resembled the popular image of arduous, lengthy journeys—those men who found themselves hundreds of miles and multiple states from home when the war ended. For example, how did a Texan get home from Virginia? How did a resident of Middle Tennessee or Kentucky travel from North Carolina? How did a prisoner of war who ended the conflict in Camp Douglas in Illinois—or Johnson's Island in Ohio, or Point Lookout in Maryland—reach his home state?

Despite the improvised nature of individual travel and the countless courses followed by men from all corners of the South, certain routes emerged as the primary travel corridors for demobilized Confederates for significant portions of their journeys. The availability of railroad and water-based travel frequently dictated the chosen route more than any other factors. In the case of each major travel artery described below, soldiers typically followed the course until they reached a logical departure point, whereupon each followed the individual path necessary to reach his home. For lengthy stretches of the journey, however, demobilized Confederates usually followed one or more of the following courses.

At war's end the railroad still functioned southbound from Richmond, through Danville, Virginia, and into North Carolina, where it passed through Greensboro, Salisbury, and Charlotte, and at least as far as Blackstock, South Carolina. In the vicinity of Charlotte or Blackstock, many soldiers chose to walk approximately forty miles to Newberry, where they could again board a train to carry them about fifty miles to Abbeville, before walking or improvising another fifty miles to find a functioning rail line at Washington, Georgia. That line carried them westward to Atlanta. Others rejoined the railroad at Augusta, Georgia, approximately fifty miles southeast of Washington and rode the cars to Atlanta. Soldiers who began their journeys at any point along that rail corridor could, potentially, secure passage by train for most, but not all, of the distance between Richmond and Atlanta.

Atlanta, already an important transportation hub during the war, also served as a major crossroads for demobilized southern soldiers. Countless Confederates from states within the Western theater turned north in that Georgia city, but the railroad between Atlanta and Dalton had not yet been restored. Thus each travel party improvised that trek, which was at least ninety miles. Upon reaching Dalton, a soldier could again board a train and travel to Chattanooga, whereupon he might continue his rail journey northeast, deeper into East Tennessee toward Knoxville or Greeneville, or more likely, ride the rails to the northwest toward Nashville.

The Tennessee capital also became an important crossroads. For many Rebels, government transportation ended there and travel by foot began. A few others continued by rail northward toward Louisville, but far more journeyed either overland or on the Cumberland River to the northwest toward Cairo, Illinois, near the confluence of the Ohio and Mississippi Rivers. Many individuals then continued their travels on the Mississippi, occasionally north toward St. Louis, but more often south toward Memphis, Vicksburg, Baton Rouge, or New Orleans. Some disembarked at places along the way, such as the White River in

Arkansas or Red River in Louisiana or ventured through New Orleans to board a steamer into the Gulf of Mexico, bound for Galveston, Texas.

Meanwhile, back in Atlanta, a relative few headed south out of the city, but many more ventured generally west-southwest and eventually followed what was already a common route of travel across the South. From Atlanta, some soldiers journeyed to Mobile by rail via Montgomery. Others crossed into Alabama on foot and passed by Opelika, before they eventually reached Montgomery and Selma, two communities that served as crossroads similar to Atlanta and Nashville, though on a smaller scale. Some soldiers boarded vessels and traveled via the Alabama River from the Selma area to Mobile on the Gulf Coast, where they boarded oceangoing steamers for New Orleans or Galveston. Others simply continued westward out of Selma on a familiar route that passed through Demopolis, then crossed into Mississippi and passed through Meridian, on to Jackson, and eventually to Vicksburg. There they might cross the Mississippi River or board a vessel on that great waterway. Although sources vary on the consistency of rail service in the region and many soldiers indeed walked, at various points during demobilization soldiers could travel from just west of Selma to Jackson by train. However, the railroad remained out of service for the forty-five miles from Jackson to Vicksburg. Even the bridge over the Big Black River between those two cities had yet to be repaired.

Other routes proved less common but still served a meaningful number of soldiers. For example, some men who surrendered in Virginia or North Carolina simply traveled westward into the mountains along a more direct, if less convenient, route home on foot or horseback. Soldiers bound for homes in Arkansas sometimes went far out of their way to secure transport on the White River or Ouachita River to avoid walking, while their Louisiana comrades often did the same for water transport on the Red River. Still others traveled tremendous distances on vessels along the East Coast or Gulf Coast.

Coastal travel became particularly common for men who completed their service as prisoners of war and thus began their journeys home from those northern facilities. Despite their unenviable situation as prisoners, those men usually benefited from more efficient travel and typically walked only the final portion of their journey. Men released from northern prisons, particularly Camp Douglas and Johnson's Island, generally traveled by rail to within only miles of their homes, or rode the rails to a coastal port or river city and boarded a vessel for the remainder of their trek. Thus many Confederate veterans passed through cities such as Indianapolis, Pittsburgh, and even New York City on their way "south." Veterans released from Point Lookout in Maryland typically boarded a steamer for travel through the Chesapeake Bay and upriver to Richmond, whence they might follow the established routes.

Analysis of the experiences of the men whose writings form the basis of this study permits three important general conclusions concerning travel logistics. First, although soldiers from the Army of Tennessee and other western forces often faced arduous journeys home (as described in the next chapter), they benefited significantly from the experience of comrades who had surrendered before them and from the careful preparation of Union and Confederate officers. When officers and enlisted men cooperated fully, the system generally worked properly. In those cases, Army of Tennessee units remained at their posts despite surrender negotiations, retained their organization even when informed of the capitulation, and marched together to a location along the route home. There, often a small village in South Carolina or Georgia, the men received their paroles, their share of the Confederate treasury silver, and, potentially, a horse or mule.

Second, the experiences of officers and soldiers of the Army of Northern Virginia helped make possible the development of a system of Confederate demobilization. The respective commanders and subordinate officers who directed affairs at Appomattox have received justifiable praise during the generations since that historic encounter for their respectful interactions, and those officers certainly considered the needs of demobilized southern soldiers as they embarked on their homeward journeys. However, Union and Confederate officers who secured the terms of surrender for the Army of Northern Virginia failed to grasp the scope of the problem. After all, Lee's army surrendered first and, similar to chaotic scenes between unprepared forces in early battles, the officers simply had no experience with a problem of this nature.

The third general conclusion with regard to travel logistics resulted directly from the second. The journeys and general demobilization experiences of Army of Northern Virginia soldiers who hailed from western and trans-Mississippi states most closely resemble the iconic popular image of the penniless, bedraggled Rebels who somehow, through grit and determination, improvisation, and the compassionate assistance of others, managed to find their way home across great distances. As the next chapter illustrates, certainly some men found easier roads than others, but in general, western men from the great eastern army faced the most difficult circumstances of all demobilized Confederates. They traveled farther than their eastern comrades in the Army of Northern Virginia but demobilized weeks earlier than their fellow westerners who served elsewhere. Thus, many of them traveled great distances, even all the way home in some cases, before the full development and implementation of the system of Federal rations and transportation passes.

In the bigger picture, despite the eventual development of a Confederate demobilization system, each veteran, whether from the Eastern, Western, or Trans-Mississippi theaters—or a prisoner of war recently released from a facility in the North—confronted the challenge of how to reach his home. How he accomplished that, and the partnership that developed between demobilized Confederate soldiers and southern civilians, form the basis of the next chapter.

3

REBELS
& REBELS

WHEN JOHNNY REB CAME
MARCHING HOME

Into the chaos and widespread lawlessness of the former Confederacy, thousands of men trekked on their most important missions yet—to reach their homes and loved ones. As the armies melted into history after the surrenders, soldiers and officers pondered logistics and developed strategies for their homeward journeys. In numerous cases entire units maintained their organization and discipline during the initial stages of travel. The preservation of unit structure enhanced security for the men and for residents of the countryside and motivated individuals to retain discipline until the distribution of paroles.

Typically, however, such organization proved fleeting as men splintered from the group to blaze separate trails home. Obviously, men within their home state or only a few days travel from farms and families typically left their units immediately, therefore regiments composed of men more distant from their destination proved more likely to retain organization than those nearer to home. In some cases, units remained intact until they reached a logical dispersal point, whereupon officers distributed paroles, comrades said final goodbyes, and men spread across the landscape in the directions of their respective homes. Many units in the Army of Tennessee, for example, marched together initially but disbanded at Salisbury, North Carolina; Washington, Georgia; or Augusta, Georgia; or simply the nearest railroad depot. Even in the chaotic trans-Mississippi region, certain units remained unbroken for a portion of the journey home, while some elements of the Army of Northern Virginia, in the absence of a defined system, benefited from the sagacity of officers who held their charges together as long as possible.[1]

A relative few officers followed orders to maintain organization and, if possible, withhold paroles until the units reached their home states. One Arkansas infantry colonel led his men and others who followed on a perilous journey through a maze of swamps and rivers in Louisiana and portions of his home state. Another diarist recorded that he and more than two hundred fellow Missourians parted ways in St. Louis after making the trip together from Shreveport, Louisiana. Nearly one hundred of those men eventually made their way collectively to the vicinity of Rolla, Missouri. These noteworthy accounts, however, were the exceptions. Most officers actually distributed paroles either immediately subsequent to surrender or shortly thereafter because they deemed it wholly unrealistic to expect soldiers to prolong reunions with family to await a piece of paper, however important the parole.[2]

Despite the disintegration of most units within days of the respective surrenders, virtually all soldiers instantly recognized the importance of smaller-group travel.[3] One excellent study of Civil War veterans posited that demobilized Confederates traveled in groups in order to maintain a sense of collective identity and to preserve individual masculinity.[4] Perhaps on a subconscious level such considerations motivated some men, but several more practical considerations explicitly informed this decision to travel with comrades. Some soldiers explained the composition of groups based upon the speed at which each man could travel. In certain cases this thought process played out before the comrades left their final bivouac as brothers-in-arms. Other times, the group composition evolved during the journey as those healthy enough to move more quickly eventually separated from the group.[5]

Obviously, individuals who resided in the same general region readily identified the advantage of travel with known and trusted companions for the entire length of the journey. A former Arkansas infantry captain traveled by rail and water with a group of approximately ten comrades from the Johnson's Island prison in Ohio to Memphis, Tennessee, where the veterans parted ways. Another typical example was the case of a young Virginia infantryman who traveled across his home state with several companions. Over the course of one week the party gradually thinned at various crossroads as each man turned homeward. The twenty-one-year-old covered only the last two miles alone after a trip of more than two hundred miles with comrades from the same area.[6]

Group travel also provided a level of security necessary during that law-less season in 1865. Indeed, soldiers soon learned the imprudence of individual travel. As a chaplain from a Tennessee infantry regiment made his way across Georgia in a quest to reunite with his family, he confided to his diary, "I have seen evidences of social disorganization, on my route, that are alarming indeed to a lover of law and order. A number of cases of lawlessness were reported among citizens, soldiers and deserters from our armies. Oh! God have mercy on our country." Such circumstances prompted that weary wanderer to join new travel parties when necessary, desperate never to ride alone. Also in Georgia, a group of Kentucky-bound cavalrymen received their paroles at Washington, boarded a train for Atlanta, and set out on foot northward for Dalton, but not before forming a group explicitly for security. Meanwhile in Virginia, a unit of South Carolina infantrymen benefited from an escort of Union and Confeder-ate cavalry officers for the initial stages of their journey.[7]

The availability of food also factored into the formation of travel parties. Here again, much thought informed the composition of the group. Bands of travel-ers with too many men often struggled to obtain food. No matter how sympa-thetic or patriotic, the denizens of a random, isolated farmhouse could hardly feed two dozen men, but clutches of several often fared reasonably well. A few conscientious travelers even considered the burden placed upon residents in the countryside and sought to alleviate the strain endured by their hosts by limiting the size of the group.[8]

Strategies for procurement of nourishment hardly stopped at the size of the travel party. These men had survived the trials of combat, campaigns, and camp life, and were skilled in creative foraging. Men frequently relied on their vast scavenging experience gained during the war and scattered during the night in search of food, only to reunite by morning to resume their trek. Countless soldiers simply accelerated their pace of travel in order to visit farms before other sol-diers could consume scarce foodstuffs. Others marched exclusively on smaller, less traveled roads to avoid homes visited by numerous comrades. A Texas cav-alry officer who surrendered with the Army of Tennessee merits special mention for his strategic ability to secure nourishment. Traveling much of the way with an ever-changing group of five to twelve men, he and one particular comrade attempted always to remain together. Frequently the pair left the main route of travel in search of out-of-the-way farmsteads hitherto uncontacted by returning soldiers. Occasionally the tandem reunited with the group in order to share in what others had gathered, only to part again to search on their own. As the veteran remembered it, the plan worked "to a queen's taste. We would eat from three to eight meals a day at the tables of these good North Carolina people, and it got to be no surprise to us to run onto a bountiful supply of moonshine whisky." Doubtless other weary and hungry soldiers envied those Texans' success.[9]

Ultimately, the ideal travel party included men from the same general region in numbers sufficient to enhance security from bushwhackers and other ne'er-do-wells but few enough to improve the chances to obtain food. Numerous units began their journey together but typically fragmented into smaller groups as the miles passed. Regardless of the composition of the travel party, soldiers depended principally on the generosity and cooperation of southern civilians.[10]

Most soldier accounts, wartime and postwar, make it profoundly clear that the overwhelming majority of southern civilians provided some level of assistance to returning veterans when presented with the opportunity. Countless soldiers described helpful families and individuals, almost always complete strangers, and innumerable statements create an overall impression of accommodating civilians. Although the occasional individual, typically an officer, could afford hotel rooms along the way, most demobilized Confederate soldiers relied extensively upon shelter provided by southern civilians.[11]

Henry Felix Wilson, a twenty-seven-year-old private from Alabama, noted in his wartime diary multiple instances of support within a few weeks of travel. Among other examples of assistance, one night the former infantryman stayed at the home of a "clever old man," four days later lodged with a "bachelor," spent a third night with a couple that treated his cold with a home remedy, and sheltered yet another evening with a family who treated him with particular kindness.[12]

Although civilians regularly opened their actual homes to soldiers, hosts frequently offered more modest accommodations. In one such typical case, a Confederate surgeon informed his wife that he and his comrades generally were too filthy to slumber in private homes, so they usually slept in barns. Soldiers on the homeward march often slept on porches, in vacant houses, in train depots, or on hotel floors. In one case a South Carolina artilleryman recalled lodging offered by the wife of another soldier, on the condition that he carried neither smallpox nor measles. Another veteran later recalled a night spent in a church, though the officers of the group stayed in the preacher's house. Although grateful, the impatient North Carolina native recalled the parson's "interminably long grace."[13]

People along the roadway usually shared food but sometimes facilitated soldiers' travels in other ways. Women frequently cooked the meager rations that the men carried. Other individuals found creative ways to assist, such as an older man who drew a map that directed a group of soldiers through a region with plenty of food and populated by pro-Confederate residents. The memoirs of a veteran, only seventeen during demobilization, provide probably the most noteworthy account of creative assistance offered by a civilian. The youthful Georgian survived a stint at Fort Delaware military prison and journeyed most of the way home on an oceangoing vessel, at the expense of the federal government. Unfortunately, during the voyage he lost his shoes and thus found himself barefoot and responsible for the remainder of his trip from Port Royal, South Carolina, to his parents' home in Quitman, Georgia, a distance well in excess of two hundred miles. During the final stretch of his trying journey, however, one man "was very kind to me and sent me to Quitman, my home, with his little boy on a mule."[14]

As that account of a generous stranger suggests, civilians frequently assisted returning Confederate veterans in ways beyond food and shelter, particularly when soldiers encountered individuals in towns or cities rather than at isolated farmhouses. Predictably, the most common example of this aid centered on modes of transportation. As noted by soldiers in contemporary diaries and postwar memoirs, at times strangers simply offered soldiers a ride in their wagon, on a spare horse or mule, or even on a railroad handcar. At other times random individuals paid for a soldier's train ticket if the exhausted traveler could not produce a transportation pass issued at the time of parole or by a Federal provost marshal along the way, or the occasional train conductor or ship captain instituted his own policy of free travel for returning soldiers. On a few occasions veterans remembered monetary gifts from southern civilians. In one such case a Kentucky cavalryman recalled a remarkable gift of one hundred dollars from a judge to his travel party to facilitate the final leg of their journey. Meanwhile, a disabled, road-weary Texan remembered two separate monetary gifts. He received the first from a woman who had nursed his wounds in Georgia. Later a complete stranger gave him one United States dollar as he passed through Vicksburg, Mississippi.[15]

Multiple other accounts support that Texan's tale of a kind reception for Confederate soldiers as they passed through Vicksburg, a common crossroads for returning veterans. Innumerable soldiers stopped in on riverboats headed north or south, but many soldiers bound for states west of the Mississippi River passed through town and crossed the great river there. One former private remembered his experience in Vicksburg fondly. Bound for Texas, the Army of Tennessee veteran and six comrades had traveled together from North Carolina and across parts of South Carolina, Georgia, Alabama, and Mississippi. As they passed through Vicksburg they enjoyed comfortable living quarters, more than ample rations for a change, and the freedom to roam the city at will. In fact, Federal soldiers on occupation duty in the former great Confederate citadel expressed frustration and disgust that local residents hailed the defeated Rebels as conquering heroes. The sight of so many Confederate uniforms and the celebratory nature of the soldiers' reception understandably drew the ire of the victorious men in blue.[16]

Not unique to Vicksburg, Federal soldiers elsewhere chafed at the sight of Confederate veterans who wore their uniforms longer than the victors deemed appropriate. Federal authorities in North Carolina and Virginia issued directives to reduce the presence of such obvious symbols of the Confederacy. One Missouri native recalled that the Federal provost marshal in Memphis, Tennessee, required demobilized Confederates to secure a permit to wear the butternut. Only nineteen at the time, the youthful soldier judged this requirement unnecessary and contrived strictly to humiliate southern veterans. As he later recalled in his memoirs, the former artilleryman decided instead to acquire a suit of civilian clothes, on credit with his father's name as a reference, and tossed his uniform out a second-story window. Embittered by defeat and already indignant toward postwar Federal policies, he noted that "some rag picker found it, and my good old grey jacket and pants were turned into eventually into paper, 'legal cap,' perhaps, on which to write the infamous documents of the Reconstruction Period."[17]

Similar to Vicksburg, scores of other southern communities offered warm receptions to returning Confederate veterans, whether hometown boys or those just passing through. Newspaper editors sometimes urged readers to assist traveling soldiers and to offer them warm welcomes. New Orleans, Louisiana, welcomed demobilized Confederate soldiers to such an extent that observers might have been pardoned for wondering which side had actually won the war. Perhaps this can be attributed to the high-spirited reputation of that historic city or to some sort of symbolic defiance of Federal occupation.[18]

Not to be outdone, residents in other southern cities—such as Richmond, Virginia; Louisville, Kentucky; Galveston, Texas; Savannah, Georgia; and Nashville, Tennessee—received special mention in soldiers' diaries or were remembered with affection. Some such communities offered warm receptions to demobilized Rebels, notwithstanding the presence of Union occupation forces. As one officer from a Georgia infantry regiment traveled home from a prisoner-of-war camp, he passed through Louisville and confided to his diary that the kindness he received there from the female residents of the community made him begin to feel that he was once again in friendly country, despite the substantial presence of Federal troops. Though also treated well three days later in Nashville, the thirty-year-old captain sardonically noted his greater appreciation for the physical beauty of the women of Louisville.[19] In other cities soldiers received aid from institutions such as the Ladies Relief Hospital of Lynchburg, Virginia; the Soldiers' Aid Society in Churchville, Virginia; and soldier homes in locales that include Houston, Texas, as well as Chattanooga and Nashville in Tennessee.[20]

Other cities and smaller communities around the South frequently greeted soldiers warmly, often with cheers and impromptu, unsolicited meals. Two different accounts recalled tables of food placed alongside the road in eastern Alabama, one near Notasulga and the other near Opelika. In reference to the provisions provided at the latter location, described by one traveler as an "oasis in the desert," he remembered: "Placed in the shade of the oaks and surrounded by a bevy of charming women it was a pretty sight, such a one the poor fellows had not seen in many a day. Never did men eat more ravenously. The ladies smiled as they watched the performance, and doubtless excused the boys for their want of politeness." In soldiers' descriptions of these communities it was women, especially, who assisted the exhausted travelers. The abundance of evidence supports these claims, though admittedly some emotional, homesick young soldiers may have been more affected by the outward displays of support and assistance provided by female southerners.[21]

Whether male or female, denizens of large cities or small communities, civilians occasionally made particularly strong impressions on soldiers through displays of exceptional generosity. This proved especially true when the residents obviously had little to spare. In certain cases, families opened their homes to numerous passing soldiers and even spread the word to direct those in need to the house. Other veterans recorded extended stays with a particular individual or family in order to recover from wounds or illness, to save money to finance the homeward journey, or simply to wait for a river to recede to facilitate crossing. In a few remarkable instances strangers even gave passing soldiers a mule to ride home, or more often, loaned an animal or a skiff to cross a river. Often soldiers described instances in which individuals or families simply provided an unusual amount of food. In one such instance a man in Virginia gave away an entire acre of onions to homeward bound soldiers only days after the surrender at Appomattox.[22]

Other men from the Army of Northern Virginia, also just days after that surrender, gathered at a small country store that served as a distribution center for food for the needy. Soldiers assembled there among many women in need and, rather than consume meat obviously intended for the women and their families, the men agreed to eat peas and some of the women agreed to cook the vegetables for the men. Most of the solders consumed what they could and packed a small additional supply in their haversacks. One desperate chap, either for want of a haversack or out of fear of going hungry, removed his "drawers," improvised a sack, filled each leg with peas, and tied the disgusting contraption around his neck. The modern reader can only imagine the hunger necessary to consume peas from the filthy garment of a Civil War soldier.[23]

A particular example of unusual generosity that made a lasting impression on a soldier deserves special mention. Twenty-one-year-old infantry sergeant John C. Porter faced a journey of approximately 250 miles entirely within his home state of Texas, hardly a daunting expedition compared to the epic treks of many other demobilized Confederates. After covering a portion of the distance via railroad, Porter walked with two comrades across much of East Texas, before parting ways with his friends to complete the remainder of the trip alone. When he neared the small community of Callaway, in Upshur County, he shared a meal that left a lifelong impression.[24]

The family who opened their home to Porter included a woman and "six or seven little urchins, as black and dirty as anyone ever saw." From humble tableware the mother served a dinner of stewed meat, corn bread, and milk, while the sergeant could not help but notice the children's poor table manners and tendency to place their filthy hands inside the pitcher of milk. Porter wrote that he intended no mockery in his description of the family or his surroundings. He had enjoyed the meal, understood that he was in no way entitled to it, and realized that many people lived in such conditions. Porter genuinely appreciated the generosity and hoped that later generations could understand the experiences of their wartime relatives. Most important, although he never explicitly acknowledged it, the meal meant more to him because of the family's wretched living conditions. They had so little to give yet chose to share their meager provisions with a stranger in need.[25]

As Porter's experience indicates, civilian assistance often left indelible impressions on returning Confederate veterans. Frequently, despite the obvious importance of food and shelter, other types of assistance—simple acts of kindness or quasi-familial behavior—created lifelong memories. More specifically, shared experiences that made soldiers feel genuinely welcome, reminded them of home and family, and pointed to a return to normality frequently proved most memorable or worthy of repeated or extended commentary in wartime diaries. One soldier who had been fed and sheltered by an older woman who lived in a shack along the roadside witnessed the homecoming of his host's soldier son. That emotional moment reminded him of his own loved ones who desperately awaited his return. Evenings of shared music and attendance at church services along the road home comforted soldiers and hinted at a sense of the ordinary that they might regain in a postwar world.[26]

Such comforting experiences often centered upon women who provided assistance. One twenty-four-year-old Virginia diarist, for instance, confided his admiration for an attractive young woman who baked bread for him. Although she appears just once in the man's diary, he confessed instant affection for her and admitted that her kindness had made him realize that the world had not come to an end, despite his immense disappointment with the failure of the Confederate cause. Similarly, as an aide on the staff of Lieutenant General James Longstreet traveled through North Carolina with his commanding officer, he spent a night at the large home of an affluent family. Here again a young woman, the daughter of the homeowner, made an indelible impression on the soldier. Although he offered a rather insensitive and less-than-flattering assessment of her appearance, he noted that she was educated and had been raised with an understanding of business. "If the Yankees had not freed all the negroes," he quipped, "this would be the place for a young man in search of a wealthy wife." Clearly the evening spent in the woman's company directed that tactless young man's mind toward the future. Meanwhile a Mississippian related a less obnoxious account, though with the benefit of years of maturity and reflection. Still, his words indicate the direction of his thoughts and how a meeting with charming young women could leave lasting effects on an impressionable young soldier. Though he told the story later in life, his encounter with three young women in Alabama occurred at nineteen years of age. He recalled: "These girls in their old buggy looked very pretty to me: the homespun dress could not be beat, when worn by a true Southern girl. Theirs was a charm that has never been equalled since."[27]

Often these men were quite young, impressionable, homesick, perhaps traumatized by years of combat and overall defeat, a condition exacerbated by the knowledge that they had survived while countless comrades had perished. Reminders of home and family, signs of stability and normality, and suggestions of a return to a life of peace could all prove powerful to young men in such a vulnerable condition. Predictably, for many a demobilized soldier, a meeting with a woman of the same approximate age who was kind to the young man under the circumstances, produced a powerful and everlasting impression. Such encounters perhaps, even subconsciously, helped to fortify the masculine identity of defeated Rebels by reminding them that they were men, not just soldiers. Moreover, such meetings, however fleeting, evoked images of a longed-for return to a peacetime norm.

Reminders of home increased as Confederate veterans drew nearer their final destinations. Assistance provided by civilians also took on a different character because soldiers frequently stopped at the homes of old friends. Clearly a soldier was at least somewhat more likely to receive aid from an acquaintance than from a stranger, though soldiers were no more likely to comment on visits with friends than on encounters with unfamiliar people. In fact, diaries and postwar reminiscences are generally less descriptive of visits with friends or acquaintances than accounts of encounters with strangers throughout the journeys. Perhaps the personal nature of time spent with acquaintances kept the details from the pages of diaries and memoirs, though considering the intimate details provided on so many other issues, that explanation seems improbable. Instead, a soldier almost certainly expected assistance in the form of food, shelter, and companionship from people he knew and thus considered such visits less noteworthy than meals provided by poverty-stricken families and strangers. Soldiers frequently mentioned assistance received from friends but typically opted for matter-of-fact entries instead of detailed, thought-provoking discussions. Still, the sight of familiar faces and places obviously comforted the weary travelers.[28]

One particular account illustrates the concept with clarity. John Frank Edwards, a twenty-two-year-old private, journeyed more than one thousand miles from a northern military prison to his mother's home in Georgia. As the bedraggled young infantryman reached the Chattahoochee River, what he described as "my old playground," a familiar face greeted him and two ancient eyes gazed upon on him. "I could not hold back the emotions that welled up in my heart. There I met the same old darkey that had always kept the ferry." Though Edwards called him by name, the man failed to recognize the young soldier. After Edwards identified himself, he recalled, the older man embraced him but commented on his unhealthy appearance. "You look so bad and yellow, I hardly recognize this is Frank. I am sorry for you." Edwards remembered vividly the comfort provided by those sympathetic words. The ferryman continued, "Your mother will never know you unless you make yourself known. You don't look like the boy that left here four years ago. You are so poor and lean." Edwards insisted that he felt better than he apparently looked and that he "was going home to see that good mother."[29]

Many modern readers will doubtless question the young Georgian's account, and indeed one could interpret the episode in number of ways. Most obvious, the story was written years after the war, not in a wartime diary or letter. Perhaps the account is complete fiction created for the sake of a good story or to advance a Lost Cause version of southern race relations. Or perhaps the story is perfectly true. Of course a whole range of possibilities exists between those extremes. Maybe Edwards's version of events represents simple sentimentalism looking back on an important moment in his life that took place during a historic episode in American history. If so, the tale could be an innocent, even unintentional distortion colored by emotion. If not, the yarn could be an example of Lost Cause rhetoric about faithful African Americans, in which case there is nothing innocent or accidental about the misrepresentation. Most likely, that encounter happened and played out generally the way that Edwards described, but the veteran possibly exaggerated (intentionally or not), misinterpreted, or even imagined the older man's sympathy and affection for him. In other words, the story is probably an overly sentimental account of an actual meeting tinted with somewhat creative dialogue, particularly when one considers that the account was written years after the event. Edwards offers no further detail on the nature of the relationship between the two men or even an indication of whether the individual was a freedman or had been free before the war.

It should be noted that Edwards's account, other than its detailed dialogue, is hardly unique. To be sure, sources reveal examples of such encounters long before the end of the war. A group of Texans paroled as prisoners of war after the fall of Vicksburg, Mississippi, in 1863, described in unremarkable language the help provided them as they walked across northern Louisiana to their home state. The African Americans in that case, quite possibly still enslaved, insisted upon payment in northern money. "They took us in and cared for us as well as possible," according to one traveling Texan among the group. He and his comrades certainly appreciated the assistance but considered the encounter commonplace.[30]

Other returning Confederate veterans at war's end noted varied forms of assistance from African Americans during their journeys home. Examples included simple meals, a place to sleep, help crossing rivers, and assistance with transportation in general. In some cases, those who provided assistance, particularly women, might have believed that they had no choice. A woman, regardless of race, alone in an isolated house understandably might have felt obliged to feed and shelter a group of soldiers passing through. In other cases, Black men and women might have helped returning soldiers simply out of a sense of basic human compassion, just as white civilians did countless times. Some accounts of African Americans assisting Confederate soldiers cited here derive from postwar memoirs or regimental histories. Others, however, appear in wartime diary entries composed the day that the events transpired. An Alabama infantry captain, for example, described a night spent a few miles from Danville, Virginia, just days after the surrender at Appomattox. Only one day after he had left a hospital bound for another in North Carolina, the twenty-two-year-old recorded that he and a comrade "slept on the floor of a negro hut. The negro woman helped cook our rations for us. We were quite comfortable, considering that we were in a negro hut surrounded by negro children."[31]

Another veteran remembered an encounter in which the white resident of a home was less than generous to the passing soldiers. As the men continued on their journey, he wrote, an elderly enslaved couple who still resided at the home followed them to apologize for the conduct of their master. According to the soldier's memoirs published decades after the war, "The refined feelings and delicate sensibilities of those old colored people, manifested so strikingly in such substantial sympathy, made up a beautiful picture of Southern life; and wherever we eight have been we have told it as an everlasting memorial of them." Clearly the encounter made an impression upon the soldier and his seven comrades. However, nothing in his comments suggests that this was necessarily the norm. In fact, one could argue that the experience made such an impression upon them and that they continued to relate the stories years later because it might have been at least somewhat unusual and thus memorable. As discussed below, white civilians typically did not refuse assistance to soldiers, so the combination of a refusal of aid from the white resident and the kindness extended by the Black couple could certainly have been cause for comment.[32]

One Kentucky infantryman, John W. Green, recorded multiple instances of assistance provided by African Americans, but there can be no doubt about his explanation for such aid. During a journey of more than seven hundred miles across parts of Georgia, Alabama, Tennessee, and Kentucky, the soldier noted instances of Black men who helped him cross the Chattahoochee and Tennessee Rivers. In neither case, according to the soldier, would the man accept payment. Rather, Green repeatedly insisted that despite the demise of slavery southern Blacks remained loyal to southern whites, and indeed, considered themselves essentially fellow countrymen. In fact, one man who helped Green cross a river and refused payment allegedly stated that "he knowed the Confederate soldiers could not get home ef *they* own people did not help them along" [emphasis in original]. The other man who assisted Green with a river crossing but refused payment, in Green's account, remained with his former master as that very young, one-legged soldier made his way home. "This good darkey," as Green referred to him, recalled having served in the war himself alongside his young former master's father, who was killed in the Seven Days Battles near Richmond, Virginia. Upon the older man's death, he returned to care for that soldier's wife when the son went off to war. He then journeyed to Virginia again to retrieve the wounded younger man.[33]

Days after the river crossing, Green related a nighttime encounter in which he thwarted the attempted theft of his horse by one African American man, only to have more a pleasant encounter the following evening at a plantation owned by friends in northern Alabama. There Green described a man and a woman who had remained on the plantation in May 1865. The woman, who the soldier identified as the cook, insisted on feeding him because of his slight frame and gaunt appearance. The man, identified by Green as Uncle Simon, made light of the Kentuckian's appearance. "He may be little but I bet you he could shoot yankies all right." Green clearly referred to the Black and white residents of that northern Alabama plantation when he remarked that he "had found a haven of rest & a hearty welcome."[34]

Obviously, in wartime and postwar writings soldiers routinely described white civilians of all social classes, and in certain instances freedpeople, as exceedingly helpful and generous. More specifically, a relative few enjoyed truly exceptional experiences, allowed sentimentalism to shape their memories, or simply exaggerated when they claimed that *everyone* they encountered assisted the homebound veterans and that the returning Rebels were *never* refused assistance. According to those accounts, in the land of true southern hospitality soldiers in need always received assistance. Such claims should be examined individually because a close reading reveals important factors unique to the individual circumstances.

In the case of the Texan Porter, he made a perfectly realistic claim that he never missed a meal during his journey home. He traveled entirely within the state of Texas, relatively untouched by the ravages of war, and passed through a part of the Lone Star state that offered bountiful resources. Another soldier diarist mentioned that he and his comrades always found plenty of food between Shreveport, Louisiana, and Houston, Texas, during their homeward journey. Circumstances support the veracity of certain other claims of universal assistance, such as in the instance of soldiers given the run of the city in New Orleans and civilian aid provided to travel parties that included prominent figures.[35]

Other accounts, however, suggest potential cases of selective memory at best, intentional distortion at worst. A private who traveled from North Carolina to Texas, for example, recalled a hearty welcome at every stop because, he reasoned, nearly everyone had a loved one in the Army of Northern Virginia or the Army of Tennessee. Despite his seemingly sound logic, the claim—that he and his comrades received assistance at every stop through parts of North Carolina, South Carolina, Georgia, Mississippi, Alabama, Louisiana, and Texas— remains virtually impossible to believe.[36]

Two other veterans recalled drastically different experiences that better illustrate the sometimes tense interactions between hungry soldiers and weary civilians. One former soldier remembered an encounter with an older man in North Carolina determined to defend his home and possessions. As the ravenous Rebels approached the house the skeptical host greeted them with a gun and explained that area residents had developed a system of warning sounds and a network of support to protect each other amidst the chaos of the spring and summer of 1865. Eventually the soldiers eased the man's troubled mind and earned his confidence. He invited them into the house and provided them with directions for the next leg of the journey. Similarly, another veteran recalled a trek across Mississippi, where he encountered a fellow Louisianan, who had fled

New Orleans as a refugee. The man initially refused to allow the soldier to sleep at his home until he learned that he, too, hailed from Louisiana. Upon the discovery of their shared heritage, the host took in the traveler and fed him well.[37]

Those veterans' experiences point up an important reality of demobilized Confederates' homeward journeys. Although most southern civilians generously and willingly assisted returning soldiers, a meaningful portion refused to help for myriad reasons. Obviously not every civilian matched the idyllic image of the true southern patriot who charitably shared his or her last morsel of food. Certain individuals and even a relative handful of communities proved less than receptive to returning Rebels. Occasionally residents helped only reluctantly, some offered less assistance than the soldier believed them capable of, others demanded payment in exchange for whatever aid they could offer, and still others refused to help at all.

At times soldier diaries and memoirs openly discuss occasions when their fellow southerners turned them away. Such accounts point to certain important themes, to be discussed below, but could also create the mistaken impression that these represented isolated instances. Diaries and memoirs often employed language that indicates a more realistic situation. Soldiers often used phrases that indicated that "most" people were willing to help, people "often" helped, soldiers were "rarely" refused assistance, and they stopped at each house and "usually" received something. Occasionally soldiers acknowledged the need to "convince" an individual to give them a ride in a wagon and admitted to taking food or supplies from farms when the hosts refused assistance. Thus, though not the norm, traveling Confederate veterans sometimes left a house empty-handed.[38]

Now and then civilians who offered no assistance to passing soldiers simply possessed nothing to give. One Virginia infantry sergeant noted that the residents of a particular house had no food to share because of previous visits by other soldiers. A sympathetic Kentucky cavalryman remarked similarly in his diary that he and his comrades had traveled twenty-six miles in three days, had found food at only two houses during that time, and that "they all tell us they haven't got anything to eat which I expect is pretty much the case." Whether they wrote at the time or reflected years later, Confederates generally understood the severe limitations and hardships that confronted many potential hosts.[39]

Other civilians helped only grudgingly or refused help for similar reasons of self-preservation. At times inhabitants of areas hit particularly hard by the war or ravaged by the appetites of returning veterans decided that they had done their part for the Confederate war effort. Understandably they determined to retain what provisions remained on their homesteads for the survival of their families. Self-preservation as a reason to turn away soldiers manifested in other ways as well. One farmer refused to feed or shelter a passing party of soldiers because he feared that they would spread disease by drawing water from his well and that they would steal his chickens. Several individuals refused to render aid to Confederate president Jefferson Davis's travel party for fear of repercussions suffered at the hands of Federal troops. Others declined to assist a group of soldiers and officers because the color of one naval officer's uniform confused the civilians. Though perfectly reasonable, such motivations offered little comfort to hungry soldiers miles from home.[40]

One such famished veteran struggled mightily during a specific stretch of his trek from North Carolina to Alabama. Although he fared well for most of his journey, he encountered less generous hosts as he crossed part of Georgia and reserved harsh words for the denizens of his least favorite southern state. In his diary he rejoiced to spend the night on Alabama soil for the first time in months and fumed: "I have wiped the dust of Georgia off my feet, and I hope never to have it on them again. A considerable experience in this State enables me to speak, in some respects, understandingly of its people. As a general rule, the people are wanting in hospitality, and consider travelers a nuisance, exhibiting little desire to aid them." With the exception of a single kind individual, "no man has opened his cribs or heart to us." The diatribe continued to its ultimate conclusion that, for some inexplicable reason, in the mind of this single officer the people of Georgia somehow differed from the entirety of their southern brethren.[41]

Any number of factors, including plain bad luck or possibly a haughty attitude, could explain his hardship. A major, twenty-six years of age at the end of the war, the University of Mississippi graduate had worked as a lawyer and newspaper editor before the war. The simple, harsh realities of war could also explain his struggles. His travel itinerary reveals that his route took him through a part of Georgia that suffered through not only the Atlanta campaign but also William T. Sherman's March to the Sea. He even acknowledged such in his diary, yet failed to grasp that individuals who had experienced the ultimate in hard war might have been left with limited provisions and even less patience.

A minority of civilians needed no justification to deny assistance to returning soldiers. They simply refused aid for reasons known only to them, though clearly financial considerations played the central role in most cases cited here. Whether a railroad conductor who refused free transportation for soldiers or a parsimonious farmer determined to protect his corn supply, the occasional ci- vilian not only elected not to help soldiers but obviously sensed no obligation to do so. As an unidentified diarist from Arkansas opined, some people "seem to have forgotten that soldiers are compelled to eat in order to live—that they have but few friends and still less money." Similarly, an army doctor who trekked across Virginia approached the mansion of a wealthy woman with understand- able hopes of a restful stay and a bountiful meal. Unfortunately for the optimis- tic surgeon, the woman he encountered forcefully instructed him not to ascend the steps of the great house. They would host no soldiers there.[42]

That physician's experience points up an important aspect of civilian assis- tance to returning soldiers. Wartime and postwar accounts cited throughout this study demonstrate that wealthy southerners proved no more or less likely than others to offer aid and comfort to traveling veterans. Rather, when a wealthy family or individual turned away a soldier it reasonably made a powerful im- pression, just as encounters with poor people who shared their meager provi- sions left lasting imprints in the memories of veterans. Some soldiers, such as a Virginia infantry captain who initially refused to surrender in his home state and attempted to link up with Confederate forces in North Carolina, encountered wealthy families who welcomed soldiers and treated them as conquering heroes.

At one particularly noteworthy stop, he and his comrades encountered a large farm with abundant livestock and other provisions. Indeed, the idyllic scene suggested a homestead somehow untouched by war. Chickens, geese, turkeys, cattle, and more roamed the farm. The bountiful display prompted the soldier and his comrades to agree that if they could not secure a meal there, they "had better give up travelling at other people's expense." Fortune had indeed smiled upon that group because not only had they stumbled upon a home with much to offer, but the occupants possessed Confederate sentiment to the core. The family matriarch proudly affirmed that "if the Yankees *and white people* were going to be all together in heaven, she believed she'd rather not go to heaven at all." The soldier identified the host family surname as Bowe. The route of travel, itinerary information available in the diary, and census records, suggest the identity of the family in question almost certainly as that of W. B. Bowe, a Caswell County, North Carolina, resident who possessed an estate valued at an estimated $37,000.[43]

Others, of course, encountered less hospitality from their affluent southern brethren. A young Georgia native who had left school at the University of North Carolina to enlist in the military acknowledged help from wealthy residents at one stop but poor treatment at another. The refusal of aid irked the youthful soldier specifically because a poor man had previously shared what little he possessed. Similarly, as a twenty-five-year-old infantry officer crossed from South Carolina into Georgia, he stayed at the home of a "haggish" old man who, despite his considerable wealth, offered the soldiers no food and only a pallet on which to sleep.[44]

The accounts cited thus far demonstrate that most civilians of all social classes assisted returning Confederate soldiers, though a meaningful number of southern residents refused support for a variety of reasons. Close inspection of the sources further reveals an interesting middle ground of sorts. Numerous soldiers recorded instances in which civilians agreed to assist them with food, shelter, or transportation but demanded compensation in some form. A Mississippi infantryman on his way home from a Union prison camp lamented one manifestation of this theme. At multiple train stations along his route he witnessed individuals who approached soldiers with baskets of food. Unfortunately, he soon realized, the individuals sold rather than gifted the baskets. Most soldiers had no money, of course, so they could only gaze with "hungry eyes." Other soldiers noted the occasional simple charge for lodging or a meal, such as the day that an African American man charged a soldier fifty dollars in Confederate money for breakfast. Another veteran recalled that a particular resident insisted on payment in gold or silver.[45]

Sometimes, as in the case of an artilleryman who passed through war-torn central Virginia in April 1865, soldiers understood the need for recompense. At a random farmhouse the owner offered to share his last remaining food with the men, only days removed from their service in the Army of Northern Virginia. Although he insisted upon nothing in return, the soldiers ultimately left behind their mule because Yankees had taken all of his stock. In this case, the sympathetic and grateful diarist volunteered such payment and insisted that "a thousand mules would not compensate him for the kind feeling which prompted the act, nor his wife with the pleasant alacrity with which she bustled about and prepared the dinner for us."[46]

That understanding soldier proved the exception. In fact, an interesting pattern emerged among soldier accounts of such encounters. If residents of a private home demanded compensation for food or shelter, soldiers typically expressed indignation or at least a sense of disappointment. Soldiers took offense to insistence upon recompense from individual citizens simply because most made no such demands, thus the expectation of payment broke from established social custom. As one diarist bemoaned, the "meanest" man he and his travel companions encountered charged them for use of his home and provisions, but the "Shylock" still only "half-fed" the soldiers' horses. Another recalled a preacher in Virginia who provided breakfast for his party but charged them one hundred dollars, presumably in Confederate money. Mere days after the surrender at Appomattox, the parson admitted the exorbitance of his rate but, perhaps believing the men deserters or unaware of the terms of parole, he quipped that they would not need the money in prison.[47]

In stark contrast, soldiers expected to pay individuals in cases in which the assistance provided in some way involved the civilian's livelihood. For example, although hotel owners occasionally offered free rooms, soldiers typically assumed that they could not lodge in such an establishment without charge unless they slept on the porch or on the floor of the lobby. Far more common, traveling soldiers almost universally, willingly, paid private citizens who helped them cross rivers. Numerous accounts describe payments to civilians, regardless of race or gender, adults and even children, because the individuals lived along a river and obviously supplemented their income with a ferry service. Dugout canoes, skiffs, improvised rafts, and vessels of myriad other descriptions, occasionally pulled by mules, regularly conducted returning Rebels across the many riparian obstacles on their homeward journeys. Occasionally a local resident offered the service free of charge or permitted the soldiers to use the vessel to cross without assistance. Such was the case with a travel party that needed to cross the Arkansas River. A local farmer loaned the group his skiff but refused to help personally because of the high water level. Though soldiers at times quibbled over the rate charged or suspected that the local took advantage of the circumstances to command a higher rate, all parties typically understood that the service required payment.[48]

The expectation to pay individuals for transportation assistance proved so common that one soldier recalled his surprise when a young boy refused payment for use of his skiff. More revealing, another band of travelers voluntarily paid the captain of a small river boat for transportation rather than wait for the free conveyance provided by the Federals. Interestingly, most soldiers clearly considered railroads an exception to this principle. Perhaps they considered railroads nameless, faceless, big businesses rather than relatable, hardworking individual citizens. They probably reasoned that one seat on a train or open space on a freight car really cost the railroad nothing. Of course, most soldiers also knew that the U.S. government had mandated free railroad travel for soldiers with the appropriate paperwork.[49]

Despite the distribution of the remains of the Confederate treasury to soldiers and officers of the Army of Tennessee, most demobilized Rebels around the South possessed little or no money for significant stretches of the homeward march. Predictably, a barter system emerged to dictate the terms of compensation. Soldiers routinely exchanged various supplies or provisions, typically obtained from headquarters at the time of parole or scavenged during the widespread looting of government warehouses and war-torn southern cities. One soldier traded a pocket mirror for breakfast, while another swapped his horse to Federal soldiers for "a mule some larger than a rabbit." That mule helped the man and a comrade traverse part of the route home and provided an asset for future sale or trade. Others who traded specifically for mules had already turned their thoughts toward the future. The animal would be essential to the postwar recovery of their farms. One Rebel diarist recorded that his comrade favored coffee as a commodity because people in the countryside would give almost anything for it.[50]

That clever observation reveals an important aspect of the soldiers' attitudes toward the barter system. Veterans appreciated the value of scarce commodities, particularly to residents of rural communities and isolated farmhouses, and recognized that such goods functioned as a currency of sorts to facilitate travel. As one staff officer noted in his diary during his long westward journey to Alabama, "We find no difficulty in procuring forage; cotton thread, salt, tobacco, etc., will tempt any of the South Carolinians to part with corn, no matter how scarce it may be." Within two weeks, that same officer lamented "Out of bartering tricks, and will be forced to beg the rest of the way." Although cognizant of the prevalence and necessity of the barter system, at least a few returning Rebels sometimes disparaged the concept. Mere days into his homeward trek, an officer in a heavy artillery unit complained that he was already "reduced" to barter in order to secure food along the way. That diarist's social status might have contributed to his disdain for the barter system, or perhaps more accurately, his resentment of his dependence upon it. The twenty-four-year-old artillery colonel, a senior at The Citadel at the onset of hostilities, grew up at the home of his grandparents, who in 1860 boasted an estate valued at almost $300,000. In 1865 the South Carolinian purchased his own plantation in Georgia.[51]

The most revealing facet of soldiers' words and deeds on the system of haggle and trade is that, regardless of whether they embraced or resented the practice, they expected and prepared for it. In certain cases, groups of soldiers gathered materials for the purpose of future trade and stated so explicitly in their diaries. A cluster of Virginians headed east from Appomattox absconded with a mule specifically to trade for food. Farther south, when General P. G. T. Beauregard and his staff prepared to depart for home from North Carolina, they gathered an impressive cache that included nails, yarn, thread, and tobacco for the express purpose of barter. One of the general's travel companions insisted that civilians always helped and rarely accepted compensation when they realized that Beauregard was among the cadre, but the level of the group's preparation proves that they readied themselves for more arduous circumstances.[52]

Other Confederates acted similarly but elected not to state their motives explicitly. A Rebel who had traded for a mule later sold the animal in one city then sold the bridle and saddle in another. Elsewhere he and a comrade had participated in the looting of a Confederate government warehouse in Danville, Virginia, and had absconded with bacon, meal, army blankets, and a saddle. The men almost immediately traded the saddle, revealing the true reason for taking it. Later, the duo joined in a raid on a supply depot in Charlotte, North Carolina. This time feeling sufficiently fed, the twosome paid themselves with a bolt of denim, which they actually retained for the duration of their journey together and split equally when they parted ways approximately ten miles from their respective South Carolina homes.[53]

The barter system, expectations for compensation, and the occasional refusal of assistance collectively demonstrate that not all individual southerners received returning Confederate soldiers as conquering heroes entitled to whatever they desired. The same could be said for particular cities and towns and even entire regions. Similar to circumstances that greeted some returning northern veterans, in certain cases indifferent communities barely noticed the return of their local veterans. In reference to the unceremonious return of thousands of fighting men to their homes, a newspaper editor in Marshall, Texas, lamented that "if the southern people had been successful in this revolution, these noble men would have been welcomed with processions and banners, music and flowers." Every town would have thrown parades and every household would have offered its best to the returning heroes, according to the disappointed writer, who urged the people in his local community to support the returning soldiers despite the war's outcome. "Are the soldiers less meritorious because our cause has failed?"[54]

The unfriendly reception offered veterans in that East Texas town and those described below point up an important contrast between the immediate postwar experiences of northern and southern fighting men. Multiple scholars have demonstrated that Union soldiers generally arrived to mixed receptions. Some received warm welcomes, even parades, but many returned to no fanfare. More significantly, as explained in the excellent works of James Marten, Paul A. Cimbala, and Brian Matthew Jordan, northern civilian support for Union veterans waned rather quickly. Indeed, Marten described a "widening chasm" between civilians and veterans who all too often fell victim to the stereotypical imagery of addiction, poverty, and general failure. In fact, some northern civilians even came to resent volunteer soldiers' claims to pensions. As Jordan observed of the postwar North, "In the absence of any social-welfare policy, and clinging to strident, laissez-faire individualism, civilians hardly knew what to do with so many needy veterans."[55]

Although northern veterans often received honors and tributes for their service, their image over time became increasingly complex. As Marten has explained, although a greater portion of American males joined the ranks than in any previous conflict, a slight majority of military-age northern white men did not enlist. "In other words, many good, worthy men did not fight for the Union, ensuring that northerners could perceive multiple paths to fulfilling a citizen's duty." Thus circumstance provided northern civilians multiple lenses through which to view both noncombatants and those who donned the blue. Meanwhile, the vast majority of military-age white men served the Confederacy in some capacity and accordingly became the most revered members of southern society. Confederate veterans typically arrived to heroes' welcomes and, unlike their erstwhile opponents, their stature in society grew greater with each passing year.[56] The shared sacrifice and experience with defeat, wartime devastation, and hatred for an invasive enemy fueled the overwhelmingly celebratory nature of southern communities' receptions of Confederate veterans. Consequently, even the experience of demobilization, simply the trek home and the greeting received by fellow southerners, helped to plant the seeds and nourish the mindset that would blossom into the Lost Cause.

Despite the overwhelmingly celebratory nature of Confederate veterans returning from war, some exceptions occurred. Similar to the events in Marshall, a group of soldiers who returned to Waxahachie, Texas, met with a cold reception. As they rode down the street residents offered no cheers or indeed any greeting at all. They simply stared in silence. Meanwhile, the city council in Galveston, Texas, where chaos had reigned supreme during the aftermath of war, temporarily refused soldiers entrance into the island city, but treated them well thereafter. Obviously, defeat and general war weariness shaped the attitudes of civilians, though another factor further contributed to the indifferent reception of Confederate veterans in certain towns. Marshall, for example, suffered heavily and witnessed looting and pillaging on a scale that most communities fortuitously avoided. Doubtless citizens there and in other communities recalled the chaos and plunder that befell their hometowns and understandably viewed additional returning soldiers with a cautious eye.[57]

Indifferent receptions gave way to harsh treatment of returning soldiers in a relative few communities. One veteran recalled his surprise at the poor treatment that he and his comrades received as they passed through the cradle of secession in Charleston, South Carolina. Another veteran, near the end of his lengthy journey from Appomattox to his home in Georgia, recalled an inhospitable reception in Atlanta. The twenty-two-year-old private remembered vividly, "As we passed along the ruined streets desperate-looking men peeped at us from cellars with the eyes of hawks. They looked like desperadoes who had followed the wake of Sherman's army to rob, steal, or murder as opportunity offered. But if they had injured one of our men, it would have cost the offender his life."[58]

Similar to the experience of that infantryman in Atlanta, soldiers who returned to certain regions encountered an insecure state of affairs and the potential for violence. In particular, men from Missouri, Kentucky, and East Tennessee faced not only uncertain receptions but genuine physical danger once they reached home. Missouri and Kentucky, of course, had been slave states but not Confederate states and had supplied regiments to both belligerents during the war. In both regions, instability had reigned for years, and demobilized Confederate soldiers understandably questioned the wisdom of returning. Even more serious, East Tennessee, which boasted a large Unionist population, proved a legitimately dangerous destination for former Rebels. Numerous veterans recalled that they waited various lengths of time for postwar emotions to soothe before they returned home, some returned briefly but left soon thereafter, while others literally never went back. One veteran referred to East Tennessee as "hostile country" during his return trek, while another remembered the region as "not being a healthy place for 'Rebels'" at the end of the war. Another Tennessee veteran recalled that when he returned home after the war his Unionist neighbors "were so bitter that I had to leave home. I went first to Ga. Then to Texas and stayed until the bitter feeling had passed away to some extent."[59]

That Rebel's decision to relocate in order to avoid the danger that confronted him at home highlights a final, important aspect of demobilized Confederates' final journeys. Most of the men profiled in these pages traveled home as rapidly as possible. After prolonged absence and burdened by the psychological trauma of defeat, most veterans moved heaven and earth to reach those whom they held most dear. Mental images of wives and children—perhaps struggling without him, certainly vulnerable amid the postwar chaos—motivated veterans to travel at a tortuous pace. However, a meaningful portion of the men under consideration here chose not to travel home immediately, and some never went home at all. More than one soldier explicitly stated that he traveled at a leisurely pace simply because he had no family at home. Two youthful South Carolina infantrymen lingered in Charlotte, North Carolina, "for we wanted to see and hear what might be going on in the world. . . . We loafed around town taking in the sights." The unhurried pace continued for the remainder of the homeward march. "We were faring right well, and, as neither of us had a wife and children awaiting our coming, we did not push hard after leaving Charlotte."[60]

Unlike so many family men discussed throughout this study, the youthful, unmarried South Carolina tandem escaped the interminable pressure to resume the masculine role of protector and provider for wives and children. Scholars of gender and masculinity among Civil War combatants have identified the concept of mastery as a pillar of the masculine ethos and have suggested that the return to home and family presented defeated Confederate veterans the opportunity to restore mastery at least on the domestic front. That contention is compelling and clearly correct, though it remains equally obvious that the quest to restore mastery occurred on a subconscious level. Southern veterans considered themselves providers and protectors, even masterful heads of households, and sought immediately to return to that role. However, combat veterans who had survived the crucible of war and the arduous journeys home never pondered the gendered implications of their resumption of domestic normality.[61]

Less typical than those casual young South Carolinians described above, veteran Victor Murat Locke recalled that he never went home to Tennessee.

Rather, that diehard Rebel had made up his mind to flee to Mexico. After a skirmish with freedmen near the Texas-Louisiana line, however, he opted to settle in Indian Territory, where he later worked as a cowboy, a merchant, and ultimately as superintendent of education for the Choctaw Indian nation, for whom his eldest son later served as chief.[62]

Several considerations, from the mundane to the tragic, explain the divergence from the typical narrative of the desperate journey to reunite with loved ones. In certain cases, soldiers simply delayed the start of their journey. One individual with the Army of Tennessee, for example, found himself mentally overwhelmed by the chaos and simply unsure of what to do next. Others postponed their trip to avail themselves of ill-gotten gains during the looting of southern cities. Other units remained behind temporarily to provide security while some of their comrades plundered and the remainder started for home. The occasional Rebel delayed the start of his journey or moved exceedingly slowly because he took odd jobs to pay his way home or struggled to find the means. Whether those men were less resourceful or less motivated than their comrades—or perhaps simply misunderstood how to avail themselves of the system for disbursing rations and transportation assistance—remains unclear.[63]

Transportation also figured into the delayed start or slow progress for other demobilized Confederates, who strategically waited for the best possible means of conveyance. One patient traveler, an artillery sergeant from Tennessee, waited one month in Georgia for the repair of a nearby railroad rather than walk a substantial portion of his journey home. A group of Kentuckians meanwhile spent a few weeks in a town along their route, in part to purchase horses to avoid a lengthy march. Perhaps most noteworthy, a Texan spent two months at the home of a random stranger, he recalled, while he waited for the Mississippi River to recede at his desired crossing point.[64]

Recovery from wounds and illness explains the delayed journey for other veterans. Even weeks after the surrenders, some convalescing soldiers remained in hospitals and private homes. Doctors and other soldiers sometimes postponed their own journeys home so that they could care for their weakened comrades. In addition to combat wounds and pneumonia, myriad other types of mishaps befell many veterans, prolonging their separation from loved ones. One unlucky Louisiana infantryman suffered injuries in an explosion, while an Arkansas private on his way home from North Carolina made it as far as Tennessee before a train wreck sent him to a hospital for several weeks. In the cases of those who recuperated in hospitals or at private homes along the way, it was not uncommon for soldiers to reach home as late as July or August 1865. Sadly, others who spent weeks in recovery never made it home. The father of a Georgia officer received the notice of his son's death from a nurse in Petersburg, Virginia, in early June. The same day, a different nurse sent a lengthy, detailed, and heartrending letter to the deceased man's wife. He had suffered his wound in late March, and doctors had predicted a rapid recovery. He soon faced reality, however, and died with his brother at his bedside. The nurse shared the fallen soldier's final words of love and appreciation for his wife and his assurance that the couple must meet again in the afterlife. Though not typically perceived as an overt expression of nineteenth-century masculinity, family bonds created a fundamental building block for the identities of thousands of similar Confederate veterans.[65]

More joyful and benign developments explain the belated homecoming of many demobilized Confederates. In one such case, a Tennessee veteran married immediately after the war and remained in Alabama for two years. Far more common, numerous soldiers stopped to visit friends and family along the way and in some cases even altered their route to reach those loved ones. One Kentuckian spent a week in a town where he had a "sweetheart." Soldiers frequently traveled to the homes of parents or grandparents to rest before continuing their journey, to borrow a horse or other means of transportation, or simply to visit. Typically, these reunions lasted only a few days before the footsore warrior continued on his way. Circumstances occasionally dictated longer visits. One twenty-three-year-old cavalryman ended the war in Virginia and began his long journey home to Missouri. Along way, however, he stopped at his uncle's home in Kentucky, where he found his sister. The duration of his visit extended to two months, during which time he worked his uncle's farm. After two months of plowing, planting, cutting wood, and performing sundry other tasks, he resumed his trek to reunite with his parents in Missouri, where he arrived in mid-July.[66]

The experience of a soldier from Arkansas who also visited family along the way illustrates another intriguing example of delays and detours in the homeward march of demobilized Confederates. After a visit with his ailing mother in Kentucky, the soldier made travel arrangements, via correspondence, for his wife and young son. In many such cases circumstances forced soldiers to reunite with their relatives in places other than home. At times a soldier's family had fled chaos or destitution as refugees, thus presenting a war-weary veteran with the additional challenge of locating his loved ones. In another example a young Louisiana cavalryman from a prominent planter family journeyed to East Texas to assist his widowed mother who had fled the plantation. The young soldier supervised the completion of the crop before returning the family to Louisiana and heading off to college. In other cases, loved ones had relocated to shelter with extended family. In such instances the soldier journeyed to that location, collected his clan, and continued his trek with family in tow. One veteran recalled that he met up with his sister at a friend's home, then rode to his uncle's house where his brother soon arrived. He then traveled to a nearby town to relocate another sister, before finally he, his brother, and a cousin rode for home. Even prominent officers shared such experiences. Lieutenant General Alexander P. Stewart reunited with his family in Georgia before the entire party returned days later to the family home in Tennessee.[67]

One other important consideration influenced the delayed return of certain veterans. In reaction to surrender and overall defeat, numerous soldiers cited earlier admitted to feelings of shame and embarrassment. A reluctance to face family, friends, and neighbors in the wake of failure doubtless slowed the pace of some meaningful number of veterans, yet almost none explicitly acknowledged the fact. Perhaps feelings of shame and dishonor in the face of defeat embody the ultimate manifestation of emasculation, but the dearth of confessions of such sentiments certainly exemplifies a masculine refusal to evince weakness. Veterans understandably wanted their loved ones to be proud of them, and doubtless some remained unconvinced by such assurances in the face of defeat. As one North Carolina woman proclaimed, "God bless you all; we are just as proud of you, and thank you just as much as if it had turned out differently."[68]

A Tennessean who served in infantry and cavalry units and surrendered at Gainesville, Alabama, recalled years later that "I did not want to go home, felt like I never wanted my people to see me. We had failed and laid down our arms." James C. Bates, a Texas cavalry officer who brooded during the final days of the war, recorded similar sentiments in his wartime diary and letters. Disfigured by a severe facial wound and devastated by the failure of the Confederate cause, he simply could not bring himself to face his family. According to one historian, "The dark bitterness and deep disappointment that invaded his soul after the surrender left him confused and disoriented. He did not want to stay among the Yankees now swarming over Mississippi, he did not want to go home, he did not want to do anything. All he wanted was to get away from everything." Bates promised his mother that he would return to her Texas home by Christmas and, though it remains unclear whether he honored the pledge that holiday season, he eventually made his way home.[69]

Many veterans of the First World War remained in the liminal state thrust upon them by war. Such men often retreated into a defensive posture among other veterans because they returned to a society so transformed that it seemed to offer them no place. Similarly, the American Civil War proved so transformative, or in some cases traumatic, that certain Confederate veterans simply chose not to go home. In some well-known cases those with the means left the country for Cuba, Mexico, or elsewhere. Others remained in a radically altered United States but sought a new home. An Alabama infantryman, for example, left a military prison in 1865 but elected to settle in Dayton, Ohio, for a number of years rather than return to his native state because, he recalled years later, "I didn't have no home. Father was killed in the war." Meanwhile a Texan who at the end of the war was in Kentucky elected to revisit Middle Tennessee, "where I had made quite an acquaintance during the war." He remained there from May until November of 1865 before his eventual return to Texas.[70]

Two other examples of individuals who did not return home provide a powerful contrast. Constantine A. Hege, a North Carolina infantryman, left a Union military prison during the summer of 1864, but rather than return to his unit to resume military service to the Confederate cause, he swore an oath of allegiance to the United States and remained in the North. Hege differed from the vast majority of those profiled throughout these pages in at least two ways. First, specific religious convictions indicate his likely identity as a pacifist who had never ardently supported the Confederate war effort. Second, he concluded his service in the summer of 1864, not the spring–summer of 1865, as in the case of the others under consideration in this study. His letters to his mother and siblings reveal a man at peace with his decision to remain in the North and illustrate his happiness with his newfound identity. He informed his mother that he considered it an honor rather than an insult to be called a Yankee and teased his sister about the prospects of marriage. "You say the southern girls are marrying the yankeys. I am verry sorry to hear that they think more of the yankey than of their own people, but be that as it may I am now also a yankey and perhapse I may stand a better chance to get a southern wife." Though atypical of the men studied here, his tale reflects the diversity of character among Confederate soldiers and their many experiences with the transformative power of the war.[71]

By comparison, the story of Missouri infantry officer Avington Wayne Simpson presents the picture of a dedicated Rebel, although, like Hege, he sought and found a new home as a result of the war. Paroled at Meridian, Mississippi, in May 1865, Simpson traveled approximately sixty miles north to Macon, Mississippi, and remained in the area for the duration of the summer. Upon receiving indeterminate news from home in late July, he embarked on the journey to reunite with loved ones he had not seen for four years. After visits with siblings along the route, he finally arrived at his mother's home for what turned out to be a brief visit. "Glad to meet," he noted in his diary in August, "but doubtless will part again. How true that 'every sweet has its bitter.'" Not mere sentimental tripe, the diary entry proved prophetic. The Missourian soon returned to Mississippi, where he married and settled.[72]

Overall, a remarkable consistency emerged between wartime and postwar written sources cited throughout this chapter. Although predictable in certain cases, the uniformity proves somewhat surprising with regard to other topics. For example, the twenty-first-century reader probably would expect wartime accounts to be more likely than postwar writings to acknowledge the refusal of assistance by southern civilians. An individual who published a memoir or regimental history was almost certainly a proud Confederate veteran, intense in his southern patriotism, and unlikely to acknowledge many things, consciously or subconsciously, that would undermine the image of a unified South during or after the war. Furthermore, those veterans wrote either during the violent, chaotic, and vengeful years of Reconstruction, or later, when age had possibly soothed their anger, time had moved the nation to other concerns, and the sentiment of reconciliation had led the nation to celebrate veterans of both sides. In any case, modern readers would understandably expect powerfully pro-southern accounts from such authors. To whatever extent all of this might be true—and to the degree that such factors help explain the dearth of sentiments critical of the Confederacy in postwar writings—the fact remains that wartime and postwar accounts proved remarkably similar regarding *most* of the topics addressed in this chapter.

Analysis of the sources for certain specific themes discussed in this chapter reveals near uniformity. Most obviously, wartime and postwar sources universally support the general idea that most southern civilians assisted passing Confederate soldiers during their journeys home. The same can be said for the generally positive reception offered by most communities, the various types of assistance provided, and the expectations for compensation or barter. Interestingly, no significant difference emerged between wartime and postwar sources pertaining to the occasionally cold reception that met soldiers in certain towns and cities. One might have expected postwar sources to avoid or minimize this topic in an effort to advance a Lost Cause viewpoint in which all southern towns opened their arms and graciously received their returning heroes. No such discrepancy exists in the sources, and in fact, postwar accounts and wartime descriptions coincide, particularly on the unwelcoming climate for Confederate veterans who returned to East Tennessee. Everyone recognized the anti-Rebel sentiment in that region, and the well-documented presence of unionists there likely explains the willingness of veterans to criticize their fellow southerners, though not fellow Confederates, in this instance. The pattern remains clear regardless of when the account was written. The similarity also applies to those who acknowledged that the shame of facing friends, neighbors, and loved ones in the aftermath of defeat delayed their return home. In that instance, perhaps the greater point is that exceedingly few admitted to such an emotional state.

On one issue a slight discrepancy between wartime and postwar sources likely means nothing. In instances of civilian refusal to offer aid to soldiers for reasons other than simply having nothing to give, soldiers who wrote during the war proved somewhat more likely to acknowledge being turned away. The discrepancy remains slight and, to be sure, some postwar accounts reference a lack of cooperation from civilians. Considering the number of memoirs and regimental histories that discuss the homeward journey, and the fact that some wartime and postwar sources acknowledge the issue, civilian refusal of assistance to demobilized soldiers probably should appear more often in postwar accounts. Perhaps some memoirists intentionally omitted such subject matter because it suggested cracks in the Lost Cause foundation, or perhaps because some consciously considered it unremarkable and thus unworthy of comment, or possibly because of its unremarkable nature some veterans never gave the matter much thought and thus subconsciously omitted it from their reminiscences.

More meaningful discrepancies emerge between wartime and postwar accounts with reference to two themes. First, predictably, soldiers who claimed to have received aid from every person they encountered during their homebound journey almost always made such claims years after the war. A closer examination further reveals that one wartime diarist who made a similar but perfectly realistic claim referred to a specific stretch of his journey during which time he technically claimed always to have had plenty to eat. Moreover, two accounts, one written during wartime, the other published later but based upon wartime documents, alleged never to have been refused assistance. Those accounts referred to the travel parties of two famous generals. Thus the wartime accounts that made such claims could not be considered representative of the typical demobilized Confederate's experience because of the celebrity of those generals.

The second theme to reveal a divergence between wartime and later accounts centers on the stories of assistance that African Americans provided homebound Confederates. Such encounters proved relatively common, in no way surprising, and appear in the pages of both wartime and postwar accounts. The question, however, remains not on the matter of whether the individuals in question offered the aid, but rather in the descriptions of such meetings. Wartime sources tended to offer brief, matter-of-fact entries that simply mention the offer of food or shelter without any implication that the act in any way deviated from the norm. The exception, the famous diary of Johnny Green, included extraordinarily detailed descriptions of his encounters with multiple African Americans during his trip home. Green's account, however, is drawn from the last chapter of the journal. Unlike previous chapters that feature sequentially dated diary entries, the chapter in question appears to have been written from memory.[73]

Predictably, postwar accounts sometimes offered more descriptive versions, complete with dialogue either impressive in its creativity or indicative of a remarkable memory on the part of the author. Confederate veterans who left such accounts might have intentionally portrayed freedmen and -women as unfailingly loyal to white southerners, to advance a Lost Cause, moonlight-and-magnolias image of a unified South. If so, such accounts contradict the many others cited throughout this study that portray fierce conflict between races, at least in certain areas, during the immediate postwar years. Doubtless the explanation varies from one individual to the next, but the possibility remains, in at least some cases, that postwar writers left more verbose accounts simply because they had the time and opportunity to write at length.

One other important aspect of the story of Confederate demobilization could not be more obvious. Although most Confederate soldiers returned home immediately after the war, the experiences of numerous veterans discussed above illustrate that some southern veterans genuinely did not want to go home for myriad reasons. Of course many others shared these sentiments but left no written account, and those who left diaries, letters, or memoirs possibly held back, or were themselves unaware of other factors that influenced their reluctance to return home. In particular for young, single soldiers, the length and timing of service should be considered. These men often served multiple years during formative stages of their lives. Away from home and family, fighting to survive, during their late teens and early twenties, all while witnessing the most transformative event in American history that turned southern society on its head, these men could have genuinely questioned their entire existence. A twenty-one-year-old man who had been a soldier since the age of seventeen or eighteen might question returning to his old identity that no longer existed. Perhaps, just as the war transformed the nation, the conflict fundamentally changed these young men and forced them to forge a new identity.

Twenty-year-old veterans rarely saw fit to discuss such sentiments in diaries and letters for the benefit of modern historians. Generally, more practical, immediate, real-world matters dominated their thoughts and the pages of their journals. In particular, numerous soldiers documented or reflected upon the final step of their homeward journeys and the first phase of their postwar lives—the homecoming moment. But before Johnny Reb could experience that joyful reunion, he had to navigate the chaotic, lawless, and dangerous conditions that enveloped much of the immediate postwar South.

4

EVERY REBEL
FOR HIMSELF

THE LAWLESS SUMMER OF 1865

Many years after the war a veteran who had traveled from Asheville, North Carolina, to his parents' home in East Tennessee remembered the harrowing closing stages of the conflict: "The excitement was great, and neither life nor property was safe." Confederates who journeyed home during the spring and summer of 1865 overcame material deprivation and immense logistical challenges. They also underwent a tremendous trial in the form of sheer chaos that swept the cities, towns, and countryside of much of the former Confederacy in the immediate aftermath of war. Although cases of rioting and plunder during the war's closing scenes are well known to modern scholars of the era, the scale of the anarchy might surprise some readers. If a pattern could be imposed upon the study of disorder, two fundamental points emerge. First, the presence or absence of Federal troops, more than any other factor, determined the state of affairs. Second, although demobilized Confederates often added to the disorder, the arrival of those veterans to their homes typically added to the restoration of law and order in their respective communities.[1]

Those two developments further explain the structure of this chapter, which addresses events in the Eastern, Western, and Trans-Mississippi theaters in that order. Besides the largely regional chronological pattern, the scale of bedlam generally increased as events moved west. For example, the absence of Federal troops in vast areas west of the Mississippi River helps to explain why that region witnessed more widespread lawlessness than the others. Moreover, many soldiers who served in the Eastern theater and who hailed from eastern regions faced shorter homeward journeys and therefore reached home more quickly. Soldiers in the Western theater frequently benefited from travel assistance provided by their erstwhile enemies that allowed them to cover many miles by rail or water and thus also reached home sooner than the distance of their travel might suggest. Once soldiers reached home they protected their property, began their transition to peace and a new postwar normal, and of course, they no longer contributed to the chaos themselves. Therefore, although riots and general lawlessness swept across many parts of the South, the intensity and duration proved worse in trans-Mississippi regions.

Frequently those veterans who surmounted countless obstacles during their homeward journeys also contributed to the crippling chaos that gripped the immediate postwar South. Sources of the time typically blamed specific segments of society for the riots that swept southern communities. In those accounts, deserters rather than soldiers, the poor or rabble rather than the more respectable elements of the community, the dregs of society, jayhawkers, freedmen and -women, or anyone else received blame rather than returning soldiers or respectable common folk. One Confederate officer blamed that ambiguous demographic, "stragglers," for an attempted theft of the stock animals from his travel party, while a chaplain more than once protected his home from stragglers. The latter observer also echoed the sentiments of multiple others with a particularly blunt appraisal of the role of the poorest members of society. From Georgia he confided to his diary, "The stores in town were all pillaged, chiefly by the poor of the town and the scenes were indescribably disgusting. The poor people of this section are the meanest of the poor and their outrages show very clearly that we have not as a people reached a very high degree of civilization."[2]

As so often proved the case, a veteran who composed his memoirs years after the conflict expressed sentiments consistent with those recorded by wartime observers. Also typical, he offered a more verbose description from the comfort of his home and with all the advantages and perils of hindsight. A Tennessee native, reared in Texas from childhood and a veteran of an infantry regiment from the Lone Star State, he offered the most succinct version of the tendency to cast blame upon the allegedly undesirable elements of society and thus, at least implicitly, deflect possible culpability for the chaotic scenes from returning Rebels of the proper sort. As he described his three-month journey from Kentucky to Texas he recalled: "Bands of freed Negroes depredated over the countryside inspiring terror in the white women. Bushwhackers were almost as great a plague to the southern families as were the Yankees, on account of their pillaging. Deserters had conducted a reign of terror during the latter part of the war, many of them in Texas, and were still doing so."[3]

In reality, all segments of society looted and pillaged stores and warehouses or at least took possession of government or private property when availed of the opportunity. Voluminous sources, including wartime and postwar words of the soldiers themselves, demonstrate beyond any reasonable doubt that demobilized Confederate soldiers participated in riots, robbery, and general theft all across the very country that they had endeavored to protect, and in the process, seized public and private property. Motivated by various factors discussed below, Johnny Reb ultimately adopted an anything-to-get-home mindset. If a pilfered pony or a misappropriated mule could help a returning soldier reach home, and perhaps pull a plow afterward, so be it.

The disorder that reigned over the South began in Virginia with the fall of the capital city of Richmond. Between the evacuation of the Confederate government and most Rebel soldiers and the arrival of Federal troops, anarchy descended upon the streets. The temporary absence of authority in the smoldering city set the stage for unbridled lawlessness fueled by a desperate sense of self-preservation that would play out in cities and villages across the crumbling Confederacy. Those most in need alongside mere opportunists swarmed the streets and for days thereafter sorted through the rubble and ashes of the many burned homes and buildings. One witness insisted that the three days of mayhem seemed to last three months. On the worst day of disorder individuals of all classes poured into the streets and absconded with whatever goods they could seize from the flames or from unprotected buildings and dwellings. Provisions of meat and flour, bolts of cloth, and boxes of shoes proved especially popular. Men, women, and children—Black and white alike—roamed the streets, some as if in a daze. Meanwhile others watched helplessly as the flames spread toward their homes and, of course, the chaos and uncertainty of it all drew additional onlookers. A discomforting silence descended upon the city, broken only by the occasional explosion of munitions, exultations of individuals who pilfered something especially valuable, or the desperate cries of terrified children.[4]

Disquieting sights of vulnerable women, tearful children, and desperate parents acting upon their natural protective instincts made lasting impressions on those who witnessed the fall of Richmond. Amidst the initial collapse of order, according to one account, "upon the grassy slopes, under the trees, were groups of frightened children, homeless and houseless, shrinking in abject fear from the fierce conflict of the elements of destruction, while parents strove in vain to patch up some sort of protection for them from broken tables, dilapidated chairs and carpets hurriedly torn from floors." One soldier, a Richmond native, looked back at his hometown in flames as he fled the approaching enemy, "but I didn't imagine that my own people were being driven out by the flames and my precious diary going up in smoke. . . . Our females were in battle like their brothers."[5]

For one battle-hardened South Carolina cavalry officer the temporary breakdown of structured society in the fallen capital proved powerful enough to shake his faith in humanity. As he and his comrades passed through the city amidst the sights and sounds of bedlam and desperation, he questioned his fellow man. "We could scarcely get through the mob at the commissary's; we came near being hemmed in by the flames which had been started in several directions. To witness the apparent madness and recklessness with which the women were pillagers and the skulking and deserting men also is enough to give us a contemptible opinion of human nature, but thank God we do sometimes meet pure characters which bolster up our respect for mankind." The cavalryman obviously attempted to remain positive, though an older officer informed him that "when I am forty I will think as poorly of human nature as he does. God forbid."[6]

Just as the fall of Richmond marked the symbolic beginning of the end of the Confederacy, the bedlam that befell the city began a trend that ultimately spread across the South. In one sense Richmond's story typified the broader narrative. People of all ages and social classes participated in the lawless behavior amidst crumbling or absent authority. In another sense, however, the dramatic and iconic scenes of the fallen capital deviate from the norm soon established. In Richmond, most soldiers had already vacated before the descent into pandemonium. Thus in that case the city was looted primarily by civilians. This demonstrates that despite the prominent role played by Johnny Rebs in the riots and general disorder that plagued so much of the South in the spring and summer of 1865, such activity befell some communities even in the absence of returning Rebel soldiers.

Still, as soldiers traveled homeward chaos predictably followed, particularly during the initial days of uncertainty, because the sight of defeated Rebel legions headed for home sent shockwaves through so many communities. Confusion reigned as residents in the path of those first waves of demobilized troops understandably wondered what the ensuing weeks would bring. This actually began during the immediate aftermath of the fall of Richmond, days before the surrender of the Army of Northern Virginia. As soldiers and the Confederate cabinet fled south-southwest along the railroad, Danville, Virginia, suffered through the same disorder that befell Richmond. Individuals in Danville witnessed both the symbolic and literal flight of their government and essentially the disappearing ghost of the Confederate States of America. Residents saw the remnants of authority fade away, and with it, any semblance of law and order. Virtually no one, military or civilian, seemed to know what to do. Organized military units that had not yet surrendered were kept under guard in train cars in order to keep them together and to prevent the mass disintegration of the last vestiges of organization. In the face of such obvious signs of the Confederacy's demise, the looting of Danville began.[7]

Unfortunately for the denizens of Danville, the reign of confusion continued for approximately two weeks, exacerbated by the demobilization of Robert E. Lee's defeated soldiery. Every man for himself became the rule as citizen and soldier alike pounced upon government and private property. Large crowds particularly targeted government storehouses, where bacon, meal, molasses, and blankets proved most popular. A pair of South Carolina infantrymen acquired some of those materials but also left town with a new saddle, which they soon traded for more practical goods to facilitate their homeward journey. After an explosion rocked the city and scattered a large crowd that had gathered near the depot, an unnamed Texan boarded the train and identified himself as an engineer. A large group of soldiers and others then absconded with the train, headed southward, and refused to stop until they were well into North Carolina.[8]

During the ensuing days similar trouble gripped the surrounding countryside and other Virginia communities. Residents of Amelia Court House, Lynchburg, Lexington, and Winchester reported outrages perpetrated by passing soldiers. Inhabitants of rural areas focused their attention on home defense, not against dreaded Yankee invaders or shadowy figures in the night, but against returning Confederate soldiers or those ill-defined bushwhackers. One veteran from southwest Virginia even recalled that he returned home and put in a crop, only to flee a group of bushwhackers who had established a camp near his farm.[9]

Another veteran who served in Virginia described in graphic detail the unstable conditions that plagued the countryside in that state during the weeks that followed the war, at least until the arrival of Federal troops. "Our principal danger was from the lawless bands of marauders who infested the country, and our greatest difficulty in dealing with them lay in the utter absence of constituted authority of any sort." Apparently unwilling to cast aspersions on the average Johnny Reb, the veteran laid the blame at the feet of various others. "Highwaymen," as he described them, who "were simply the offscourings of the two armies and of the suddenly freed negro population,—deserters from fighting regiments on both sides, and negro desperadoes, who found common ground upon which to fraternize in their common depravity."[10]

That veteran also pointed not only to the lack of established government authority but also to the absence of men from their homes during the initial postwar days. Circumstances remedied the latter concern relatively quickly as compared to many other regions across the South. Although danger persisted to some degree throughout the summer, order generally returned in Virginia sooner than in areas to the south and west. The presence of Federal troops and the fact that Virginia soldiers typically reached their homes sooner than their western comrades helped to restore a semblance of stability. As soldiers reached home conditions improved to some degree, in part because the men were home to protect their families and belongings and to deter potential thieves, and in part because they no longer preyed upon others to assist in their own travel.[11]

Of all regions east of the Mississippi River, the North Carolina–South Carolina–Georgia corridor witnessed the most widespread and persistent chaos because of the high concentration of soldiers during the earliest stages of demobilization. As men from the Army of Northern Virginia traveled south they brought news of the Confederacy's demise, contributed directly to the tumult, and mingled with soldiers from the Army of Tennessee, also soon to be surrendered and demobilized. One Richmond native recognized the general southward spread of instability and lawlessness and opted to travel northward toward his devastated hometown. Without friends or a support system of any kind, he concluded: "I think the best thing for me to do is to go back to Richmond; but suppose I can do that, what then? Will not they be all beggars like myself? Oh, what a wretched condition of affairs we are all plunged in by this unfortunate war." Despite the uninspiring prospects of a return to Richmond, amidst the swirling confusion in North Carolina, the twenty-two-year-old infantry captain probably made a wise decision. "It is madness to go farther South, and going back does not present a very encouraging prospect. Imprisonment, starvation, all kinds of dangers, sufferings, and death in many forms stare me in the face."[12]

The upheaval in North Carolina undermined security and threatened property throughout the countryside. Tensions increased in areas populated by unionists, doubtless emboldened by the collapse of the Confederacy. Predictably, horse theft proved especially common because thousands of disbanded soldiers hailed from western states and frequently stole the animals to facilitate their journeys home. Particularly brazen bandits absconded with new mounts even from General Joseph E. Johnston's headquarters. Neighbors in rural areas sometimes justifiably banded together to protect property. Observers of the chaos in Salisbury attributed the looting of a government warehouse primarily to men from the Army of Northern Virginia. In mid-April an officer making his way across the state en route to Greensboro described the miserable state of affairs: "A stream of vagabonds passing—some Lee's men—many deserters who are seizing horses, & otherwise robbing & plundering as they go." In the big picture, statewide looting, particularly that carried out by Confederate soldiers, prompted a missive from states-rights-minded Governor Zebulon Vance to Johnston insisting upon remuneration for the loss of good earmarked for state troops. Ultimately, soldiers and civilians had looted so many supply depots around the state that upon surrender Johnston appealed to his Federal counterpart Sherman for assistance with rations for his defunct army.[13]

Despite the widespread danger that swept across the countryside, the disorder of the largest scale in North Carolina centered in Greensboro and Charlotte. In the former locale, approximately fifty miles west of the site of Johnston's surrender of the Army of Tennessee, the trouble began even before the general's capitulation. Greensboro's soldier population increased significantly when Johnston evacuated Raleigh and sent many units there and to Charlotte. Greensboro's proximity to the general's headquarters, the number of soldiers posted there further augmented by those passing through from Virginia, and its location on the railroad line made the city a veritable powder keg. The vast amount of supplies and horses there only added to the combustible circumstances. In fact, Greensboro served as a supply base for other depots in the region. As in the countryside, horses drew the notice of countless would-be thieves, but in this case, soldiers and civilians could not resist large numbers of the animals held together in government-owned corrals. One Rebel soldier assigned to protect the stock reported that local citizens besieged him with pleas to allow them to take the animals, and he actually expressed relief when Federal forces arrived to take possession of the valuable mounts.[14]

To make matters worse, unlike most communities where soldiers passed through as quickly as possible on their way home, in Greensboro many remained in the city for days even after they had received their paroles. The frenzied atmosphere, almost an immense manifestation of relief bordering on celebratory, and access to massive storehouses probably explain why so many men remained there longer than usual. Flush with fresh supplies and relieved to have survived the war, soldiers exploded gun powder as makeshift fireworks during alcohol-fueled benders. One historian has concluded that the chaotic scenes at Greensboro more accurately depicted the end of the war than the romanticized, almost halcyon scenes associated with Appomattox. The point of comparison is generally correct, but the scale and duration of disorder in Greensboro ranks among the most extreme in the entire South and thus cannot be considered representative.[15]

Other cities around the South experienced difficulties similar to those afflicting Greensboro. However, Greensboro was unique in that chaos reigned for weeks, despite the efforts of Confederate officials, officers, and some soldiers. Inconsistency likely explains the difficulty. In some cases, Confederate officers distributed goods from government warehouses to crowds. One soldier who passed through in late April witnessed guards disperse a crowd in one case but saw officers distributing shoes to citizens in another. In certain instances, Rebel units fired on the mobs. In one such case organized units of Confederate cavalry raided government stores and private homes, only to be fired upon by comrades reassigned from other duties in the surrounding countryside. The willful distribution of goods and the use of force against comrades both occurred frequently during the chaotic closing scenes of the war, but officials' inconsistent enforcement must have confused soldiers and civilians and further undermined efforts to restore stability. However, law and order returned as homebound Johnny Rebs departed the city, and on the afternoon of May 2 a Federal garrison of three hundred Billy Yanks arrived.[16]

The sight of Greensboro in shambles provoked introspection on the part of one melancholy Rebel. "I walk around the town this morning and the relics of the departed Confederacy remind me of the abandoned remains of some *large circus* which sometimes when a child I used to move when the tents had been struck, the horses gone, their gaudy trappings no longer visible, and feelings akin to sadness would creep into my young heart, as I looked upon the remnants of what had been its glories, now all, departed."[17]

Though he wrote in tones of a man in the winter of his life, in reflection upon on his youth, the infantryman recorded his lamentation in his diary at twenty-two years of age. Youthful but educated and hardly naïve, the homebound veteran understood the historic moment that he witnessed. "But now in the bitterness of an older and more disappointed heart I gaze on the ruins of a fallen Republic. Countless fragments of papers, etc., etc. strew the ground in front, in hopeless confusion. Ah! proud land, what hast thou suffered, struggling in the throes of a mighty revolution, and for what hast thou endured thy agonies!" The self-described "war-worn veteran" continued his philosophical reflection but ultimately turned his thoughts to postwar life under the rule of his erstwhile enemies. "From this mournful wreck and frightful ruin the foul and unseemly head of despotism towers above its destined victims, and like some polluting monster with sharp rapacious claws clutches its shrinking prey and trails its accursed and venomous slime over all it grasps and sways and destroys."[18]

Disarray in Greensboro signified the end of the war and the beginning of life under tyranny for that disillusioned Rebel, but fewer than one hundred miles to the southwest, Charlotte fared little better. In both cities the disorder began before the surrender of Johnston's army but after official negotiations had begun. From Charlotte, one officer noted the rapid disintegration of the army and that officers of all ranks left for home as early as April 21. In both locales, troops from the Army of Tennessee sent from Raleigh swelled the population, while additional Johnny Rebs passed through on their way home from the Army of Northern Virginia. The pair of South Carolina infantrymen who had procured provisions and a saddle in Danville, Virginia, also joined in as a large crowd raided a warehouse in Charlotte. This time the young men possessed plenty of food, and instead focused their efforts on the acquisition of other materials. An influx of refugees unsure of where to go, what to do, or how to provide for themselves and their families further contributed to the sense of desperation that gripped the city.[19]

As in Greensboro, the remnants of the Confederate government passed through town and added to the confusion. The sight of President Jefferson Davis and several cabinet officials in flight—even as Lee's defeated legions limped through town—contributed to the feeling of finality and conveyed a sense of desperation. Such obvious signs of the demise of the Confederacy emboldened individuals with Unionist sympathies or those who at least resented their former leaders. Indeed, one group of Confederate soldiers who passed through the city agreed to remain for a few days to assist with the maintenance of order in exchange for much needed provisions and supplies, but served only reluctantly because of the anti-Confederate sentiments of certain Charlotte residents. As one soldier recalled, "The party were very glad to obtain the rations and shoes, but disliked very much to assist in doing guard duty for the protection of such people as the citizens of Charlotte appeared to be." Another proud Rebel who accompanied Confederate first lady Varina Davis through Charlotte shared that unflattering assessment of segments of the local population. "The news of Mrs. Davis's arrival in Charlotte quickly spread through the city, which by that time was thronged with straggler and deserters—conscripts—the very scum of the army, and a mob of these wretches gathered round the car in which she sat. The wretches reviled her in most shocking language."[20]

As demobilized Confederates made their way into South Carolina, similar chaos swept through the countryside and ravaged select communities. In certain areas witnesses and victims identified the perpetrators as Federal soldiers or random bushwhackers. In others, however, they explicitly accused Confederate soldiers. One resident of Anderson expressed relief that she resided within the village because those who lived in the countryside suffered terribly and worried more about passing Johnny Rebs than vengeful Yankees. One Rebel soldier and South Carolina native who made his way home witnessed firsthand the devastation wrought by some of his wayward former comrades. As his travel party neared his family home they checked on an elderly neighbor, whom they found in a daze sitting on his porch. Attackers identified variously as "cavalry" and "bummers" looted the man's home, stole all of his food, destroyed and scattered his belongings, and killed his livestock and his dog. Elsewhere, as a dedicated and unrepentant Rebel officer crossed into Georgia, he encountered a group of Federal troops guarding the bridge over the Savannah River. He reluctantly admitted that the behavior of returning Johnny Rebs had necessitated the Yankee presence.[21]

Similar conditions prevailed across the river in Georgia, where once again even rural communities sometimes fell victim to lawlessness. One veteran recalled that he and his travel companion who trekked home across Georgia made an arrangement with another pair, including a former Federal soldier. He and his comrade helped the others locate horses, and protected them in Georgia, and in exchange the Union man and his companion promised protection for the Rebels in a pro-Union region of Tennessee. Soldiers who crossed the state kept close watch on their horses and mules and, as one Texas-bound Rebel recalled, eluded outlaws with regularity. Another confronted horse thieves in an area he deemed a "rural paradise" near Kingston, where "we halted in a meadow in which fat cows were resting over full stomachs and lazily browsing beneath the pendant branches of bushy trees. Here there gushes from the foot of a small hill a bold stream as clear as crystal and so cool and refreshing that I could hardly determine when to refrain from heavy draughts of its delicious nectar."[22]

Meanwhile one hundred fifty miles away in Columbus, a chaplain literally defended his home against attacks by would-be robbers. Sixty miles away, civilians and Confederate guards looted the meager remaining quartermaster and commissary stores at Camp Sumter, the infamous prison camp better known as Andersonville. In far southern Georgia officers turned over government stores to the local court judge, who voluntarily dispersed the materials to community members as a manifestation of humanitarian and practical impulses. According to an officer who endorsed the action, "The object in view is to protect the stores from plunder by the lawless and to appropriate them as far as I can to the poor and needy."[23]

As in Virginia and North Carolina, cities along major travel routes experienced more frequent trouble at the hands of demobilizing soldiers, local residents, and sundry other elements who passed through. At Augusta, where Confederate units stood guard against citizens and comrades, the efforts of officials to clear North Carolina of soldiers exacerbated conditions. On at least one occasion a local militia unit also defended the home of a prominent merchant against a large group of freedmen and -women intent on plunder.[24] Athens fared little better. At different times Federal and Confederate soldiers as well as Black and white civilians pillaged the town. A mob emptied the commissary strictly to keep the remaining goods out of northern hands, and each group apparently considered themselves entitled to the material. Poor residents grew angry in response to a rumor that the wealthy had been given first access, while Rebel soldiers who arrived later became agitated because so little remained for them.[25]

Meanwhile, during the first several days of May 1865, Washington, Georgia, suffered terribly because of its location along a major travel route, and because it served as a designated parole cite for demobilized soldiers. Thus the number of individuals who passed through the small town that summer far exceeded the norm. One witness there described Confederate cavalry as "little better than a mob" and civilians barricaded themselves inside their homes. Perhaps those citizens possessed a great deal worthy of protection, based upon a Kentucky infantryman's characterization of many of those local denizens as "very aristocratic." After a raid on the court house, commissary depot, and the quartermaster's department, by a passing regiment of Texans, "they threw out writing paper, thread, buttons, etc., on the streets, by the wagon load. The little negroes and citizens soon had wheel-barrows on the ground to take the plunder home. After the 'Rangers' had gone, the Q. M. had a guard stop the pillagers. The guards were chasing the little negroes around for some time."[26]

A local resident, the educated daughter of a prominent planter, confirmed the destructive behavior of the Texans with remarkably similar detail. The disgusted young woman noted that the "provost guard refused to interfere, saying they were too good soldiers to fire upon their comrades, and so the plundering went on unopposed. Nobody seemed to care much, as we all know the Yankees will get it in the end, any way, if our men don't." Just two days after the scene described by the young woman, one Union officer requested the assignment of a garrison of Federal troops to Washington, Georgia, because of the vast amount of government property there and because residents particularly feared demobilized Confederate cavalry.[27]

Approximately one hundred miles to the west, Atlanta, predictably, suffered a similar fate as a major crossroads, parole center, and commissary station for traveling soldiers. Individuals who passed through during their homeward journeys protected their scant possessions, especially horses and mules, primarily from each other. In an act repeated frequently across the collapsed Confederacy, disparate travel parties sometimes banded together for protection as they left Atlanta, particularly those who traveled north between Atlanta and Dalton, a war-torn stretch where the railroad had yet to be repaired. By May 3, passing soldiers and civilians had ravaged the city to the point that Federal officers wondered whether enough materials remained to supply paroled Confederates. Events soon proved the officers' concerns justified. Just two days later, virtually nothing remained except meager supplies of meat, and an individual on the scene wrote his comrades that paroled Rebels should secure rations elsewhere before they reached Atlanta. Indeed, also on May 5, one Union officer in Atlanta wrote that "Many citizens are passing through going home; having no money, they cannot go farther. Negroes are here in some numbers, who wish to go back home. Shall I furnish transportation for all those at Government expense, or shall I cause the railroad to carry them gratis?"[28]

Similar chaos gripped other states in the Western theater, but by the time disbanded soldiers reached those regions they had typically dispersed in the directions of their respective homes and usually traveled in smaller groups. Moreover, the soldiers stationed in Mississippi and Alabama had already surrendered and started for home when westerners who had capitulated in Virginia or North Carolina passed through. Still, chaos reigned in certain areas, including Tallahassee, Florida, and surrounding communities. The Federal commander in that district asked the governor to call out militia units to protect government property that remained. Demobilized Confederates also encountered problems at various points across Tennessee. One travel party on their way to Middle Tennessee met a group of women who directed the travelers to a point down the road where they could secure feed for their horses, only to meet armed men who stole the animals. Another veteran recalled that he traveled across Alabama and into western Tennessee without incident, but lost his horse to bushwhackers only four miles from home.[29]

Thus emerged a similar pattern of chaos in larger communities along travel routes and lawlessness in the countryside, but Mississippi, Alabama, and Tennessee avoided the large concentration of forces as witnessed in the corridor that connected Virginia, North Carolina, South Carolina, and Georgia. Moreover, the powerful presence of Federal garrisons in Tennessee and parts of Mississippi contributed to the maintenance of order in portions of those states. To be sure, violence continued between Rebels, Unionists, and Federal occupation troops in Tennessee, but the Volunteer State generally avoided the lawlessness and widespread looting that ravaged regions to the east. In fact, one report from East Tennessee indicated that by early May armed bands in the countryside had dispersed, and even the "worst men" had left the country and the others had headed for their homes. Despite his confidence, the officer who wrote the report acknowledged, "This may not be true."[30]

Meanwhile, in northern Alabama, Huntsville suffered at the hands of a mob, while guerrillas infested the countryside between that town and Florence. Horse theft again pervaded, while disorder and the constant threat of violence interrupted mail service and left many rural residents dangerously isolated. Similar troubles afflicted rural residents in other portions of the state. In one small community a livery stable full of mules fell victim to passing raiders. Weeks earlier, at the southern end of the state, the larger city of Mobile witnessed an attack on the commissary by a short-lived mob. Unfortunately in Alabama, uncertainty and a relative state of insecurity reigned well into the summer months. Indeed, in mid-June one plantation owner in Talladega County in the east central portion of the state lamented the gloom, loss of life, insecurity, and general lack of order that prevailed.[31]

Circumstances proved even worse west of the Mississippi River, where vast portions of the Trans-Mississippi Confederacy—including Arkansas and Indian Territory, but particularly parts of Louisiana and virtually the entire eastern half of Texas—endured more than a month of lawlessness. In Arkansas horse theft and general lawlessness plagued the people, and there as elsewhere returning soldiers strategically traveled in groups for security. Citizens begrudgingly came to expect demobilized Johnny Rebs to help themselves to food and supplies. One Arkansas infantryman acknowledged such behavior elsewhere weeks before he even reached his home state and certainly continued the practice during the last leg of his journey. Earlier he had noted sardonically that he and his comrades "bade farewell to 'the Chivalry of the South' and commended ourselves to the land of 'Goobers and Sorghum.'" Having served the Confederate cause and struggled to return to his home, the bedraggled veteran mustered little sympathy for civilian croakers and complainers. The complete collapse of authority in the state in May 1865 prompted the governor, quite reasonably, to declare his intention to conduct his state's affairs as though no organized Confederate military force existed.[32]

To the west in Indian Territory, Native American Johnny Rebs behaved in similar fashion. After soldiers seized government property at the Confederate commissary at Boggy Depot in the Choctaw Nation, Major Isaac Asbury Clarke endeavored to protect the supplies entrusted to him by Creek Colonel Daniel N. McIntosh. In early June, Clarke—a college professor and a dedicated Rebel even after the demise of the Confederacy—insisted that no bribe could have interfered with the prosecution of his duty. He sought to transport the goods to a refugee camp where the bounty could be distributed among Creek soldiers and civilians.[33]

En route to his destination he reached Robinson's Academy, a small school in the Chickasaw Nation, under the protection of a group of soldiers whose intentions he suspected were less than noble. Some of those men, Clarke noted, "came near proving to be more dangerous as *enemies* than useful as *guards*." When confronted by a group of Seminoles, described by Clarke as "ripe for the lawless move," who sought possession of wagons and mules, he warned that if they disobeyed his orders they would not receive a share of the property upon distribution by McIntosh. A leader of the would-be looters reasoned that the supplies would be captured anyway, perhaps even by a group of Cherokees expected to pass through the area, thus the major should simply hand over the property.[34]

"I was not disposed to accept his *sage* advice," Clarke assured Colonel McIntosh. Clarke, who also had private property in the wagon train, refused to submit, and insisted that he would fight to protect the supplies. When some of the men under his command vehemently refused to risk their lives to protect a wagon train, Clarke proclaimed that he would do just that and the others could simply do nothing if they wished. He and another officer stood guard overnight while the others soon calmed and went to sleep. After he reasoned with the group of Seminoles, they "determined not to go into the 'Jayhawking' business." The wagon train never made it to the Creek refugee camp, however. Clarke and another officer distributed the property among the men only days later.[35]

Officers' correspondence provides at least a semblance of a timeline to illustrate the state of affairs in the territory. On May 17, 1865, brigadier general and Indian Territory district commander Douglas H. Cooper worked feverishly to continue the war effort, at least in part to maintain order. Clearly mindful of the reality of impending defeat, the general urged his Indian officers to hold together their units and to advise "the warriors to stand to their colors, obey orders, refrain from plunder, and protect the country until the storm is over and things settle down in peaceful channels." The next day, however, in a confidential missive to an officer in north Texas, Cooper asked for assistance from white troops stationed in the Lone Star State to preserve order and protect property in Indian Territory. Three days later, May 21, the general sent an Indian brigade to drive away stock to keep it out of Yankee hands. Cooper also ordered his subordinate officer to keep an eye out for his stolen horse. Only weeks later, on June 26, from Fort Washita near the southern boundary of the Choctaw Nation in the southeastern portion of Indian Territory, did Cooper once again breathe easy. Expecting Federal representatives within days, the general closed, "The country is quiet, and no danger in travelling alone."[36]

Meanwhile, similar circumstances prevailed in Confederate-controlled portions of Louisiana. The disintegration of Confederate forces there began in Alexandria in the central portion of the state, where on May 5 the commander decried the demoralization of his forces to such an extent that he called for the replace-

ment of the entire garrison. He estimated that fifty men had deserted the previous night and that the remainder simply could not be relied upon. One week
later the same officer called upon the men in the ranks to stand by their colors,
though oddly, he admitted that he could not force them to do so. By May 17
chaotic conditions in the Alexandria area reached a critical point, at which officers weighed the demands of duty and continued resistance versus the physical
safety of soldiers' families. As one officer wrote, "Indeed, with the whole country
filled with deserters with arms in their hands, the question would naturally arise
whether many of those who have thus far remained true and fast to their colors
should not be allowed to go home to defend their families." Clearly by this point,
the denizens of Alexandria faced enemies beyond the dreaded Yankee hordes.
Reality had set in for that officer, who regretfully concluded, "All is confusion
and demoralization here, nothing like order or discipline remains."[37]

During the next few days most soldiers still under arms around Alexandria
headed for home and absconded with whatever they could carry or ride. On
May 19 an officer reported all government transportation stolen and a complete dearth of rations for the dedicated few troops who remained at isolated
outposts. He expected even those garrisons to depart for home at any moment.
The next day another officer advised a comrade not to bring his wagon train of
valuable supplies to Alexandria for safekeeping. "It would be worse than useless
to attempt to bring your train here. Every wagon and mule would be stolen in
less than four hours after your arrival."[38]

Chaos and lawlessness also, predictably, swept through the heavily traveled
corridor across northern Louisiana from the Mississippi River opposite Vicksburg to Shreveport, the headquarters of the Confederate Trans-Mississippi Department until May 18, 1865. Amidst the disintegration of the army, officers attempted to concentrate forces near Shreveport, only to witness regiments melt
away into history before they reached their assigned destination. Difficulties
along the travel route continued for weeks. In early June, near Monroe on the
Ouachita River in northeast Louisiana, a group of soldiers confronted a prominent Confederate surgeon and his family as they traveled home. The soldiers
demanded supplies from the boat, on the mistaken assumption that the materials had been purchased through the sale of government cotton.[39]

Farther west soldiers looted Mansfield, site of an important battle during
the 1864 Red River campaign. Amid multiple reports that the troops intended
to disband without orders and raid the commissary and ordnance stores, one

officer and his closest comrades hid their horses and mules in the woods and sank wagons in the bayou to secrete them from disbanding soldiers eager to expedite impending homeward journeys. Most such efforts proved unsuccessful. In fact in certain instances the very soldiers entrusted to hide the animals absconded with the prized mounts. A disgusted colonel on the scene deemed the command "a mob and rabble, disregarding the authority of their superiors and governed alone by a spirit of lawless plunder and pillage. Predatory bands were formed, and in many instances led by officers, for the seizure and appropriation of all public property. The Quartermaster, Commissary, and Ordnance depots, both with the Division and in Mansfield, were sacked, the mules and wagons forcibly taken and appropriated." Local residents, too, took special precautions to protect their horses.[40]

One desperate officer called for volunteers to preserve order. When no one stepped forward to accept the assignment, the dismayed leader bemoaned: "I thought it strange my faithful boys would desert me in this extremity." When assured by a comrade that the men of the regiment would respond to a direct order, the commander issued the directive and some portion of the regiment indeed formed ranks to protect what property they could. In the face of such unstable conditions, men from other regiments availed themselves of the secure line established by that regiment.[41]

The war had taken on a different and darker tone for these men. After years of arduous service in camp and in battle, they now gathered to defend themselves not against hated Yankee invaders, not against roving bands of bushwhackers who haunted the shadows, but against their comrades. Moreover, this occurred not in the no-man's-land of the rural countryside but in the relative safety of camp. Rebel had turned on Rebel.

On May 18, 1865, as other communities in northern Louisiana descended into bedlam, General Edmund Kirby Smith announced the relocation of the headquarters of the Confederate Trans-Mississippi Department from Shreveport to Houston. Even before his departure from the former locale, the threat of instability weighed heavy there. As early as late April one soldier perceived a restive spirit among the troops. Plagued by bad water, lice, and oppressive heat, and recently made aware of Robert E. Lee's surrender in Virginia, the soldier noted ominously that something was "going on" among the troops in town. Throughout the first three weeks of May, as regiments disintegrated and authorities loaded ammunition and supplies into wagons for relocation, citizens crowded into Shreveport and rumors swirled that the city would be pillaged. At least one warehouse burned May 18, destroying a vast supply of cotton and sugar in the blaze. Kirby Smith hesitated to move about town without a guard during his final days in Shreveport, and one outbreak of looting began two days before the announcement of the headquarters change.[42]

On May 21 a great crowd gathered in the streets and the sack of Shreveport began in earnest. Soldiers and civilians carried away all they could from government storehouses. One witness commented on the particular role played by women in the looting, while a veteran recalled that excessively hot day as "a scene which beggared description. Government stores, of every imaginable description, were seized, the streets filled with goods, official papers, etc., scattered everywhere. It was awful, terrible beyond portrayal. Large quantities of these goods were eagerly bought for silver by rapacious speculators." In a tone dripping with sarcasm, the veteran recalled that "Confederate officers disappeared very suddenly; the stars and bars mysteriously departed, but citizens in fine apparel became quite numerous. Passing strange!"[43]

Severe troubles beset the city until Federal troops arrived in early June and continued even afterward in the surrounding countryside. Other than the sparse Confederate command that remained, no law of any kind had existed for more than two weeks. Clerks at the headquarters, established in the residence of an officer, remained armed at all times. Legitimate businesses struggled to reopen their doors amid the tense atmosphere and a shortage of currency. One landlord evicted an officer who lacked the ability to pay. That officer and his ill child moved into the residence of a comrade, where the child soon perished. In a scene rife with symbolism, Federal forces arrived in Shreveport during the funeral procession.[44]

As the remaining diehard Rebels began their homeward journeys, horse theft became the norm, and bandits swarmed the surrounding countryside. Soldiers from neighboring Arkansas and Texas in particular absconded with new mounts. Those who traveled to the Lone Star State journeyed into a scene of chaos and lawlessness unparalleled anywhere else in the disintegrating Confederacy. In fact a travel party of seven Johnny Rebs received a warning as they passed through Shreveport toward the end of their long trek home from Camp Douglas prison in Chicago. The travelers heeded the warning and kept a gun at the ready.[45]

Despite the surrender of Confederate armies east of the Mississippi River, Kirby Smith continued resistance with the apparent primary objective to attain more desirable terms of capitulation. The general insisted to Federal officers that "his sense of honor and duty" could not allow him to accept the terms of surrender offered to Rebel forces to the east. Instead, he organized a conference of Confederate trans-Mississippi governors in Marshall, Texas, where he urged civil leaders to help him devise a plan to cease hostilities and maintain order yet preserve the soldiers' honor. Predictably, under the chaotic circumstances that descended upon the trans-Mississippi region, the conference failed to achieve anything noteworthy. The state executives proposed rather improbable terms to Federal authorities, including the restoration of full United States citizenship to all Confederates and the disbandment of the army without the requirement of paroles. Only days later, after hearing of great disaffection among his units in Texas, Kirby Smith announced the relocation of his headquarters from Shreveport to Houston. While the commander traveled, however, his army disintegrated. All across the entire eastern half of Texas soldiers threw down their arms and made their way home, plundering government and private property as they went.[46]

Four days before the announcement of the headquarters relocation, approximately four hundred Confederates in Galveston attempted to organize a mutiny. The commanding officer on the scene, obviously forewarned of the insurrection, employed parts of two regiments to suppress the uprising. He posted soldiers at both ends of the bridge that connected the island to the mainland, and the guards stood ready to operate the drawbridge if the would-be mutineers boarded the railroad cars. Colonel Ashbel Smith, the officer in command, arrived that evening and prevailed upon the insurrectionists to abandon the scheme. He then arrested ninety-eight ringleaders, put them to work on fortifications, and ordered the others back to their posts. Rumors of further mutinous behavior, including the takeover of a train, continued to circulate in the increasingly unstable island city.[47]

During the ensuing days the infamous breakup of the Texas portion of the Confederate Army of the Trans-Mississippi commenced. Even most of the remaining diehards now accepted the certainty of defeat and endeavored to return to their farms and families. Officers prepared to disband their forces in an organized fashion, but Texas Confederates seized the initiative. They planned to take government property as compensation for months of unpaid service rather than concede the valuable materials to their hated Yankee vanquishers. A communication from Major General John B. Magruder in Houston to General Kirby

Smith confirmed the rapidity with which the situation deteriorated. Similar to officers in other theaters of the war, Magruder proposed to divide the property and send the soldiers home. Only that, he concluded, would spare Texas cities and towns from complete anarchy. The missive's final words, "for God's sake act or let me act," reveal the desperation.[48]

Prudent officers in several locales around the state, as far south as Brownsville on the Mexican border, echoed the call to disband the troops, divide the property, and send the men home peaceably. Thus the remaining soldiers parted from comrades and headed home, without waiting for Kirby Smith's approval. By the time he reached Houston, no army remained for the general to command. All of this set the stage for chaos on a scale not witnessed in any other state at the end of the war. During the last week of May, civilians and ex-soldiers plundered Texas communities from the Rio Grande in the south to the Red River in the north.[49]

Galveston and Houston hosted the largest garrisons in the state and thus witnessed some of the most significant rioting. Exactly one week after the attempted Galveston mutiny, Magruder ordered the evacuation of the island. His directive issued on May 21 offered explicit directions for the conveyance of regiments, arms, stores, and slaves. The order further directed Ashbel Smith to send the "most unmanageable regiment" to Houston and to keep the commander informed of the location of every unit. Officers promised honorable discharges to those who retained discipline and additional clothing to individuals who assisted with the preservation of order. Rightfully apprehensive that soldiers would pillage private property, Smith divided regiments into small groups. Despite admirable efforts on the part of Magruder and Smith to accomplish an organized withdrawal from Galveston, Johnny Rebs ransacked the quartermaster and commissary stores on the very day of the evacuation order.[50]

Two days later, on the morning of May 23, a child who witnessed the disturbances in Galveston remarked to a Confederate naval officer that "the whole thing is busted up." By that point opportunistic civilians had joined the fracas. A mob descended upon a government warehouse while a gang of ex-soldiers purportedly appropriated a locomotive and local youths exploded ammunition. By the following day the mayhem had spread to the wharf, where a throng ransacked a blockade runner. A small detachment of one dozen men arrived with instructions to disperse the crowd but instead joined the festivities. When the ship's crew moved the vessel away from the docks, the resourceful horde simply procured small boats and rowed out to continue their property acquisition. Soon thereafter individuals, reportedly including elderly women, flaunted their swag throughout the city.[51]

Conditions reached such crisis levels that some citizens begrudgingly looked to the blockading Federal fleet for deliverance. One veteran who had returned home to the Lone Star State during the immediate aftermath of the breakup in Galveston recollected that the mayor required the soldiers to remain on board until a train could be prepared to transport them to the mainland. The city council even enacted a temporary ordinance that banned soldiers within the city limits. It was during this surreal postwar period that a witness described Galveston as a "city of dogs and desolation."[52]

Nearby Houston, the location of Magruder's headquarters, had already witnessed the disintegration of troop discipline and the beginnings of general disorder, but descended into chaos as the Galveston troops passed through. Inexplicably and wildly uninformed, officials expected three hundred men, but approximately one thousand men arrived by train May 23. City officials formed a committee to issue rations to passing Johnny Rebs in an effort to preserve order and to keep the soldiers moving. Astute public officials closed all saloons, temporarily banned liquor within the city limits, and enforced the policies aggressively. Magruder reportedly positioned cannons in the streets to prevent a repeat of Galveston's troubles in Houston.[53]

Despite admirable and sensible actions on the part of military and civil officials, disorder swept Houston as early as eight o'clock on the morning of May 23, when a massive horde estimated at two thousand people, including women and children, Black and white, stormed government buildings that housed ordnance and clothing. By noon the crowds had stripped those warehouses, leaving little for the next wave of soldiers who arrived from Galveston that afternoon. Similar to events witnessed elsewhere, the dearth of remaining goods angered the late-arriving soldiers, who threatened to invade private homes until others shared the provisions. According to one account, officers reclaimed materials collected by civilians to redistribute to soldiers. One disappointed diehard bemoaned how future generations would judge the participants. "God, how will this appear on page of history? Gen Magruder powerless & the rabble tell him to his face they will take horses &c."[54]

Bolts of gray cloth became common sights around town and some enterprising pillagers appropriated trains to transport their ill-gotten gains. Other ingenious opportunists immediately sold the excess bounty. Predictably, as with many communities through which demobilized Confederate soldiers passed, horse theft spiked, though in Houston, civilians frequently robbed the soldiers. The pillagers' acquisitions prompted a discerning newspaper editor to remark that throughout the war Confederate officials had been more effective in "preserving supplies than in issuing them," a sentiment thousands in the South would no doubt have echoed during the spring and summer of 1865.[55]

One dyed-in-the-wool Rebel penned candid descriptions of the scenes in several communities as he traveled away from Houston. In the small community of Hockley to the northwest of Houston, the twenty-six-year-old cavalry officer noted that "swarms of soldiers press & appropriate everything. All day we hear nothing & are in anxiety lest all is lost & we have to abandon our baggage &c. The livelong day crowds of soldiers loaded down with every variety of plunder go push on mules, horses, cars, wagons &c." Two days later, having turned to the southwest en route to San Antonio, he passed through Columbus, where he complained of roads still crowded with plunder-laden soldiers, whom he deemed "a motley mass, . . . , seizing whatever belonged to Gov't & eagerly moving on towards home." Only when he reached the historic town of Gonzales did he once again encounter stable circumstances: and the reason could hardly be more evident. "The town perfectly orderly—no soldiers to be seen." Despite rumors of more trouble in San Antonio and continued anxiety, the remainder of the cavalryman's journey home proved relatively uneventful.[56]

The same could not be said for countless other communities, particularly those along the railroad and other popular travel routes. Northwest of Houston, the railroad town of Hempstead—site of a relatively large garrison and close to a former prisoner-of-war camp—experienced especially intense activity. More so than in many locations, soldiers ignored the distinction between private and public property and thus invaded and robbed residences. An aide on the staff of Major General John G. Walker stood aghast at the destruction of the town, an action he deemed "disgraceful . . . the darkest chapter in the gloomy history of the War." He successfully protected his horses from a group of soldiers, only to lose the mounts to another party who, though thieves by any definition, reasonably wondered why Walker "who was now no better than any other man [should] have four wagons & an ambulance & they return afoot." The aide remained disgusted with the entire state of affairs, though he derived a certain pleasure from the experience of an African American man from a nearby plantation who entered camp one night to steal what he could. While the would-be robber considered potential bounty, other camp invaders stole *his* horse.[57]

Multiple communities along travel routes that carried soldiers away from Houston and Hempstead suffered substantial damage. Approximately 20 miles north of Hempstead an explosion rocked the small town of Navasota; it was blamed on a passing soldier. The mischievous Johnny Reb allegedly ignited powder near a warehouse that stored a substantial quantity of the same, a ridiculous action that took the lives of 8 people, damaged an entire city block, shattered windows throughout the town, and caused an estimated $70,000 in damages. Meanwhile, to the northeast, soldiers looted the state penitentiary and escaped with a stunning amount of cloth, some 16,880 yards of the valuable commodity. Kirby Smith stopped in Huntsville on his way to Houston but delayed for more than a day because so many soldiers blocked the roads.[58]

Demobilized Confederates who traveled a more westerly course from Houston and Hempstead wreaked havoc on the community of La Grange. The local newspaper editor anticipated trouble weeks ahead of the soldiers' arrival and encouraged the community to prepare. Locals even formed a committee with the intention to distribute government property in the county among passing soldiers and civilians in need. Despite such best-laid plans, on May 22 soldiers sacked the town on a scale reminiscent of much larger cities. Mules and wagons especially attracted the soldiers' attention, though looters also absconded with military uniforms, wool, and leather. Soldiers even ransacked a hat factory, pilfering approximately twenty-five hundred items in an action that clearly strayed from the notion of an equal distribution of public property to those in need.[59]

That unfortunate development followed a pattern witnessed elsewhere in Texas and around the crumbling Confederacy—some portion of the attacks on private property were carried out by soldiers who arrived after the plunder of government property. In La Grange several store owners lost everything in the melee. In fact, officials estimated that private property comprised two-thirds of the ninety thousand dollars in lost assets. Although community members supported the distribution of government property to ex-soldiers as payment for their arduous service, the local newspaper made clear the communal condemnation of the loss of private property to "*military hocus pocus.*" Unfortunately, numerous veterans "had not a very nice sense of discrimination between *meum* and *tuum,* and private rights were not sacredly regarded in all cases."[60]

Other communities in the general vicinity—including Gonzales, Bellville, Alleyton, and Columbus—suffered smaller raids during the same period, though those appear to have focused on public property, specifically government mules. The pattern appeared brutally obvious to one area resident, who in June cautiously described a sense of calm that had returned to the region. Although clearly concerned that the serene conditions might not last, he explicitly stated that no trouble had befallen the area since the last soldiers passed though on their way home. With an apparent eye toward postwar reconstruction, or perhaps simply weary of any military presence, he hoped that the return to normality precluded the necessity for occupation troops.[61]

Comparable events transpired in central and south-central Texas, particularly in and around San Antonio and Austin. At the former locale, demobilized soldiers confiscated and distributed among themselves government stores of gold and silver, while a raucous crowd of soldiers and civilians alike looted other public property and despoiled and burned a commissary train. One witness insisted that noncombatants of questionable character played a particularly large role in San Antonio's suffering. Residents eventually determined to feed passing Johnny Rebs in an organized fashion to keep them moving, an act that eventually contributed to the restoration of order. Despite reports of relatively limited damage to private property in the city, residents of the surrounding countryside suffered more substantial losses. In the area of New Braunfels, northeast of the Alamo City, groups of demobilized soldiers, and probably other unknown assailants, robbed private dwellings and routinely stole horses, even in daylight in front of witnesses. One perceptive observer compared the last days of Confederate Texas to those of a fatally wounded animal, remarking that "the last convulsions are always the most dangerous."[62]

Perhaps the most famous actions of the breakup occurred approximately fifty miles north of New Braunfels in the capital city of Austin, where soldiers and numerous others wreaked havoc for more than two weeks. Initial activity focused on quartermaster and commissary stores, and as one witness wrote, "the citizens are as bad as the soldiers." Mobs made away with cotton cards, quinine, lead, and powder, along with massive stores of flour, sugar, bacon, and salt. Government stables fell prey as soldiers seized horses and saddles. The pillage soon shifted to private property, and individuals eventually turned on each other. One appalled witness decried the robbery of private citizens whether the target "was going to a wedding or funeral, for the doctor or to church, no difference if a hundred miles from home." On the night of June 11, more than two weeks after pandemonium had initially stricken Austin, approximately forty soldiers—still proudly displaying their unit colors—stormed the capitol building, broke into the state treasury vault, and absconded with an estimated seventeen thousand dollars in gold despite admirable efforts of locals to repel the raiders.[63]

By all accounts the group that raided the state treasury descended upon the capital city from South Texas, where the breakup brought lawlessness especially to the border community of Brownsville and the vast open surrounding countryside. Travelers in the region suffered the roadside holdups that had by this point become all too typical around the postwar South. Soldiers who disbanded at Brownsville seized public property, particularly cotton, as they departed. In fact, although the commanding officer on the scene cooperated with the distribution of government property, soldiers arrested and detained him until they received what they deemed a more appropriate share. For some time, however, soldiers remained in the region, robbing indiscriminately, though one witness quipped that the ex-soldiers found distinct amusement in targeting northern merchants in Brownsville and across the Mexican border in Matamoros.[64]

Meanwhile, disorder and confusion on an even greater scale swept across the more populous and heavily traveled corridor across northern and northeast Texas. Here communities from Dallas in the north-central area to Marshall near the Louisiana border suffered terribly. Geography and logistics created a combustible situation for residents. Returning veterans from all three theaters resided in the region. Countless individuals traveled the corridor from Dallas to Shreveport because of the former location of Confederate Trans-Mississippi headquarters in the latter city, a significant supply depot and prisoner-of-war camp in Tyler, and an important Confederate arsenal at Marshall.[65]

Discipline and order collapsed quickly in Tyler when prisoners at Camp Ford were released May 13, most Confederate soldiers who served as guards left for home, and certain officers enjoyed a drinking binge with those prisoners who had not immediately left town. Soldier appropriation of government property began a week later when Johnny Rebs sacked transportation facilities, then later in the day distributed food and other public stores to civilians. Trouble continued in Tyler for several days as soldiers turned their attention to the quartermaster supplies and, on consecutive days, a large assemblage of women unsuccessfully attempted to ransack the commissary. During one five-day period, the officer in command of the ordnance works decried his lack of orders from above, called for an additional officer, pleaded for more guards, and eventually admitted that he would not be able to maintain a garrison much longer. His letters not only illustrate the chaotic scene and desperate mindset of an officer who hoped to preserve some semblance of order, but they also reveal that even the diehards who remained on duty during the breakup had their limits. Eventually they, too, left their posts and headed for hearth and home.[66]

Disturbances continued to plague Tyler for at least another week, despite the efforts of Confederate officers and local officials. A young woman whose family resided in the area as refugees from their plantation in Louisiana recorded the ongoing tumult and acknowledged that "Anarchy and confusion reign over all. Jayhawking is the order of the day." She chronicled the continuous looting of public property by soldiers but also recognized the involvement of other men not affiliated with any Confederate army. Moreover, she clearly blamed some of the disorder on officers whom she deemed too quick to leave their posts and abandon their responsibilities. "The officers are scattering to the four winds, and Jayhawkers and private soldiers are stopping and robbing them whenever found."[67]

Even more severe conditions prevailed sixty miles to the east in Marshall, site of not only a Confederate arsenal but also approximately three hundred wagons and twelve hundred mules that reportedly had been captured from Federal forces during the ill-fated Red River Campaign of 1864. Such prizes proved too tempting for soldiers and civilians to ignore. As word of the breakup and demobilization of forces in Marshall spread, civilians from the community and the surrounding countryside descended upon the East Texas town. An officer who received orders to protect the public property until it could be disposed of in some organized fashion endeavored to accomplish just that but mocked the very concept of official authority amidst the dying Confederacy. "The authority and rank of a colonel with 800 effective muskets behind him was vastly superior to the authority and rank of any general with no other support than a vacant command and a dead commission."[68]

Circumstances in Marshall had been unsteady for at least several weeks, even before the commencement of the breakup. Strained relations between soldiers and residents and alleged soldier depredations against the civilian population had prompted action by military authorities in mid-April. Brigade commanders posted guards at each command to keep soldiers in camp even when off duty, and ordered daily cavalry patrols to arrest offenders. Confederate commanders issued twelve-hour passes only to those judged deserving and only with written explanation. At least one mutiny occurred among soldiers in camp outside of town less than two weeks after that directive.[69]

Again similar to developments in Tyler, general discipline and the basic command structure in Marshall crumbled for several days as men gradually drifted homeward, often with officers' blessings. When all order collapsed a crowd of soldiers, Black and white civilians, and even children immediately targeted the powder mill and ammunition factory. Mobs raided even the soldiers' home operated by the Ladies Aid Society, meaning that soldiers who passed through during ensuing weeks found little comfort and aid in the town. With an eye toward assistance to those in need and the termination of the chaos as quickly as possible, officers in Marshall simply opened other government warehouses to the public. Unfortunately, in a pattern repeated many times over throughout the South, when late-arriving soldiers and citizens found no remaining government bounty they turned their attention to private property. Indeed, residents in and around Marshall continued to suffer significant property damage and loss until the arrival of Federal troops in June.[70]

Numerous other communities in northern portions of Texas suffered significant loss as well. A Confederate doctor who spent an extended period in the area witnessed chaos in Dallas and multiple other towns and described the general conditions in northern Texas as "wholesale robbery." On three separate occasions raiders appropriated the sugar supply at Clarksville, where the doctor operated a hospital, near the Red River adjacent to Indian Territory. Mobs variously identified as citizens and soldiers destroyed a shoe factory in Gilmer and made away with a staggering amount of corn, flour, wheat, bacon, and salt from Mt. Pleasant, Rusk, and Jefferson. When Kirby Smith passed through Crockett during the relocation of his headquarters, he witnessed firsthand the forcible seizure of public property by his soldiers.[71]

Kirby Smith reached Houston May 27 and famously acknowledged that no army remained for him to command, yet defiantly refused to surrender or yield whatever authority he imagined that he retained, demanding a report from Magruder on the conduct of the army, and even calling for a court of inquiry. The pointless inquest predictably and correctly absolved Confederate officers of wrongdoing related to the riotous actions of their erstwhile subordinates, but condemned the soldiers' actions as those of a mob, inconsistent with honor and duty, a sentiment adamantly reinforced in the general's final address to the troops on May 30. Though clearly in the minority, one former Rebel shared Kirby Smith's condemnation of the soldiery. The veteran of Brigadier General Joseph Shelby's irrepressible unit blasted his comrades and insisted that "History must dam to all eternity these last days of the Trans-Mississippi army, when it tells how sixty-thousand well-armed, well-appointed, well-fed, healthy and well-officered men, with not an enemy within two hundred miles, spontaneously gave way to a universal desire for desertion . . . without the exhibition of a single heroic impulse or the exercise of one manly virtue."[72]

During surrender negotiations Kirby Smith summarized the breakup of his army in Texas and explicitly clarified his condemnation of his former troops and the civilian population. "From one extremity of the department to the other the troops, with unexampled unanimity of action, have dissolved all military organization, seized the public property, and scattered to their homes. Abandoned and mortified, left without either men or material, I feel powerless to do good for my country and humiliated by the acts of a people I was striving to benefit." Three days later Kirby Smith officially surrendered his department on board a Union steamer in Galveston Harbor.[73]

Although other regions of the South witnessed considerable chaos, looting, and lawlessness, obviously the demise of the Confederate Trans-Mississippi Army differed considerably from that of other Rebel forces in the Eastern and Western theaters. Kirby Smith admitted as much, if begrudgingly and indirectly. A similar assessment came from an interesting source, Federal commander and notorious opponent of all things Texas, Major General Phillip Sheridan. With great annoyance, that famously expressive officer found "nothing practical in the surrender of Texas troops of Kirby Smith's command. It looks more like a move than anything else." Sheridan expressed abhorrence with the general chaos throughout the theater, the lack of a formal surrender, and probably most of all, the fact that the defeated Johnny Rebs effectively left the field on their own terms.[74]

Without question the absence of Federal troops in Texas, more than anything else, explains why the scale of disorder in Texas outstripped that witnessed elsewhere in the collapsed Confederacy. However, the want of that source of stability and the actions of those who sought to fill the void actually highlights one important aspect of the story, not merely in Texas, but in all three theaters. Certain southern officers, soldiers, and civilians from Virginia to Texas and numerous points in between attempted to maintain order, and those stories should be told to provide a balance to the many accounts of riotous conduct.

No national or state military or police force existed to protect the people of Texas during the three weeks between the Trans-Mississippi Army's surrender and the arrival of Federal troops. To their credit, senior officers and officials—including Generals Kirby Smith, John Magruder, and Governor Pendleton Murrah—attempted to maintain order, though they ultimately fled the country for fear of the unknown fate that awaited high-ranking Confederates. Murrah issued a proclamation to encourage action and cooperation among local law enforcement officials around the state, while Kirby Smith oddly requested that the governor mobilize virtually nonexistent state troops. Magruder attempted to arrange transportation of troops out of Galveston as quickly as possible to minimize the damage and employed certain units to preserve order, an action that in one instance the general reasoned might "save Houston." Despite the best of intentions, those senior officers and officials failed to enforce any semblance of law in most cases.[75]

Interestingly, local citizens around Texas seem to have been more effective, probably due in part to the motive of self-preservation and in many cases supplemented by returning veterans. For example, in Huntsville, where the state penitentiary had been ransacked with such devastating effect, area residents joined together to protect the prison and the town and even repelled a subsequent attack. In San Antonio citizens formed a vigilance committee that conducted nightly patrols. Galveston famously enacted city ordinances that temporarily excluded soldiers from the city and eventually restored a sense of calm as a result of cooperation between local residents and officials, soldiers, and officers. Numerous communities around the state formed home guards, with particular success in Tyler, Marshall, and Clarksville. Multiple cities supplemented their security forces with organized groups of former Confederate regiments.[76]

Authorities in the capital city of Austin formed a volunteer police force in early June, just one week before the infamous looting of the state treasury. Locals performed heroically in a failed attempted to prevent the robbers from absconding with the loot and, depending upon which account is to be believed, received some measure of aid from the command of Shelby, the officer who famously refused to surrender and instead led his men to Mexico. Whatever the extent and nature of their involvement, Shelby's men certainly were present during the raid on the treasury and participated sometimes as protectors and other times as looters at numerous other communities around Texas, including Tyler, Marshall, Waxahachie, and Waco. The group also acquired a veritable war chest of arms including ten artillery pieces, thousands of rounds of small arms ammunition, and an estimated five hundred sabers.[77]

Residents of Clarksville in northeast Texas personified the self-help attitude adopted by numerous civilian and veteran Texans. Locals there formed a protective squad christened the Red River Guards who met each morning at 9:00 in the town square. Those who shirked duty were deemed unfit for the Guards' protection. Some residents expressed pride in the unit's ability to restore law and order and to prevent further looting at the hands of passing soldiers and others. The local newspaper editor shrewdly advertised that all subsistence supplies had been distributed to deserving soldiers and the needy. He also warned potential ne'er-do-wells that locals stood vigilant and prepared to defend their small city. Residents stood armed and ready, he warned, "and if are any who still feel like trying the experiment, they are officially invited to come. Their reception shall be very warm, and prompt—a true soldiers' greeting. . . . We have plenty of arms, and ammunition, and some tried soldiers to use them."[78]

Elsewhere in the trans-Mississippi South, officers, soldiers, and locals also endeavored to protect property and lives. Shreveport proved especially problematic, but several units maintained their organization and patrolled the streets with some effect. In late May the post officer of the day reported that he attempted to maintain order in the city with a garrison force of 115 men and officers. One unit reportedly even confiscated property appropriated during the mass looting of the city and stored the recovered materials in the courthouse.[79]

Only days earlier, in nearby Indian Territory, an officer had called for additional units to help maintain order. That astute brigadier general demonstrated his grasp of the reality that he faced the disintegration of authority amidst a tenuous alliance between white and Native American Confederate regiments. "I want prudent officers and steady men, who will do just enough and not get into difficulties with the people or allow themselves to be made use of to gratify private malice or avarice."[80]

Although the chaotic atmosphere and near-total absence of authority in the trans-Mississippi South necessitated the actions of southerners who attempted to protect their homes and communities more so than elsewhere, residents in other regions took similar actions. Multiple units served as guards in an around the troubled city of Greensboro, North Carolina, for example. One veteran recalled that he guarded a large number of horses until Federal troops arrived, while an infantry captain from Alabama recorded a particularly violent encounter in his diary. When Confederate cavalrymen raided houses and stores in the city, those units who policed the streets opened fire on their comrades, reportedly wounding some and killing others. To the south in Mobile, Alabama, armed local citizens joined together to halt looting on at least one occasion. To the north, in the Old Dominion, another soldier remembered that veterans in his home county banded together during the immediate postwar period to provide some semblance of order and security for residents.[81]

Despite the admirable efforts of certain civilians, local officials, Confederate officers, and individual units, in many places only the arrival of Federal troops restored order. Many studies chronicle the story of Union occupation of the defeated South, but the point here remains that the scale of anarchy around an entire region of the country necessitated the mobilization of Federal soldiers to reestablish order. Moreover, once everyone recognized the certainty of overall Confederate defeat, at least some southerners openly welcomed their erstwhile enemies out of a desperate bid for peace, stability, and the return of lawful society. One Texan—whose fire-breathing Rebel credentials compared favorably to those of even the most diehard Confederate—by late May actually hoped to see Federal troops. "We will pray for a detachment of Yankee soldiers before long to stay lawlessness. French Revolution." A veteran in Virginia echoed those sentiments when he remarked "Those districts in which the Federal armies were stationed were peculiarly fortunate."[82]

Elsewhere the arrival of Federal troops proved equally fortuitous for the reestablishment of law and order. In the vanquished Confederate capital of Richmond, Virginia, a witness vividly described the arrival of Union forces amidst the chaos and fires, though he might have questioned their prowess in the face of such commotion. "Then, like phantoms against the background of the burning city, the sudden appearance of the first Yankee cavalry scouts: they came galloping sword in hand and pistol in belt giving the impression, as they looked neither to the left nor to the right, that they were even more frightened than frightening." Meanwhile hundreds of Federal troops marched into Greensboro, North Carolina, to curtail the turmoil in that troubled locale. Civilians and soldiers recorded similar observations in other locations, including Washington, Georgia, and Shreveport, Louisiana, both stops on common travel routes for soldiers and civilians at war's end.[83]

The arrival of Federal troops in Texas provides a case study in the process and further illustrates the necessity of the presence of the men in blue. Despite the commendable efforts of certain civilians, local officials, Confederate officers, and individual units, their collective actions yielded results only in certain communities. Overall, widespread lawlessness continued throughout most of the settled portion of Texas during the three weeks between the department's official surrender and the appearance of Union forces. Sheridan assumed command of the new Federal Military Division of the Southwest on May 29, 1865, with two major directives—to carry out the formal surrender of the Confederate Trans-Mississippi Department, and more important in the big picture, to establish and preserve order in Texas until civil government could be restored.[84]

Sheridan's subordinate, Major General Gordon Granger directed the initial occupation of Texas, beginning in mid- to late June. Federal soldiers occupied Galveston on the Gulf Coast and entered the state in the northeast corner and in South Texas along the Rio Grande. An additional force of 9,500 cavalrymen also entered the state in two columns. One occupied San Antonio while the other, commanded by Major General George A. Custer, traveled to Austin. Although most Texans resented the presence of occupation troops, some residents, at least initially, welcomed their onetime enemies as the only hope for the restoration of law and order.[85]

Union officers identified numerous locales around the state where Texas Confederates who, unlike most of their brethren east of the Mississippi River, had not bothered to wait for paroles, could secure those important documents and take the oath of allegiance to the United States. Interestingly, Federal authorities announced that public property taken during the breakup should be returned to the parole sites. Although unlikely to recover any substantial amount of property, Federal officers intended to enforce the directive and threatened imprisonment and property confiscation for offenders. Moreover, Granger also announced plans to pursue all lawbreakers with vigor. "All persons committing acts of violence, such as banditti, guerillas, jayhawkers, horse-thieves, &c.," the general announced with a flair for the dramatic, "are hereby declared outlaws and enemies of the human race, and will be dealt with accordingly."[86]

Federal soldiers went to work quickly under the directives of Sheridan and Granger. Units spread across the state to establish order and to scour the countryside for Confederate government property in the hands of private citizens. By the end of June, Sheridan concluded that the presence of his men had made the state safe for the return of refugees and, as further evidence of his confidence in Federal occupation, he declared that Union troops were sufficient to maintain order and thus outlawed home guards, with certain exceptions. Consistent with Federal occupation policies enacted earlier in the war, Sheridan called upon residents to cooperate with Union forces and to work together to help restore stability to their respective communities. Failure to do so or the rendering of assistance to lawbreakers would result in punitive action against the residents of that area. Clearly satisfied with his work, on July 1, 1865, Sheridan declared Texas ready for a provisional governor.[87]

As the material presented throughout this chapter demonstrates, demobilized Confederates hardly acted alone when they contributed to the chaotic scenes that plagued the South during the spring and summer of 1865. However, those same sources illustrate that soldiers played a prominent role, alongside civilians of all classes, deserters, and those ill-defined elements of society upon which many observers blamed the looting. Other accounts simply divulged details or pointed up the commonplace character of soldier depredations. One such case concerned a soldier who, like thousands of his former comrades, passed through Atlanta during his homeward journey. In that city the clever chap slept under the same tree to which he tied his mule to protect his mount from other traveling veterans, "many of whom doubtless would not be averse to riding." Fortunately for that careful traveler, the mule "was polite enough not to intrude on my humble bed."[88]

More important, many candid soldiers acknowledged their own actions or those of comrades in wartime and postwar accounts. One veteran recalled that he and his companions availed themselves of the fruits of a private orchard near Montgomery but could not recall whether they had "obtained permission to invade the orchard or not." In a less light-hearted confession of an incident, also in Alabama, a soldier and his comrades happened upon a family in a remote cabin. The residents reluctantly traded fifty ears of corn for the soldier's gold dollar. Despite the Rebel's promise to leave after the transaction, "I saw an oven on the hearth, with fire in the lid. They said I had promised to go if they would let me have the corn. I sat down and told them I would leave directly; I wanted to see what was in that oven. When she raised the lid, the fumes came my way and smelled fine; so I told her to give me half that pone of bread and I would go, so she sawed a butcher knife across it and put half in my haversack and we left."[89]

Theft of public and even private property by soldiers during the closing scenes of the war proved so commonplace that observers simply assumed that Johnny Rebs would steal from them. One such Virginia family expressed genuine dismay when a passing group of soldiers returned horses to them, while a Georgia civilian conveyed utter shock when cavalrymen simply rested on the family property without stealing horses. "We had seen three horsemen ride to the spring," she wrote, "and the most natural thing to expect was that when they went away, some of our own horses would be missing." As the men of the house prepared to defend hearth and home from alleged marauders, however, they found that they had been pleasantly mistaken. "But, oh, most lame and impotent conclusion! not a shot was fired. The three cavalrymen were sleeping quietly in the shade."[90]

Despite vindication for that trio of traveling soldiers, two other cases illustrate just how routine such activity had become. One pair of enterprising Trans-

Mississippi soldiers fit the profile formed in the mind of the suspicious Georgia civilian. Three hundred miles from home at the time of capitulation, the two-some concocted a scheme to secure mules for the journey. In exchange for an unnamed price the pair arranged for two teamsters, one unwittingly, to saddle and ride two mules along a specific road where the schemers would "rob" them of their mounts. While less dramatic than a fake robbery, the story of a twenty-four-year-old infantry private who walked from Georgia to Arkansas provides a far simpler example. When the exhausted traveler came upon an acquaintance near the end of his journey, the local man's initial comment illustrates the state of affairs as well as any account possibly could. "You have walked all the way . . . and have not stolen a horse?"[91]

The numerous accounts of theft and looting by soldiers and civilians not only establish the widespread and commonplace nature of such activity but also help to explain lawless behavior that would not have been tolerated under normal circumstances. Several considerations illuminate the uncharacteristic actions of so many typically law-abiding citizens. First, some individuals simply took advantage of the general collapse of societal norms to prey upon the vulnerability of others. Examples of such disagreeable conduct occurred throughout the crumbling Confederacy. Similar events transpired in more isolated instances in Civil War prisons, where soldiers frequently victimized weaker comrades. This particularly helps to explain the targeting of private property.

Furthermore, hardly unique to disbanding Confederates, soldiers in other conflicts displayed disobedient, mutinous, even riotous conduct to express dissatisfaction with aspects of demobilization. American and British soldiers chafed at the "pace and principles" of demobilization at the conclusion of both world wars. Those victorious combatants, often with civilian support, demanded immediate transportation home, while officers and officials struggled to balance postwar security concerns and the immense logistical nightmare of transportation for so many soldiers thousands of miles from home. While they waited idly, American and British troops alike mutinied in multiple theaters.[92]

Not unique to the former Confederacy nor even to the American Civil War, increased crime during the aftermath of war has afflicted numerous countries. One study revealed that significant increases in crime plagued numerous countries during the aftermath of other conflicts, including the German Revolution of 1848, the Crimean War, the Franco-Prussian War, and the First World War. Moreover, that study documented significantly increased crime rates in the northern United States for several years after the American Civil War. Analysis of

crime statistics in certain northern states revealed a predictable decline in wartime incarceration of men but an increase in wartime incarceration of women.
Further, statistical analysis also illustrated an increase in wartime juvenile de-
linquency and an overall spike in crime during the immediate postwar period.[93]

In reference to soldiers during the immediate aftermath of the Crimean
War, a London police commissioner described young British soldiers who had
no occupation before their military service and turned to crime afterward:
"When they come home they think it very fine to take up this means of livelihood. The have been accustomed and encouraged to take life lightly, and you
cannot expect every individual to go back to the normal state in a minute." That
point could apply especially to ex-Confederates, for whom the old normal had
largely ceased to exist. Speaking in 1919 on the subject of crime in Britain immediately after the First World War, Winston Churchill remarked ominously:
"Never was there a time when people were more disposed to turn to courses of
violence, to show scant respect for law and country and tradition and procedure
than the present." Here again, Churchill's comment could apply particularly to
demobilized Johnny Rebs who witnessed and helped to cause a complete breakdown in law and order, experienced the destruction of the "country" they had
endeavored to create, and searched in vain for any semblance of the tradition
that they had always known, though they would soon work diligently to restore
as much of the Old South as possible.[94]

In his classic study of First World War combatants, historian Eric J. Leed
argued that the war functioned as a liminal event for fighting men in that prolonged combat experience altered the relationship between soldiers and society.
Leed describes the veteran as a "liminal type" who "derives all of his features
from the fact that he has crossed the boundaries of disjunctive social worlds,
from peace to war, and back." Ultimately, some veterans retained violent ten-
dencies precisely because they had lived "beyond civilian social categories."
Confederate soldiers had also functioned outside the norms of civilian expectations before their return to society but also initially confronted a lawless, chaotic
postwar South. Johnny Rebs who experienced the liminal event of war returned
to a society in flux. During the summer of 1865, even southern civilians often
lived beyond the typical social and legal norms. Confederate veterans experienced the liminal, transitional forces of warfare similar to that encountered by
veterans of numerous other conflicts, but at least initially confronted an unstable and disorderly world where no law existed. Johnny Reb therefore continued

to conduct himself and to ensure his survival as he knew best—as a soldier who foraged when necessary.[95]

Recent scholarship argues that many Confederate veterans during the immediate postwar period refused to shed their soldier identity and continued to forage and make demands on southern civilians as though the war still raged. Excellent studies by Joan E. Cashin and Caroline E. Janney further highlight the conclusions presented here, that during and immediately after demobilization, ex-Confederates occupied a liminal space, caught between defeat and grave doubts about a post-emancipation South under the rule of an embittered North bent upon vengeance. (See chapter five for further discussion of the fears of postwar conditions held by some Confederate veterans.) This further reinforces the belief among southerners that wartime service and sacrifice effectively entitled demobilized veterans to forage in order to facilitate their homeward journeys.[96]

Although some Confederates, a former governor for example, insisted that the theft of private property by soldiers constituted the rare exception, the multitude of accounts cited throughout this chapter indicates otherwise. Two particularly flagrant examples stand out: The case of soldiers in a Louisiana camp who turned on each other, and the instance of Rebel cavalrymen who stole the last supply of meat from a large North Carolina family. Equally abhorrent, three soldiers took a horse from a boy as he watered the animal at a river. This was no unfortunate accident, because the men knew that the child and the horse would be in that spot.[97]

More often, whether they targeted private or public property, those who absconded with ill-gotten gains acted less out of a careless compulsion to victimize others and more out of what they considered fundamental necessity. Johnny Reb proved willing to do quite literally almost anything to get home. The war had ended, the country he had fought to establish had ceased to exist, the government he had served had collapsed, and he faced many miles and innumerable dangers between himself and his home and loved ones. No longer a matter of nationalism or patriotism, it had become every man for himself. Although Johnny Reb frequently received assistance from southern civilians, comrades, and even Federal soldiers and officials, he could not always guarantee sustenance for the next leg of his homeward journey. If a government mule or wayward pony would help him reach those who needed him most and provide vital assistance to begin the postwar phase of his life, he took the animal. If valuable supplies appropriated from the warehouse of a defunct government could provide barter during his long trek, the acquisition of such commodities simply made good sense. Finally, and perhaps most obvious and reasonable, if rations in the possession of a nonexistent government could provide nourishment for a desperate veteran traversing a barren, war-torn landscape, he took the food. After all, most soldiers had become adept at the art of creative forage during countless marches throughout the course of the war.[98]

Accounts of soldiers who took over trains and large river vessels to facilitate their homeward journeys provide extreme examples of this "anything to get home" mentality, precisely because no soldiers involved considered the actions actual theft. Though clearly examples of misappropriation of property and the very definition of opportunism amidst the chaotic situation, demobilized soldiers carried out such dramatic escapades exclusively to hasten their travel.[99]

Many Confederate combatants and civilians also adopted a rather flexible definition of theft under such frenzied and desperate conditions. Demobilized fighting men, for example, sometimes continued to target Federal materials because they still considered it enemy property, thus the confiscation simply constituted action taken against an adversary despite the obvious termination of hostilities.[100]

Soldiers and civilians often applied a malleable meaning to theft with regard to Confederate public property. Several justifications proved widespread. Although General Johnston stated that Confederate military property not already distributed to soldiers should be left for United States officials, one common refrain held that the Confederate States of America no longer existed, and so proper ownership of the materials was far from certain. Some even proclaimed the property abandoned and thus free for the taking. Perhaps this explains the soldier who acquired a new pair of shoes during the riots in Greensboro, but insisted that he had not stolen the footwear, only "prowled" them. Moreover, any remaining materials would fall into the hands of the hated Yankee invaders, and that thought proved too much to bear for many southerners. Additionally, the countless occasions upon which Confederate officers willfully distributed supplies in the streets of southern cities during the disintegration of the war effort understandably strengthened the impression that soldiers and civilians acted correctly when they took possession of government property. A woman in East Texas personified these sentiments. A diehard Rebel by any standard, the young woman proudly proclaimed that the Federals would not find anything to confiscate when they arrived. "'To the victor belongs the spoils,' but he will not get his dues in this Department."[101]

The fiery twenty-four-year-old daughter of a planter also voiced another common outlook. Although she took immense delight in the denial of southern property to northern invaders and mockingly expressed pride in the substantial cache of materials that she received during the collapse, including furniture and, for some reason, a large amount of ammunition, she adamantly insisted that soldiers deserved the property more so than did civilians. Others expressed and even acted upon similar opinions. Soldiers who patrolled the chaotic streets of Shreveport, Louisiana, for example, confiscated looted materials from white civilians and freedmen and -women to redistribute to soldiers.[102]

In northeast Texas a newspaper editor illustrated the hierarchy when he denounced local members of a reserve force who allegedly participated in the looting of a local sugar supply. "We understand that an officer of that bloodless body, the *reserve* corps, who never faced a more dangerous enemy than these Sugar barrels, has been prominent in the action. . . . On Wednesday last, these heroes captured a wagon load of Sugar which had been purchased . . . by REAL soldiers . . . men who had not been fed regularly on Sugar, but somewhat on lead; and these heroes of victorious campaigns against private property pounced upon and divided it."[103]

The common thread through virtually all of these accounts suggests that most Johnny Rebs and other observers saw nothing objectionable about the appropriation of public property, particularly by soldiers. In fact, the general consensus assumed that their arduous service entitled the fighting men to the materials. The vast number of soldier accounts cited throughout this chapter, particularly postwar admissions of such conduct, point to a widespread, though not universal, acceptance. Because they had nothing to hide, civilians and soldiers alike admitted in wartime and even postwar accounts that they had absconded with various amounts of property. Although not overtly political in nature, the widespread support for such riotous behavior echoed the sentiments of Americans of previous generations who, according to one historian, espoused the "plebian belief that crowd action represented the true interests of the community."[104]

Individuals who justified the appropriation of government property with the insistence that soldiers' service entitled them to it most often proffered one of two explanations. The first pointed to the immense sacrifice and material deprivation endured by soldiers in the field, often without pay for months, only to find government warehouses full of supplies at war's end. Ironically, then, in the minds of many, such activity aligned with, rather than undermined, Confederate nationalism. Soldiers and observers saw nothing unpatriotic about veterans taking possession of property that they deserved and that might otherwise end up in the hands of northerners. As the former governor of Louisiana recalled of soldiers who had looted a government storehouse, the men became enraged at the discovery of such ample materials. "They thought they had been allowed to become ragged and naked in the midst of abundance. They had been deprived of their pitiful pay, unnecessarily, it seemed." Why would those materials not rightfully belong to southern soldiers and even civilians who had supported and served the defunct government that had amassed the cache?[105]

Second, because rightful ownership of the property remained undefined, some individuals, such as a North Carolina cavalry sergeant who came into possession of a wagon that had belonged to the Army of Tennessee, reasoned that his claim to the property possessed as much validity as that of anyone else. Already having reached his home, he took his cue from a group of passing soldiers who had abandoned the wagon when an axle broke. Recognizing the potential value of a fine wagon for the farmer-sergeant, the soldiers reportedly advised him, "Go and get that wagon. It is as much yours as anybody else's." Unsure whether he could keep the prized item, the sergeant chose not to make the repair until weeks later, when he secured approval from Federal officers to maintain possession. Apparently at least some Union authorities endorsed the ambiguous definition of rightful possession, or perhaps considered the issue insignificant.[106]

Two additional accounts effectively represent the typical mindset that individuals considered themselves entitled to public property, in particular if the materials could help them with the next stage of life. In one case, a soldier who participated in the looting of Salisbury, North Carolina, fled with Confederate money, shoes, flour, bacon, socks, and a roll of denim. He later traded the denim to a baker in his hometown of Aiken, South Carolina, in exchange for enough bread to feed his family for the remainder of the summer. A second veteran and his travel companions not only appropriated government cotton that they "found" in the woods, but twice robbed other groups during their journey across Arkansas. In the first instance the infantry officer and his comrades seized two Confederate-branded mules at gunpoint and justified the action by reasoning that the men they confronted were close to home, while they still had many miles to travel. In the second incident, the Arkansas men took a large amount of equipment from another party because they "very easily came to the conclusion that these men had more than their share of Government property."[107]

Thoughts of postwar life with families indeed motivated demobilized Confederate soldiers to appropriate government and sometimes private property just as such powerful sentiments compelled most to travel home as quickly as possible. Numerous soldiers explicitly stated that the lure of loved ones compelled them to push through hunger, illness, difficult weather, transportation challenges, and roving gangs of highwaymen. One veteran remained emotional about the subject forty-five years later, when he described his journey home from prison. He focused specifically on the chance to reunite with his mother. Exhausted and painful from his travels and travails, he refused to complain as he neared home. That former prisoner-of-war's story exemplifies the tale of thousands. Understandably, then, demobilized soldiers from across the former Confederacy pushed through the final miles with one thing in mind—homecoming.[108]

5

REBELS REUNITED

HOMECOMING, REBIRTH, AND REDEMPTION

"I go now to share with the people of the south the deep humiliation which will be dictated by yankee vindictiveness."[1] A Confederate prisoner of war penned those words to his wife just days before he departed for home. Similar to countless comrades around the nation, that Johnny Reb longed for a joyous reunion with loved ones. Although most homecoming moments indeed resulted in predictably joyful affairs, the actual homecoming of former Confederate soldiers frequently presented a staggering range of emotions for veterans and their families. Moreover, upon return, Confederate veterans quickly faced the reality of the postwar world as they began the transition back to civilian life. Thoughts of immediate survival, the question of how to move on with life, and concerns for what life would be like in the newly defeated occupied South dominated the thoughts of Confederate veterans in the spring and summer of 1865.

Many demobilized Confederates chose not to write about their homecoming moment. We cannot know why some omitted that part of their wartime experience, and doubtless very often the soldier had no particular reason to exclude the tale. The omission appears glaring, however, in light of the descriptive, even exhaustive, nature of so many firsthand soldier accounts. Readers learn of exploits in battle, adventures with comrades, and minutiae such as daily weather reports and the names of random creeks from which the traveling soldier drank. Countless common soldier narratives cited throughout this and other studies routinely emphasize the powerful and perfectly reasonable desire to reunite with loved ones. Yet many of those same accounts abruptly stop just before the family reunion or even skip over that moment and resume discussions of post-war life.

A select few cases point to one explanation—at least some veterans considered that moment too personal for public consumption. A thirty-two-year-old Virginia infantry captain, for example, witnessed the homecoming of another soldier at a small roadside shack where a woman had graciously fed him and his horse. However, he deemed the reunion of mother and son too personal for him to remain on the scene. He recorded in his diary that "While they were mingling their tears of love, and giving expressions of their joy with embraces, too sacred for observation, I silently rode away, with heart too full to give utterance to my feelings." Meanwhile, a Kentucky cavalryman who traveled more than thirteen hundred miles remembered: "I arrived at home and found the dear ones alive. I cannot and will not attempt to describe the meeting." A colorful Texan said it best and most explicitly when he recalled, "The tears and thanksgiving shed by my mother and father at my safe return are too sacred to be described." Considering the countless other things that soldiers often discussed in diaries, letters, memoirs, and regimental histories, it seems unlikely that most would deem this particular fleeting moment too personal for readers. Still, for at least some Confederates, that proved to be the case. Perhaps a detailed portrait of that moment would reveal Johnny Reb at his most vulnerable. Or, just possibly, for once he considered it none of our business.[2]

Fortunately, a meaningful number of Confederates thought otherwise and shared vivid descriptions of the homecoming moment. Several common themes emerged in those accounts. One such topic, however, appears conspicuous for how few soldiers mentioned it specifically. Sometimes family members anticipated the soldier's return because a passing comrade or recently returned neighbor informed them that their husband, son, brother, or nephew would soon be there. He had survived the war and had received his parole at the same location as the neighbor, or he had been seen at a train station or river crossing along the route. One youthful Alabama infantryman recalled such a scene and the longing, watchful eyes of his mother that gazed upon him in May 1865. "O! how happy I was, found all well and mother looking for me. She had been told that I was spared and was on my way home. She was looking by day and listening at night for the sound of footsteps from her only soldier boy. I was not twenty-one till August."[3]

Sometimes word arrived by design rather than by happy accident. A North Carolinian who survived a northern prison camp noted that, "I think that I was the last of the boys to get out of the pen. Sam was just one day ahead of me and he let my people know that I was coming." All of this makes perfect sense in light of what we know about varied rates of travel. Logically, some soldiers would reach their home counties before their comrades reached their own, so they were able to spread the word about the impending arrival of others. Indeed, this practice probably proved so common that few soldiers even thought it worthy of mention.[4]

The same cannot be said for certain more noteworthy themes of homecoming accounts. For example, a number of men lamented that their loved ones, including and especially children, failed to recognize them upon arrival. A soldier who reached his central Texas home in September 1865 found an anticlimactic moment when even his dog initially mistook him for a passing stranger. Months earlier the canine companion of a soldier from Mississippi also greeted his master with something less than enthusiasm. Luckily the dog quickly recognized its human, though the same could not be said for the family gathered inside the house. As the twenty-one-year-old private approached the home, the family greeted him as though he were just another passing Rebel in need of a meal. The patriarch welcomed him inside and asked his name so that he might introduce him to the others. Amused by the spectacle of being introduced to his relatives by his unknowing father, the soldier could no longer continue the charade and laughed aloud. That gave him away, and the family swarmed him for the long-awaited joyous reunion.[5]

Although always ephemeral in nature, those seconds of confusion and the lack of instant recognition could have been devastating to a ragged soldier who had survived so many trials, traveled so far, and dreamed so long of that cherished moment. Significant change in appearance obviously explains the misidentification in certain instances. In one such case a Texas infantry sergeant had left home four years earlier as a self-described "fleshy" boy of seventeen. He returned a thin, twenty-one-year-old mustachioed man, unrecognizable to his mother. Similarly, a twenty-year-old North Carolina sharpshooter lamented his father's inability to recognize him but acknowledged that he had lost thirty-eight pounds. Even a Mississippian in his mid-thirties surprised his unknowing wife and children. They initially could not identify him without the beard that he had worn for many years.[6]

The experience of seventeen-year-old Samuel Lewis Moore most vividly illustrates the phenomenon of physical appearance altered by the ravages of war to the extent that even the boy-soldier's mother failed to recognize him. A member of the Georgia Reserves who served only briefly before his confinement at Fort Delaware prison, Moore traveled approximately thirteen hundred miles almost exclusively by water, before hitching a ride on a mule for the final stretch to his parents' home. Years later his penned an autobiography that included a colorful description of his homecoming moment. "When I got home my mother did not know me, and I was indeed a sad looking spectacle. I had on a U.S. blue shirt, a pair of pants 44 inches in the waist, buttoned around to the suspender button. One leg of my pants was torn off half way to the knee, and the other leg rolled up to match it. I had on a Confederate gray hat with the visor torn off. I was barefooted, and my hair was down to my shoulders." Despite his appearance the family celebrated his return and his mother set about restoring the unsoiled, youthful facade of her beloved boy. He recalled that "The first thing my mother did, of course, was to fix me a bath, and give me some clean clothes. She burned the ones I wore home because they had 'things' [lice] on them."[7]

The fact that the confusion typically lasted a matter of only seconds adds to the believability of accounts of loved ones unable to recognize their returning Rebel. Moreover, the war occurred during formative years for many fighting men, who would have undergone meaningful physical changes regardless of the conflict. In cases of Civil War soldiers, those natural changes, exacerbated by the trials of camp and combat, occurred during lengthy absences from home. Bouts of illness or years of poor diet in camp or prison obviously exacted a toll from many young men. Significant weight gain, or more likely weight loss, and the growth or removal of facial hair could alter the appearance of an individual to such an extent that they were unrecognizable to their loved ones.

Subconscious defense mechanisms also might have been in play. A family member might have stiffened themselves against the constant disappointment of staring down the road awaiting the return of their soldier. Thus a mother, father, or wife might have conditioned themselves not to assume the best upon the approach of every ragged Rebel. Of course, one other development sometimes hindered recognition. In the case of a Georgia private whose parents and siblings recognized him only after he drew a drink of water from the well and spoke directly to them, the family had a powerful reason for misidentifying the soldier. "No one ever expected to see me again. They had been told by several parties that I had been killed at the battle of Petersburg."[8]

That Georgian's family suffered the terrible fate of wondering whether their loved one had even survived the war, and sadly, others shared that heartrending experience. Families frequently lived with the worst uncertainty imaginable. Parents sometimes speculated not merely when but whether their son would appear on the horizon. Some parents questioned every returning veteran for any information about their soldier, and wives often did the same. A Mississippian still in a northern prison in late May 1865 confirmed by letter his survival to his desperate wife, who had questioned paroled comrades that had already returned home. A more poignant example manifested with the story of a Mississippi mother who mistook another for her son. The soldier in question soon learned that his own mother had refused to believe reports of *his* demise.[9]

Such accounts point to a more extreme version of such postwar confusion. Whereas those families remained uncertain of their respective soldier's fate, others received mistaken reports of their loved one's death. Thousands of families North and South received such devastating news, but in certain cases the reports proved untrue. Friends and families mourned the loss of their companion and loved one, only later to learn of his survival. Though not as common as those instances in which the families simply remained in the dark as to the fate of their soldier, Confederate veterans certainly recalled some cases of mistaken reports. A twenty-year-old Georgian who traveled approximately seven hundred miles to reach home noted that his parents had presumed him dead. After all, his older brothers had been killed and even a younger sister had died the same year. Upon the young man's return his father remarked, "Well, this boy is all the war has left us."[10]

Others recalled similar, if sometimes more dramatic accounts. One would be hard pressed to find a Johnny Reb with a greater tale to tell than the South Carolinian who insisted that he happened upon his own funeral. Regardless of the veracity of that story, a North Carolinian captured and paroled in Virginia told a comparable but less melodramatic account. Unaware of his capture, his comrades quite plausibly presumed him dead, and, he recalled, even erected a grave marker for him. "I had been mourned as dead. Some of my company had taken the description, given by a burying detail, of a young fellow resembling me, and marked his grave with a board on which they carved my name." The alleged dead man, however, made his way from Virginia to North Carolina by rail and reached his parents' home in just a couple of days. "My welcome home can be imagined."[11]

Besides the astonishment implied in that soldier's pronouncement, the reader can easily imagine the joyous response of family and friends upon his arrival. Returning veterans knew the happiness that their return would bring and sometimes prepared for the moment as they neared home. In some cases, the soldier attempted to avoid friends and neighbors during those last several miles in order to surprise his family. One soldier even slept in the woods near his home that last night to preserve the surprise for the next day, only for his dogs to discover him during his slumber. Some soldiers attempted to clean themselves up and change into better clothing, or in some cases at least wished that they could do so, for the long-awaited reunion. One individual insisted upon changing clothes in the barn before entering the house even after his family had spotted him coming down the road.[12]

All of these accounts indicate not only that the soldiers wanted the moment to be perfect but also that the savvy veterans comprehended the historical significance of the homecoming to their own life stories. One former artillerist in the Army of Northern Virginia who had traveled from Point Lookout prison in Maryland to his home in the Shenandoah Valley in Virginia, paused atop a mountain on his last day of travel, ironically July 4, 1865. He gazed briefly at the lush and beautiful valley as if to take in the moment and to prepare himself for the reunion.[13]

Many Confederates described such jubilant arrivals in diaries or recalled them in memoirs. Perhaps some soldiers considered the blissful character of most reunions so obvious that they offered banal summary comments that simply denote the happiness of the moment with no further commentary. Despite the predictable character of most descriptions of the homecoming moment as joyful, even the less descriptive accounts illustrate important context for those once-in-a-lifetime experiences. Often the veteran was relieved, indeed overjoyed, to have survived the war to reunite with loved ones, and to know that his beloved had also survived and now once again rested safely in his arms. In one such case, an officer literally ran up the stairs to greet his wife in his father's Georgia home, while a Texan who returned to his family in mid-June 1865 captured the moment in his final, poignant diary entry that illustrates the bliss of reunion and the relief that all had survived the crucible: "Here I find my mother, and brothers, who soon tell me where my wife and children are, not more than three hundred yards off," the Texan wrote, "so I go on until I find her who has been my guiding star in all my travels, my wife."[14]

Escape from the presence of hated Yankees also informed the character of some homecoming accounts. See for example the case of a particular young man who had left college during his senior year to join a South Carolina infantry unit. Upon his return to his hometown in May 1865, he retorted that he was "Very glad to be again within the pale of civilization." A few hundred miles to the north, as a fellow artillerist returned to his parents and their Virginia home, he remarked upon the quiet, pastoral scene. The former prisoner-of-war lamented that he expected a Yankee guard to emerge from the bushes at any moment to spoil the prospect. The specter of the enemy loomed in his mind even as the young man took his final steps toward his home, his family, and his former life in peace. Still, a joyful reunion followed even for that apprehensive Rebel.[15]

The most emotional and descriptive accounts of homecomings focused on young soldiers who reunited with parents. Wartime diaries and postwar memoirs share accounts of mothers and fathers waiting on the porch, watching wistfully down the path for the return of their beloved son. One such veteran traveled about a thousand miles from Virginia—across the Carolinas, Georgia, and Alabama—before he reunited with his family in Mississippi. His father had waited for him on the piazza for many painful, lonely nights, and insisted that he had had a premonition that his son would return that evening. The youthful Rebel remarked in his diary: "Once again, all of us who are alive are together."[16]

In Georgia, a twenty-one-year-old cavalry private who had survived not only combat but months in a northern prison reunited with his widowed father during the final spring of the war. Years later the veteran recalled: "There was no mother to welcome me to her bosom, as it had been my irreparable misfortune to lose her gentle admonition and loving caresses in my early youth, but there was somewhere the manly heart of a devoted father whom I well knew was more than ready to greet his soldier boy." The relieved and overjoyed father greeted his son with outward displays of emotion that the young man had never seen from his elder, who embraced his grown child with teary eyes and an unsteady voice. As the appreciative son recollected later: "Reader, have you ever experienced a warm loving embrace of a father's love, after a long absence, in which his yearning soul was depressed with doubt or elated with a hope as to whether he would ever meet you again?"[17]

Similar scenes unfolded around the South, where parents—conditioned to cautious optimism about the fate of their soldier sons—allowed the emotions to pour forth upon confirmation of his return. Two similar reunions occurred states apart. In one case, a Mississippi native arrived at his parents' home one night in late July. When he reached the front gate, he hailed the house and received an answer from his father who was sitting on the porch. The older man asked the identity of the man at his gate, to which the young veteran answered, "your lost boy." The father called into the house, "Emily, William is here." That message brought an exclamation from the mother who quickly moved to embrace her son.[18]

Hundreds of miles away and a few weeks earlier, a nineteen-year-old Missouri Rebel and his brother returned to their parents' St. Louis home. As the young veterans rang the bell to announce their arrival they heard their mother's voice, "It's the boys! It's the boys! I know it, I tell you! It's the boys." Next they heard their father, in a trembling voice, attempt to calm his wife, perhaps to shield her from possible disappointment. They heard their father descend the stairs, and when he finally opened the door, "An indescribable, overwhelming moment of emotion for us all! About 6 o'clock, Sunday morning, June 18, 1865." By their own count the young brothers had survived a combined forty-seven battles and skirmishes, yet were now, finally, safe and sound at the family home. Their proud mother insisted that the family attend church that day. "Her heart was bursting with pride for her boys and she was determined to show us off. Not a very proper motive for church going, but at such a moment, deserving indulgent judgment, I hope. Devoutly thankful too, I know she was."[19]

The previous several examples illustrate the predictable, probably even natural responses of parents, and as the last two accounts make clear, sometimes Johnny Reb received a particularly effusive welcome from his mother. Another such story comes from an Alabama infantry officer, also a former delegate to the secession convention of that state, who arrived at his parents' plantation in July 1865. Upon hearing the news of her son's approach, the mother "at once put out in a run to meet me, and ran through the branch without knowing it, meeting me near the branch. This was one of the happy periods of my life." Three states away a humble, teenage Texas private had reached his parents' Austin home several weeks earlier and recalled that he "was soon locked in my mother's arms, who wept with joy over her soldier boys safe return." An Arkansas infantry private probably said it best when he noted that after his return, "Mother would look at me for hours and could not talk for joy. Her dear soul was never happier than now with her dear soldier boy safe at home, surrounded by loved ones."[20]

Some Confederate veterans also recalled hearty greetings from slaves or freedmen and women who remained at the family home. Several such accounts relate joyful embraces, particularly from older individuals. As one Louisiana infantryman, musician, and strident Rebel insisted, specifically of the house slaves, "They loved me and were glad I was home again, and that home heretofore their home." Elsewhere a Missouri fighting man returned home and years later recalled a more effusive welcome from an elderly cook, "deeply colored but with a very white heart, a slave when I left her, a free citizeness now, answered the bell, and when she saw who it was, with many explosive expressions of delight, grasped me in her ponderous arms and gave me a hug that would have done credit to an Ethiopian bear." A cook also loomed in the memory of a twenty-four-year-old Kentucky cavalry sergeant. She prepared him such a hearty meal upon his return that he reminisced fondly, "Had I eaten to her satisfaction I would not be here now to tell of it."[21]

Most of the above accounts of emotional welcomes from African Americans, written years after the war, drew upon memory. In no way does that necessarily undermine the veracity of the narratives, but the postwar character of the accounts must be considered. Perhaps the meetings occurred exactly as the veterans remembered and the accounts accurately describe genuine emotion from all parties. Or, maybe slaves or freedmen emoted as they thought the soldier and his family would expect, and the soldier believed the emotions genuine. In other words, perhaps the stories rang completely true in the mind of an aging veteran. Perhaps the authors subconsciously tinged the accounts with a degree of sentimentalism or even consciously aimed at a Reconstruction-era audience. Almost certainly some combination of all of these explanations played a role, and one case differed from another. In defense of at least some southern veterans, enslaved or freed men and women who had known the soldier since his childhood would have rejoiced upon his safe return from war. Although clearly not the norm, such accounts do not necessarily constitute Lost Cause apologia.

One perceptive young Virginia artillerist, Henry Robinson Berkeley, whose wartime diary described his homecoming moment and noted that numerous African Americans gathered to greet him, recalled: "Old Francis, among the servants, was very hearty, and I believe, very sincere in his welcome." The significance here lies not in the claim that slaves who had been freed welcomed him. In that way his account hardly differs from that of comrades who wrote from memory. Rather, the significance rests with his insistence, writing in June 1865, upon the earnestness of the greeting from the older man. Private Berkeley perceived a need to assure the reader, or himself, of the genuine character of the welcome.[22]

Whatever the explanation for that soldier's assertion, his account and those of his comrades illustrate that the homecoming moment for Confederate soldiers frequently involved individuals beyond immediate family. Often the returning Rebel visited friends and members of his extended family during the ensuing days. Sometimes neighbors descended upon the family home for an impromptu celebration. One Alabama infantry captain, despite failing health and intensely painful neuralgia in his jaw that forced him to rely on morphine to sleep, attended days of picnics and dances as a celebration for his homecoming and probably for that of other soldiers in the area. Though joyful and celebratory, such large social gatherings occasionally made the returning Rebel uncomfortable because he had become accustomed to camp life and to the company of comrades. As one veteran recalled, "Happy day, when I could bless God at home. I met my father, mother, brothers and sisters at home, and a great many of my friends. The girls came from all around home. I sat there very quietly, and had very little to say; they did all the talking."[23]

One Kentucky cavalryman reunited with friends and family twice, but his second homecoming proved less triumphant than the first. The twenty-three-year-old corporal spent weeks at his uncle's farm in Kentucky, where he visited his sister and assisted his uncle with numerous chores around the homestead. Although overjoyed to spend time with his sister, the young cavalryman admitted that those days were not as blissful as they might have been because he had not yet made his way to his parents and other siblings in Missouri. Finally, in early July, he began the trek toward what he hoped would be a second happy homecoming. Although he indeed rejoiced at the reunion with his parents and other sisters, the sight of his aged, feeble father immediately robbed the younger man of his happiness. The elder man had aged significantly during his son's absence, and the cavalryman immediately recognized that his father would soon perish.[24]

As that soldier's experience illustrates, not every individual enjoyed a pleasant homecoming. Often poignant, occasionally devastating, the reunions of some Confederate soldiers severely disappointed men who had longed to return to home and loved ones to begin life anew. The brutality of war denied some fighting men the triumphant homecoming moment: instead, they had to face the task of informing the families of less fortunate comrades that their own Johnny Reb would never again cross their threshold. One such Rebel traveled from Appomattox to his rural Mississippi home and encountered the unknowing mother of a fallen comrade. Agony befell the mother who would never again see her son. Even years later the infantry veteran recalled with melancholy: "But such is the cruelty of war." For some soldiers the mere act of returning home was a painful reminder of those departed comrades who had perished, at least with the masculine honor of death in service to their country.[25]

The deep disappointment of overall defeat, the demise of the Confederacy, and the ominous mystery of what postwar life would bring also sometimes undermined the expected revelry of homecoming. A South Carolina cavalry officer who returned to his family in late April 1865 personified just such a case. He had long imagined a triumphant return, the conquering hero marching back to the loving arms of his proud family. His surrender at Appomattox dashed those dreams and he straggled back to his home a beaten and deeply disappointed man. On April 30 he parted ways with a comrade and marched the final stretch to his home. That day he penned his final diary entry, an explicit admission of his devastated emotional condition. "I feel as if I am one of a disgraced army and unable to control myself at meeting my family under such circumstances. I had expected the day I could put off my armor to be the proudest of my life, but alas, how different."[26]

A similar scene unfolded on the other side of the crumbled Confederacy, as a young Louisiana soldier trekked to his family who had fled their home state for the relative safety of East Texas. When he finally arrived his sister, who had long watched and waited for his return, recorded the scene in her diary: "Jimmy came home Thursday no longer a soldier but a poor discouraged boy." A Rebel at heart, the failure of the Confederate experiment devastated the young man, but so too did the condition of his family. His sister admitted the painful reality. "We are so glad to have Jimmy safe at home, but oh, what a different homecoming from what we anticipated when he enlisted. No feasting. No rejoicing. Only sadness and tears." The next day another relative began a journey back to the family plantation in Louisiana in an attempt to salvage a corn crop.[27]

Many other accounts mirrored that downhearted tale. Confederate veterans frequently endured unhappy homecomings because of the condition of family and home at war's end. For example, the Texan who found his father in a rented house with only a couple of cows and a pony to his name; the Kentuckian who was immediately troubled by the signs of stress so apparent in his mother's face; or the Arkansas infantry captain who returned to find his family living in the stable because the house had been burned during the war. Elsewhere, a prominent Mississippian returned to his plantation to find his wife and daughter chopping weeds in the field, a sight that according to family oral tradition moved the soldier to tears. A Georgian recalled his return to find a desperate family. His father was on his deathbed amidst a crumbling home, with the corn crib and smokehouse both empty. That Georgia veteran published his account many years after the war in *Confederate Veteran Magazine,* and thus clearly wrote to a sympathetic southern audience. Perhaps the aged veteran exaggerated for posterity, maybe he told the perfect truth, or perchance time had influenced his memory of the homecoming in ways that even he did not recognize. Whatever the case, without question a joyous reunion eluded that ex-soldier and his family.[28]

Collectively those experiences indicate that painful sights deeply affected Confederate veterans upon their return, and often those young soldiers' minds turned almost immediately to the future. Confronted by the reality of defeat, news of lost loved ones, the changes undergone by those still living, and a society turned on its head, some Rebel soldiers managed to hope for the best, while others pondered a rather bleak future indeed. One veteran perfectly summarized the sentiments of many comrades when he described his own homecoming moment: "This was a happy family reunion after four years of separation. The two boys were restored to the family, safe and well, after passing through many battles and the dangers of the march and camp for four years. We were all very happy—in spite of the Confederacy's downfall, which of course we had to deplore, in spite of 'free niggers,' that we had to endure."[29]

That pointed commentary almost perfectly highlights the three prominent concerns and adjustments for Confederate veterans that characterize the final part of our story—immediate short-term economic survival; the rapidly evolving place of freed slaves in southern society; and postwar life under "Yankee rule." Johnnies returned home after the most revolutionary event in American history, amidst massive death and devastation in almost every direction, to a southern society turned on its head. Despite the gravity of the situation that confronted them, most demobilized Rebels immediately turned their thoughts to the question of how to restart their civilian lives and how to provide for themselves and their families.

Before demobilized Confederates could begin life anew in a material sense, they encountered challenges of the mind and spirit. Civil War veterans on both sides confronted numerous mental health difficulties, including but not limited to unshakable memories of traumatic events, lingering pain from severe wounds, and even sleep deprivation. Mangled bodies and severe disabilities presented physical and psychological obstacles for some veterans, though, in a tragic irony, at least some disabled veterans considered their visible trauma proof of their courageous service rather than evidence of emasculation. Thus, in response to physical and emotional disabilities, here again, Confederate veterans redefined their own masculinity. According to one study, even Confederate veterans who perished via suicide acted in part out of defiant, masculine determination to retain or recover mastery of their own lives. In light of such prevalent mental health challenges, permanent readjustment to civilian life proved a struggle for countless former combatants, as did the fear of a failure to do so. Families instantly recognized the changes that the war had wrought on their loved ones, particularly the onset of what might be deemed severe and unrelenting depression.[30]

In addition to families, broader communities also played fundamental roles in restoring the mental health and reshaping the masculine identity of Confederate veterans. Dianne Sommerville discovered that local communities typically mourned veteran suicides and treated those deaths as honorably as those of individuals who had fallen in battle. In his excellent study of veteran amputees, Brian Craig Miller argues that disabled ex-soldiers and their home communities together negotiated new concepts of southern masculinity. Southern white women, in particular, provided substantial mental and physical support in the process. Moreover, Jeffrey W. McClurken's exceptional study of veterans in certain Virginia counties illustrates that former soldiers often found considerable support not only among families but through institutions administered at the local and state levels. Certainly the proliferation of soldiers' homes and asylums, the advent of various relief agencies, and the necessity for pensions and other forms of state aid indicate the extent of the struggle for thousands of veterans, both Yankee and Rebel. Still, unlike Billy Yank, Johnny Reb encountered certain obstacles unique to the men in gray, including the legitimate fear of an unknown future.[31]

The uncertainty of the postwar South and the dread of an inability to provide for loved ones tormented Confederate veterans of all social classes from the very day of their homecoming. Arguably no measure of masculinity outweighed that of a man's sense of himself as a provider for his family, and countless Confederate veterans confronted a crippling fear of an inability to do so because of the indeterminate future that loomed. One such Rebel, a Mississippi cavalry officer of above-average means, recalled the anxiety that instantly befell him upon his return. "I spent the night quietly talking over the future, which looked gloomy indeed, for I had on my hands to care for, educate and support, at that time seven children, the youngest nearly four years old. The negroes, I knew, would be free, my stock of horses and mules were nearly all gone . . . but I knew I had a brave wife, and together we looked the future in the face and determined to conquer fate, and not let it conquer us." Despite his determination to press forward and his insistence upon a brave face, the former officer acknowledged that with the choice of the worrisome future or the Yankee army, he would have preferred to fight the enemy.[32]

For some recently demobilized Confederate soldiers, the unstable circumstances and the fear of the unknown left them in a sense paralyzed, utterly unsure of what to do next. Some veterans found solace in the knowledge that they would face the challenging postwar world with the support of their loved ones. Moreover, the notion that families evinced pride in the veteran's service helped some readjust to civilian life, while soldier-fathers sometimes eased the painful transition by focusing on their children. Of course, others had no home or family to return to. Thousands faced the prospect of unemployment or barren farms. That grasping, desperate search for the proper course of action pervaded the thoughts of countless such former soldiers. Whether to head west, abandon the family farm for a wage in a city, or attempt to scratch out a living on a desolate homestead stripped of resources, such indecision and a crippling sense of helplessness often plagued Confederate veterans. As one member of the Army of Northern Virginia noted only nine days after Appomattox, the soldiers appeared "much exercised" as to the appropriate course to follow.[33]

The loss of loved ones further reinforced that instability for some returning Confederate soldiers. Amidst the palpable uncertainty that weighed heavy on virtually all demobilized combatants, those who confronted deaths in the family also suffered that obvious sense of loss and, perhaps more important in the long term, were denied an additional source of emotional support that the cherished relative would have provided. One such veteran returned to his war-ravaged hometown in northern Mississippi only days after the murder of his father in early May 1865. According to family records, the young man learned the news on board a train during the last leg of his homeward journey. Meanwhile, a twenty-year-old Georgia infantry private returned home to find a family virtually eviscerated by the war. "When the war started we were a happy family of eight children and when it ended four were gone, three brothers and one sister."[34]

Depression and general malaise assailed many southern veterans during the days and weeks immediately after their arrival at home. The fears, uncertainty, and personal losses discussed above, as well as overall Confederate defeat, physical illness, and lingering wounds, all coalesced to fuel a depression that some Rebels simply could not escape. Wartime diaries and letters reveal such painful sentiments recorded during those difficult times. Veterans who wrote years later confessed similar emotions. Some suffering individuals even wondered whether fate had dealt them a more severe blow than that which had befallen dead comrades, while a nineteen-year-old infantry private from Georgia took a poetic bent in his diary. The youthful bard who had survived a northern prison and traveled roughly a thousand miles to reunite with his family, thereafter compared his brief but eventful life to a "shattered wreck" and a "blighted oak."[35]

The actual physical and economic conditions encountered by demobilized Confederate soldiers exacerbated the depression and anxiety suffered by many, and mercilessly reminded them of the challenging difficulties that awaited them on their path to postwar recovery. Moreover, the extent of economic disruption throughout the South meant that financial recovery would be more than a simple matter of being determined or having a strong work ethic. A report submitted to Congress in late 1865 by a Republican inspector described in graphic detail what confronted the former Confederate soldier. Unlike their northern counterparts, the report concluded, southern veterans found no prosperous communities ready and willing to offer meaningful employment. Rather, the defeated Rebel "found, many of them, their homesteads destroyed, their farms devastated, their families in distress; and those that were less fortunate found, at all events, an impoverished and exhausted community which had but little to offer them. Thus a great many have been thrown upon the world to shift as best they can."[36]

The report ultimately deemed the southern people overall not merely defeated in a military sense, but also "economically ruined." Individuals from all social classes had been reduced to poverty and even some who at least retained ownership of land "cross their arms in gloomy despondency, incapable of rising to a manly resolution." Others who possessed greater means struggled to make use of those resources in part because the old ways had been destroyed. The inspector noted, perhaps as an ominous warning to those who sought to direct Reconstruction policy, that southern men "must do something honest or dishonest, and must do it soon, to make a living, and their prospects are, at present, not very bright. Thus that nervous anxiety to hastily repair broken fortunes, and to prevent still greater ruin and distress, embraces nearly all classes, and imprints upon all the movements of the social body a morbid character."[37]

The author of that report inspected conditions in five southern states, but modern scholarly studies have found similar conditions throughout the former Confederacy, including trans-Mississippi regions such as Indian Territory and the border state of Kentucky. In addition to general economic disruption, four years of warfare wrought environmental devastation upon the landscape. The destruction of forests, farmlands, and fences contributed to a mutually reinforcing cycle of mental and economic depression. As one historian has astutely observed, Confederate soldiers not only returned home to devastated circumstances but observed such living conditions along the way. They knew the massive challenges that awaited them even before they completed those bittersweet homeward journeys.[38]

Scholars have examined the effects of such sights on demobilized soldiers on both sides. Federal troops who marched toward the Grand Review in Washington, DC, traveled through the battlefields at places such as Fredericksburg, Chancellorsville, Cold Harbor, and others. During the trek to a joyous national celebration of their triumphant service, Union veterans thus encountered the horrific sights of human bones, haunting reminders of death on a massive scale. For those northern men, the grisly images reinforced the immense sacrifice of so many men in blue, dampened the ardor of the great celebration for many, and doubtless caused deep introspection among countless Union veterans on the meaning of it all. Meanwhile, demobilized Confederates encountered similarly gruesome scenes at battlefields, breathed the foul stench of former campgrounds, and—more importantly—gazed upon devastated farms, missing fences, deforestation, and empty homes where families had been driven away by war. Consequently, in addition to the legal and social upheaval and financial uncertainty that faced demobilized Confederate soldiers, war had altered both the natural and built environments. The very land so fundamentally important to the southern existence had been disfigured by war. For some men, even areas close to home that should have brought comfort instead appeared almost unrecognizable, and further impeded the veterans' escape from the devastation of war.[39]

For Johnny Reb, such grim reminders of the massive destruction inflicted upon his section of the country, the grisly sights of war brought to the doorsteps of their homes within the immediate personal sphere of wives and children, and

the uncertain financial reality that confronted them all, served as incessant reminders that so much heartbreak and devastation was inflicted by hated invaders. Southern culpability in the conflict notwithstanding, Confederate veterans
understood all too well that those homes did not burn themselves. The visceral
sights and smells of the trek home fueled the continued Confederate identity
of now ex-Confederates, and therefore even from the closing days of the war
helped to create what would become the mindset of the Lost Cause.

Generations before scholars examined postwar conditions in the South,
Confederate soldiers themselves recorded the daunting, sometimes desperate
circumstances that confronted them. The sight of loved ones living in destitution deeply troubled returning veterans. The sight of his mother and sisters
wearing homespun garments shocked one well-to-do southerner. Dilapidated
or burned-out houses, damaged fences, empty cupboards, and nonexistent livestock undermined initial hopes of success. A dearth of viable currency further
complicated recovery efforts. Residents in some low-lying areas encountered
flooded fields and roads, while denizens of certain southern cities returned to
find entire neighborhoods virtually destroyed. One Alabama soldier and diarist who traveled through Georgia on his way home observed actual starvation
conditions in one area.[40]

Such widespread difficulties not only reminded Confederate veterans of the
task before them but also served up a painful and bitter dose of reality to those
southerners unaccustomed to financial insecurity. Months after the war the sister of one recently returned combatant witnessed poverty heretofore unknown
to her. A plantation mistress before the war, but a refugee during the conflict,
she and her family enjoyed the gracious hospitality of the numerous residents
of a small, two-room cabin. The hosts had recently survived primarily on bread,
milk, and butter, but "killed their last chicken for us yesterday, an old, old hen,
but the people are as kind as they can be, and as hospitable. They give us their
best and are really sorry for us. There are two women and a girl and not a scrap
of ribbon or lace or any kind of adornment in the house. I never saw a woman
before without a ribbon. They have not even a comb. They are the poorest people I ever saw."[41]

How did southern veterans confront such overwhelming economic challenges? Interestingly, a relative few initially had no intention of returning to
work or at least questioned their ability to do so. A Virginia infantry sergeant
who surrendered on that fateful April day at Appomattox opined "All I know is

to drill, and march, and fight. How can we get interested in farming or working in a store or warehouse when we have been interested day and night for years in keeping alive, whipping the invaders, and preparing for the next fight?" Weeks later in Louisiana, other confused Rebels expressed a comparable, if more determined outlook. As one former private recalled, he and his comrades discussed their postwar fate and what they should do upon reaching home. Just before their departure the comrades defiantly insisted that "they would be d—d if they were going to work; they had lived four years without working. And for five or six years after the war there was more horse stealing than I had ever seen in these parts and I guess that is what some of them did for a living."[42]

Obviously most former soldiers understood that they must return to work, but many despaired of finding success back home. Some veterans therefore pulled up stakes and headed west in search of a new start. Of course, many more discussed the idea but never followed through. Texas became a popular destination in both the actual and hypothetical solutions. He probably spoke for countless comrades when an Alabama veteran wrote of relocating to Texas one year after the war. After a stalled attempt to restart his life in his home state, he declared, Alabama had nothing left to offer him. The war had destroyed it all. He reasoned that wheat farming in north Texas might provide the new life he sought, while another former Rebel looked to Texas because it was so far from the United States government in Washington.[43]

The general concept of the West, broadly defined, appealed to Confederate veterans for both economic and political reasons. In the minds of many southern soldiers the West offered some nebulous prospect of profit. Others simply could not abide the thought of life under Yankee rule within their southern homeland. Those who migrated to Mexico were the only truly free southerners, one veteran later insisted. Many wrote of moving to Mexico, Central America, or simply somewhere to the west, far from the scene of the last four years of trauma. Veterans from both sides embraced the lure of the West, and those who suffered with traumatic memories of the war often sought the company of other veterans.[44]

Practical considerations took precedence over philosophy for other erstwhile Rebels. Different destinations offered opportunity, albeit generally without the exciting allure of the West. Southern veterans reasoned that Canada, Cuba, Bermuda, and even the dreaded northern United States promised at least the prospect of a fresh start. Although less desirable and romantic than land ownership or western adventure, at least the North boasted an established economy, stable currency, and the probability of steady employment as a wage earner. Some equally practical Rebels simply sought to escape the devastation in their local areas, while others recognized that they had almost literally nothing to lose through relocation.[45]

Dreams of a fresh start elsewhere, whether out West, up North, or in the Confederate settlements in South America, obviously appealed to countless southern veterans, but equally evident, only a minority acted on the impulse. Physical debilitation or lingering illness prevented migration for some. Love, whether romantic interests or familial responsibilities, kept other veterans at home. One Louisiana Rebel wrote at the close of the war that he would flee to Mexico if not for a certain young woman in his life. Years later a Mississippi veteran recalled that he rejected any scheme to leave the country, specifically so that he could care for his children. "For myself, I could not have gone without basely deserting these helpless ones." Ultimately, most former Confederate soldiers lacked the resources or even the desire to leave the South. Even a twenty-year-old Texas private, penniless and recently released from a Union prison, turned down a job complete with room and board on a northern farm in order to make his way home to start anew. Indeed, the vast majority of Confederate veterans seemed never to entertain the idea of relocation.[46]

Rather, most understood that the war had wrought a new world, an altered reality that confronted them, and that they must move forward with their lives in their familiar homelands. In the words of one South Carolina officer who explained his thoughts during his homeward trek, "I could see the future . . . a country already desolated and drained by war . . . its people on their knees . . . would be held there by revenge. Could I rebuild my life here? Why not Brazil . . . or Mexico? But I knew that I would not leave my State . . . that I would go down on my knees and put the bricks back, one by one, and build the house again. . . . I was smiling as I rode into the dawn."[47]

Although perhaps melodramatic, that officer's words reflect a widespread sense of determination and an essential point about the attempts of Confederate veterans to restart their lives. That they must return to work and face reality became obvious to almost all as a matter of simple survival. More important, Confederate veterans often consciously endeavored to begin anew as part of a defiant effort to appear resilient and unconquered. Here notions of individual masculinity merged with collective Confederate pride to bolster that unwavering Rebel intransigence. In other words, they started over not merely to survive but also to divest themselves of the traumatic sufferings of the war and to show their erstwhile enemies that resolute southerners would persevere, thus denying the Yankee victors the satisfaction of seeing Confederate veterans as broken men.[48]

In that resolute and buoyant spirit, a former captain in a Virginia cavalry regiment wrote to his wife in July 1865: "I look forward to the future with resolution and with hope. I do not need help, except the help of an occasional loving and encouraging word from you, to give me success, and God willing, I will yet gather around you every blessing of which I dreamed in the far away years of my boyhood." Veterans such as that former cavalryman recognized the possibility of recovery and a return to their antebellum norm, at least for those of relatively modest means such as the average laborer or small farmer.[49]

Southern veterans who returned to the family farm typically went to work immediately, sometimes tending the fields literally the day after their homecoming with the hope that they might still produce a crop. In fact, a jarring transition characterizes many wartime diaries. Dramatic descriptions of battles, campaigns, and war almost instantly give way to mundane registers of daily drudgery. Men and their families worked to repair homes, clean chimneys, mend fences, recover livestock, and in countless cases, adjust to living with less. The land remained the only resource left to some families, and upon that they set to work to rebuild their lives.[50]

During the summer of 1865 demobilized Confederate soldiers returned to work in a wide range of occupations. Those with means to do so pursued education, law, and politics. Some took in lodgers to make ends meet, while others boarded with relatives out of necessity. Innumerable former soldiers found themselves working as store clerks, house painters, or general laborers on farms or in cities. Still others traveled around the South to scour the cities and countryside in search of employment. One young former artillery private, for example, resided with his grandmother in Richmond and spent months in search of steady work.[51]

Improvisation and adaptation became necessary skills for returning veterans that summer. Certain resourceful southerners produced and sold items on the farm or out of the home, while others, probably many others, bartered their services with neighbors. One Louisiana veteran recalled: "I had a wife and two baby boys, and my wife owned a cow and a dog. These were our earthly possessions." In search of a way to provide for his young family, the resourceful veteran made shoes for laborers on a nearby plantation in exchange for corn and bacon. Another ex-soldier faced the reality that the postwar South offered dim prospects for his antebellum occupation of music teacher. He therefore decided to become a doctor, but eventually settled on postmaster.[52]

The story of twenty-four-year-old former infantry sergeant James Edward Whitehorne epitomizes soldiers' rapid transition back to civilian life. After four years of service, at least two wounds, and multiple severe illnesses, Whitehorne traveled one hundred miles with comrades from Appomattox to his family home in Greensville County, Virginia. On April 16, 1865, just three miles from his home, he parted ways with his companions for the final time: "Well, I never expected to see these familiar lanes again. There's the house." One week later he noted that food was scarce and that he was hard at work on a crop "before we all starve to death." Despite the struggle, all around him signs pointed to a community prepared to resume its peacetime existence. The local Masonic Lodge had reorganized, a Boston Yankee reportedly had plans to open a general store, and church services were scheduled to resume the next day. A local informed Whitehorne that the soldiers in the area had already formed a "Confederate Veterans Organization" just two weeks after the surrender at Appomattox. "I'm a veteran," he reasoned, "supposed I'll attend the meeting." Ever the diehard Rebel, like so many other comrades, he concluded his diary with one final demonstration of defiance: "I wish General Lee (may heaven bless him forever) had ordered our (Mahone's) brigade to burst through the invaders back in Appomattox. So endeth this scribbling." Even in the immediate aftermath of defeat, that obstinate Confederate veteran dictated the narrative that he would have continued the fight if given the opportunity.[53]

As it had during the chaotic closing weeks of the war and the stressful uncertainty of economic survival, the fear of the unknown dominated another facet of Johnny Reb's postwar mind. What would be his new relationship with former slaves? Although a civilian, one Alabama planter voiced the sentiments common to many returning soldiers in his diary. In May 1865 he wrote: "There is great gloom hanging over the people by reason of the destruction of the labor system of the Country." Freedmen and -women in the vicinity had begun to leave some area plantations, while at others productivity had diminished dramatically. The planter lamented that "with reduced stock and negroes demoralized a crop looks impossible."[54]

The encumbrance of the unknown that so burdened former Confederate soldiers, according to the Rebels, also weighed heavily upon freed slaves in two ways. First, much like white southerners, former slaves frequently groped about for guidance or some solution as to what to do next. In the opinion of one former major in the Army of Northern Virginia, not only did former slaves look to southern whites for assistance during that fateful summer, but Confederate veterans, freedmen, and freedwomen actually faced comparable challenges. The North Carolina native bemoaned the ravages of war wrought by Federal general William T. Sherman's troops when he observed, "Sherman's bummers had carried off, and what they could not carry away, had wantonly destroyed all the supplies of food for white and black. The darkeys came to their owners and sought at the hands of those, who had always supplied their wants, food and sustenance to be told they had none for them."[55]

Second, Confederate soldiers frequently deemed freedmen deluded about their postwar prospects. What did freedom really mean to them? According to the white southern appraisal, the African American version of freedom often meant simply that they never had to work again. In fact, some openly asserted such intentions and according to some veterans, mocked others who returned to manual labor. A thirty-year-old Georgia infantry captain recorded his observations in his diary as he made his way home from a northern prison in June 1865. As he passed through Tennessee he noted significant numbers of freedmen "pretending" to work on the railroad. "They are the worst deluded people in the world," he sneered. Years later a senior officer recalled his travel across Virginia soon after Appomattox. He witnessed "a plow stopped in the midst of a furrow and a negro plowman lying behind the plow asleep, with his face upturned to the broiling sun. Here was a picture of freedom to the negro."[56]

African Americans' alleged delusion, according to Confederate veterans, stemmed in part from a deeply flawed perception of white northerners. In the minds of Confederate veterans, second only to the true nature and implication of freedom, Yankees constituted the foremost source of confusion for recently freed slaves. Simply put, according to white southern observers, Black people in the South mistakenly believed that they had found nurturing friends and powerful allies among the northerners. A Virginia infantry captain complained in his diary in May 1865 that so many former slaves looked for support and salvation "so liberally promised them by Uncle Abraham and the whining hypocrites of N. England." Meanwhile, a former Mississippi infantryman bemoaned the futility of trying to persuade former slaves of alleged Yankee tricks. A fellow Mississippi native probably best encapsulated the overall sentiment when he wrote of freedpeople in his diary in May 1865, "Poor, deluded, people do not know who their real friends are."[57]

The observer obviously implied that freedpeople in search of friendship and guidance should look no further than their white southern neighbors. Interestingly, in the opinion of some former Confederates, the war overall, and emancipation specifically, disrupted what had been a proper, functional, and even loving relationship between the two races in the South. Invaders from the outside disrupted that relationship by force, southern veterans reasoned, only to abandon freedpeople within less than one generation. Even wartime assessments, without the perspective and bitterness of the Reconstruction years, concluded that African Americans would soon live under worse conditions than anything that they had experienced during the antebellum period. As one soldier concluded in April 1865, northerners had "gone forth to poison the happiness of black and white."[58]

Generally, even Confederate veterans' complimentary assessments of African Americans focused on concepts such as perceived loyalty to southern whites or on the potential of freedmen and -women to attain education sufficient to make them worthy neighbors and fellow citizens. A typically verbose former regimental musician and infantryman deemed Black people "naturally shrewd" individuals who would align themselves with southern whites, whom they genuinely loved, rather than carpetbaggers and other northern meddlers if permitted to chart their own course. Another soldier who witnessed African American children walking to school during his long trek home applauded that revolutionary development because, he reasoned, education might improve Black people's sense of honor and moral advancement.[59]

False admiration and claims of a mutually affectionate relationship notwithstanding, a number of Confederate veterans penned damning assessments of African Americans overall, particularly with regard to how the war and emancipation allegedly altered their character. Decades after the war a former Virginia cavalryman authored perhaps the most pointed and egregious example of such amateur anthropology. Before northern intervention, Blacks' loyalty to southern whites knew no bounds, and slaves even considered themselves Confederate allies, despite knowledge that Union victory meant freedom, he insisted. Slaves could be trusted to protect white men, women, and children before and indeed during the war. Black men often escorted white women away from home, sometimes over great distances, "but the kinky-headed, pigeon-heeled colored man always delivered his charge safely, and would have died in his footsteps to do it if the occasion required." Unfortunately, the Virginian lamented, the war, freedom, education, and Yankee intervention in general forever altered former slaves. He retained respect and a "tender spot" in his heart for African Americans, despite their allegedly altered character, because of their immense service, loyalty, and sacrifice for whites for generations, particularly during the crucible of war.[60]

Predictably, Confederate veterans sometimes mocked the notion of emancipation and African American advancement, particularly as a result of the most devastating conflict in American history. For Black freedom, "a nation was abolished" one soldier remarked contemptuously. Southern veterans scoffed at the mere concept and chafed at so much death, destruction, and widespread devastation for such a ridiculous concept as the advancement of African American civil rights, particularly when so many southerners who suffered most were nonslaveholders. The war, Johnny Reb insisted, ended chattel slavery but solved nothing with regard to Black inequality.[61]

Such condemnation on the part of some white southerners extended even to African American religious expressions. Ironically, as one influential study has demonstrated, some observers considered the immediate postwar rise of the Black church a sign of moral deterioration, and deemed the actual worship style of former slaves essentially a false religion. For their part, Black people had dealt with white suspicions toward religious practices for generations, and the end of the war provided a long-sought opportunity for free expression. The rise of Black denominations, separate from white southern institutions, represented a celebration of both emancipation and a newfound freedom of worship. The establishment of separate African American churches, characterized by the flight of so many recently emancipated slaves from established southern bodies, concerned whites in the South and the North as an alarmingly bold expression of Black independence.[62]

Whatever the meaning of freedom and its implications for African Americans, beginning in 1865 some southern veterans judged emancipated slaves as somehow unfit for liberty or at best unprepared for its advantages. One Confederate soldier who passed through South Carolina on his way home to Arkansas in May 1865 described individuals apparently still enslaved on a large plantation as happy and content. He contrasted that image with miserable, decrepit conditions that he witnessed among former slaves in camps along his journey. In his opinion the detestable state of affairs demonstrated the inhumanity of the

Federals because they insisted upon bestowing freedom upon people who were "morally and intellectually unfit to enjoy its' blessings."[63]

Others who deemed freedmen and -women unfit for freedom contended that former slaves simply would not and could not fend for themselves, a circumstance that would unavoidably lead to their misery as well as concerns for law and safety among southern whites. In the minds of some Confederate veterans, during the immediate aftermath of war and years later, emancipation was both inappropriate and unfair to the Black and white populations of the South. Federal policy thrust millions of individuals unprepared for liberty into the postwar world. It has been argued that the sight of freedmen moving about the countryside at their leisure undermined the masculine concept of mastery among white southern males. The men examined here at least considered it a sign of the chaos and instability that threatened their future. Moreover, such sights doubtless fueled white southern desires to block Congressional Reconstruction efforts and to seize control of the legal, political, social, and economic development of the postwar South. As one former officer bewailed, "What assurance can we have of law and order and the safety of our families with four million slaves suddenly emancipated in the midst of us and the restraints to which they have been accustomed entirely removed?"[64]

Although such sentiments could be found in the hearts and minds of white southerners regardless of social class, and all residents of the South confronted a society forever altered after the war, emancipation obviously affected a specific class of ex-Rebels most directly. Former slaveholders immediately found themselves at the center of the most revolutionary consequence of the Civil War. Planters and smaller farmers alike obviously confronted the reality of life without slave labor, but at least some claimed to be relieved by the development. Interestingly, in such cases emancipation effectively unburdened former slaveholders. No longer would they provide for those who labored for them, or more to the point, for those *no longer able* to work. As an added benefit, young whites from certain families would have to learn a new level of self-reliance.

Moreover, some white southerners examined here accepted the new postwar, free labor South and, without the slightest sense of irony, in effect considered themselves freed from the encumbrances and responsibilities of the peculiar institution. Some planters even gave former slaves gifts as incentives to leave. Though obviously embittered by defeat, southerners who adopted this perspective, through a powerful combination of contempt and liberation now considered newly emancipated people to be someone else's problem. The resentful and frustrated mother of one veteran told him in the summer of 1865 that she wished for all former slaves to be "hung around the necks of the abolitionists."⁶⁵

Other former slaveholders occupied a sort of philosophical middle ground. They moved forward with remarkable adaptability and informed their ex-slaves that they could stay, obviously under dramatically altered circumstances, or that they could leave to strike out on their own. In such cases, the planter or farmer determined to adjust to the postwar South and to survive regardless of the actions of his former labor force. Those planters and farmers typically advised ex-slaves to stay, at least temporarily, but seemingly had little time or patience for deep introspection or philosophical contemplation about the meaning of the last four years. Life continued, crops needed to be tended, and expenses had to be paid. They would employ their former slaves or hire new laborers.⁶⁶

On countless farms and plantations and in certain cities around the South, African Americans once again constituted the primary labor force in the period immediately after the war. In some cases, freed slaves remained on or returned to the plantations where they had long lived and labored. Others moved on, only to take up similar duties in a comparable field elsewhere. Perhaps they secured better wages or general working conditions. Perchance they relocated simply because they could. Whatever the case, at thousands of homesteads around the South, white landowners made the conscious decision to move forward with white and Black together again. Just as Confederate veterans refused to submit to a northern redefinition of southern masculinity, they immediately seized the opportunity to establish control of working conditions on their own farms.⁶⁷

At least some former slaveholders made immediate provisions for the continued care of those former slaves, particularly the very young or old, who remained at their antebellum home. In one such case, a former officer in Georgia took special interest in the welfare of the children of freedmen and -women on his property, while elsewhere a South Carolinian loaned a mule to his ex-foreman so that the man could search for his missing teenaged son. Elsewhere in the Palmetto State, upon his return to the family home an eighteen-year-old sergeant carefully administered smallpox vaccinations to Black and white residents.⁶⁸

This altered world obviously demanded newfangled arrangements, and all around the South former Confederates adjusted quickly. Necessity demanded that former masters, now employers, adapt and improvise with rapidity. Typically, former slaveholders offered freedmen and -women continued food and shelter and either wages or a share of the finished crop. Planters usually advised their former slaves to remain at the plantation, at least for the remainder of the year, and insisted that laborers must maintain discipline and follow instructions in order to honor the contract. Some employers even forbade their workers from inviting others to settle on the premises, under threat of termination. The relevance to the present study centers not on the wide range of terms of service agreed upon. Rather, the significance lies in the fact that white southerners adapted quickly during the chaotic spring and summer of 1865, before the establishment of widespread influence of the Freedman's Bureau, and consciously endeavored to set the agenda as much as possible.[69]

The case of James Griffin, a planter and former officer from South Carolina, provides a detailed example of the life-changing adjustments made by some southern veterans in their relationship with their former slaves. On the eve of the war, he possessed a large estate of approximately 1,500 acres, more than 60 slaves, and overall assets valued in excess of $80,000. Only thirty years old by the fall of 1860, Griffin boasted remarkable wealth for such a young individual.[70]

The war and time reduced Griffin's labor force considerably. By the summer of 1865 he listed 42 former slaves as resident on his plantation, only 22 of whom he identified as "workers," though 10 of those he described as "half hands." In a letter to a Federal officer who oversaw the transition from slaveholding planters to employers with compensated workers, Griffin proposed three arrangements with his former slaves. In the first the planter offered to compensate his employees with provisions, minus their expenses. In the second he proposed to divide among the workers one-quarter of all crops produced that year, again minus expenses. The third proposal, deemed best by Griffin, called for him to provide food and clothing for the freedpeople and to permit them time to burn coal, their antebellum source of income. Griffin intended to provide the wood and the former slaves would keep the profits from coal sold in the nearby village.[71]

Most revealing of the new reality for all parties, Griffin inquired of the Federal officer of his responsibilities for a "non-worker" former slave who had fled the plantation during the war, only to return afterward. The officer's order required local planters to provide for infirm freedpeople who resided on the respective plantation at the time that the order was issued. Griffin noted, however, that the former slave had fled before the issuance of the order and now sought to return. The recovering planter hoped to divest himself of the responsibility of another individual who could not produce anything for the plantation.[72]

Overall, Confederate veterans' assessments of African American reactions to emancipation during the summer of 1865 most pointedly illustrate the white southern concern with regard to the altered and unknown dynamic between the races. As explained above, former Confederates often believed that a substantial portion of emancipated slaves intended never to work again. Therefore, predictably, some southerners presumed a need to instill order and to seize the initiative in the struggle to redefine Black rights in the South, even as early as summer 1865. Accordingly, this action began with an attempt to compel freedmen and -women to labor under the conditions deemed appropriate by white southerners, an obvious step toward the restoration of mastery, that all-important pillar of southern masculinity.[73]

Such aggressive and concerted efforts suggest more than merely angry white southerners, bitter about defeat and emancipation. That predictable resentment appears throughout the soldier accounts, written both during and after the war. Rather, more specifically, southern veterans questioned the very character of the new relationship. What would be a former slave's place in society, and how would he or she interact with former planters? How would freedpeople compare to poor or average southern whites? Even the most diehard Rebel understood that emancipation was the new reality, but also recognized—by the summer of 1865, correctly as it turned out—that virtually everything else with regard to Reconstruction overall and African American civil rights specifically, remained unresolved and could be influenced by continued, determined southern defiance.

Although this present study focuses on the immediate end of the war rather than Reconstruction per se, some Confederate veterans wrote of their homeward journeys years later, and thus produced accounts clearly informed by that controversial period. Interestingly, wartime accounts sometimes presaged the same sentiments that appeared in later reminiscences, memoirs, and regimental histories. One former South Carolina artilleryman, a twenty-two-year-old private at the end of the war, published his account forty years later. In his mind the arrival of African American occupation troops the day after he returned home marked the beginning of Reconstruction, which he remembered as "a course of negro domination, corruption, robbery, and outrages; and which steadily increased in intensity until in 1876 it was overthrown by the general uprising of the white people."[74]

The Johnny Reb version of Reconstruction depicted a period defined by the emancipation of lazy and undeserving former slaves, the extension of Black civil liberties at the end of Federal bayonets, and the oppression of southern whites via tyrannical rule by a carpetbagger-scalawag-Black triumvirate of corruption. In fact, one veteran described the pursuit of Black civil rights, the presence of African American troops, and the implementation of Black education as the three bitter pills of Reconstruction. Ultimately, however, former Confederates banded together to "Redeem the South" and restore white southern dominance through perseverance, political reorganization, and in a minority of cases, the formation of secretive groups such as the Ku Klux Klan. Some Confederate veterans quite candidly proclaimed the end of Reconstruction and the overthrow of Republican (i.e., pro-emancipation) state governments a triumph of right over might.[75]

That last achievement points to the final phase of Johnny Reb's story—his genuine fear and resentment of life under Yankee domination and his determination to resist northern rule. Uncertainty once again plagued former Confederates as recently returned soldiers contemplated the impending actions of their vanquishers. As one Arkansas Rebel confided to his diary in May 1865: "What is reserved for the survivors none can tell." Genuine anxiety afflicted countless southerners, who, according to a Texas cavalryman writing in the same period, expected no mercy from "an enemy whose vile and atrocious deeds of cruelty and inhumanity have transcended those of the most barbarous nations of the heathen times."[76]

As that Texan's ominous words illustrate, although many southerners feared the unknown, a great many soldiers and civilians from all across the former Confederacy expected the worst. That same month, a fellow Lone Star State soldier penned his gloomy prediction and even wondered whether those who died in battle might have secured the better fate. "No longer will we be a free people, no longer have our rights, but must submit to the cruel relentless yoke of Yankee Tyranny. Far better to have fell on the Gory battle field than to witness what is now going on. Thrice happy are they whose bodies bleach on the plains of Shiloh, Murfreesboro, and Chickamauga, and whose spirits now rest from strife."[77]

Certain Confederate veterans expressed specific concerns about expected postwar treatment at the hands of northerners. Former Confederates anticipated intentional and repeated acts designed to humiliate southerners. In one case a local newspaper reported that the commander of occupation forces promised not to employ African American garrisons unless local lawlessness necessitated the measure. Elsewhere, a veteran fumed that northern civil officials placed former slaves in position of authority merely to humiliate southerners. Like so many others, however, he quietly accepted what he deemed the temporary reality but planned a return to power when he noted ominously that "for the present we must be harmless as doves but wise as serpents." Meanwhile, a minister and former officer clashed repeatedly with Union soldiers in Virginia throughout the summer of 1865. He complained bitterly that northern troops allegedly desecrated the grave of his son, a Confederate officer who had been killed in battle. The minister's persistent and public support of the dismantled Confederacy doubtless contributed to his poor relations with northern officers and soldiers in the region.[78]

A second very specific fear of northern retribution concerned the threat of property confiscation. Wartime confiscation legislation and potential punishments for southerners who failed to secure pardons under the amnesty proposals of both Abraham Lincoln and Andrew Johnson gave rise to such trepidation. Individuals disapproved for pardons under the amnesty proclamations were potentially subject to death, disfranchisement, property confiscation, imprisonment, and heavy fines. Those fears weighed heavy on civilians as well as veterans. In fact, hundreds of southern women applied for pardons, primarily to avoid property confiscation.[79]

Most significant, some Johnny Rebs expected merciless treatment at the hands of northern politicians and occupation troops intent on vengeance. A prominent South Carolinian conveyed that concern vividly when he recalled, "I could see the future . . . a country already desolated and drained by war . . . its people on their knees . . . would be held there by revenge." Indeed, as early as summer 1865 some Rebels suggested, or in certain cases warned, that moderation and forbearance might better achieve the goals of Reconstruction than what countless former Confederates already considered harsh and vindictive policies toward the southern populace.[80]

Southerners issued predictable but largely unrealistic calls for leniency from northern occupation forces. Since early 1863 Union military treatment of white southern civilians had transitioned away from conciliation both in practice and in official policy. Northern officers, soldiers, and officials shifted toward a hard war approach in response to determined, often violent, white southern resistance. As the war closed, Federal officers and officials typically had long since ceased to care about winning over southern hearts and minds.[81]

Such concerns presented southern veterans with the dilemma of how to respond in a manner that would allow them to seize the initiative and control the agenda. At the extreme a small minority of former Confederates formed or joined organizations such as the Ku Klux Klan. Interestingly, of the men examined here, in each case the veteran insisted that tyrannical, abusive Federal actions and policies necessitated the formation of such organizations. Southern men banded together to instill order and to protect themselves and their families from vindictive Yankees, empowered freedpeople, and in some regions, southern Unionists. One Tennessee veteran referred to the immediate postwar years in his home region as a Reign of Terror that forced Confederate veterans to defend themselves vigorously. So many individuals victimized Johnny Rebs there, he insisted, that "I could not longer remain in the country without either killing a lot of them or being killed."[82]

Violent extremists notwithstanding, most former Confederates reacted to the new postwar South and northern occupation in one of two ways. First, many admitted that the Confederacy had lost the war and insisted that they would like to move on with their lives *if permitted to do so in peace.* Such individuals genuinely embraced the return of peace and hoped never to witness warfare again but also remained watchful of the federal government. One excellent study of Virginians found that the war-weary population accepted the end of slavery but remained determined to resist anything that smacked of federal control. Similar individuals under consideration here also rejected any semblance of African American equality. They focused on immediate economic recovery and insisted that as long as they acknowledged the results of the war they should be allowed to carry on with their lives without further interference from federal authorities. The vast majority of Confederate veterans thus avoided violence, eagerly returned to work, and concentrated initially on the recovery of their individual households but, as an excellent study of southern emotions concluded, ultimately refused to concede to northern visions of a new social hierarchy in the defeated South.[83]

As one veteran observed in June 1865: "If the U.S. Government treats the South with a noble magnanimity I shall glory in their prosperity, if not, I shall glory in their ruin." Those former Rebels were willing to concede defeat but, to be sure, expressed no remorse and admitted no wrongdoing. Even a veteran who endeavored to follow federal law faithfully after the war maintained that "I have not yet lived long enough to regret my action. I still feel that we fought for a principle and for a just and righteous cause, and I still believe that all governments should rest upon the consent of the governed. But we submitted our cause to the arbitrament of the Sword and lost."[84]

That sentiment proved almost universal among ex-Confederates who constituted the second, more vocal group. Many southern veterans not only remained adamant in defense of their actions but continued to identify with the defunct Confederacy. Many such men remained embittered, even angry, and determined to combat federal Reconstruction efforts and regain control of their respective states. One manifestation of that attachment to the Rebel identity centered upon the insistence of southern veterans to wear their Confederate uniforms in public after the war. Although some Confederate soldiers wore their uniforms immediately after the cessation of hostilities out of simple necessity, many others clearly did so as a public display of Confederate pride and identity, an action obviously conceived at least in part to irritate Federal authorities. Such stubborn refusal to discard the treasured gray uniforms doubtless represented a conscious display of masculinity, but the simpler political statement remains palpable and explicit. Moreover, the continued attachment to uniforms presaged later veterans' emphasis on material culture such as muskets, uniforms, and wartime documents. In this instance Confederate veterans in effect combined politics and masculinity with yet another refusal to accept northern efforts to redefine them as men. Authorities in numerous occupied localities issued regulations against wearing Confederate uniforms, a perfectly reasonable action but one that typically only exacerbated the demobilized Rebels' resentment of all things northern.[85]

Scholarly studies of Confederate veterans have found that a shared insistence upon the justness of the pursuit of southern independence, fueled by Lost Cause rhetoric and ultimately manifested in organizations such as the United Confederate Veterans, illustrates the determined but nonviolent nature of continued southern resistance to what they deemed northern rule. The Lost Cause portrayed southern veterans as heroic survivors of a conflict that never truly could have been won against such a numerous foe, thus southern fighting men bore no shame in defeat. Veterans' organizations not only helped ex-soldiers come to terms with defeat in battle but also provided important community support and political guidance and mobilization. The direction provided by such organizations also helped to build community and business networks that prized a reputation for loyalty and meritorious service to the Confederacy. Most Confederate veterans therefore continued to resist northern rule by working and socializing together, valuing each other's military service records, and by returning to the polls with a dogged obedience to conservative white southern

Democratic candidates. Those powerful unifying sentiments existed immediately after the war, and the shared experience of demobilization provided early stimulation for what became Lost Cause ideology.[86]

James J. Broomall's insightful analysis of the emotional world of Confederate soldiers found that southern fighting men dedicated themselves absolutely to the war effort but emerged unprepared for the consequences of the conflict, and thus continued to rely on each other for support as they confronted the chaotic postwar world. Military service defined such men, Broomall concluded, but that experience also undermined the veterans' ability to function in society as they confronted severe depression and anxiety. Bonds formed during military service, however, actually strengthened after the conflict, fueled by the collective experience of sacrifice and defeat, and helped ex-Confederates muster the strength to remain defiant of federal rule. According to Broomall, veterans essentially chose a "restrained, if still volatile, manliness." In time that unity of purpose forged the foundations of the Lost Cause and thus allowed ex-Confederates to transform "their military tragedy into a historical triumph."[87] The conclusions presented throughout this study support Broomall's conclusions but also demonstrate that those developments began immediately during demobilization. Certainly, Confederate veterans, like most other Americans, entered the postwar years unprepared for the revolutionary consequences. However, former Johnny Rebs immediately responded to the myriad challenges that confronted them, and demonstrated that the war had inhibited but not destroyed their ability to function. From the initial moments of demobilization, Confederate veterans endeavored, at times with almost religious zeal, to control their postwar fate and indeed to formulate the historical narrative of the conflict.

Although scholars have long debated the connection between Lost Cause rhetoric and religion, a general consensus holds that most former Confederates during the immediate postwar period accepted the harsh reality of defeat but remained steadfast in the righteousness of their actions. As one important study concluded, white southerners remained advocates of state sovereignty and white supremacy but recognized the need to move forward with their lives. Thus for some scholars the Lost Cause became a southern civil religion, another has deemed it "quasi-religious," while still others recognize the movement as culturally significant but not of a religious nature. The latter two interpretations are generally more convincing with regard to the individuals and the time period under consideration here and likely help to explain the relative dearth of reli-

gious references among the Confederate veterans examined during the immediate postwar days.[88]

Ex-Confederates who retained their Rebel identity after the war not only
remained adamant about the justness of the southern cause but blamed northerners for the vast devastation and death wrought by the war. Moreover, genuine hatred for all things Yankee constituted a significant portion of that postwar
Rebel identity and the revulsion remained palpable. One former infantryman
who spent much of the summer of 1865 in search of work mocked an Independence Day celebration held by Union sympathizers in the streets of Richmond.
The Declaration of Independence was read aloud to an "admiring & appreciat-
ing audience of poor white folks niggers & Yankees." Also during the summer
of 1865 that Texan wrote to his cousin: "There is no love in my soul for Yankees,
neither can there ever be."[89]

Many Confederate veterans and their families deemed reconciliation with
their former opponents unthinkable during the immediate aftermath of the war.
Those individuals insisted that defeat in no way undermined the legitimacy of
their cause and thus they apologized for nothing. For example, in a resolution
to his people upon official surrender in 1865, the principal chief of the Choctaw Nation adamantly refuted any notion of remorse. Moreover, Reconstruction efforts, both legislative actions and military occupation, only intensified the
separatist sentiments among some former Confederates. During the summer
of 1865, one former officer and dyed-in-the-wool Rebel bemoaned the invasive northern sentiments that had crept into local Virginia newspapers, two of
which he considered "so thoroughly arrogant, abusive, grandiloquent . . . false
& deceptive, that I find them nothing short of nauseating." He reserved particular venom for newspapers published in the former Confederate capital of
Richmond. Those had become "so entirely Yankeeized and Anti-Virginian, and
subservient to the northern tyranny" that he considered them more objectionable than any paper published north of the Potomac River. In later years such
men proudly identified as unreconstructed Rebels. Many southern veterans remained Confederates long after the demise of the Confederacy.[90]

Persistent efforts to resist Congressional Republicans' control of Reconstruction and ultimately to determine the fate of the postwar South indicate
Confederate veterans' preservation of the masculine virtue of mastery. After all,
such single-minded resistance, political and social, violent and peaceful, along
racial and sectional lines, hardly reflects emasculation. Therefore, defeat on the

battlefield in no way constituted a loss of manhood. Rather, Confederate veterans employed a new strategy defined by an immediate shift of the conflict to a new front. Once again Confederates' adaptability made possible the conscious transition to postwar resistance and the redefinition of southern manhood. Clearly defeat on the battlefield undercut mastery, temporarily at least, more so than it undermined individual honor. The power of the Lost Cause assuaged the sting of defeat and allowed southern men to reshape the contours of manhood and individual honor to focus on meritorious service against allegedly insurmountable odds. Free from potential shame of defeat, veterans then emphasized their roles as husbands, fathers, and providers, and, on the collective level, their shared resistance to northern rule and the advancement of African American civil rights. In other words, although martial defeat, emancipation, and financial strains challenged Johnny Rebs' masculine ethos, the fierce resistance that continued from the war itself and into Reconstruction demonstrates that Confederate veterans never submitted and instead seized control of their postwar economic fate, Reconstruction, and the Civil War narrative.[91]

Amidst the war's closing scenes one Confederate soldier managed to express all the sentiments typical of his comrades in an emotional but thoughtful letter to his wife. As he prepared, finally, to leave a northern prison camp he insisted that "I have performed my duty and now abandon the cause as (at present) hopeless, without in the least having changed my opinion as to the justness of that cause." More important, the young Rebel even claimed that the dream of southern independence remained perfectly viable and could be achieved within a decade. One week before his thirty-first birthday and soon to begin his homeward journey, the former Virginia Military Institute cadet penned a defiant and prophetic entry: "The present, thank God, is only the 'beginning of the end.' The military power of the South is broken, the spirit is not."[92]

APPENDIX

SAMPLE & METHODOLOGY

The interpretations and conclusions throughout this book draw upon the writings of approximately 1,100 Confederate soldiers. Roughly 400 of those left diaries, letters, memoirs, or regimental histories, while more than 700 others answered questions about their homeward journeys in the Tennessee Civil War Veterans' Questionnaires. Those documents include the accounts of men who resided in the Volunteer State at the time of the questionnaires' distribution, not merely veterans from Tennessee regiments.

The overall sample size of approximately 1,100 individuals stands in accordance with that of two influential works of scholarship. James McPherson's *For Cause and Comrades: Why Men Fought in the Civil War* (1997) utilized a sample of more than 1,000 men, fewer than half of whom were Confederate. McPherson thus analyzed motivation for Confederate soldiers for the entire war period based on the writings of those 429 men. Kenneth W. Noe's fine study *Reluctant Rebels: The Confederates Who Joined the Army after 1861* (2010) employed a sample of 320 men to analyze the motivations for Rebels who enlisted after the war's early months. Thus the sample employed in the present study of approximately 400 manuscript and published accounts supplemented by another 700 questionnaires to examine the experiences of individuals who remained in the ranks at the end of the war adheres to the standard established by those two excellent studies.

Within the overall sample, this appendix identifies 200 men who provided enough information to track their entire journeys home, not simply starting point and destination. The beginning point identified in the table below identifies the place where they began their actual journey home. Some men in the sample had traveled during previous days but had not yet made the decision to go home. Moreover, some men followed indirect routes for various reasons, as discussed in chapters two and three. Therefore, simply mapping the distance between beginning point and final destination will often yield a dramatically different total from that which appears in the appendix. Instances of men who traveled significant distances in order to secure railroad or water-based transport provide the most common explanation for this development. Mileage totals for river and ocean travel draw upon data assembled by the U.S. Army Corps of Engineers. All defining characteristics—including rank, unit affiliation, age, and marital status—reflect the soldier's situation at the end of the war.

Analysis of that sample of two hundred men for whom the complete journeys remain available yields the following results: 93 privates; 14 corporals; 20 sergeants; 3 musicians; 2 chaplains; 1 surgeon. Thus, 133 men collectively can be defined as enlisted men or noncommissioned officers. The remaining 67 include officers of various higher ranks, staff officers, and adjutants. Clearly, those totals somewhat overrepresent officers, but officers proved more likely to leave a written record of their journey and, more important, the distances traveled did not differ from those of enlisted men. Overall, at the end of the war, 167 men were single, 3 others were widowers, and 30 were married. The average age among those 200 men at the end of the war was 25, and the average number of miles traveled to reach home was 586.

NAME	AGE	UNIT	RANK	MARITAL STATUS	HOME STATE	STARTING LOCATION	DESTINATION	MILES	SOURCE	NOTES
Adair, Robert President	23	13th SC Infantry	private	single	SC	Danville, VA	Laurens County, SC	250	postwar questionnaire	
Alexander, Edward P.	29	Army of Northern Virginia	brig. general	married	GA	Appomattox Court House, VA	Washington, GA	1,700	memoir	indirect route while trying to arrange travel to Brazil
Alexander, Thomas Benton	26	1st TN Heavy Artillery	sergeant	single	TN	Barnesville, GA	Maury County, TN	350	diary	
Allen, John Benton	20	2nd TN Cavalry	private	single	TN	Fort Delaware Prison	Chattanooga, TN	1,000	postwar questionnaire	
Alston, Warren J.	19	2nd Battalion, GA Infantry	private	single	GA	Point Lookout Prison, MD	Stewart County, GA	1,100	diary	
Anderson, Ephraim M.	21	2nd MO Infantry	corporal	single	MO	Selma, AL	St. Louis, MO	1,400	memoir	
Andrews, John Oliver	20	14th GA Infantry	private	single	GA	Point Lookout Prison, MD	Butts County, GA	750	memoir	
Andrews, Welburn J.	21	23rd SC Vols	private	single	SC	Point Lookout Prison, MD	Sumter, SC	600	memoir	
Atkins, Lucullus Can	21	7th KY Cavalry	private	single	TN	Washington, GA	Montgomery County, TN	425	postwar questionnaire	
Bahnson, Henry T.	20	1st NC Battalion Sharp Shooters	private	single	NC	Farmville, VA	Salem, NC	250	memoir	
Bailey, Joseph M.	24	16th AR Infantry	captain	single	AR	Shreveport, LA	Carroll County, AR	350	memoir	

NAME	AGE	UNIT	RANK	MARITAL STATUS	HOME STATE	STARTING LOCATION	DESTINATION	MILES	SOURCE	NOTES
Ballanfant, Josiah Turner	19	3rd/4th TN Cavalry	private	single	TN	Greensboro, NC	Maury County, TN	600	postwar questionnaire	
Barfield, Mills T.	19	67th NC Infantry	private	single	NC	Kinston, NC	Green County, NC	20	postwar questionnaire	
Bates, James C.	28	9th Texas Cavalry	lieut col	single	TX	Jackson, MS	Paris, TX	400	letters/ diary	After prolonged recovery period
Beasley, Charles D.	18	19th AL Infantry	private	single	AL	Kingston, GA	Cherokee County, AL	50	postwar questionnaire	
Beauregard, Pierre G. T.	47	Army of Tennessee	general	widower	LA	Greensboro, NC	New Orleans, LA	1,000	memoir	
Benson, Berry	22	1st SC Infantry	sergeant	single	GA/ SC	Appomattox Court House, VA	Augusta, GA	400	memoir	Parents in GA, lived some with grandparents in SC
Benson, Blackwood	20	1st SC Infantry	corporal	single	GA/ SC	Appomattox Court House, VA	Augusta, GA	400	memoir	parents in GA, lived some with grandparents in SC
Berkeley, Henry Robinson	25	Kirkpatrick Batt., Light Art, ANV	private	single	VA	Fort Delaware Prison	Hanover County, VA	350	diary	
Betts, Alexander Davis	32	30th NC Infantry	chaplain	married	NC	Petersburg, VA	Chapel Hill, NC	150	memoir	went home on leave; war ended while home
Bevens, William E.	24	1st AR Infantry	private	single	AR	Augusta, GA	Jacksonport, AR	800	memoir	

Name	Age	Unit	Rank	Marital	State	Location 1	Location 2	Miles	Source	Notes
Bigger, James A.	22	2nd MS Cavalry	corporal	single	MS	Artesia, MS	Cherry Creek, MS	80	diary	
Boyd, William Townes	21	First Co. Richmond Howitzers	private	single	VA	Farmville, VA	Mecklenburg County, VA	50	postwar questionnaire	
Bradwell, Isaac G.	22	31st GA Infantry	private	single	GA	Appomattox Court House, VA	Bainbridge, GA	750	postwar article	
Brett, Martin W.	25	12th GA Infantry	corporal	single	GA	Point Lookout Prison, MD	Drayton, Georgia	800	memoir	
Brockman, Henry	41	10th Missouri Infantry	captain	married	MO	Shreveport, LA	Cole County, MO	1,300	diary	
Brown, James Welsman	24	2nd SC Heavy Artillery	colonel	single	SC	Greensboro, NC	Camden, SC	150	diary	From Charleston but went to Camden
Bryant, John David	21	44th TN Infantry	private	single	TN	Point Lookout Prison, MD	Bedford County, TN	1,000	postwar questionnaire	
Burke, Curtis	23	2nd KY Cavalry	private	single	KY	Richmond, VA	Lexington, KY	2,000	diary/memoir	Additional travel from Camp Douglas to Richmond on parole; war ended while still in Richmond
Cannon, Newton	19	11th TN Cavalry	sergeant	single	TN	Gainesville, AL	Williamson County, TN	250	memoir	
Carson, William Waller	20	4th LA Cavalry	sergeant-major	single	LA	Shreveport, LA	Tyler, TX	100	postwar questionnaire	
Casler, John Overton	26	33rd VA Inf; 11th VA Cav	private	single	VA	Fort McHenry Prison, MD	Harrisonburg, VA	175	memoir	

NAME	AGE	UNIT	RANK	MARITAL STATUS	HOME STATE	STARTING LOCATION	DESTINATION	MILES	SOURCE	NOTES
Cater, Douglas John	24	19th LA Infantry	chief musician	single	LA	Meridian, MS	Desoto Parish, LA	750	memoir	
Cavaness, Isaac F.	23	46th NC Infantry	corporal	single	NC	Appomattox Court House, VA	Randolph County, NC	150	diary	
Chambers, Henry Alexander	24	49th NC Infantry	captain	single	NC	Appomattox Court House, VA	Iredell County, NC	350	diary and postwar questionnaire	
Chambers, William Pitt	25	46th MS Infantry	sergeant	single	MS	Meridian, MS	Covington County, MS	100	diary	diary had some postwar edits
Clark, Carroll Henderson	23	16th TN Infantry	2nd lt.	single	TN	Greensboro, NC	Van Buren County, TN	550	postwar questionnaire	
Cline, G. H.	21	8th NC Infantry	private	single	NC	Greensboro, NC	Cabarrus County, NC	60	postwar questionnaire	
Coakley, James	21	10th KY Cavalry	private	single	TN	Washington, GA	Sparta, TN	300	postwar questionnaire	
Coalson, Charles	42	11th Texas Infantry	2nd lt.	married	TX	Crockett, TX	Rusk County, TX	200	diary	very indirect route
Coffin, James Park	25	2nd TN Cavalry	1st lt.	single	TN	Charlotte, NC	Hawkins County, TN	300	postwar questionnaire	
Cole, David L.	45	61st AL Infantry	private	married	AL	Point Lookout Prison, MD	Chambers County, AL	650	diary	
Coles, Robert T.	22	4th AL Infantry	adjutant	single	AL	Appomattox Court House, VA	Huntsville, AL	1,000	memoir	indirect route while seeking free transport

Name	Age	Unit	Rank	Marital	State	Location 1	Location 2	Number	Source
Collins, Robert M.	36	15th TX Cavalry	lieutenant	married	TX	Greensboro, NC	Decatur, TX	2,400	memoir
Coltrane, Daniel B.	22	5th NC Cav	sergeant	single	NC	Clover Station, VA	Guilford County, NC	100	memoir
Conner, Presley Neville	24	9th TN Infantry	captain	single	TN	Opelika, AL	Ripley, TN	850	postwar questionnaire
Copley, John M.	19	49th TN Infantry	private	single	TN	Camp Douglas Prison, IL	Dickson County, TN	450	memoir
Cowles, R. S.	21	45th TN Infantry	sergeant	single	TN	Greensboro, NC	Triune, TN	550	postwar questionnaire
Cox, Abner	23	Palmetto Sharpshooters	lieutenant	single	SC	Appomattox Court House, VA	Belton, SC	400	diary
Crenshaw, Edward	22	58th AL Infantry	captain / 1st lt.	single	AL	Greensboro, NC	Butler County, AL	600	diary
Crosland, Charles	19	20th SC Infantry	private	single	SC	Albemarle, NC	Bennettsville, SC	70	memoir
Dacus, Robert H.	21	1st AR Mounted Rifles	private	single	AR	Jamestown NC	Dardanelle, AR	1,050	memoir
Darsey, William Henry	21	32nd GA Infantry	private	single	GA	Point Lookout Prison, MD	Clay County, GA	1,000	postwar questionnaire
Davis, William V.	36	30th MS Infantry	captain	single	MS	Richmond, VA	Attala County, MS	1,000	diary
Denton, Frank Desha	24	8th AR Infantry	2nd lt.	single	AR	Atlanta, GA	Independence County, AR	1,400	postwar questionnaire
De Saussure, Charles Alfred	18	Beaufort Artillery	private	single	SC	Greensboro, NC	Camden, SC	250	postwar questionnaire
Devereux, Thomas P.	19	43rd NC Infantry	private	single	NC	Appomattox Court House, VA	Wake County, NC	150	memoir

NAME	AGE	UNIT	RANK	MARITAL STATUS	HOME STATE	STARTING LOCATION	DESTINATION	MILES	SOURCE	NOTES
DeWitt, Marcus Bearden	30	8th TN Infantry	chaplain	married	TN	Greensboro, NC	Houston County, GA	400	diary	
Diamond, James	24	1st SC Infantry	private	single	SC	Appomattox Court House, VA	Barnwell, SC	400	memoir	
Dixon, William Daniel	26	1st GA Infantry	captain	single	GA	High Point, NC	Savannah, GA	400	diary	
Donaldson, Lauchlan	21	12th KY Cavalry	lieutenant	single	TN	Johnson's Island Prison, OH	Obion County, TN	600	postwar questionnaire	
Dooley, John E.	22	1st VA Infantry	captain	single	VA	Charlotte, NC	Richmond, VA	300	diary	
Drake, W. B.	18	1st VA Artillery	private	single	VA	Appomattox Court House, VA	Powhatan County, VA	60	postwar questionnaire	
Dunlop, William S.	31	12th SC Infantry	major	married	SC	Johnson's Island Prison, OH	Rock Hill, SC	1,700	memoir	
Durham, Henry Farmer	22	7th AL Cavalry	private	single	AL	Iuka, MS	Franklin County, AL	10	postwar questionnaire	
Dyer, John Will	24	1st KY Cavalry	sergeant	single	KY	Washington, GA	Union County, KY	550	memoir	
Edwards, John Frank	22	35th GA Infantry	private	single	GA	Point Lookout Prison, MD	Troup County, GA	850	memoir	
Falconer, Kinloch	26	AOT HQ, asst adj gen	major	single	MS	Greensboro, NC	Bridgeville, AL	700	diary	
Fergus, John Tyler Constant	23	45th TN Infantry	private	single	TN	Augusta, GA	La Vergne, TN	400	postwar questionnaire	
Fielder, Alfred Tyler	51	12th TN Infantry Consolidated	captain	married	TN	High Point, NC	Friendship, TN	850	diary	

Name	Age	Unit	Rank	Marital status	State	From	To	Amount	Source
Fields, Charles B.	24	1st VA Cavalry	private	single	VA	Appomattox Court House, VA	Abingdon, VA	200	diary
Firth, Thomas Julian	22	13th TN Infantry	chief musician	single	TN	Augusta, GA	La Grange, TN	900	postwar questionnaire
Fletcher, William A.	26	8th Texas Cavalry	private	single	TX	Greensboro, NC (vicinity)	Beaumont, TX	1,000	memoir
Ford, Arthur P.	22	Manigualt's Batt., SC Artillery	private	single	SC	Greensboro, NC	Aiken, SC	350	memoir
Forrest, Douglas French	27	Gen. John G Walker's staff	staff officer	single	VA	Houston, TX	Richmond, VA	2,400	diary
Foster, Samuel T.	35	24th TX Cav (dismounted)	captain	married	TX	Greensboro, NC	Hallettsville, TX	2,200	diary
Fowler, S. W.	21	26th AL Infantry	private	single	AL	Selma, AL	Fayette County, AL	100	postwar questionnaire
French, George D.	21	51st VA Infantry	captain	single	VA	Dublin, VA	Russell County, VA	100	postwar questionnaire
Gardner, Edwin Maximillian	19	6th MS Cavalry	private	single	MS	Okolona, MS	Tupelo, MS	30	postwar questionnaire
Gibbons, Alfred R.	19	1st GA Cavalry	private	single	GA	Michigan City, Indiana	Floyd County, GA	700	memoir
Goodloe, James Camp	26	4th AL Infantry	sergeant	single	AL	Pond Spring, AL	Colbert County, AL	30	postwar questionnaire
Goodloe, William Henry	21	11th AL Cavalry	private	single	AL	Pond Spring, AL	Colbert County, AL	30	postwar questionnaire
Gordon, William Osceola	20	11th LA Cavalry	private	single	LA	Mobile, AL	Baton Rouge, LA	200	postwar questionnaire

NAME	AGE	UNIT	RANK	MARITAL STATUS	HOME STATE	STARTING LOCATION	DESTINATION	MILES	SOURCE	NOTES
Gorham, Robert Townshend	20	2nd KY Cavalry	private	single	TN	Washington, GA	Clarksville, TN	400	postwar questionnaire	
Graber, Henry W.	24	8th TX Cavalry	private	single	TX	Greensboro, NC	Hempstead, TX	1,600	memoir	
Green, John W.	24	9th KY Infantry	sergeant-major	single	KY	Washington, GA	Henderson, KY	600	memoir	
Green, Thomas Wallace	23	12th KY Cavalry	private	single	KY	Huntsville, AL	Hopkinsville, KY	200	postwar questionnaire	
Grisamore, Silas T.	40	18th LA Infantry	major; asst. qm.	single	LA	Mansfield, LA	Thibodaux, LA	300	memoir	
Gross, Simeon	22	20th SC Infantry	corporal	single	SC	Greensboro, NC	Lexington, SC	250	diary	
Haggard, William S.	23	7th KY Cavalry	corporal	single	MO	Lynchburg, VA	Boone County, MO	1,000	diary	
Hall, James E.	23	31st VA Infantry	adjutant	single	VA (WV)	Farmville, VA	Elk Creek, WV	300	diary	
Hamilton, David H.	21	1st Texas Infantry	sergeant	single	TX	Appomattox Court House, VA	Groveton, TX	1,300	memoir	
Hart, Harvey L.	19	12th SC Infantry	private	single	SC	Fort Delaware Prison	York County, SC	1,000	postwar questionnaire	
Herndon, Thomas	25	14th TN Infantry	2nd lieutenant	single	TN	Augusta, GA	Clarksville, TN	450	diary	
Hinson, William G.	27	7th SC Cavalry	2nd lieutenant	single	SC	Appomattox Court House, VA	James Island, SC	450	diary	

Name	Age	Regiment	Rank	Marital status	State	Surrender/Prison	Home	Number	Source	Notes
Holt, David E.	21	16th Mississippi Infantry	private	single	MS	Point Lookout Prison, MD	Woodville, MS	1,300	memoir	trip home on furlough just before end of war
Hooper, James Henry	20	13th NC Infantry	private	single	NC	Appomattox Court House, VA	Caswell County, NC	100	postwar questionnaire	
Howard, McHenry	26	Maj. Gen. GWC Lee's staff	lieutenant / staff officer	single	MD	Johnson's Island Prison, OH	Baltimore, MD	600	memoir	
Houghton, William R.	22	2nd GA Infantry	sergeant	single	AL	Appomattox Court House, VA	Smiths Station, AL	600	memoir	
Hubbard, John Milton	30	7th TN Cavalry	private	widower	TN	Gainesville, AL	Bolivar, TN	200	memoir	
Hudson, Joshua H.	33	26th SC Infantry	lt. col.	married	SC	Five Forks, VA	Bennettsville, SC	350	memoir	
Hundley, George J.	27	15th VA Cavalry	private	single	VA	Lynchburg, VA	Amelia County, VA	100	memoir	former militia general; former 2nd lieutenant in 19th VA Infantry
Inzer, John Washington	31	58th AL Infantry	lt. col.	single	AL	Johnson's Island Prison, OH	St. Clair County, AL	1,000	diary	
Jackman, John S.	23	9th KY Mounted Infantry	private	single	KY	Washington, GA	Bardstown, KY	700	memoir/ diary	
Johnson, Isaiah Woody	19	2nd TX Infantry	private	single	TX	Galveston, TX	Burleson County, TX	150	postwar questionnaire	
Johnston, David E.	21	7th VA Infantry	private	single	VA	Point Lookout Prison, MD	Giles County, VA	550	memoir	

NAME	AGE	UNIT	RANK	MARITAL STATUS	HOME STATE	STARTING LOCATION	DESTINATION	MILES	SOURCE	NOTES
Johnston, John	23	14th TN Cavalry	private	single	TN	Sumterville, AL	Denmark, TN	250	diary/ memoir	
Jones, Charles C.	33	Chatham Artillery (GA)	lieutenant	married	GA	Greensboro, NC	Savannah, GA	400	memoir	
Jones, R. W.	18	2nd KY Cavalry	private	single	KY	Camp Douglas Prison	Owen County, KY	400	postwar questionnaire	
Keen, Newton A.	20	6th TX Cavalry	private	single	TX	Camp Douglas Prison	Dallas County, TX	1,350	memoir	traveled farther than notes in memoir suggest because took water route, Vicksburg to Shreveport
Kees, Martin Van Buren	24	33rd MS Infantry	private	single	MS	Greeneville, SC	Brookhaven, MS	700	diary	
Key, Thomas J.	34	15th AR Infantry	captain	married	AR	Macon, GA	St. Charles, AR	900	diary	
Keysaer, John Conrad	27	10th VA Infantry	private	single	VA	Harrisonburg, VA	Rockingham County, VA	10	postwar questionnaire	
King, John H.	21	6th GA Cavalry	private	single	GA	Richmond, VA	Canton, GA	550	memoir	
Lambert, Joel	24	27th AL Infantry	corporal	single	AL	Pond Spring, AL	Rodgersville, AL	10	postwar questionnaire	
LaMotte, Thomas J.	34	17th SC Infantry	sergeant	married	SC	Petersburg, VA	Columbia, SC	350	diary	
Lavender, John W.	28	4th AR Infantry	captain	single	AR	Johnson's Island Prison, OH	Prairie County, AR	950	memoir	

Name	Age	Unit	Rank	Status	State	Place 1	Place 2	Number	Type	Notes
Lee, George Taylor	17	VMI Cadets	private	single	VA	Richmond, VA	Powhatan County, VA	25	postwar questionnaire	
Leon, Louis	23	53rd North Carolina	private	single	NC	Elmira Prison, NY	New York City	250	diary	
Leuschner, Charles A.	19	6th Texas Infantry	sergeant	single	TX	Camp Douglas Prison	Victoria, TX	2,300	diary	
Lewis, John A.	23	9th KY Cavalry	1st lieutenant	single	KY	Washington, GA	Frankfort, KY	600	memoir	
Lewis, John Henry	29	9th VA Infantry	2nd lieutenant	married	VA	Fort Delaware Prison	Portsmouth, VA	250	memoir	
Lightsey, Ransom J.	27	16th Mississippi Infantry	private	single	MS	Appomattox Court House, VA	Jasper County, MS	900	memoir	
Luster, James Henry	22	16th VA Cavalry	private	single	VA/WV	Appomattox Court House, VA	Wayne County, WV	300	postwar questionnaire	appears as Lester in Tennessee Civil War Veterans Questionnaire; Wayne Co. became part of WV
Maiden, William Franklin	20	48th VA Infantry	private	single	VA	Elmira Prison, NY	Washington County, VA	800	postwar questionnaire	
Marshall, Thomas J.	32	6th GA Infantry	captain	married	GA	High Point, NC	Monroe County, GA	500	diary	
Martin, George A.	32	38th VA Infantry	captain	married	VA	Augusta, GA	Norfolk, VA	700	diary	
Maverick, Lewis	26	36th TX Cavalry	major/captain	single	TX	Houston, TX	San Antonio, TX	200	diary	
McClure, Joseph	21	18th TX Cavalry	private	single	TX	Griffin, GA	Alvarado, TX	850	memoir	

NAME	AGE	UNIT	RANK	MARITAL STATUS	HOME STATE	STARTING LOCATION	DESTINATION	MILES	SOURCE	NOTES
McCollum, Duncan	27	4th MS Cavalry	captain	single	MS	Gainesville, AL	Mount Olive, MS	150	diary	
McCoy, Charles W.	21	6th AL Infantry	corporal	single	AL	Appomattox Court House, VA	Lee County, AL	2,100	postwar questionnaire	
McKnight, William Thomas	18	Armstead's Cavalry	private	single	AL	Gainesville, AL	Livingston, AL	20	postwar questionnaire	
McMichael, James Robert	30	12th GA Infantry	captain	single	GA	Fort Delaware Prison	Marion County, GA	1,400	diary	
McPheeters, William M.	49	General Sterling Price's staff	surgeon	married	MO	Spring Hill, AR	St. Louis, MO	1,550	diary	indirect route
Mewborn, Joshua Wilson	21	13th TN Infantry	private	single	TN	Augusta, GA	Fayette County, TN	850	postwar questionnaire	
Miller, John M.	26	20th MS Infantry	private	single	MS	Greensboro, NC	Scott County, MS	700	memoir	
Mixson, Frank	18	1st SC Infantry	sergeant	single	SC	Appomattox Court House, VA	Joyce's Branch, SC	400	memoir	
Montgomery, Frank A.	35	1st MS Cavalry	lt. col.	married	MS	Columbus, GA	Bolivar County, MS	450	memoir	
Montomery, Walter A.	20	12th NC Infantry	2nd lieutenant	single	NC	Appomattox Court House, VA	Warrenton, NC	100	memoir	
Moore, Samuel Lewis	17	Georgia Reserves	private	single	GA	Fort Delaware Prison	Quitman, GA	1,200	memoir	
Morgan, William Henry	28	11th VA Infantry	captain/ 1st lt.	married	VA	Fort Delaware Prison	Campbell County, VA	700	memoir	
Morris, William G. B.	26	64th NC Infantry	captain	single	NC	Johnson's Island Prison, OH	Henderson County, NC	1,200	diary	

Name	Age	Unit	Rank	Marital	State	Location 1	Location 2	Number	Source	Notes
Mosteller, William David	18	4th GA Reserves	private	single	GA	Montgomery, AL	Cherokee County, GA	200	postwar questionnaire	
Mullen, James M.	19	13th Battalion NC Artillery	private	single	NC	Nash County, NC	Hertford, NC	125	memoir	
Murphree, Joel	37	57th AL Infantry	qm. sergeant	married	AL	Greensboro, NC	Troy, AL	550	memoir	
Nance, David C.	22	12th Texas Cavalry	private	single	TX	Robertson County, TX	Dallas County, TX	150	secondary source	
Nash, Francis H.	40	42nd GA Infantry	private	married	GA	High Point, NC	Alpharetta, GA	350	diary	
Neese, George M.	26	Thompson's Battery, Virginia Horse Artillery	corporal	single	VA	Point Lookout Prison, MD	Shenandoah County, VA	450	diary	
Nicholson, James William	21	12th LA Infantry	sergeant	single	LA	Greensboro, NC	Claiborne Parish, LA	1,450	memoir	
Nolen, William H.	21	12th LA Infantry	private	single	LA	Point Lookout Prison, MD	Claiborne Parish, LA	2,200	postwar questionnaire	aka Noland
Owen, William M.	32	Washington Artillery, LA	1st lieutenant	single	LA	Appomattox Court House, VA	New Orleans, LA	2,500	memoir	
Paine, Smith Ferguson	28	64th NC Infantry	sergeant	single	NC	Asheville, NC	Madison County, NC	15	postwar questionnaire	
Palmer, Joseph B.	39	18th TN Infantry	brig. general	widower	TN	Greensboro, NC	Murfreesboro, TN	550	secondary source	
Perkins, Thomas F.	18	11th VA Infantry	private	single	VA	Point Lookout Prison, MD	Bedford County, VA	475	postwar questionnaire	
Pickens, Samuel	24	5th AL Infantry	corporal	single	AL	Point Lookout Prison, MD	Greensboro, AL	1,200	diary	

NAME	AGE	UNIT	RANK	MARITAL STATUS	HOME STATE	STARTING LOCATION	DESTINATION	MILES	SOURCE	NOTES
Pinnell, Eathan Allen	30	8th MO Infantry	captain	single	MO	Shreveport, LA	Crawford County, MO	1,250	diary	
Poche, Felix Pierre	29	LA scout / partisan	captain	married	LA	Donaldsonville, LA	St. James Parish, LA	20	diary	
Polley, Joseph B.	24	4th TX Infantry	corporal	single	TX	Richmond, VA	Houston, TX	1,650	wartime letters with postwar edits	
Porter, Albert Quincy	39	22nd MS Infantry	private	married	MS	Greensboro. NC	Meadville, MS	900	diary	
Porter, John C.	21	18th TX Infantry	sergeant	single	TX	Hempstead, TX	Upshur County/ Camp County, TX	250	memoir	
Porter, John M.	25	9th KY Cavalry	2nd lieutenant	single	KY	Richmond, VA	Sugar Grove, KY	1,350	memoir	indirect route
Powers, James Madison	19	37th VA Infantry	private	single	VA	Appomattox Court House, VA	Washington County, VA	175	postwar questionnaire	
Prewitt, Milton Williamson	18	18th MS Cavalry	private	single	TN	Gainesville, AL	Hardeman County, TN	200	postwar questionnaire	
Pullen, Archibald Benton	21	2nd KY Infantry	sergeant	single	KY	Washington, GA	Graves County, KY	500	postwar questionnaire	
Reynolds, Abram David	18	5th VA Reserves	major (reserve / cadets)	single	VA	Danville, VA	Patrick County, VA	60	postwar questionnaire	
Ridley, Bromfield	22	Gen. AP Stewart staff's, Army of TN	1st lieutenant	single	TN	Greensboro, NC	Murfreesboro, TN	650	memoir/ diary	

Name	Age	Unit	Rank	Marital status	State	Surrender/Prison location	Home	Distance	Source	Notes
Riley, Franklin Lafayette	30	16th MS Infantry	private	married	MS	Point Lookout Prison, MD	Lawrence County, MS	1,600	diary	
Rowell, Samuel Benjamin	21	42nd MS Infantry	private	single	MS	Fort Delaware Prison	Senatobia, MS	1,450	postwar questionnaire	
Sanders, Lorenzo J.	26	30th TN Infantry/4th TN Consolidated	private	single	TN	Salem, NC	Sumner County, TN (now Macon County)	500	postwar questionnaire	
Segle, Louis M.	21	1st NC Cavalry	private	single	NC	Culpeper, VA	Burke County, NC	350	postwar questionnaire	
Semmes, Raphael	55	Naval Brigade	rear admiral / temporary brig. general	married	AL	Greensboro, NC	Mobile, AL	700	diary	
Shaver, Robert G.	34	Shaver's Infantry Regt. (AR)	colonel	married	AR	Marshall, TX	Jacksonport, AR	800	memoir	indirect route
Simpson, Avington W.	30	5th MO Infantry	1st lieutenant	single	MO	Meridian, MS	Bevier, MO	675	diary	did not go home immediately; brief visit home to MO, returned to MS to settle
Smith, Daniel Elliott Huger	19	Marion Artillery (SC Light Artillery)	private	single	SC	Greensboro, NC	Athens, GA	400	memoir	
Sorrel, G. Moxley	27	Mahone's Division, Army of Northern VA	brig. general	single	GA	Lynchburg, VA	Savannah, GA	1,500	memoir	indirect route
Stephenson, Philip D.	19	Washington Art., AOT	private	single	MO	Demopolis, AL	St. Louis, MO	750	memoir	

NAME	AGE	UNIT	RANK	MARITAL STATUS	HOME STATE	STARTING LOCATION	DESTINATION	MILES	SOURCE	NOTES
Taylor, Richard	39	Dept AL, MS, and East LA	lt. gen.	married	LA	Meridian, MS	New Orleans, LA	400	memoir	
Telford, Robert C.	32	1st SC Rifles	sergeant	married	SC	Hart's Island Prison, NY	Anderson County, SC	900	diary	
Terrell, William Alexander	20	3rd VA Cavalry	private	single	VA	Elmira Prison, NY	Goochland County, VA	550	postwar questionnaire	
Thompson, Isaac	22	64th VA Infantry	private	single	VA	Camp Douglas Prison, IL	Lee County, VA	700	postwar questionnaire	
Tillman, James Adams	23	24th SC Infantry	captain / 1st lt.	single	SC	High Point, NC	Edgefield County, SC	225	diary	
Todd, Samuel Newton	21	16th AL Infantry	private	single	AL	Macon, GA	Lauderdale County, AL	400	postwar questionnaire	
Townsend, Harry C.	22	Richmond Howitzers	corporal	single	VA	Charlotte, NC	Richmond, VA	300	diary	
Turner, James M.	21	6th Texas Infantry	corporal	single	TX	Camp Douglas Prison, IL	Travis County, TX	2,100	memoir	indirect route
Waldrop, John	25	1st VA Artillery	private	single	VA	Appomattox Court House, VA	Richmond, VA	125	diary	
Walker, Thomas Jefferson	23	9th TN Infantry	private	single	TN	Greensboro, NC	Haywood County, TN	1,000	memoir	
Walters, John H.	30	Norfolk Light Artillery Blues	private	single	VA	Appomattox Court House, VA	Norfolk, VA	250	diary	
Walthall, Howard Malcolm	23	1st VA Infantry	private	single	VA	Lynchburg, VA	Richmond, VA	100	memoir	

Name	Age	Regiment	Rank	Status	State	Location	Location	Number	Source
Weaks, Andrew Jackson	19	2nd KY Cavalry	private	single	TN	Washington, GA	Cumberland City, TN	425	postwar questionnaire
Wheaton, John F.	43	Chatham Artillery (GA)	captain	married	GA	Greensboro, NC	Savannah, GA	400	memoir
Wheeler, Samuel V.	25	51st VA Infantry	sergeant	single	VA	Fort Delaware Prison	Wythe County, VA	550	postwar questionnaire
Whitehorne, James E.	24	12th VA Infantry	sergeant	single	VA	Appomattox Court House, VA	Greensville County, VA	100	diary
Wilson, Henry Felix	27	3rd AL Infantry	private	single	AL	Appomattox Court House, VA	De Kalb, MS	1,000	diary
Wise, John S.	18	Army of Northern VA	lieutenant	single	VA	Greensboro, NC	Richmond, VA	200	memoir
Wood, James H.	23	37th VA Infantry	captain	single	VA	Fort Delaware Prison	Gate City, VA	650	memoir
Woolwine, Rufus J.	24	51st VA Infantry	captain	single	VA	Fort Delaware Prison	Patrick County, VA	600	diary
Worsham, John H.	25	21st VA Infantry	private	single	VA	Richmond, VA	Richmond, VA	0	memoir
Worsham, William J.	25	19th TN Infantry	musician	single	TN	Greensboro, NC	Knox County, TN	300	memoir
Wright, Thomas Clark	27	1st Regt Thomas Legion	private	single	TN	Indianapolis, IN	Oliver Springs, TN	400	postwar questionnaire
Zimmerman, John Robert	26	17th VA Infantry	private	single	VA	Appomattox Court House, VA	Alexandria, VA	350	diary

NOTES

INTRODUCTION

1. Martin Whitlock, "A Confederate Soldier Returns after the War to Hear of His Funeral Preached," in *Recollections and Reminiscences, 1861–1865* (South Carolina Division, United Daughters of the Confederacy, 1990), vol. 1, 270.

2. Whitlock, "A Confederate Soldier Returns," vol. 1, 270; Compiled Records Showing Service of Military Units in Confederate Organizations, Record Group 109, War Department Collection of Confederate Records, National Archives, Washington, DC; United States Bureau of the Census, Eighth U.S. Census, 1860, Schedule 1 (Free Inhabitants).

3. Dixon Wecter, *When Johnny Comes Marching Home* (Cambridge, MA: Houghton Mifflin, 1944), 104–21; William B. Holberton, *Homeward Bound: The Demobilization of the Union and Confederate Armies, 1865–1866* (Mechanicsburg, PA: Stackpole Books, 2001), xii–xvi, 7, 15–16, 28, 37; John C. Sparrow, *History of Personnel Demobilization in the United States Army* (Washington, DC: Department of the Army, 1952), 5–8; Yael A. Sternhell, *Routes of War: The World of Movement in the Confederate South* (Cambridge, MA: Harvard University Press, 2012), 164–67; Brian Matthew Jordan, *Marching Home: Union Veterans and Their Unending Civil War* (New York: W. W. Norton, 2014), 7, 31–32, 34; Gary W. Gallagher, *The Confederate War: How Popular Will, Nationalism, and Military Strategy Could Not Stave Off Defeat* (Cambridge, MA: Harvard University Press, 1997), 168–72; Holberton, "Confederate Demobilization," in Larry M. Logue and Michael Barton, eds., *The Civil War Veteran: A Historical Reader* (New York: New York University Press, 2007), 22–30; James M. McCaffrey, *This Band of Heroes: Granbury's Texas Brigade, CSA* (Austin, TX: Eakin, 1985), 156; Ida M. Tarbell, "Disbanding the Confederate Army" (1901; reprint, *Civil War Times Illustrated* 6, no. 9 (January 1968): 10–19); James Nicholson, *Stories of Dixie* (New York: American Books, 1915), 238–39.

For just a small sample of firsthand accounts written by soldiers that advance some version of this interpretation, see Valerius C. Giles, *Rags and Hope: The Recollections of Val. C. Giles, Four Years with Hood's Brigade, Fourth Texas Infantry, 1861–1865* (New York: Coward-McCann, 1961), 278–79; Ada Christine Lightsey, *The Veteran's Story* (Meridian, MS: Meridian News, 1899), 44; W. A. McClendon, *Recollections of War Times: By an Old Veteran While under Stonewall Jackson and Lieutenant General James Longstreet: How I Got In, and How I Got Out* (Montgomery, AL: Paragon Press, 1909), 234–35; Frank Mixson, *Reminiscences of a Private* (Columbia, SC: State Company, 1910),

123; Bromfield L. Ridley, *Battles and Sketches of the Army of Tennessee* (Mexico, MO: Printing and Publishing, 1906), 483–84; William Alexander Smith, *The Anson Guards: Company C Fourteenth Regiment North Carolina Volunteers, 1861–1865* (Charlotte, NC: Stone Publishing, 1914), 306–9; George C. Underwood, *History of the Twenty-Sixth Regiment of the North Carolina Troops in the Great War, 1861–1865* (Goldsboro, NC: Nash Bros., 1901), 91; W. A. Callaway, "Reminiscences of War at the Close," *Confederate Veteran Magazine* 17, no. 10 (October 1909): 504–5.

4. Eric J. Leeds, *No Man's Land: Combat & Identity in World War I* (London: Cambridge University Press, 1979), 12–29.

5. For a small sample of the best scholarship on common Civil War soldiers, see James M. McPherson, *For Cause and Comrades: Why Men Fought in the Civil War* (New York: Oxford University Press, 1997); Kenneth W. Noe, *Reluctant Rebels: The Confederates Who Joined the Army after 1861* (Chapel Hill: University of North Carolina Press, 2010); Aaron Sheehan-Dean, ed., *The View from the Ground: Experiences of Civil War Soldiers* (Lexington: University of Kentucky Press, 2007); Earl J. Hess, *The Union Soldier in Battle: Enduring the Ordeal of Combat* (Lawrence: University Press of Kansas, 1997); Larry J. Daniel, *Soldiering in the Army of Tennessee: A Portrait of Life in a Confederate Army* (Chapel Hill: University of North Carolina Press, 1991); Joseph T. Glatthaar, *The March to the Sea and Beyond: Sherman's Troops in the Savannah and Carolinas Campaign* (New York: New York University Press, 1985).

For studies of Civil War veterans, see Paul A. Cimbala, *Veterans North and South: The Transition from Soldier to Civilian after the American Civil War* (Santa Barbara, CA: Praeger, 2015); James Marten, *Sing Not War: The Lives of Union and Confederate Veterans in Gilded Age America* (Chapel Hill: University of North Carolina Press, 2011); Brian Matthew Jordan and Evan C. Rothera, eds., *The War Went On: Reconsidering the Lives of Civil War Veterans* (Baton Rouge: Louisiana State University Press, 2020); Caroline E. Janney, *Remembering the Civil War: Reunion and the Limits of Reconciliation* (Chapel Hill: University of North Carolina Press, 2013); Jordan, *Marching Home*; Eric T. Dean, *Shook Over Hell: Post-Traumatic Stress, Vietnam, and the Civil War* (Cambridge, MA: Harvard University Press, 1999); David W. Blight, *Race and Reunion: The Civil War in Memory* (Cambridge, MA: Harvard University Press, 2001); Barbara A. Gannon, *The Won Cause: Black and White Comradeship in the Grand Army of the Republic* (Chapel Hill: University of North Carolina Press, 2011); Logue and Barton, eds., *The Civil War Veteran*; Larry M. Logue, *To Appomattox and Beyond: The Civil War Soldier in War and Peace* (Chicago: Ivan R. Dee, 1996); Jeffrey W. McClurken, *Take Care of the Living: Reconstructing Confederate Veteran Families in Virginia* (Charlottesville: University of Virginia Press, 2009); David Silkenat, *Moments of Despair: Suicide, Divorce, and Debt in Civil War Era North Carolina* (Chapel Hill: University of North Carolina Press, 2011).

For a thorough summary of the state of the field of veterans' studies, see Marten, "Civil War Veterans," in Aaron Sheehan-Dean, ed., *A Companion to the U.S. Civil War* (Chichester, West Sussex: John Wiley & Sons, 2014), vol. 1, 608–28.

6. Lightsey, *The Veteran's Story*, 44 (first quotation); James I. Longstreet, *From Manassas to Appomattox: Memoirs of the Civil War in America* (Philadelphia: J. B. Lippincott, 1896), 631 (second quotation).

7. Joseph McClure, "A Wounded Texan's Trip Home on Crutches," *Confederate Veteran Magazine* 17 (April 1909): 162–63.

8. *Tennessee Civil War Veteran Questionnaires* (5 vols.) (Easley, SC: Southern Historical Press, 1985), vol. 1, 163 (quotation) (hereafter cited as *TCWVQ*); Logue, *To Appomattox and Beyond*, 81; Holberton, *Homeward Bound*, 37, 39–52.

9. John Overton Casler, *Four Years in the Stonewall Brigade* (Guthrie, OK: State Capital Printing, 1903), 289.

10. John H. Worsham, *One of Jackson's Foot Cavalry* (New York: Neale Publishing, 1912), 342 (quotation); Nora Fontaine M. Davidson, *Cullings from the Confederacy* (Washington, DC: Rufus H. Darby Printing, 1903), 141–42.

11. Paul Fussell, *The Great War and Modern Memory* (London: Oxford University Press, 1975), see esp. 310–35 (quotations 310 and 326).

12. James J. Broomall, *Private Confederacies: The Emotional Worlds of Southern Men as Citizens and Soldiers* (Chapel Hill: University of North Carolina Press, 2019), 1–11.

13. Sparrow, *History of Personnel Demobilization in the United States Army;* Rex Pope, "British Demobilization after the Second World War," *Journal of Contemporary History* 30, no. 1 (January 1995): 65–81; John F. Shortal, "20th-Century Demobilization Lessons," *Military Review* 78 (5) (September–November 1998): 66–71; R. Alton Lee, "The Army 'Mutiny' of 1946," *Journal of American History* 53 (December 1966): 555–71; Daniel Eugene Garcia, "Class and Brass: Demobilization, Working Class Politics, and American Foreign Policy between World War and Cold War," *Diplomatic History* 34, no. 40 (2010): 681–98; W. Butler, "'The British Soldier Is No Bolshevik': The British Army, Discipline, and the Demobilization Strikes of 1919," *20th Century British History* 30, no. 3 (September 2001): 321–46.

14. Nicholson, *Stories of Dixie,* 206.

15. Johnson Hagood, *Memoirs of the War of Secession* (Columbia, SC: State Company, 1910), 372.

16. Joseph E. Johnston to Major General Lovell, May 5, 1865, in United States War Department, *The War of the Rebellion: A Compilation of the Official Records of the Union and Confederate Armies,* 128 vols. (hereafter cited as *Official Records*), (Washington, DC: Government Printing Office, 1880–1901), ser. 1, vol. 47, pt. 3, 872.

17. John H. Lewis, *Recollections from 1860 to 1865* (Washington, DC: Peake & Company Publishers, 1895), 91.

18. For the best studies of Civil War veterans' postwar adjustments over the course of generations, see Marten, *Sing Not War,* and Jordan, *Marching Home.*

19. For the most recognized explanation of the hibernation thesis, see Gerald Linderman, *Embattled Courage: The Experience of Combat in the American Civil War* (New York: Free Press, 1987), 266–97. For correctives to that thesis, see Brian Matthew Jordan, *Marching Home,* 68–69, 86, 99–100; Marten, *Sing Not War,* 8–11; and Broomall, *Private Confederacies,* 109–10.

20. The two important books in question are Blight, *Race and Reunion,* and Janney, *Remembering the Civil War.*

21. Brian Matthew Jordan, "Veterans in New Fields: Directions for Future Scholarship on Civil War Veterans," in Jordan and Rothera, eds., *The War Went On,* 311.

22. Excerpt from "When Will Papa Come?," *Confederate Veteran Magazine* 4 (1897): 311.

1. REBELS RESOLUTE: THE MIND OF JOHNNY REB UPON SURRENDER

1. James Edward Whitehorne Diary, April 9, 1865, Southern Historical Collection, University of North Carolina, Chapel Hill (hereafter cited as SHC).

2. Numerous studies support the general point that Lee's surrender shocked most southerners.

For examples that collectively illustrate a cross section of views from various parts of the Confederacy, see Joseph T. Glatthaar, *General Lee's Army: From Victory to Collapse* (New York: Free Press, 2008), 470–71; Thomas W. Cutrer, *Theater of a Separate War: The Civil War West of the Mississippi River, 1861–1865* (Chapel Hill: University of North Carolina Press, 2017), 427; William A. Marvel, *Lee's Last Retreat: The Flight to Appomattox* (Chapel Hill: University of North Carolina Press, 2002), 178, 183; Bradley R. Clampitt, *The Confederate Heartland: Military and Civilian Morale in the Western Confederacy* (Baton Rouge: Louisiana State University Press, 2011), 150–51; Robert M. Dunkerly, *The Confederate Surrender at Greensboro: The Final Days of the Army of Tennessee* (Jefferson, NC: McFarland, 2013), 108–12; Jason Phillips, *Diehard Rebels: The Confederate Culture of Invincibility* (Athens: University of Georgia Press, 2007), 169–72.

3. Robert G. Evans, ed., *The 16th Mississippi Infantry: Civil War Letters and Reminiscences* (Jackson: University Press of Mississippi, 2002), 307 (quotation); W. A. McClendon, *Recollections of War Times: By an Old Veteran While Under Stonewall Jackson and Lieutenant General James Longstreet: How I Got In, and How I Got Out* (Montgomery, AL: Paragon Press, 1909), 233–34; Susan Williams Benson, ed., *Berry Benson's Civil War Book: Memoirs of a Confederate Scout and Sharpshooter* (Athens: University of Georgia Press, 1962), 200; James Edward Whitehorne Diary, April 9, 1865, SHC; Edward M. Boykin, *The Falling Flag, Evacuation of Richmond, Retreat and Surrender at Appomattox, by An Officer of the Rear-Guard* (New York: E. J. Hale & Son, 1874), 61.

4. William C. Davis and Meredith L. Swentor, eds., *Bluegrass Confederate: The Headquarters Diary of Edward O. Guerrant* (Baton Rouge: Louisiana State University Press, 1999), 686; Lawrence R. Laboda, *From Selma to Appomattox: The History of the Jeff Davis Artillery* (Shippensburg, PA: White Mane Publishing, 1994), 313; Ruth Woods Dayton, ed., *The Diary of a Confederate Soldier: James E. Hall* (Lewisburg, WV, 1961), 135–36; John H. Worsham, *One of Jackson's Foot Cavalry: His Experience and What He Saw During the War 1861–1865, including a History of "F Company," Richmond, Va., 21st Regiment Virginia Infantry, Second Brigade, Jackson's Division, Second Corps, A. N. Va.* (New York: Neale Publishing, 1912), 290; William E. Bahlmann, "Down in the Ranks," *Journal of the Greenbrier Historical Society* 2, no. 2 (October 1979): 93.

5. William Sylvester Dillon Diary, April 18, 1865, Georgia Archives, Morrow (hereafter cited as Georgia Archives); John Porter Fort, *John Porter Fort, A Memorial and Personal Reminiscences* (New York: Knickerbocker Press, 1918), 35–36, 36 (first quotation); Johnson Hagood, *Memoirs of the War of Secession* (Columbia, SC: State Company, 1910), 368 (second quotation); Charles Crosland, *Reminiscences of the Sixties* (Columbia, SC: State Company, 1910), 50–51; Franklin Alexander Montgomery, *Reminiscences of a Mississippian in Peace and War, by Frank A. Montgomery, Lieutenant-Colonel First Mississippi Cavalry* (Cincinnati, OH: Robert Clarke Co. Press, 1901), 251–52; W. F. Pendleton, *Confederate Diary of Captain W. F. Pendleton, January to April 1865* (Bryn Athyn, PA, 1957), 19; A. D. Kirwan, ed., *Johnny Green of the Orphan Brigade: The Journal of a Confederate Soldier* (Louisville: University of Kentucky Press, 1956), 195; Roger S. Durham, ed., *The Blues in Gray: The Civil War Journal of William Daniel Dixon and the Republican Blues Daybook* (Knoxville: University of Tennessee Press, 2000), 276; Hambleton Tapp, ed., "A Sketch of the Early Life and Service in the Confederate Army of Dr. John A. Lewis of Georgetown, Ky.," *Register of the Kentucky Historical Society* 75 (April 1977): 137.

6. Richard Taylor, *Destruction and Reconstruction: Personal Experiences of the Late War* (New York: D. Appleton, 1879), 222; John Q. Anderson, ed., *Brokenburn: The Journal of Kate Stone, 1861–*

1868 (Baton Rouge: Louisiana State University Press, 1955), 330–31; S. B. Barron, *Lone Star Defenders: A Chronicle of the Third Texas Cavalry, Ross' Brigade* (New York: Neale Publishing Company, 1908), 274–75; Cutrer, *Theater of a Separate War,* 427; Clampitt, "The Breakup: The Collapse of the Confederate Trans-Mississippi Army in Texas, 1865," *Southwestern Historical Quarterly* 108 (April 2005): 502–3.

7. Warren J. Alston Diary, April 6 (quotation), 10, 1865, Georgia Archives; Miles Vance Smith, Reminiscences of the War," p. 65, Civil War Document Collection, United States Army Heritage and Education Center, Carlisle, Pennsylvania (hereafter cited as USAHEC); G. Ward Hubbs, ed., *Voices from Company D: Diaries by the Greensboro Guards, Fifth Alabama Infantry Regiment, Army of Northern Virginia* (Athens: University of Georgia Press, 2003), 366–71; Charles D. Spurlin, ed., *The Civil War Diary of Charles A. Leuschner* (Austin, TX: Eakin Press, 1992), 53; William Clyde Billingsley, ed., "'Such is War': The Confederate Memoirs of Newton Asbury Keen," pt. 4, *Texas Military History* 7 (Fall 1968): 183; John M. Copley, *A Sketch of the Battle of Franklin; with Reminiscences of Camp Douglas* (Austin, TX: Eugene von Boeckmann, 1893), 203; John S. McNeilly, "A Mississippi Brigade in the Last Days of the Confederacy," *Publications of the Mississippi Historical Society* 7 (1903): 53–54; Donald C. Pfanz, *Richard S. Ewell: A Soldier's Life* (Chapel Hill: University of North Carolina Press, 2000), 444.

8. William S. Haggard Diary, April 8–9, 1865, Special Collections Research Center, University of Kentucky Libraries, Lexington (hereafter cited as UK); Lavender R. Ray Diary, April 20, 23, 1865, Lavender R. Ray Papers, Georgia Archives; Winfield Scott Featherston Manuscript, Civil War Document Collection, USAHEC; Sarah Rousseau Espy Diary, May 14, 1865, Alabama Department of Archives and History (hereafter cited as ADAH); Arthur W. Bergeron Jr., ed., *The Civil War Reminiscences of Major Silas T. Grisamore, CSA* (Baton Rouge: Louisiana State University Press, 1993), 181; James T. Lambright, *History of the Liberty Independent Troop During the Civil War, 1862–1865* (Brunswick, GA: Press of Glover Brothers, 1910), unnumbered pages; Randolph H. McKim, *A Soldier's Recollections* (New York: Longmans, Green, 1910), 264; Jay F. Taylor, ed., *Reluctant Rebel: The Secret Diary of Robert Patrick, 1861–1865* (Baton Rouge: Louisiana State University Press, 1959), 27–28; Francis W. Dawson, *Reminiscences of Confederate Service, 1861–1865* (Charleston, SC: News and Courier Book Presses, 1882), 145; George Mitchell, "Memories of Surrender and Journey Home," *Confederate Veteran Magazine* 17, no. 4 (April 1909): 172; James M. Mullen, "Last Days of Johnston's Army, a Comrade's Experience with General L. S. Baker's Command at Weldon, N. C., During the Fifteen Days Preceding Johnston's Surrender at Greensboro, N.C.," *Southern Historical Society Papers* 18 (1890): 105.

9. James Edward Whitehorne Diary, April 1–10, 1865, SHC.

10. Howard Malcolm Walthall Reminiscences, 41–42, Civil War Document Collection, USAHEC; Sanford Venable Hughstone to wife, April 6, 1865, Sanford Venable Hughstone Letters, Mississippi Department of Archives and History, Jackson (hereafter cited as MDAH); James E. Green Diary, April 12, 13, 1865, SHC; William N. Still, ed., "The Civil War Letters of Robert Tarleton," *Alabama Historical Quarterly* 32 (Spring and Summer 1970): 51, 78–79, 80 (quotation).

11. Royce Gordon Shingleton, ed., "'With Loyalty and Honor as a Patriot': Recollections of a Confederate Soldier," *Alabama Historical Quarterly* 33 (Fall/Winter 1971): 262; Thomas Anthony Head, *Campaigns and Battles of the Sixteenth Regiment, Tennessee Volunteers, in the War Between the States* (Nashville, TN: Cumberland Presbyterian Publishing House, 1885), 155; J. A. Stikeleather,

"Recollections of the Civil War in the United States," 97 (first quotation), Bryan Grimes Papers, SHC; Bergeron, ed., *Reminiscences of Major Silas T. Grisamore*, 180–81; Kent Masterson Brown, ed., *One of Morgan's Men: Memoirs of Lieutenant John M. Porter of the Ninth Kentucky Cavalry* (Lexington: University of Kentucky Press, 2011), 195 (second quotation); John Overton Casler, *Four Years in the Stonewall Brigade* (Guthrie, OK: State Capital Printing, 1903), 284; Henry George, *History of the 3d, 7th, 8th, and 12th Kentucky, CSA* (Louisville, KY: C. T. Dearing Printing, 1911), 143.

12. George B. Guild, *A Brief Narrative of the Fourth Tennessee Cavalry Regiment, Wheeler's Corps, Army of Tennessee* (Nashville, TN: n. p., 1913), 145.

13. Vicki Betts, ed., "The Civil War Letters of Elbridge Littlejohn," *Chronicles of Smith County, Texas* 18 (Summer 1979): 35–36; Jacob Allison Frierson letters, April 18 (quotation), April 26, 1865, Jacob Allison Frierson Correspondence, Louisiana and Lower Mississippi Valley Collections, Hill Memorial Library, Louisiana State University, Baton Rouge (hereafter cited as LLMVC).

14. Benjamin R. Glover to Betty, April 10, 1865, Benjamin R. Glover Letters, ADAH; United States Bureau of the Census, Eighth U.S. Census, 1860, Schedule 1 (Free Inhabitants); Compiled Records Showing Service of Military Units in Confederate Organizations, Record Group 109, War Department Collection of Confederate Records, National Archives, Washington, DC.

15. Mark Grimsley, "Learning to Say 'Enough': Southern Generals and the Final Weeks of the Confederacy," in Grimsley and Brooks D. Simpson, eds., *The Collapse of the Confederacy* (Lincoln: University of Nebraska Press, 2001), 40–79; William B. Feis, "Jefferson Davis and the 'Guerilla Option': A Reexamination," in Grimsley and Simpson, eds., *The Collapse of the Confederacy*, 104–28; Clampitt, *Confederate Heartland*, 148–51; Marvel, *Lee's Last Retreat*, 183–84; J. Cutler Andrews, *The South Reports the Civil War* (Princeton, NJ: Princeton University Press, 1970), 503–5; Burke Davis, *The Long Surrender* (New York: Random House, 1985), see chapter 5.

16. Bell I. Wiley, ed., *This Infernal War: The Confederate Letters of Edwin H. Fay* (Austin: University of Texas Press, 1958), 441–42; Earl Schenck Miers, ed., *A Rebel War Clerk's Diary* (New York: Sagamor Press, 1958), 535; Paula Mitchell Marks, ed., *When Will the Weary War Be Over? The Civil War Letters of the Maverick Family of San Antonio* (Dallas: The Book Club of Texas, 2008), 228.

17. Henry Clay Dickinson, *Diary of Henry Dickinson, CSA, Morris Island, 1864–1865* (Denver, CO: Press of the Williamson-Haffner Co., n.d.), 179–83; George Peddy Cuttino, ed., *Saddle Bag and Spinning Wheel: Being the Civil War Letters of George W. Peddy, M. D., Surgeon, 56th Georgia Volunteers Regiment, CSA, and His Wife Kate Featherston Peddy* (Macon, GA: Mercer University Press, 1981), 313; Betts, ed., "The Civil War Letters of Elbridge Littlejohn," 36; Jacob Allison Frierson to Allison, April 26, 1865, Jacob Allison Frierson Correspondence, LLMVC; Fort, *John Porter Fort*, 35–36; Montgomery, *Reminiscences of a Mississippian in Peace and War*, 252; William S. Haggard Diary, April 10, 1865, UK.

18. Evan Shelby Jefferies to wife, April 15, 1865, 16th Mississippi Infantry File, Simpson History Complex, Hill College, Hillsboro, TX (hereafter cited as Hill College); George Lee Robertson to Julia, May 8, 1865 (quotation), George Lee Robertson Papers, Dolph Briscoe Center for American History, University of Texas, Austin (hereafter cited as DBCAH); Jacob Allison Frierson to Ma, April 18, 1865, Jacob Allison Frierson Correspondence, LLMVC; Joseph B. Polley, *Hood's Texas Brigade: Its Marches, Its Battles, Its Achievements* (New York: Neal Publishing, 1910), 277–78; Carlton McCarthy, *Detailed Minutiae of Soldier Life in the Army of Northern Virginia* (Richmond: Carlton McCarthy, 1894), 161; James I. Longstreet, *From Manassas to Appomattox: Memoirs of the Civil War in Amer-*

ica (Philadelphia: J. B. Lippincott, 1896), see chapter 43; Nat S. Turner III, ed., *A Southern Soldier's Letters Home: The Civil War Letters of Samuel A. Burney, Cobb's Georgia Legion, Army of Northern Virginia* (Macon, GA: Mercer University Press, 2002), 291–92.

19. Feis, "Jefferson Davis and the 'Guerilla Option,'" 104–28; Gary W. Gallagher, *The Confederate War: How Popular Will, Nationalism, and Military Strategy Could Not Stave Off Defeat* (Cambridge, MA: Harvard University Press, 1999), 140–53; Earl J. Hess, *The Civil War in the West: Victory and Defeat from the Appalachians to the Mississippi* (Chapel Hill: University of North Carolina Press, 2012), 291–94, 301–4; Cutrer, *Theater of a Separate War,* 435; Mary Elizabeth Sanders, ed., *Diary in Gray: Civil War Diary and Letters of Jared Young Sanders II* (Baton Rouge: Louisiana Genealogical & Historical Society, 1994), 93–95; George Alexander Martin Diary, April 9, 1865, Virginia Historical Society, Richmond (hereafter cited as VHS); Cullen A. Battle Manuscript, 133–34, ADAH; Charles Woodward Hutson Diary, April 8, 1865, Charles Woodward Hutson Papers, SHC; Lawson Jefferson Keener, *Letters from Lawson Jefferson Keener Written During His Confederate Service to Alcesta (Allie) Benson Carter* (Longview, TX: Mrs. Rogers Lacy, 1963), unnumbered pages, see May 13 entry; Richard Lowe, ed., *A Texas Cavalry Officer's Civil War: The Diary and Letters of James C. Bates* (Baton Rouge: Louisiana State University Press, 1999), 332; Wiley, ed., *This Infernal War,* 443–44; Joshua Hilary Hudson, *Sketches and Reminiscences* (Columbia, SC: State Company, 1903), 70; James Troy Massey, ed., *Memoirs of Captain J. M. Bailey* (James Troy Massey, 1994), 103.

20. Thomas L. Connelly, *Autumn of Glory: The Army of Tennessee, 1862–1865* (Baton Rouge: Louisiana State University Press, 1971), 531–34; Perry D. Jamieson, *Spring 1865: The Closing Campaigns of the Civil War* (Lincoln: University of Nebraska Press, 2015), 179–83; Davis, *The Long Surrender,* see chapter 5. For a detailed assessment of the motives and proposals of Davis and the various officers and cabinet officials during the closing weeks of the war, see William C. Davis, *An Honorable Defeat: The Last Days of the Confederate Government* (New York: Harcourt, 2001).

21. Joseph T. Durkin, ed., *John Dooley: Confederate Soldier. His War Journal* (Washington, DC: Georgetown University Press, 1945), 181–85; Charles Woodward Hutson Diary, April 11, 1865, SHC; Benson, ed., *Berry Benson's Civil War Book,* 200–201; James M. McCaffrey, ed., *Only a Private: A Texan Remembers the Civil War: The Memoirs of William J. Oliphant* (Houston: Halcyon Press, 2004), 86–88; George Dallas Mosgrove, *Kentucky Cavaliers in Dixie; or The Reminiscences of a Confederate Cavalryman* (Louisville, KY: *Carrier-Journal* Job Printing Co., 1895), 262–63; R. M. Collins, *Chapters from the Unwritten History of the War Between the States; or, the Incidents in the Life of a Confederate Soldier* (St. Louis: Nixon-Jones Printing, 1893), 300; George C. Underwood, *History of the Twenty-Sixth Regiment of the North Carolina Troops in the Great War, 1861–1865* (Goldsboro, NC: Nash Bros., 1901), 91, 100–101; John Sergeant Wise, *The End of an Era* (Boston: Houghton Mifflin, 1899), 448; Laboda, *From Selma to Appomattox,* 312; John Herbert Roper, ed., *Repairing the "March of Mars": The Civil War Diaries of John Samuel Apperson, Hospital Steward in the Stonewall Brigade, 1861–1865* (Macon, GA: Mercer University Press, 2001), 614; Davis and Swentor, eds., *Bluegrass Confederate,* 686–87.

22. Jubal A. Early, *A Memoir of the Last Year of the War for Independence in the Confederate States of America Containing an Account of His Commands in the Years 1864 and 1865* (Toronto: Lovell & Gibson, 1866), 138 (quotation); Guild, *A Brief Narrative of the Fourth Tennessee Cavalry Regiment,* 145; Thomas W. Cutrer and T. Michael Parrish, eds., *Brothers in Gray: The Civil War Letters of the Pierson Family* (Baton Rouge: Louisiana State University Press, 1997), 259–60; Lavender

Ray Diary, April 20, 1865, Georgia Archives; George Alexander Martin Diary, April 9, 25, 26, May 9, 1865, VHS; Michael E. Banasik, ed., *Serving with Honor: The Diary of Captain Eathan Allen Pinnell, Eighth Missouri Infantry (Confederate)* (Iowa City: Camp Pope Bookshop, 1999), 217–21; Marks, ed., *When Will the Weary War Be Over?*, 184–98, 215–29; Miers, ed., *A Rebel War Clerk's Diary*, 536; Francis R. Lubbock, *Six Decades in Texas* (Austin, TX: Ben C. Jones, 1900), 575; William Physick Zuber, *My Eighty Years in Texas* (Austin: University of Texas Press, 1971), 226; Kirwan, ed., *Johnny Green of the Orphan Brigade*, 195; Howell Carter, *A Cavalryman's Reminiscences of the Civil War* (New Orleans: American Printing, 1900), 126; Arch Frederic Blakey, Ann Smith Lainhart, and Winston Bryant Stephens Jr., eds., *Rose Cottage Chronicles: Civil War Letters of the Bryant-Stephens Families of North Florida* (Gainesville: University of Florida Press, 1998), 365–66; Patricia J. Bennett, ed., "Curtis R. Burke's Civil War Journal" (pt. 4) *Indiana Magazine of History* 67 (June 1971): 159–63.

For less descriptive discussions of continued resistance in the Trans-Mississippi theater, see Mosgrove, *Kentucky Cavaliers in Dixie,* 262–63; Collins, *Chapters from the Unwritten History of the War Between the States,* 300; Hubbs, ed., *Voices from Company D,* 381; Mauriel Phillips Joslyn, ed., *Charlotte's Boys: Civil War Letters of the Branch Family of Savannah* (Berryville, VA: Rockbridge Publishing, 1996), 302; W. J. Lemke, ed., *The War-time Letters of Captain T. C. Dupree, CSA, 1864–1865* (Fayetteville, AR: Washington County Historical Society, 1953), unnumbered pages; John Preston Young, *The Seventh Tennessee Cavalry (Confederate), A History* (Nashville, TN: Publishing House of the Methodist Episcopal Church, South, 1890), 136–37.

23. Banasik, ed., *Serving with Honor,* 217–19, 220 (quotation), 221; Marks, ed., *When Will the Weary War Be Over?*, 184–98, 215–29; Winchester Hall, *The Story of the 26th Louisiana Infantry in the Service of the Confederate States* (n.p., 1890), 133; Bell I. Wiley, ed., *Fourteen Hundred Ninety-one Days in the Confederate Army* (Jackson, TN: McCowat-Mercer Press, 1954), 239; George Lee Robertson to Julia, May 8, 1865, George Lee Robertson Papers, DBCAH.

24. George T. Todd, *Sketch of History: The First Texas Regiment, Hood's Brigade, Army of Northern Virginia* (Waco, TX: Texian Press, 1963), 27; Polley, *Hood's Texas Brigade,* 277–78; Richard Taylor, *Destruction and Reconstruction: Personal Experiences of the Late War* (New York: D. Appleton, 1879), 226.

25. Grimsley and Simpson, eds., *Collapse of the Confederacy,* 1–8; Hess, *The Civil War in the West,* 286–303; Cutrer, *Theater of a Separate War,* 427–37; Clampitt, *Confederate Heartland,* 148–51; Michael L. Bradley, *This Astounding Close: The Road to Bennett Place* (Chapel Hill: University of North Carolina Press, 2000), 200–205; Dunkerly, *The Confederate Surrender at Greensboro,* 107–12; John H. Worsham, *One of Jackson's Foot Cavalry,* 290; W. J. Worsham, *The Old Nineteenth Tennessee Regiment, CSA June 1861–April 1865* (Knoxville, TN: Press of Paragon Printing, 1902), 177 (quotation).

26. George E. Pickett, *The Heart of a Soldier, as Revealed in the Intimate Letters of Genl. George E. Pickett, CSA* (New York: Seth Moyle, 1913), 176–79 (quotation 179); Thomas P. Nanzig, ed., *The Civil War Memoirs of a Virginia Cavalryman: Lt. Robert T. Hubbard, Jr.* (Tuscaloosa: University of Alabama Press, 2007), 213–14, 220; Lewellyn A. Shaver, *A History of the Sixtieth Alabama Regiment, Gracie's Alabama Brigade* (Montgomery, AL: Barrett & Brown, Publishers, 1867), 100–101; William Miller Owen, *A Soldier's Story, Including the Marches and Battles of the Washington Artillery and of Other Louisiana Troops* (New Orleans: Clark & Hofeline, Book Printers, 1874), 211; Maurice S. Fortin, ed., "Colonel Hilary A. Herbert's 'History of the Eighth Alabama Volunteer Regiment, CSA,'" *Alabama Historical Quarterly* 39 (1977): 184.

27. William Alexander Smith, *The Anson Guards: Company C Fourteenth Regiment North Carolina Volunteers, 1861–1865* (Charlotte, NC: Stone Publishing, 1914), 306 (quotation); Walter Alexan-

der Montgomery, *The Days of Old and the Years That Are Past* (Charlottesville, VA: Michie, 1939), 60; Evans, ed., *The 16th Mississippi Infantry*, 307; George Jefferson Hundley, "Beginning and the Ending, Reminiscences of the First and Last Days of the War, by Gen. George Hundley," *Southern Historical Society Papers* XXIII (1895): 312; Bahlmann, "Down in the Ranks," 93.

28. Robert H. Dacus, *Reminiscences of Company "H," First Arkansas Mounted Rifles* (Dardanelle, AR: Post-Despatch Printing, 1897), 26; Winfield Scott Featherston Manuscript, Civil War Document Collection, USAHEC; R. B. Meadows, "Experiences and Recollections of R. B. Meadows" 46, ADAH; H. W. Barclay Reminiscences, unnumbered pages, DBCAH; William Campbell Preston Breckinridge, "The ex-Confederate and What He Has Done in Peace," *Southern Historical Society Papers* 20 (1892): 227; Mullen, "Last Days of Johnston's Army," 105; Tapp, ed., "A Sketch of the Early Life and Service in the Confederate Army of Dr. John A. Lewis," 137; Walter Augustus Clark, *Under the Stars and Bars; or, Memories of Four Years Service with the Oglethorpes, of Augusta, Georgia* (Augusta, GA: Chronicle Printing, 1900), 198–99; Valerius C. Giles, *Rags and Hope: The Recollections of Val. C. Giles, Four Years with Hood's Brigade, Fourth Texas Infantry, 1861–1865* (New York: Coward-McCann, 1961), 276–77; W. J. McMurray, *History of the Twentieth Tennessee Regiment Volunteer Infantry, CSA* (Nashville, TN: Publication Committee, 1904), 358; Bromfield L. Ridley, *Battles and Sketches of the Army of Tennessee* (Mexico, MO: Printing and Publishing, 1906), 458; Taylor, *Destruction and Reconstruction*, 222–23.

29. John C. Porter, "The Life of John C. Porter and Sketch of His Experiences in the Civil War," Simpson History Complex, Hill College, Hillsboro, Texas (hereafter cited as Hill College); John Bateman Rushing Autobiography, 11, Civil War Document Collection, USAHEC; X. B. Debray, *A Sketch of the History of Debray's 26th Regiment of Texas Cavalry* (Waco, TX: Waco Village Press, 1961), 25; Thomas North, *Five Years in Texas; or, What You Did Not Hear During the War from January 1861 to January 1866* (Cincinnati, OH: Elm Street Printing, 1871), 183; Thomas Benton Reed, *A Private in Gray* (Camden, AR: T. B. Reed, 1905), 117; Mamie Yeary, ed., *Reminiscences of the Boys in Gray, 1861–1865* (Dallas: Smith and Lamar, M. E. Church, South, 1912), 832; Zuber, *My Eighty Years in Texas*, 226.

30. G. Moxley Sorrel, *Recollections of a Staff Officer* (New York: Neale Publishing, 1905), 289.

31. William D. Alexander Diary, April 9, 1865, SHC; Charles Woodward Hutson Diary, April 11, 18, 1865, SHC; J. E. Whitehorne Diary, April 22, 1865, SHC; William S. Haggard Diary, April 9–23, 1865, UK; George H. Murphy Diary, April 12, 1865, Hesburgh Libraries, Special Collections, University of Notre Dame, Notre Dame, Indiana (hereafter cited as UND); Edward Crenshaw, "Diary of Captain Edward Crenshaw of the Confederate States Army," *Alabama Historical Quarterly* 2 (Winter 1940): 466; Jack Sullivan, ed., "'The Dark Clouds of War': The Civil War Diary of John Zimmerman of Alexandria. Part II The Journey Toward Appomattox," *The Alexandria Chronicle* (Fall 2014): 12; Archie P. McDonald, ed., *Make Me a Map of the Valley: The Civil War Journal of Stonewall Jackson's Topographer* (Dallas: Southern Methodist University Press, 1973), 265–66; Miers, ed., *A Rebel War Clerk's Diary*, 535–36; Roper, ed., *Repairing the "March of Mars,"* 612; Festus P. Summers, ed., *A Borderland Confederate* (Pittsburgh, PA: University of Pittsburgh Press, 1962), 104–6.

32. Gaines M. Foster, *Ghosts of the Confederacy: Defeat, the Lost Cause, and the Emergence of the New South* (New York: Oxford University Press, 1987), 104–7.

33. Edwin C. Bearss, ed., *A Louisiana Confederate; Diary of Felix Pierre Poche* (Natchitoches: Louisiana Studies Institute, Northwestern State University, 1972), 237 (quotation); Richard A. Baumgartner, ed., *Blood and Sacrifice: The Civil War Journal of A Confederate Soldier* (Huntington,

WV: Blue Acorn Press, 1994), 219–23; Lemke, ed., *The War-time Letters of Captain T. C. Dupree*, unnumbered pages; Turner, ed., *A Southern Soldier's Letters Home*, 291–92; Wiley, ed., *This Infernal War*, 441–42; W. A. Johnson, "Closing Days with Johnston," *National Tribune*, June 5, 1902. Johnson's article is a 1902 reprint of his wartime diary.

34. James Bennington Irvine Diary, April 10, 21 (quotation), 1865, Newberry Library, Chicago, Illinois (hereafter cited as Newberry Library); James Robert McMichael Diary, April 9, 20, 26, May 2, 7, 1865, SHC; Warren J. Alston Diary, June 22, 1865, Georgia Archives; Dickinson, *Diary of Henry Dickinson*, 179–87; Anne King Gregorie, ed., "Diary of Captain Joseph Julius Westcoat, 1863–1865" (pt. 2), *South Carolina Historical Magazine* 59 (April 1958): 94–95; Robert E. Park, "Diary of Captain Robert E. Park, Twelfth Alabama Regiment," *Southern Historical Society Papers* 3 (January–June 1887): 244–53; Louis Leon, *Diary of a Tar-Heel Confederate Soldier* (Charlotte: NC: Stone Publishing, 1913), 69–71; George M. Neese, *Three Years in the Confederate Horse Artillery* (New York: Neale Publishing, 1911), 352–53; William H. Runge, ed., *Four Years in the Confederate Artillery: The Diary of Henry Robinson Berkeley* (Richmond: Virginia Historical Society, 1991), 133, 135, 142; Thomas R. Campbell, ed., *Southern Service on Land and Sea: The Wartime Journal of Robert Watson, CSA/CSN* (Knoxville: University of Tennessee Press, 2002), 162; Maddie Lou Teague Crow, ed., *The Diary of a Confederate Soldier: John Washington Inzer* (Huntsville, AL: Strode Publishers, 1977), 132–43; McHenry Howard, *Recollections of a Maryland Confederate Soldier and Staff Officer Under Johnston, Jackson, and Lee* (Dayton, OH: Morningside Bookshop, 1975), 402–3; Hubbs, ed., *Voices from Company D*, 368, 371, 377–78; Terry L. Jones, ed., *Campbell Brown's Civil War: With Ewell in the Army of Northern Virginia* (Baton Rouge: Louisiana State University Press, 2001), 295–96; W. H. Morgan, *Personal Reminiscences of the War 1861–5* (Lynchburg, VA: J. P. Bell, 1911), 266–69; Dan Oates, ed., *Hanging Rock Rebel: Lt. John Blue's War in West Virginia and the Shenandoah Valley* (Shippensburg, PA: Burd Street Press, 1994), 312.

35. James E. Green Diary, April 12–May 8, 1865, SHC; S. M. Gross Journal, April 16–May 2, 1865, South Caroliniana Library, University of South Carolina, Columbia (hereafter cited as USC); Blakey, Lainhart, and Stephens, eds., *Rose Cottage Chronicles*, 363; Norman D. Brown, ed., *One of Cleburne's Command: The Civil War Reminiscences and Diary of Captain Samuel T. Foster, Granbury's Texas Brigade, CSA* (Austin: University of Texas Press, 1980), 163–64, 167–70; William C. Davis, ed., *Diary of a Confederate Soldier: John S. Jackman of the Orphan Brigade* (Columbia: University of South Carolina Press, 1990), 166–67; Cutrer and Parrish, eds., *Brothers in Gray*, 256–58; Durham, ed., *The Blues in Gray*, 276–77; Kirwan, ed., *Johnny Green of the Orphan Brigade*, 195; Cynthia Dehaven Pitcock and Bill J. Gurley, eds., *I Acted from Principle: The Civil War Diary of Dr. William M. McPheeters, Confederate Surgeon in the Trans-Mississippi* (Fayetteville: University of Arkansas Press, 2002), 295–300; William A. Fletcher, *Rebel Private Front and Rear: Memoirs of a Confederate Soldier* (New York: Dutton, 1995), 194; John Wetmore Hinsdale, *History of the Seventy-Second Regiment of the North Carolina Troops in the War Between the States, 1861–1865* (Goldsboro, NC: Nash Brothers, 1901), 30; Charles C. Jones Jr., *Historical Sketch of the Chatham Artillery during the Confederate Struggle for Independence* (Albany, NY: Joel Munsell, 1867), 215–16; Massey, ed., *Memoirs of Captain J. M. Bailey*, 103; D. H. Cooper to T. M. Scott, May 10, 1865, in United States War Department, *The War of the Rebellion: A Compilation of the Official Records of the Union and Confederate Armies*, 128 vols. (hereafter cited as *Official Records*), (Washington, DC: Government Printing Office, 1880–1901), ser. 1, vol. 48, pt. 2, 1297; Clampitt, *Confederate Heartland*, 148–60.

For eastern theater soldiers, including prisoners of war, see Chris Fordney, ed., "Letters from the Heart," *Civil War Times Illustrated* 34 (September/October 1995): 81–82; Morgan, *Personal Reminiscences of the War,* 266–67; Harry C. Townshend, "Townshend's Diary—January–May, 1865; From Petersburg to Appomattox, Thence to North Carolina to Join Johnston's Army," *Southern Historical Society Papers* 34 (1906): 111–25; Laboda, *From Selma to Appomattox,* 312; Wise, *The End of an Era,* 448.

36. Robert G. Shaver, "Recollections and Reminiscences of the Last Days of the Confederate Trans-Mississippi Department, Marshall, Texas," 2, Robert G. Shaver Papers, Arkansas History Commission, Little Rock (hereafter cited as AHC); Unknown Confederate Soldier Diary, May 14, 1865, AHC.

37. Park, "Diary of Captain Robert E. Park," 251–52; Joseph P. Blessington, *The Campaigns of Walker's Texas Division* (New York: Lange, Little, 1875), 303–6; John Bell Hood, *Advance and Retreat: Personal Experiences in the United States and Confederate States Armies* (Bloomington: Indiana University Press, 1959), 311.

38. William Nelson Pendleton to Major J. G. Payton, May 5, 1865, William Nelson Pendleton Papers, SHC; Lavender R. Ray Diary, April 20, 22, 23, 28, 1865, Lavender R. Ray Papers, Georgia Archives; William S. Haggard Diary, April 9–23, 1865, UK; Henry Brockman Journal, April–May, 1865 entries, AHC; George Lee Robertson to Julia, May 8, 1865, George Lee Robertson Papers, DBCAH; Frederick W. Moore, ed., "Diary of Maj. Kinloch Falconer," *Confederate Veteran Magazine* 9 (September 1901): 408; Banasik, ed., *Serving with Honor,* 222–23; John K. Bettersworth, ed., *Mississippi in the Confederacy: As They Saw It* (Baton Rouge: Louisiana State University Press, 1961), 358; Collins, *Chapters from the Unwritten History of the War Between the States,* 300; Sarah Anne Dorsey, ed., *Recollections of Henry Watkins Allen, Brigadier General Confederate States Army, ex-Governor of Louisiana* (New York: M. Doolady, 1866), 286–94; Durkin, ed., *John Dooley,* 181–82, 185, 195; Carter, *A Cavalryman's Reminiscences,* 126; Cuttino, ed., *Saddle Bag and Spinning Wheel,* 313; Hall, *The Story of the 26th Louisiana Infantry,* 133; Marks, ed., *When Will the Weary War Be Over?,* 184–98, 218–29; W. Stanley Hoole, ed., "Admiral on Horseback: The Diary of Brigadier General Raphael Semmes, February–May, 1865," *Alabama Review* 28 (April 1975): 131–32, 141; Max Lale, "The Military Occupation of Marshall, Texas, by the 8th Illinois Volunteer Infantry U.S.A., 1865," *Military History of Texas and the Southwest* 13, no. 3 (1976): 41; Ralph A. Wooster and Robert Wooster, eds., "'Rarin' for a Fight': Texans in the Confederate Army," *Southwestern Historical Quarterly* 84 (April 1981): 426.

39. George Cary Eggleston, *A Rebel's Recollections* (New York: Hurd and Houghton, 1874), 229 (quotation), 229–44; William Sylvester Dillon Diary, April 30, May 5, 6, 1865, Georgia Archives; Fort, *John Porter Fort,* 35–36; Charles G. Williams, ed., "A Saline Guard: The Civil War Letters of Col. William Ayers Crawford, CSA, 1861–1865" (pt. 2), *Arkansas Historical Quarterly* 32 (Spring 1973): 90–92; Jon Harrison, ed., "The Confederate Letters of John Simmons," *Chronicles of Smith County, Texas* 14 (Summer 1975): 49–51; James Dinkins, *1861 to 1865, by an Old Johnnie, Personal Recollections and Experiences in the Confederate Army* (Cincinnati, OH: Robert Clarke, 1897), 256; Wiley, ed., *Fourteen Hundred Ninety-one Days,* 239–45; Young, *The Seventh Tennessee Cavalry,* 136–37; Hall, *The Story of the 26th Louisiana Infantry,* 133–35; John D. Winters, *The Civil War in Louisiana* (Baton Rouge: Louisiana State University Press, 1963), 418–25; Rod Andrew Jr., *Wade Hampton: Confederate Warrior to Southern Redeemer* (Chapel Hill: University of North Carolina Press, 2008), 293–301; Clampitt, "The Breakup," 499–507, 534; Clampitt, "'An Indian Shall Not Spill an Indian's Blood': The Confederate-Indian Conference at Camp Napoleon, Indian Territory, 1865," *Chronicles of Oklahoma*

83 (Spring 2005): 34–42; Gayle Ann Brown, "Confederate Surrenders in Indian Territory," *Journal of the West* 12 (1973): 458.

40. Crenshaw, "Diary of Captain Edward Crenshaw," 468–69; James Bennington Irvine Diary, May 1, 1865, Newberry Library (quotation); Baumgartner, ed., *Blood and Sacrifice*, 219–21; William T. Alderson, ed., "The Civil War Reminiscences of John Johnston, 1861–1865" (pt. 6), *Tennessee Historical Quarterly* 14 (June 1955): 170–72; Bradley, *This Astounding Close*, 200–203.

41. Clampitt, "The Breakup," 503–8, 534; Harrison, ed., "The Confederate Letters of John Simmons," 53 (quotation); Cutrer and Parrish, eds., *Brothers in Gray*, 256–57; Minetta Altgelt Goyne, ed., *Lone Star and Double Eagle: Civil War Letters of a German Family* (Fort Worth: Texas Christian University, 1982), 168–69; Banasik, ed., *Serving with Honor*, 221 24; M. Jane Johansson, *Peculiar Honor: A History of the 28th Texas Cavalry, 1862–1865* (Fayetteville: University of Arkansas Press, 1998), 135; William W. White, "The Disintegration of an Army: Confederate Forces in Texas, April–June, 1865," *East Texas Historical Journal* 26, no. 2 (1988): 41–43; *Houston Tri-weekly Telegraph*, April 24, 25, 26, May 3, 4, 1865.

42. For a sample of secondary sources that have examined Confederate reactions to defeat, see James J. Broomall, *Private Confederacies: The Emotional Worlds of Southern Men as Citizens and Soldiers* (Chapel Hill: University of North Carolina Press, 2019), 88–94; Clampitt, *Confederate Heartland*, 150–51; Dunkerly, *The Confederate Surrender at Greensboro*, 108–12; Phillips, *Diehard Rebels*, 169–75; Glatthaar, *General Lee's Army*, 470–71; Jamieson, *Spring 1865*, 215.

43. Broomall, *Private Confederacies*, 2, 8–9, 88–94, 102 (quotation); Eric J. Leed, *No Man's Land: Combat & Identity in World War I* (London: Cambridge University Press, 1979).

44. Bearss, ed., *A Louisiana Confederate*, 237 (quotation); Lavender R. Ray Diary, April 23, 1865, Lavender R. Ray Papers, Georgia Archives; William Sylvester Dillon Diary, May 6, 1865, Georgia Archives; James Edward Whitehorne Diary, April 9, 1865, SHC; J. W. Yale to daughter, May 17, 1865, J. W. Yale Letters, Civil War Miscellany, DBCAH; Henry F. Wilson Diary, April 29, 1865, ADAH; Thomas T. Munford to Sallie Munford, May 21, 1865, Thomas T. Munford Civil War Letters, Virginia Military Institute, Lexington (hereafter cited as VMI); Winfield Scott Featherston Manuscript, Civil War Document Collection, USAHEC; James Robert McMichael Diary, April 20, 1865, SHC; Charles Bickem Fields Diary, April 9, 1865, VHS; Charles Woodward Hutson Letters, April 18, 1865, SHC; John Taylor Wood Diary, April 1865 entries, John Taylor Wood Papers, SHC; Sullivan, ed., "The Dark Clouds of War," 12; Joseph I. Waring, ed., "The Diary of William G. Hinson During the War of Secession" (pt, 2), *South Carolina Historical Magazine* 75 (April 1974): 119; Baumgartner, ed., *Blood and Sacrifice*, 221–25; Bobbie Swearingen Smith, ed., *A Palmetto Boy: Civil War–Era Diaries and Letters of James Adams Tillman* (Columbia: University of South Carolina Press, 2010), 148; Summers, ed., *A Borderland Confederate*, 104–6; Kenneth Wiley, ed., *Norfolk Blues: The Civil War Diary of the Norfolk Light Artillery Blues* (Shippensburg, PA: Burd Street Press, 1997), 223–24; Brown, ed., *One of Cleburne's Command*, 169–70.

For postwar sources, see Warren J. Alston, "My Life is Like Shattered Wreck" (first quotation) in Alston Diary, Georgia Archives, see postwar poem immediately following wartime diary; Hurrieosco Austill to Cousin Leila, August 8, 1872, Hurrieosco Austill Memoir and Diary, ADAH; Miles Vance Smith Reminiscences, 65, Civil War Document Collection, USAHEC; Russell B. Bailey, ed., "Reminiscences of the Civil War by T. J. Walker," *Confederate Chronicles of Tennessee* 1 (1986): 73; John Alexander Sloan, *Reminiscences of the Guilford Grays, Co. B, 27th NC Regiment* (Washington, DC: R. O. Polkinhorn, 1883), 115–16; B. P. Gallaway, *Ragged Rebel: A Common Soldier in Parsons's*

Texas Cavalry, 1861–1865 (Austin: University of Texas Press, 1988), 130; Jeffrey D. Stocker, ed., *From Huntsville to Appomattox: R. T. Coles's History of the 4th Regiment, Alabama Volunteer Infantry, CSA, Army of Northern Virginia* (Knoxville: University of Tennessee Press, 1996), 192; Worsham, *The Old Nineteenth Tennessee,* 175; Young, *The Seventh Tennessee Cavalry,* 137; Benson, ed., *Berry Benson's Civil War Book,* 201; Crosland, *Reminiscences of the Sixties,* 51; Wharton J. Green, *Recollections and Reflections: An Autobiography of Half a Century and More* (Raleigh, NC: Edwards and Broughton Printing, 1906), 195–96; McCarthy, *Detailed Minutiae of Soldier Life,* 161–62, 164; Frank Mixson, *Reminiscences of a Private* (Columbia, SC: State Company, 1910), 118–19; William Miller Owen, *In Camp and Battle with the Washington Artillery of New Orleans: A Narrative of Events during the Late Civil War from Bull Run to Appomattox and Spanish Fort* (Boston: Ticknor, 1885), 391, 393.

45. Thilbert H. Pearce, ed., *Diary of Captain Henry A. Chambers* (Wendell, NC: Broadfoot's Bookmark, 1983), 262 (first quotation), 263; Warren J. Alston Diary, June 22, 1865, Georgia Archives (second quotation); Bearss, ed., *A Louisiana Confederate,* 237; James Edward Whitehorne Diary, April 9, 1865, SHC; Sullivan, ed., "'The Dark Clouds of War,'" 12 (third quotation); Adam Fulkerson to wife, May 7, 1865, Adam Fulkerson Civil War Letters, VMI; C. T. Hardman to wife, April 10, 1865, Hardman Family Letters, Civil War Soldiers' Letters, ADAH; William Sylvester Dillon Diary, May 6, 1865, Georgia Archives; Mark Lyons Letters, April 10, 1865, ADAH; J. W. Yale to daughter, May 17, 1865, J. W. Yale Letters, Civil War Miscellany, DBCAH; John Q. Anderson, ed., *Campaigning with Parsons' Texas Cavalry Brigade, CSA* (Hillsboro, TX: Hill Junior College Press, 1967), 159; Waring, ed., "The Diary of William G. Hinson," 119; Lowe, ed., *A Texas Cavalry Officer's Civil War,* 333; Roper, ed., *Repairing the "March of Mars,"* 613; Smith, ed., *A Palmetto Boy,* 148; Daniel Elliott Huger Smith, ed., *Mason Smith Family Letters, 1860–1868* (Columbia: University of South Carolina Press, 1950), 197–99; Wiley, ed., *Norfolk Blues,* 223–24; J. Keith Jones, ed., *The Boys of Diamond Hill: The Lives and Civil War Letters of the Boyd Family of Abbeville County, South Carolina* (Jefferson, NC: McFarland, 2011), 136–37.

For postwar sources, see Robert G. Shaver, "Recollections and Reminiscences," 2, Robert G. Shaver Papers, AHC; Winfield Scott Featherston Manuscript, Civil War Document Collection, US-AHEC; Ridley, *Battles and Sketches,* 458; W. H. Tunnard, *A Southern Record: The History of the Third Regiment Louisiana Infantry* (Dayton, OH: Morningside Bookshop, 1866), 335–36; Wise, *The End of an Era,* 453–54.

46. Drew Gilpin Faust, *This Republic of Suffering: Death and the American Civil War* (New York: Random House, 2008), 5, 24–26, 48–49; Aaron Sheehan-Dean, *Why Confederates Fought: Family and Nation in Civil War Virginia* (Chapel Hill: University of North Carolina Press, 2007), 83–85; Brian Craig Miller, "Manhood," in Sheehan-Dean, ed., *A Companion to the U.S. Civil War* (2 vols.) (Chichester, West Sussex, UK: John Wiley & Sons, Ltd., 2014), 802–3.

47. Runge, ed., *Four Years in the Confederate Artillery,* 133 (quotation), 145–46; Brown, ed., *One of Cleburne's Command,* 169–70; Baumgartner, ed., *Blood and Sacrifice,* 221–24; William Sylvester Dillon Diary, May 6, 1865, Georgia Archives; Smith, ed., *Mason Smith Family Letters,* 197–98; Gregorie, ed., "Diary of Captain Joseph Julius Westcoat," 94; Williams, ed., "A Saline Guard," 91–92.

48. Leon, *Diary of a Tar-Heel Confederate Soldier,* 70 (first quotation), 71 (second quotation).

49. Runge, ed., *Four Years in the Confederate Artillery,* 137.

50. Carter, *A Cavalryman's Reminiscences,* 128 (quotation); Thornton Bowman, *Reminiscences of an ex-Confederate Soldier; or, Forty Years on Crutches* (Austin, TX: Gammel-Statesman, 1904), 46; Ulysses R. Brooks, *Butler and His Cavalry in the War of Secession, 1861–1865* (Columbia, SC: State

Company, 1909), 477; David E. Johnston, *The Story of a Confederate Boy in the Civil War* (Portland, OR: Glass & Prudhomme, 1914), 347–48, 351–54; Fordney, ed., "Letters from the Heart," 81; Samuel R. Watkins, *"Co. Aytch": A Side Show of the Big Show* (New York: Collier Books, 1962), 229; J. M. Miller, *Recollections of a Pine Knot* (Greenwood, MS: Commonwealth Publishing, 1900), 23; Morgan, *Personal Reminiscences of the War*, 270; John Alexander Sloan, *Reminiscences of the Guilford Grays, Co. B, 27th N. C. Regiment* (Washington, DC: R. O. Polkinhorn, 1883), 117–19; James H. Wood, *The War: "Stonewall" Jackson, His Campaigns, and Battles, the Regiment as I Saw Them* (Cumberland, MD: Eddy Press, 1910), 180; John Frank Edwards, *Army Life of Frank Edwards, Confederate Veteran, Army of Northern Virginia, 1861–1865* (La Grange, GA: F. Edwards, 1911), 59–61; Shingleton, ed., "With Loyalty and Honor," 263.

51. Isaac Asbury Clarke to D. N. McIntosh, June 15, 1865 (first quotation), Isaac Asbury Clarke Papers, AHC; Adam Fulkerson to wife, May 7, 1865 (second quotation), Adam Fulkerson Civil War Letters, VMI; James Robert McMichael Diary, May 7, 1865, SHC; George Alexander Martin Diary, May 9, 1865, VHS; Annie to "My Dearest Aunt," May 7, 1865, John M. Bracey Collection, AHC; Banasik, ed., *Serving with Honor*, 224–25; Bearss, ed., *A Louisiana Confederate*, 237; Fordney, ed., "Letters from the Heart," 81–82; Waring, ed., "The Diary of William G. Hinson," 119; Betts, ed., "The Civil War Letters of Elbridge Littlejohn," 36; Durkin, ed., *John Dooley*, 181, 185; Hubbs, ed., *Voices from Company D*, 368; Bell I. Wiley, ed., *Fourteen Hundred Ninety-one Days*, 246; Wiley, ed., *Norfolk Blues*, 223–24; Edward B. Williams, ed., *Rebel Brothers: The Civil War Letters of the Truehearts* (College Station: Texas A&M University Press, 1995), 217–18.

For postwar sources, see Miles Vance Smith, "Reminiscences of the War," 65, Civil War Document Collection, USAHEC; Underwood, *History of the Twenty-Sixth Regiment*, 91; Bowman, *Reminiscences of an ex-Confederate Soldier*, 46; Carter, *A Cavalryman's Reminiscences*, 126; Collins, *Chapters from the Unwritten History of the War Between the States*, 301; Guild, *A Brief Narrative of the Fourth Tennessee Cavalry Regiment*, 145; John Milton Hubbard, *Notes of a Private* (Memphis: E. H. Clarke & Brother, 1909), 176; Early, *A Memoir of the Last Year of the War*, 138; Young, *The Seventh Tennessee Cavalry*, 137; Taylor, *Destruction and Reconstruction*, 222–23, 226.

52. For the leading studies of southern honor, begin with Bertram Wyatt-Brown's two classic volumes, *Southern Honor: Ethics and Behavior in the Old South* (New York: Oxford University Press, 1982), and *The Shaping of Southern Culture: Honor, Grace, and War, 1760s–1880s* (Chapel Hill: University of North Carolina Press, 2000). See also Gerald Linderman, *Embattled Courage: The Experience of Combat in the American Civil War* (New York: Free Press, 1987), 7–16, 156–57, 297; James McPherson, *For Cause and Comrades: Why Men Fought in the Civil War* (New York: Oxford University Press, 1997), 77–84; Earl J. Hess, *The Union Soldier in Battle: Enduring the Ordeal of Combat* (Lawrence: University Press of Kansas, 1997), 74–80; Reid Mitchell, *Civil War Soldiers* (New York: Penguin Books, 1988), 17–18, 42; Lorien Foote, *The Gentlemen and the Roughs: Manhood, Honor, and Violence in the Union Army* (New York: New York University Press, 2010); Angel M. Riotto, "Remembering 'That Dark Episode': Union and Confederate Ex-Prisoners of War and Their Captivity Narratives," in Brian Matthew Jordan and Evan C. Rothera, eds., *The War Went On: Reconsidering the Lives of Civil War Veterans* (Baton Rouge: Louisiana State University Press, 2020), 122–23; Miller, "Manhood," 793–810.

53. Broomall, *Private Confederacies*, 113 (quotation), 118.

54. For the most recognized explication of the hibernation thesis, see the influential Linderman, *Embattled Courage*, 266–97. For thoughtful correctives to that thesis, see Brian Matthew Jordan,

Marching Home: Union Veterans and Their Unending Civil War (New York: W. W. Norton, 2014), 68–69, 86, 99–100; Marten, *Sing Not War,* 8–11; and Broomall, *Private Confederacies,* 109–10.

55. Carter, *A Cavalryman's Reminiscences,* 126.

56. Larry M. Logue, *To Appomattox and Beyond: The Civil War Soldier in War and Peace* (Chicago: Ivan R. Dee, 1995), 80–81; McPherson, *For Cause and Comrades,* 131, 168–70; Clampitt, *Confederate Heartland,* 149–51; Guild, *A Brief Narrative of the Fourth Tennessee Cavalry Regiment,* 145–48; Harrison, ed., "The Confederate Letters of John Simmons," 51, 53; Goyne, ed., *Lone Star and Double Eagle,* 171; Andrew, *Wade Hampton,* 301–2; Betts, ed., "The Civil War Letters of Elbridge Littlejohn," 36 (quotation); Evan Shelby Jefferies to wife, April 15, 1865, 16th Mississippi Infantry File, Hill College; Mullen, "Last Days of Johnston's Army," 108. Many other sources cited throughout this chapter, particularly in notes 43–44, reinforce this concept.

57. Williams, ed., *Rebel Brothers,* 217 (first quotation); Banasik, ed., *Serving with Honor,* 222 (second quotation).

58. For examples of rather general expressions of relief, see Augustus Pitt Adamson, *Brief History of the Thirtieth Georgia Regiment* (Griffin, GA: Mills Printing, 1912), 137; Benson, ed., *Berry Benson's Civil War Book,* 201; Collins, *Chapters from the Unwritten History of the War Between the States,* 301; Hubbard, *Notes of a Private,* 175–77; Hubbs, ed., *Voices from Company D,* 368; Alderson, ed., "The Civil War Reminiscences of John Johnston, 1861–1865," 173; McNeilly, "A Mississippi Brigade in the Last Days of the Confederacy," 54; Christopher Lyle McIlwain, *Alabama 1865: From Civil War to Uncivil Peace* (Tuscaloosa: University of Alabama Press, 2017), 126–27; Pickett, *The Heart of a Soldier,* 176–79; Ridley, *Battles and Sketches,* 468; Zuber, *My Eighty Years in Texas,* 227–28; Douglas Hale, *The Third Texas Cavalry in the Civil War* (Norman: University of Oklahoma Press, 1993), 272; Christopher Losson, *Tennessee's Forgotten Warriors: Frank Cheatham and His Confederate Division* (Knoxville: University of Tennessee Press, 1989), 248.

59. William T. Alderson, ed., "The Civil War of Captain James Litton Cooper, September 30, 1861, to January 1865," *Tennessee Historical Quarterly* 15 (June 1956): 173 (first quotation) (Cooper's "diary" was actually written in August 1866); Blakey, Lainhart, and Stephens, eds., *Rose Cottage Chronicles,* 366 (second quotation); Crosland, *Reminiscences of the Sixties,* 51 (third quotation).

60. Natalie Jenkins Bond and Osmun Latrobe Coward, eds., *The South Carolinians: Colonel Asbury Coward's Memoirs* (New York: Vantage Press, 1968), 180–81.

61. Jeffrey C. Lowe and Sam Hodges, eds., *Letters to Amanda: The Civil War Letters of Marion Hill Fitzpatrick, Army of Northern Virginia* (Macon, GA: Mercer University Press, 1998), 209–11; Harrison, ed., "The Confederate Letters of John Simmons," 50–51; Austin V. Dobbins, ed., *Grandfather's Journal: Company B, Sixteenth Mississippi Infantry Volunteers, Harris' Brigade, Mahone's Division, Hill's Corps, A. N. V. May 27, 1861–July 15, 1865* (Dayton, OH: Morningside House, 1988), 246; McClendon, *Recollections of War Times,* 234–35.

62. Harrison, ed., "The Confederate Letters of John Simmons," 50–53; Alderson, ed., "The Civil War Diary of Captain James Litton Cooper," 173; Mullen, "Last Days of Johnston's Army," 111; Runge, ed., *Four Years in the Confederate Artillery,* 133; Still, ed., "The Civil War Letters of Robert Tarleton," 80; McCarthy, *Detailed Minutiae of Soldier Life,* 165–66.

63. Mark Lyons Letters, April 1–6, 1865, ADAH; Alfred Tyler Fielder, *The Civil War Diaries of Capt. Alfred Tyler Fielder, 12th Tennessee Regiment Infantry, Company B, 1861–1865* (Louisville, KY: Ann York Franklin, 1996), 228 (quotation); Warren J. Alston Diary, June 12, 1865, Georgia Archives; Evan Shelby Jefferies to wife, April 15, 1865, 16th Mississippi Infantry File, Hill College; James Robert

McMichael Diary, May 7, 1865, SHC; Hubert L. Ferguson, ed., "Letters of John W. Duncan, Captain Confederate States of America," *Arkansas Historical Quarterly* 9 (1960): 311; Fordney, ed., "Letters from the Heart," 80–81; Moore, ed., "Diary of Maj. Kinloch Falconer," 408; Bearss, ed., *A Louisiana Confederate,* 234–36; Brown, ed., *One of Cleburne's Command,* 173; Wirt Armistead Cate, ed., *Two Soldiers: The Campaign Diaries of Thomas J. Key, C.S.A., December 7, 1863–May 17, 1865, and Robert J. Campbell, U.S.A., January 1, 1864–July 21, 1864* (Chapel Hill: University of North Carolina Press, 1938), 213; Dickinson, *Diary of Henry Dickinson,* 179–83; Williams, ed., "A Saline Guard," 91–92.

For postwar sources, see Hurrieosco Austill to Cousin Leila, August 8, 1872, Hurrieosco Austill Memoir and Diary, ADAH; John Bateman Rushing Autobiography, 11, Civil War Document Collection, USAHEC; Brown, ed., *One of Morgan's Men,* 196; Debray, *A Sketch of the History of Debray's 26th Regiment,* 25; Dinkins, *1861 to 1865, by an Old Johnnie,* 256–57; Hubbard, *Notes of a Private,* 175; Oates, ed., *Hanging Rock Rebel,* 312; Hall, *The Story of the 26th Louisiana Infantry,* 133.

64. James Bennington Irvine Diary, April 11, 1865, Newberry Library (quotation); Benjamin Glover to Betty, April 10, 1865, Benjamin Glover Letters, ADAH; Arthur W. Hyatt to Lieutenant L. L. Conrad, May 19, 1865, Arthur W. Hyatt Papers, LLMVC; Adam Fulkerson to wife, May 13, 1865, Adam Fulkerson Civil War Letters, VMI; Montgomery, *The Days of Old,* 60–61.

65. For two excellent studies, see Foote, *The Gentlemen and the Roughs,* and Stephen W. Berry II, *All That Makes a Man: Love and Ambition in the Civil War South* (New York: Oxford University Press, 2003).

66. James Marten, "Fatherhood in the Confederacy: Southern Soldiers and Their Children," *Journal of Southern History* 63 (May 1997): 269–92; Stephen M. Frank, "'Rendering Aid and Comfort': Images of Fatherhood in the Letters of Civil War Soldiers from Massachusetts and Michigan," *Journal of Social History* 26 (Fall 1992): 5–32; LeeAnn Whites, *The Civil War as a Crisis in Gender: Augusta, Georgia, 1860–1890* (New York: Palgrave Macmillan, 2005), 144, 174–75.

67. George Rable, *Civil Wars: Women and the Crisis of Southern Nationalism* (Urbana: University of Illinois Press, 1989), 231–32, 244; Jordan, *Marching Home: Union Veterans and Their Unending Civil War,* 51–52; Kurt Hackemer, "Civil War Veteran Colonies on the Western Frontier," in Jordan and Roberts, eds., *The War Went On,* 62–63; Frank, "Rendering Aid and Comfort," 12; Marten, "Fatherhood in the Confederacy," 276–77.

68. Mitchell, Civil War Soldiers, 42.

69. Cate, ed., *Two Soldiers,* 213.

70. Adam Fulkerson to wife, May 7 (quotation), 13, 1865, Adam Fulkerson Civil War Letters, VMI; Warren J. Alston Diary, June 22, 1865, Georgia Archives; Miles Vance Smith, "Reminiscences of the War," 65, Civil War Document Collection, USAHEC; James Robert McMichael Diary, March 6, April 26, May 2, 7, June 16, 1865, SHC; Gregorie, ed., "Diary of Captain Joseph Julius Westcoat," 94–95; Park, "Diary of Captain Robert E. Park," 244–53; Campbell, ed., *Southern Service on Land and Sea,* 162; Crow, ed., *The Diary of a Confederate Soldier,* 137–43; Dickinson, *Diary of Henry Dickinson,* 179–87; Howard, *Recollections of a Maryland Confederate,* 403; Hubbs, ed., *Voices from Company D,* 368, 371, 377–78; Jones, ed., *Campbell Brown's Civil War,* 295–96; Morgan, *Personal Reminiscences of the War,* 266–69; Oates, ed., *Hanging Rock Rebel,* 312; Runge, ed., *Four Years in the Confederate Artillery,* 135, 142.

71. James Bennington Irvine Diary, April 10 (quotation), 11, 21, 26, 27, 30, 1865, Newberry Library.

72. McCarthy, *Detailed Minutiae of Soldier Life,* 159 (quotation); Evan Shelby Jefferies to wife, April 15, 1865, 16th Mississippi Infantry File, Hill College; Ferguson, ed., "Letters of John W. Duncan," 311; Fordney, ed., "Letters from the Heart," 80–81; Montgomery, *The Days of Old,* 60–61; Oates, ed., *Hanging Rock Rebel,* 312; Wood, *The War: "Stonewall" Jackson, His Campaigns, and Battles,* 180; Hale, *The Third Texas Cavalry,* 272.

73. Williams, ed., "A Saline Guard," 92; United States Bureau of the Census, Eighth U.S. Census, 1860, Schedule 1 (Free Inhabitants); United States Bureau of the Census, Seventh U.S. Census, 1850, Schedule 1 (Free Inhabitants). The young man in question was Thomas Walker Crawford, nephew of William Ayers Crawford.

74. Jeffrey W. McClurken, *Take Care of the Living: Reconstructing Confederate Veteran Families in Virginia* (Charlottesville: University of Virginia Press, 2009), 68–70 (quotation 69); Whites, *The Civil War as a Crisis in Gender,* 132–36.

75. Crosland, *Reminiscences of the Sixties,* 51 (first quotation); John B. Gordon, *Reminiscences of the Civil War* (New York: Charles Scribner's Sons, 1904), 445–50, 447 (second quotation); Wiley, ed., *Fourteen Hundred Ninety-one Days,* 239–46; Young, *The Seventh Tennessee Cavalry,* 136–37.

76. Evan Shelby Jefferies to wife, April 15, 1865, 16th Mississippi Infantry File, Hill College.

77. Shelby to wife, April 15, 1865.

78. Jordan, *Marching Home,* 45–50; Paul A. Cimbala, *Veterans North and South: The Transition from Soldier to Civilian after the American Civil War* (Santa Barbara, CA: Praeger, 2015), 51–55.

79. United States Bureau of the Census, Eighth U.S. Census, 1860, Schedule 1 (Free Inhabitants); Kenneth W. Noe, *Reluctant Rebels: The Confederates Who Joined the Army after 1861* (Chapel Hill: University of North Carolina Press, 2010), 2–18, 23–39.

80. Compiled Records Showing Service of Military Units in Confederate Organizations, Record Group 109, War Department Collection of Confederate Records, National Archives, Washington, DC. See the records of Evan Shelby Jefferies and T. G. Smith, 16th Mississippi Infantry; *The Statutes at Large of the Confederate States of America, Passed at the Fourth Session of the First Congress, 1863–4* (Richmond, VA: R. M. Smith, 1864), 172.

2. YANKEES AND REBELS: THE SYSTEM OF CONFEDERATE DEMOBILIZATION

1. Michael L. Bradley, *This Astounding Close: The Road to Bennett Place* (Chapel Hill: University of North Carolina Press, 2000), 206–42; Elizabeth Varon, *Appomattox: Victory, Defeat, and Freedom at the End of the Civil War* (New York: Oxford University Press, 2014), 55–78; William A. Marvel, *Lee's Last Retreat: The Flight to Appomattox* (Chapel Hill: University of North Carolina Press, 2002), 178–99; Lieutenant General U. S. Grant to General Robert E. Lee, April 9, 1865, in United States War Department, *The War of the Rebellion: A Compilation of the Official Records of the Union and Confederate Armies,* 128 vols. (hereafter cited as *Official Records*), (Washington, DC: Government Printing Office, 1880–1901), ser. 1, vol. 46, pt. 3, 665; Sherman-Johnston Convention, *Official Records,* ser. 1, vol. 47, pt. 3, 313; Military Convention of April 26, 1865—Supplemental Terms [Revised], *Official Records,* ser. 1, vol. 47, pt. 3, 482.

2. Bradley, *This Astounding Close,* 234–37; Varon, *Appomattox,* 71–77; Chris M. Calkins, *The Final Bivouac: The Surrender Parade at Appomattox and the Disbanding of the Armies, April 10–May*

20, 1865 (Lynchburg, VA: M. E. Howard, 1988), 6–9, 54; Thomas L. Connelly, *Autumn of Glory: The Army of Tennessee, 1862–1865* (Baton Rouge: Louisiana State University Press, 1971), 534–35; Mark M. Boatner, *The Civil War Dictionary* (New York: David McKay, 1959), 619–20.

3. Anita B. Sams, ed., *With Unabated Trust: Major Henry McDaniel's Love Letters from Confederate Battlefields as Treasured in Hester McDaniel's Bonnet Box* (Monroe, GA: Historical Society of Walton County, 1994), 219–26; Joseph E. Johnston, *Narrative of Military Operations Directed During the Late War Between the States* (Bloomington: Indiana University Press, 1959), 415–16; George B. Guild, *A Brief Narrative of the Fourth Tennessee Cavalry Regiment, Wheeler's Corps, Army of Tennessee* (Nashville: n.p., 1913), 150; James P. Pate, ed., *When This Evil War is Over: The Correspondence of the Francis Family, 1860–1865* (Tuscaloosa: University of Alabama Press, 2006), 210; Varon, *Appomattox*, 71–72.

4. Johnson Hagood, *Memoirs of the War of Secession* (Columbia, SC: State Company, 1910), 372–73.

5. Bradley R. Clampitt, "The Breakup: The Collapse of the Confederate Trans-Mississippi Army in Texas, 1865," *Southwestern Historical Quarterly* 108 (April 2005): 498–534, see esp. 531–32; Robert G. Shaver, "Recollections and Reminiscences of the Last Days of the Confederate Trans-Mississippi Department, Marshall, Texas," 3, Robert G. Shaver Papers, Arkansas Historical Commission, Little Rock (hereafter cited as AHC); William A. Fletcher, *Rebel Private Front and Rear: Memoirs of a Confederate Soldier* (New York: Dutton, 1995), 195–209; Edwin C. Bearss, ed., *A Louisiana Confederate; Diary of Felix Pierre Poche* (Natchitoches: Louisiana Studies Institute, Northwestern State University, 1972), 337; Gary D. Joiner, Marilyn S. Joiner, and Clifton D. Cardin, eds., *No Pardons to Ask nor Apologies to Make: The Journal of William Henry King, Gray's 28th Louisiana Infantry Regiment* (Knoxville: University of Tennessee Press, 2006), 215–16; Davis Bitton, ed., *The Reminiscences and Civil War Letters of Levi Lamoni Wight; Life in a Mormon Splinter Colony on the Texas Frontier* (Salt Lake City: University of Utah Press, 1970), 39; W. H. Tunnard, *A Southern Record: The History of the Third Regiment Louisiana Infantry* (Dayton, OH: Morningside Bookshop, 1866), 338; Enclosure No. 4, July 19, 1865, *Official Records,* ser. 1, vol. 48, pt. 2, 1101–102; General Orders No. 6, July 15, 1865, *Official Records,* ser. 1, vol. 48, pt. 2, 1102; J. L. Brent to Major General H. T. Hays, May 30, 1865, *Official Records,* ser. 1, vol. 48, pt. 2, 1321; Circular, May 5, 1865, *Official Records,* ser. 1, vol. 49, pt. 2, 620.

6. Mamie Yeary, ed., *Reminiscences of the Boys in Gray, 1861–1865* (Dallas: Smith and Lamar, M. E. Church, South, 1912), 722–23; William S. Haggard Diary, April 8–May 5, 1865, Special Collections Research Center, University of Kentucky Libraries, Lexington (hereafter cited as UKY).

7. Varon, *Appomattox*, 73–76; Bradley, *This Astounding Close*, 240–42.

8. Richard A. Baumgartner, ed., *Blood and Sacrifice: The Civil War Journal of a Confederate Soldier* (Huntington, WV: Blue Acorn Press, 1994), 223–24; Douglas John Cater, *As It Was: Reminiscences of a Soldier of the Third Texas Cavalry and the Nineteenth Louisiana Infantry* (Austin, TX: State House Press, 1990), 212; Nathaniel Cheairs Hughes Jr., ed., *The Civil War Memoir of Phillip Daingerfield Stephenson, D. D.* (Conway: University of Central Arkansas Press, 1995), 371; Archie P. McDonald, ed., *Make Me a Map of the Valley: The Civil War Journal of Stonewall Jackson's Topographer* (Dallas: Southern Methodist University Press, 1973), 266; DeWitt Boyd Stone, ed., *Wandering to Glory: Confederate Veterans Remember Evans's Brigade* (Columbia: University of South Carolina Press, 2002), 223; Roger S. Durham, ed., *The Blues in Gray: The Civil War Journal of William Daniel Dixon and the Republican Blues Daybook* (Knoxville: University of Tennessee Press, 2000), 285.

9. Baumgartner, ed., *Blood and Sacrifice,* 223–24; Richard Taylor, *Destruction and Reconstruction: Personal Experiences of the Late War* (New York: D. Appleton, 1879), 225–28.

10. Cater, *As It Was,* 212.

11. Hughes, ed., *The Civil War Memoir of Phillip Daingerfield Stephenson,* 371.

12. James K. Turner, ed., *My Dear Emma: War Letters of Col. James K. Edmondson, 1861–1865* (Verona, VA: McClure Press, 1978), 135–36; William S. Haggard Diary, April 8, 1865, UKY; Michael E. Banasik, ed., *Serving with Honor: The Diary of Captain Eathan Allen Pinnell, Eight Missouri Infantry (Confederate)* (Iowa City: Camp Pope Bookshop, 1999), 222; Mary Elizabeth Sanders, ed., *Diary in Gray: Civil War Letters and Diary of Jared Young Sanders II* (Baton Rouge: Louisiana Genealogical & Historical Society, 1994), 94–95; W. J. Andrews, *Sketch of Company K, 23rd South Carolina Volunteers in the Civil War from 1862–1865* (Richmond, VA: Whittet and Shepperson Printers, n.d.), 28; Durham, ed., *The Blues in Gray* 276–77; William C. Davis and Meredith L. Swentor, eds., *Bluegrass Confederate: The Headquarters Diary of Edward O. Guerrant* (Baton Rouge: Louisiana State University Press, 1999), 685–86; R. Thomas Campbell, ed., *Southern Service on Land & Sea: The Wartime Journal of Robert Watson, CSA/CSN* (Knoxville: University of Tennessee Press, 2002), 162–63; Valerius C. Giles, *Rags and Hope: The Recollections of Val. C. Giles, Four Years with Hood's Brigade, Fourth Texas Infantry, 1861–1865* (New York: Coward-McCann, 1961), 278–79; W. R. Houghton and Mitchell Bennett Houghton, *Two Boys in the Civil War and After* (Montgomery, AL: Paragon Press, 1912), 234; James Morris Morgan, *Recollections of a Rebel Reefer* (Boston: Houghton Mifflin, 1917), 231–32; Carlton McCarthy, *Detailed Minutiae of Soldier Life in the Army of Northern Virginia, 1861–1865* (Richmond, VA: Carlton McCarthy, 1894), 173–74; Bell I. Wiley, ed., *Fourteen Hundred Ninety-one Days in the Confederate Army* (1876; reprint, Jackson, TN: McCowat-Mercer Press, 1963), 239; John Herbert Roper, ed., *Repairing the "March of Mars": The Civil War Diaries of John Samuel Apperson, Hospital Steward in the Stonewall Brigade, 1861–1865* (Macon, GA: Mercer University Press, 2001), 613; William B. Holberton, *Homeward Bound: The Demobilization of the Union and Confederate Armies, 1865–1866* (Mechanicsburg, PA: Stackpole Books, 2001), 18–21, 29; Reid Mitchell, *Civil War Soldiers* (New York: Penguin Books, 1988), 42.

13. Hagood, *Memoirs of the War of Secession,* 371 (first quotation); Winchester Hall, *The Story of the 26th Louisiana Infantry in the Service of the Confederate States* (n. p., 1890), 134 (second quotation).

14. Sherman to Johnston, April 27, 1865, *Official Records,* ser. 1, vol. 47, pt. 3, 320; General Orders No. 23, May 2, 1865, *Official Records,* ser. 1, vol. 47, pt. 3, 864; Special Orders No—, May 2, 1865, *Official Records,* ser. 1, vol. 47, pt. 3, 865; Bradley, *This Astounding Close,* 239; Johnston, *Narrative of Military Operations,* 417–18; John M. Schofield, *Forty-Six Years in the Army* (New York: Century Company, 1897), 351–52.

15. *Western Democrat* (Charlotte, NC), May 29, 1865; Frederick W. Moore, ed., "Diary of Maj. Kinloch Falconer," *Confederate Veteran Magazine* 9 (September 1901): 451; Johnston to McLaws, May 6, 1865, *Official Records,* ser. 1, vol. 47, pt. 3, 872; Wilson to Upton, May 3, 1865, *Official Records,* ser. 1, vol. 49, pt. 2, 587; Upton to Wilson, 587; Whipple to Stoneman, May 15, 1865, *Official Records,* ser. 1, vol. 47, pt. 3, 793; Tillson to Bascom, May 15, 1865, *Official Records,* ser. 1, vol. 47, pt. 3, 793–94.

16. For unpublished sources, see James W. Brown Diary, May 5, 1865, Georgia Archives; R. C. Telford Diary, June 30, 1865, Georgia Archives; S. M. Gross Journal, May 5, 8, 1865, South Caroliniana Library, University of South Carolina, Columbia (hereafter cited as USC); William S. Haggard

Diary, April 29, 1865, UKY; Marcus Morton Rhoades Diary, June 1, 1865, State Historical Society of Missouri, Springfield (hereafter cited as SHSM); Avington Wayne Simpson Diary, May 14, 1865, Southern Historical Collection, Wilson Library, University of North Carolina, Chapel Hill (hereafter cited as UNC); Martin Van Buren Kees Diary, April 22–26, 1865, Mississippi Department of Archives and History, Jackson (hereafter cited as MDAH); Henry Brockman Journal, June 6, 14, 22, 23, 1865, AHC; Shaver, "Recollections and Reminiscences," 10, AHC.

For published sources, see Banasik, ed., *Serving with Honor,* 228; Norman D. Brown, ed., *One of Cleburne's Command: The Civil War Reminiscences and Diary of Captain Samuel T. Foster, Granbury's Texas Brigade, CSA* (Austin: University of Texas Press, 1980), 181; Wirt Armistead Cate, ed., *Two Soldiers: The Campaign Diaries of Thomas J. Key, C.S.A., December 7, 1863–May 17, 1865, and Robert J. Campbell, U.S.A., January 1, 1864–July 21, 1864* (Chapel Hill: University of North Carolina Press, 1938), 215–16; Thomas D. Cockerell and Michael B. Ballard, eds., *A Mississippi Rebel in the Army of Northern Virginia: The Civil War Memoirs of Private David Holt* (Baton Rouge: Louisiana State University Press, 1995), 337; Robert H. Dacus, *Reminiscences of Company "H," First Arkansas Mounted Rifles* (Dardanelle, AR: Post-Despatch Printing, 1897), 29; Ruth Woods Dayton, ed., *The Diary of a Confederate Soldier: James E. Hall* (Lewisburg, WV: 1961), 137–38; Alfred Tyler Fielder, *The Civil War Diaries of Capt. Alfred Tyler Fielder, 12th Tennessee Regiment Infantry, Company B, 1861–1865* (Louisville, KY: Ann York Franklin, 1996), 234; James M. McCaffrey, ed., *Only a Private: A Texan Remembers the Civil War: The Memoirs of William J. Oliphant* (Houston: Halcyon Press, 2004), 89; J. M. Miller, *Recollections of a Pine Knot* (Greenwood, MS: Commonwealth Publishing, 1900), 23–24; James Nicholson, *Stories from Dixie* (New York: American Books, 1915), 207; William H. Runge, ed., *Four Years in the Confederate Artillery: The Diary of Henry Robinson Berkeley* (Richmond: Virginia Historical Society, 1991), 142; Kenneth Wiley, ed., *Norfolk Blues: The Civil War Diary of the Norfolk Light Artillery Blues* (Shippensburg, PA: Burd Street Press, 1997), 226–28; Ted R. Worley, ed., *The War Memoirs of John W. Lavender, CSA* (Pine Bluff, AR: Southern Press, 1956), 136–37; Patricia J. Bennett, ed., "Curtis R. Burke's Civil War Journal" (pt. 4), *Indiana Magazine of History* 67 (June 1971): 161; William Clyde Billingsley, ed., "'Such Is War': The Confederate Memoirs of Newton Asbury Keen," (pt. 4), *Texas Military History* 7 (Fall 1968): 189; Moore, ed., "Diary of Maj. Kinloch Falconer," 451–52.

17. Varon, *Appomattox,* 48–72; Marvel, *Lee's Last Retreat,* 178–99; Grant to Lee, April 9, 1865, *Official Records,* ser. 1, vol. 46, pt. 3, 665; Appomattox Surrender Terms, April 10, 1865, *Official Records,* ser. 1, vol. 46, pt. 3, 685–86; Special Orders No. 73, *Official Records,* ser. 1, vol. 46, pt. 3, 687; Runge, ed., *Four Years in the Confederate Artillery,* 144–45.

18. Bradley, *This Astounding Close,* 214–17; Sherman-Johnston Convention, *Official Records,* ser. 1, vol. 47, pt. 3, 313, 872; Supplementary Terms, *Official Records,* ser. 1, vol. 47, pt. 3, 321; *Official Records,* ser. 1, vol. 47, pt. 3, 350; Military Convention of April 26, 1865—Supplemental Terms [Revised], *Official Records,* ser. 1, vol. 47, pt. 3, 482; Johnston, *Narrative of Military Operations,* 412–14; Schofield, *Forty-Six Years in the Army,* 351–52; Perry D. Jamieson, *Spring 1865: The Closing Campaigns of the Civil War* (Lincoln: University of Nebraska Press, 2015), 199–200.

19. Johnston, *Narrative of Military Operations,* 412–14; Schofield, *Forty-Six Years in the Army,* 351–52; Bradley, *This Astounding Close,* 214–17; Jamieson, *Spring 1865,* 200; Military Convention of April 26, 1865—Supplemental Terms [Revised], *Official Records,* ser. 1, vol. 47, pt. 3, 482; Circular, May 3, 1865, *Official Records,* ser. 1, vol. 47, pt. 3, 864. See also exchanges between Brigadier Gen-

eral E. W. Pettus and Assistant Adjutant General Archer Anderson in *Official Records,* ser. 1, vol. 47, pt. 3, 868; *Tennessee Civil War Veteran Questionnaires* (5 vols.) (Easley, SC: Southern Historical Press, 1985) (hereafter cited as *TCWVQ*), vol. 3, 1118; *TCWVQ,* vol. 5, 1823.

20. Schofield, *Forty-Six Years in the Army,* 352 (quotation); Johnston, *Narrative of Military Operations,* 413–18.

21. *Western Democrat* (Charlotte, NC), May 29, 1865.

22. Stoneman to Thomas, April 29, 1865, *Official Records,* ser. 1, vol. 49, pt. 2, 519.

23. William D. Whipple to Rear-Admiral S. P. Lee, May 18, 1865, *Official Records,* ser. 1, vol. 49, pt. 2, 828 (quotation); Lee to Whipple, *Official Records,* ser. 1, vol. 49, pt. 2, 828.

24. Phil Gottschalk, *In Deadly Earnest: The History of the First Missouri Brigade, CSA.* (Columbia, MO: Missouri River Press, 1991), 527; George L. Andrews to Major General George H. Thomas, May 8, 1865, *Official Records,* ser. 2, vol. 8, 540; Major General E. S. Canby to Major General N. J. T. Dana, May 9, 1865, *Official Records,* ser. 2, vol. 8, 549; C. T. Christensen to Brigadier General T. Kilby Smith, May 11, 1865, *Official Records,* ser. 2, vol. 8, 552; Canby to Edwin M. Stanton, May 4, 1865, *Official Records,* ser. 1, vol. 49, pt. 2, 610 (quotation); Thomas to Brigadier General E. Hatch, May 15, 1865, *Official Records,* ser. 1, vol. 49, pt. 2, 791; S. Meredith to Stanton, May 16, 1865, *Official Records,* ser. 1, vol. 49, pt. 2, 809.

25. Gottschalk, *In Deadly Earnest,* 527; Grant to Stanton, May 18, 1865, *Official Records,* ser. 1, vol. 49, pt. 2, 827 (quotations).

26. Natalie Jenkins Bond and Osmun Latrobe Coward, eds., *The South Carolinians: Colonel Asbury Coward's Memoirs* (New York: Vantage Press, 1968), 180; J. Luke Austin, ed., *General John Bratton: Sumter to Appomattox in Letters to His Wife* (Sewanee, TN: Proctor's Hall Press, 2003), 268; James L. Morrison Jr., ed., *The Memoirs of Henry Heth* (Westport, CT: Greenwood Press, 1974), 197 (quotation); Taylor, *Destruction and Reconstruction,* 228.

27. Matthew Jack Davis, "A Long Journey Home," *Civil War Times Illustrated* 36, no. 2 (May 1997): 52.

28. James Edward Whitehorne Diary, April 10–12, 1865, UNC; Bearss, ed., *A Louisiana Confederate,* 244; Edward M. Boykin, *The Falling Flag, Evacuation of Richmond, Retreat and Surrender at Appomattox, by An Officer of the Rear-Guard* (New York: E. J. Hale & Son, 1874), 64–66; James W. Silver, *The Confederate Soldier* (1902; reprint, Memphis: Memphis State University Press, 1973), 191–92; Jesse Mercer Wellborn to wife, April 13, 1865, *Confederate Reminiscences and Letters* (14 vols.) (Atlanta: Georgia Division of UDC, 1995), vol. 10; Joseph I. Waring, ed., "The Diary of William G. Hinson During the War of Secession" (pt. 2), *South Carolina Historical Magazine* 75 (April 1974): 119; *TCWVQ,* vol. 1, 198; *TCWVQ,* vol. 2, 720.

29. Caroline E. Janney, *Remembering the Civil War: Reunion and the Limits of Reconciliation* (Chapel Hill: University of North Carolina Press, 2013), see esp. 42–46 and 53–55.

30. Marcus Morton Rhoades Diary, June 1, 1865, SHSM; James Edward Whitehorne Diary, April 14, 1865, UNC; Cater, *As It Was,* 218–19; Fletcher, *Rebel Private Front and Rear,* 212; Davis and Swentor, eds., *Bluegrass Confederate,* 689; John Will Dyer, *Reminiscences; or, Four Years in the Confederate Army* (Evansville, IN: Keller Printing and Publishing, 1898), 299–300; George Cary Eggleston, *A Rebel's Recollections* (New York: Hurd and Houghton, 1874), 248, 249; Thad Holt Jr., *Miss Waring's Journal: 1863 and 1865, Being the Diary of Miss Mary Waring of Mobile, During the Final Days of the War Between the States* (Chicago: Wyvern Press of S. F. E., 1964), 16; John Bell

Hood, *Advance and Retreat: Personal Experiences in the United States and Confederate States Armies* (Bloomington: Indiana University Press, 1959), 311; James Troy Massey, ed., *Memoirs of Captain J. M. Bailey* (James Troy Massey, 1994), 108–9; George M. Neese, *Three Years in the Confederate Horse Artillery* (New York: Neale Publishing, 1911), 359; Thilbert H. Pearce, ed., *Diary of Captain Henry A. Chambers* (Wendell, NC: Broadfoot's Bookmark, 1983), 264; Joseph B. Polley, *Hood's Texas Brigade: Its Marches, Its Battles, Its Achievements* (New York: Neal Publishing, 1910), 279–81; William C. Davis, ed., *Diary of a Confederate Soldier: John S. Jackman of the Orphan Brigade* (Columbia: University of South Carolina Press, 1990), 168–69; Bennett, ed., "Curtis R. Burke's Civil War Journal," 159–60; I. G. Bradwell, "Making Our Way Home from Appomattox," *Confederate Veteran Magazine* 29 (March 1921): 102–3; Edward Crenshaw, "Diary of Captain Edward Crenshaw of the Confederate States Army," *Alabama Historical Quarterly* 2 (Winter 1940): 476, 478; W. Stanley Hoole, ed., "Admiral on Horseback: The Diary of Brigadier General Raphael Semmes, February–May, 1865," *Alabama Review* 28 (April 1975): 147–48; James M. Mullen, "Last Days of Johnston's Army, a Comrade's Experience with General L. S. Baker's Command at Weldon, N. C., During the Fifteen Days Preceding Johnston's Surrender at Greensboro, N. C.," *Southern Historical Society Papers* 18 (1890): 112; Harry C. Townshend, "Townshend's Diary—January–May, 1865; From Petersburg to Appomattox, Thence to North Carolina to Join Johnston's Army," *Southern Historical Society Papers* 34 (1906): 126–27; *TCWVQ,* vol. 1, 292, 330; *TCWVQ,* vol. 2, 687.

31. Banasik, ed., *Serving with Honor,* 230; R. M. Collins, *Chapters from the Unwritten History of the War Between the States; or, the Incidents in the Life of a Confederate Soldier* (St. Louis: Nixon-Jones Printing, 1893), 308; W. E. Preston, "History of the 33rd Alabama," 72, Alabama Department of Archives and History, Montgomery (hereafter cited as ADAH); Billingsley, ed., "Such Is War," 189; *TCWVQ,* vol. 2, 666; *TCWVQ,* vol. 4, 1722.

32. Hughes Jr., ed., *The Civil War Memoir of Phillip Daingerfield Stephenson,* 380–81.

33. Samuel Lewis Moore Autobiography, 14–15, Civil War Document Collection, United States Army Heritage and Education Center, Carlisle, Pennsylvania (hereafter cited as USAHEC); Davis, "Long Journey," 15, 52; Worley, ed.. *The War Memoirs of John W. Lavender,* 136–38; Billingsley, ed., "Such Is War," 183–89.

34. Samuel Lewis Moore Autobiography, 14, Civil War Document Collection, USAHEC.

35. William S. Haggard Diary, April 10–May 1, 1865, UKY; Wiley, ed., *Norfolk Blues,* 228; Dacus, *Reminiscences of Company "H.,"* 27–29.

36. Wellborn to wife, April 13, 1865, *Confederate Reminiscences and Letters,* vol. 10; Bell I. Wiley, ed., *This Infernal War: The Confederate Letters of Edwin H. Fay* (Austin: University of Texas Press, 1958), 448; Cate, ed., *Two Soldiers,* 211–12; Henry William Graber, *The Life Record of H. W. Graber, a Terry Texas Ranger, 1861–1865: Sixty-two Years in Texas* (H. W. Graber, 1916), 244–45; Johnston, *Narrative of Military Operations,* 410; Morrison Jr., ed., *The Memoirs of Henry Heth,* 199.

37. Graber, *The Life Record of H. W. Graber,* 244–57.

38. Bradwell, "Making Our Way Home from Appomattox," 102–3; Bennett, ed., "Curtis R. Burke's Civil War Journal," 154; Townshend, "Townshend's Diary," 126–27; Brown, ed., *One of Cleburne's Command,* 180; Collins, *Chapters from the Unwritten History of the War Between the States,* 307–9; Dacus, *Reminiscences of Company "H.,"* 26–29; Joseph T. Durkin, ed., *John Dooley: Confederate Soldier. His War Journal* (Washington, DC: Georgetown University Press, 1945), 193; W. J. Worsham, *The Old Nineteenth Tennessee Regiment, CSA, June 1861–April 1865* (Knoxville, TN: Press of

Paragon Printing, 1902), 178; *Recollections and Reminiscences, 1861–1865* (12 vols.) (South Carolina Division: United Daughters of the Confederacy, 1990), vol. 10, 53; *TCWVQ*, vol. 1, 176, 426. For examples of dangerous rail travel during the demobilization of Union troops, see James Marten, *Sing Not War: The Lives of Union and Confederate Veterans in Gilded Age America* (Chapel Hill: University of North Carolina Press, 2011), 33–36.

39. Collins, *Chapters from the Unwritten History of the War Between the States*, 307–9.

40. Dacus, *Reminiscences of Company "H.,"* 26–29.

41. Holberton, *Homeward Bound*, 101–6; New Orleans *Times*, June 13, 1865; *New York Times*, June 21, 25, 1865; Marcus Morton Rhodes Diary, June 13, 1865, SHSM; Henry Brockman Journal, June 9, 10, 1865, AHC.

42. New Orleans *Times*, June 15, 1865.

43. New Orleans *Times*, June 16, 1865.

44. James T. Wallace Diary, undated entries, pp. 100–104, SHC.

45. Cater, *As It Was*, 215–16; Dyer, *Reminiscences*, 304; Bradwell, "Making Our Way Home from Appomattox," 102; R. Hugh Simmons, "The 12th Louisiana Infantry in North Carolina, January–April, 1865," *Louisiana History* 36 (1) (1995): 106; Hoole, ed., "Admiral on Horseback," 144–45; Durkin, ed., *John Dooley*, 202–3; Wiley, ed., *Norfolk Blues*, 225 (quotation).

46. Cate, ed., *Two Soldiers*, 216–17.

47. Moore, ed., "Diary of Maj. Kinloch Falconer," 409; Cate, ed., *Two Soldiers*, 209–10; John Frank Edwards, *Army Life of Frank Edwards, Confederate Veteran, Army of Northern Virginia, 1861–1865* (La Grange, GA: 1911), 72; Cater, *As It Was*, 217; Graber, *The Life Record of H. W. Graber*, 249.

48. Mullen, "Last Days of Johnston's Army," 111; Charles G. Williams, ed., "A Saline Guard: The Civil War Letters of Col. William Ayers Crawford, CSA, 1861–1865" (pt. 2), *Arkansas Historical Quarterly* 32 (Spring 1973): 91–92.

49. William Miller Owen, *In Camp and Battle with the Washington Artillery of New Orleans: A Narrative of Events during the Late Civil War from Bull Run to Appomattox and Spanish Fort* (Boston: Ticknor, 1885), 395; *TCWVQ*, vol. 1, 203, 232, 336; *TCWVQ*, vol. 3, 914–15; Ephraim McDowell Anderson, *Memoirs: Historical and Personal, Including the Campaigns of the First Missouri Brigade* (St. Louis: Times Printing, 1868), 413–14; Walter Alexander Montgomery, *The Days of Old and the Years That Are Past* (Charlottesville, VA: Michie, 1939), 62; Campbell, ed., *Southern Service on Land & Sea*, 161; Crenshaw, "Diary of Captain Edward Crenshaw," 478; Massey, ed., *Memoirs of Captain J. M. Bailey*, 104–7; Cater, *As It Was*, 213; Polley, *Hood's Texas Brigade*, 282; G. Moxley Sorrel, *Recollections of a Staff Officer* (New York: Neale Publishing, 1905), 290; Marten, *Sing Not War*, 44.

50. Samuel Lewis Moore Autobiography, 15 (first quotation), Civil War Document Collection, USAHEC; Franklin Alexander Montgomery, *Reminiscences of a Mississippian in Peace and War, by Frank A. Montgomery, Lieutenant-Colonel First Mississippi Cavalry* (Cincinnati, OH: Robert Clarke Co. Press, 1901), 243, 254 (second and third quotations); Moore, ed., "Diary of Maj. Kinloch Falconer," 409, 452.

51. Cater, *As It Was*, 213.

52. James Bennington Irvine Diary, April 15, 1865, Newberry Library, Chicago, Illinois; J. H. P. Baker Civil War Diary, April 29, 1865, State Historical Society of Missouri, Springfield; J. P. Austin, *The Blue and the Gray, Sketches of a Portion of the Unwritten History of the Great American Civil War* (Atlanta: Franklin Printing and Publishing, 1899), 168–69; Bearss, ed., *A Louisiana Confederate,*

239–40; R. S. Bevier, *A History and the First and Second Missouri Confederate Brigades, 1861–1865, and from Wakarusa to Appomattox* (St. Louis: Bryam, Brand, 1879), 470–71; Bond and Coward, eds., *The South Carolinians*, 184–86; Thornton Bowman, *Reminiscences of an ex-Confederate Soldier; or, Forty Years of Crutches* (Austin, TX: Gammel-Statesman, 1904), 57–58; Brown, ed., *One of Cleburne's Command*, 174, 179–80; Davis and Swentor, eds., *Bluegrass Confederate*, 687; Dyer, *Reminiscences*, 293; John B. Gordon, *Reminiscences of the Civil War* (New York: Charles Scribner's Sons, 1904), 450–51; David E. Johnston, *The Story of a Confederate Boy in the Civil War* (Portland, OR: Glass & Prudhomme, 1914), 339; Preston Lafayette Ledford, *Reminiscences of the Civil War, 1861–1865* (Thomasville, NC: News Printing House, 1909), 89–90; Earl Schenck Miers, ed., A Rebel War Clerk's Diary (New York: Sagamor Press, 1958), 538; Montgomery, *Reminiscences of a Mississippian in Peace and War*, 256–57; W. H. Morgan, *Personal Reminiscences of the War 1861–5* (Lynchburg, VA: J. P. Bell, 1911), 268; Owen, *In Camp and Battle*, 395; Cynthia Dehaven Pitcock and Bill J. Gurley, eds., *I Acted from Principle: The Civil War Diary of Dr. William M. McPheeters, Confederate Surgeon in the Trans-Mississippi* (Fayetteville: University of Arkansas Press, 2002), 297; Bromfield L. Ridley, *Battles and Sketches of the Army of Tennessee* (Mexico: Missouri Printing and Publishing, 1906), 459; Crenshaw, "Diary of Captain Edward Crenshaw," 469; Hambleton Tapp, ed., "A Sketch of the Early Life and Service in the Confederate Army of Dr. John A. Lewis of Georgetown, Ky.," *Register of the Kentucky Historical Society* 75 (April 1977): 137; T. Harry Williams, *P. G. T. Beauregard: Napoleon in Gray* (Baton Rouge: Louisiana State University Press, 1955), 255.

For the study of northerners' reaction to Lincoln's death and their views toward Confederate culpability, see Martha Hodes, *Mourning Lincoln* (New Haven, CT: Yale University Press, 2015), esp. 90, 129–30, 134–38, 154.

53. Vicki Betts, ed., "The Civil War Letters of Elbridge Littlejohn," *Chronicles of Smith County, Texas* 18 (Summer 1979): 36 (first quotation); Nat S. Turner III, ed., *A Southern Soldier's Letters Home: The Civil War Letters of Samuel A. Burney, Cobb's Georgia Legion. Army of Northern Virginia* (Macon, GA: Mercer University Press, 2002), 293–94; John Sergeant Wise, *The End of an Era* (Boston: Houghton Mifflin, 1899), 454–55 (second and third quotations); Durkin, ed., *John Dooley*, 195–96; Lawson Jefferson Keener, *Letters from Lawson Jefferson Keener Written During His Confederate Service to Alcesta (Allie) Benson Carter*, May 13, 1865, unnumbered pages (Longview, TX: Mrs. Rogers Lacy, 1963); Paula Mitchell Marks, ed., *When Will the Weary War Be Over? The Civil War Letters of the Maverick Family of San Antonio* (Dallas: Book Club of Texas, 2008), 195, 222; Pitcock and Gurley, eds., *I Acted from Principle*, 295–97; Ridley, *Battles and Sketches of the Army of Tennessee*, 459; Charles D. Spurlin, ed., *The Civil War Diary of Charles A. Leuschner* (Austin, TX: Eakin Press, 1992), 52; William T. Alderson, ed., "The Civil War Reminiscences of John Johnston, 1861–1865," (pt. 6), *Tennessee Historical Quarterly* 14 (June 1955): 172; Robert E. Park, "Diary of Captain Robert E. Park, Twelfth Alabama Regiment," *Southern Historical Society Papers* 3 (January–June 1887): 245; Douglas Hale, *The Third Texas Cavalry in the Civil War* (Norman: University of Oklahoma Press, 1993), 272; Mitchell, *Civil War Soldiers*, 198–201.

54. James Bennington Irvine Diary, April 15, 19, 20, 21, 23, 1865, Newberry Library; Baumgartner, ed., *Blood and Sacrifice*, 220; Bevier, *A History of the First and Second Missouri Confederate Brigades*, 473; Bond and Coward, eds., *The South Carolinians*, 186; Willene B. Clark, ed., *Valleys of the Shadow: The Memoir of Confederate Captain Reuben G. Clark, Company I, 59th Tennessee Mounted Infantry* (Knoxville: University of Tennessee Press, 1994), 69; Collins, *Chapters from the Unwritten History of the War Between the States*, 305–6; Henry Clay Dickinson, *Diary of Henry Dickinson, CSA,*

Morris Island, 1864–1865 (Denver, CO: Press of Williamson-Haffner, n.d.), 179–83; Austin V. Dobbins, ed., *Grandfather's Journal: Company B, Sixteenth Mississippi Infantry Volunteers, Harris' Brigade, Mahone's Division, Hill's Corps, A. N. V. May 27, 1861–July 15, 1865* (Dayton, OH: Morningside House, 1988), 247; William S. Dunlop, *Lee's Sharpshooters; or the Forefront of Battle* (Little Rock, AR: Tunann & Pittard, 1899), 316–18; Joseph T. Durkin, ed., *Confederate Chaplain: A War Journal of Rev. James B. Sheeran, CSA* (Milwaukee: Bruce Publishing, 1960), 161; Gary W. Gallagher, ed., *Fighting for the Confederacy: The Personal Recollections of Edward Porter Alexander* (Chapel Hill: University of North Carolina Press, 1980), 540–41; Alfred R. Gibbons, *Recollections of an Old Confederate Soldier* (Shelbyville, MO: Herald Print, 1931), 28; G. Ward Hubbs, ed., *Voices from Company D: Diaries by the Greensboro Guards, Fifth Alabama Infantry Regiment, Army of Northern Virginia* (Athens: University of Georgia Press, 2003), 372; Hughes, ed., *The Civil War Memoir of Phillip Daingerfield Stephenson*, 385; Johnston, *The Story of a Confederate Boy in the Civil War*, 339; Morgan, *Personal Reminiscences of the War*, 267; Neese, *Three Years in the Confederate Horse Artillery*, 353; Dan Oates, ed., *Hanging Rock Rebel: Lt. John Blue's War in West Virginia and the Shenandoah Valley* (Shippensburg, PA: Burd Street Press, 1994), 311; Owen, *In Camp and Battle*, 395; Pitcock and Gurley, eds., *I Acted from Principle*, 296; John H. Reagan, *Memoirs: With Special Reference to Secession and the Civil War* (Austin, TX: Pemberton Press, 1968), 208; Runge, ed., *Four Years in the Confederate Artillery*, 133–34; Spurlin, ed., *The Civil War Diary of Charles A. Leuschner*, 52; Jeffrey D. Stocker, ed., *From Huntsville to Appomattox: R. T. Coles's History of the 4th Regiment, Alabama Volunteer Infantry, CSA, Army of Northern Virginia* (Knoxville: University of Tennessee Press, 1996), 196–97; Taylor, *Destruction and Reconstruction*, 222; Lewis N. Wynne and Robert A. Taylor, eds., *This War So Horrible: The Civil War Diary of Hiram Smith Williams* (Tuscaloosa: University of Alabama Press, 1993), 134; Anne King Gregorie, ed., "Diary of Captain Joseph Julius Wescoat, 1863–1865" (pt. 2), *South Carolina Historical Magazine* 59 (April 1958): 94; Bradley, *This Astounding Close*, 239; Gottschalk, *In Deadly Earnest*, 527; Terry L. Jones, ed., *Campbell Brown's Civil War: With Ewell and the Army of Northern Virginia* (Baton Rouge: Louisiana State University Press, 2001), 286–88; Donald C. Pfanz, *Richard S. Ewell: A Soldier's Life* (Chapel Hill: University of North Carolina Press, 2000), 446–47, 462, 466.

55. Paul A. Cimbala, *Veterans North and South: The Transition from Soldier to Civilian after the American Civil War* (Santa Barbara, CA: Praeger, 2015), 14; Cater, *As It Was*, 219 (quotation); Bearss, ed., *A Louisiana Confederate*, 242–43; Martin Brett, *Experiences of a Georgia Boy in the Army of Northern Virginia, 1861–1865* (Gainesville, GA: Magnolia Press, 1988), 35; Brown, ed., *One of Cleburne's Command*, 177–78; Campbell, ed., *Southern Service on Land & Sea*, 162; Cate, ed., *Two Soldiers*, 212–13, 215, 218–21; Wellborn to wife, April 13, 1865, *Confederate Reminiscences and Letters*, vol. 10; Dacus, *Reminiscences of Company "H*,*"* 27–28; Dobbins, ed., *Grandfather's Journal*, 247; Durham, ed., *The Blues in Gray*, 287; Edwards, *Army Life of Frank Edwards*, 45, 61, 74–75; Hubbs, ed., *Voices from Company D*, 374, 383–85; Henry D. Jamison and Marguerite J. McTigue, eds., *Letters and Recollections of a Confederate Soldier, 1860–1865* (Nashville, TN: H. D. Jamison, 1964), 184; Morgan, *Recollections of a Rebel Reefer*, 245–51; Pitcock and Gurley, eds., *I Acted from Principle*, 307; Polley, *Hood's Texas Brigade*, 279–81; Stone, ed., *Wandering to Glory*, 222; Bell I. Wiley, ed., *Four Years on the Firing Line* (Jackson, TN: McCowat-Mercer Press, 1963), 249; Russell B. Bailey, ed., "Reminiscences of the Civil War by T. J. Walker," *Confederate Chronicles of Tennessee* 1 (1986): 73–74; Harry A. Hall, *A Johnny Reb Band from Salem: The Pride of Tarheelia* (Raleigh: North Carolina Confederate Centennial Commission, 1963), 106–7; W. J. Andrews, *Sketch of Company K*, 27–28.

56. Moore, ed., "Diary of Maj. Kinloch Falconer," 451–52; Morgan, *Recollections of a Rebel Reefer*,

245–51; Campbell, ed., *Southern Service on Land & Sea*, 162; Collins, *Chapters from the Unwritten History of the War Between the States*, 303–6, 317; Cater, *As It Was*, 214–15 (quotation).

57. Collins, *Chapters from the Unwritten History of the War Between the States*, 310 (quotation); Noel C. Fisher, *War at Every Door: Partisan Politics and Guerrilla Violence in East Tennessee, 1860–1869* (Chapel Hill: University of North Carolina Press, 1997), 154–71; W. Todd Groce, *Mountain Rebels: East Tennessee Confederates and the Civil War, 1860–1870* (Knoxville: University of Tennessee Press, 1999), 127–51; Stephen V. Ash, *A Year in the South: Four Lives in 1865* (New York City: Palgrave Macmillan, 2002), 171–96; Marten, *Sing Not War*, 42; Cimbala, *Veterans North and South*, 17.

58. Major General George Thomas to Major General George Stoneman, April 29, 1865, *Official Records*, ser. 1, vol. 49, pt. 2, 518; Stoneman to Thomas, April 29, 1865, *Official Records*, ser. 1, vol. 49, pt. 2, 519; Thomas to Stoneman, *Official Records*, ser. 1, vol. 49, pt. 2, 519; Stoneman to Brigadier General Davis Tillson, April 29, 1865, *Official Records*, ser. 1, vol. 49, pt. 2, 519.

59. Guild, *A Brief Narrative of the Fourth Tennessee Cavalry Regiment*, 151–52; E. Upton to J. H. Wilson, May 9, 1865, *Official Records*, ser. 1, vol. 49, pt. 2, 687; M. H. Williams to Upton, *Official Records*, ser. 1, vol. 49, pt. 2, 687; R. S. Granger to Brigadier General William D. Whipple, May 17, 1865, *Official Records*, ser. 1, vol. 49, pt. 2, 820; Whipple to Granger, *Official Records*, ser. 1, vol. 49, pt. 2, 820; Marten, *Sing Not War*, 42–43; *TCWVQ*, vol. 1, 180, 199, 207, 280, 342; *TCWVQ*, vol. 2, 481, 503, 514, 522, 539, 548, 586, 602, 615, 693, 731, 737, 743, 749, 763, 767, 776, 792, 815, 863, 867. Volumes 3–5 of the *TCWVQ* contain many additional examples of the seizure of horses from southern soldiers as they passed through East Tennessee.

60. Bailey, ed., "Reminiscences of the Civil War by T. J. Walker," 73–74; McCaffrey, ed., *Only a Private*, 156–57; Robert O. Neff, *Tennessee's Battered Brigadier: The Life of General Joseph B. Palmer CSA* (Franklin, TN: Hillsboro Press, 2000), 160–63; Dacus, *Reminiscences of Company "H*,*"* 27; Fielder, *The Civil War Diaries of Capt. Alfred Tyler Fielder*, 233; Jamison and McTigue, eds., *Letters and Recollections of a Confederate Soldier*, 184; *TCWVQ*, vol. 2, 499; Collins, *Chapters from the Unwritten History of the War Between the States*, 305–10 (quotations); Marten, *Sing Not War*, 43.

61. Bailey, ed., "Reminiscences of the Civil War by T. J. Walker," 73–74 (first quotation); Collins, *Chapters from the Unwritten History of the War Between the States*, 306 (second quotation); Fielder, *The Civil War Diaries of Capt. Alfred Tyler Fielder*, 233.

62. Brian Craig Miller, "Manhood," in Sheehan-Dean, ed., *A Companion to the U.S. Civil War* (2 vols.) (Chichester, West Sussex, UK: John Wiley & Sons, 2014), vol. 2, 807.

63. Bradley R. Clampitt, *The Confederate Heartland: Military and Civilian Morale in the Western Confederacy* (Baton Rouge: Louisiana State University Press, 2011), 141–47.

64. Cate, ed., *Two Soldiers*, 209–13, 212 (quotations); Dyer, *Reminiscences*, 299–302; Fielder, *The Civil War Diaries of Capt. Alfred Tyler Fielder*, 234; Tapp, ed., "A Sketch of the Early Life and Service in the Confederate Army of Dr. John A. Lewis of Georgetown, Ky.," 138; *TCWVQ*, vol. 2, 805.

65. Dyer, *Reminiscences*, 304–8, 307–8 (quotations); Thomas Benton Alexander Diary, May 15–17, 1865, Hesburgh Libraries, Special Collections, University of Notre Dame, Notre Dame, Indiana (hereafter cited as UND); Tapp, ed., "A Sketch of the Early Life and Service in the Confederate Army of Dr. John A. Lewis," 138; Cate, ed., *Two Soldiers*, 213–14; Collins, *Chapters from the Unwritten History of the War Between the States*, 312; Davis, ed., *Diary of a Confederate Soldier*, 168–69.

66. Kent Masterson Brown, ed., *One of Morgan's Men: Memoirs of Lieutenant John M. Porter of the Ninth Kentucky Cavalry* (Lexington: University of Kentucky Press, 2011), 200 (quotation); Brown, ed., *One of Cleburne's Command*, 181.

67. W. H. Govan to E. J. Harvie, April 28, 1865, *Official Records*, ser. 1, vol. 47, pt. 3, 850; R. H. Anderson to T. B. Gowan, May 3, 1865, *Official Records*, ser. 1, vol. 47, pt. 3, 870; Joseph E. Johnston to commanding officer, Greensboro, May 3, 1865, *Official Records*, ser. 1, vol. 47, pt. 3, 870; J. E. Green to Johnston, May 7, 1865, *Official Records*, ser. 1, vol. 47, pt. 3, 873; Johnston, *Narrative of Military Events*, 408-9; Robert Amos Jarman, "The History of Company K, 27th Mississippi Infantry, and its First and Last Muster Rolls," Mississippi Department of Archives and History (hereafter cited as MDAH); Hamilton Tapp, ed., "A Sketch of the Early Life and Service in the Confederate Army of Dr. John A. Lewis of Georgetown, Ky.," *Register of the Kentucky Historical Society* 75 (April 1977): 138; Bond and Coward, eds., *The South Carolinians*, 184; Ulysses R. Brooks, *Butler and His Cavalry in the War of Secession, 1861-1865* (Columbia, SC: State Company, 1909), 477; Walter Augustus Clark, *Under the Stars and Bars; or, memories of Four Years Service with the Oglethorpes, of Augusta, Georgia* (Augusta, GA: Chronicle Printing, 1900), 199-200; Thomas J. Marshall Diary, April 28, 1865, *Confederate Reminiscences and Letters*, vol. 8; D. Augustus Dickert, *History of Kershaw's Brigade, with Complete Roll of Companies, Biographical Sketches, Incidents, Anecdotes, etc.* (Newberry, SC: Elbert H. Aull, 1899), 530-31; Durham, ed., *The Blues in Gray*, 280; W. Eric Emerson and Karen Stokes, eds., *Faith, Valor, Devotion: The Civil War Letters of William Porcher Dubose* (Columbia: University of South Carolina Press, 2010), 334; Fielder, *The Civil War Diaries of Capt. Alfred Tyler Fielder*, 228; Hagood, *Memoirs of the War of Secession*, 372; Charles C. Jones Jr., *Historical Sketch of the Chatham Artillery during the Confederate Struggle for Independence* (Albany, NY: Joel Munsell, 1867), 221; A. D. Kirwan, ed., *Johnny Green of the Orphan Brigade: The Journal of a Confederate Soldier* (Louisville: University of Kentucky Press, 1956), 196-97; W. J. McMurray, *History of the Twentieth Tennessee Regiment Volunteer Infantry, CSA* (Nashville, TN: Publication Committee, 1904), 359; Miller, *Recollections of a Pine Knot*, 23; Nicholson, *Stories from Dixie*, 206; Ridley, *Battles and Sketches of the Army of Tennessee*, 460; Alfred Roman, *Military Operations of General Beauregard, in the War Between the States, 1861 to 1865* (2 vols.), (New York: Harper & Brothers, 1884), vol. 1, 410-11; Bobbie Swearingen Smith, ed., *A Palmetto Boy: Civil War-Era Diaries and Letters of James Adams Tillman* (Columbia: University of South Carolina Press, 1950), 149-50; Henry Lane Stone, *"Morgan's Men": A Narrative of Personal Experiences* (Louisville, KY: Brandt & Fowler, 1919), 21-22.

68. Durham, ed., *The Blues in Gray*, 280; Stone, "Morgan's Men," 21-22; Wise, *The End of an Era*, 455.

69. Isaac A. Clarke to Col. D. N. McIntosh, June 15, 1865, Isaac Asbury Clarke Papers, AHC; Shaver, "Recollections and Reminiscences," 5, AHC; John C. Porter, "The Life of John C. Porter and Sketch of His Experiences in the Civil War," 37, Simpson History Complex, Hill College, Hillsboro, Texas (hereafter cited as Hill College); John B. Magruder to E. Kirby Smith, May 16, 1865, *Official Records*, ser. 1, vol. 48, pt. 2, 1308; D. F. Boyd to L. A. Bringier, May 20, 1865, *Official Records*, ser. 1, vol. 48, pt. 2, 1314-1315; Bradley R. Clampitt, "The Breakup: The Collapse of the Confederate Trans-Mississippi Army in Texas, 1865," *Southwestern Historical Quarterly* 108 (April 2005): 512, 518, 521, 529.

70. Circular Headquarters Army of Tennessee, April 27, 1865, *Official Records*, ser. 1, vol. 47, pt. 3, 843; Circular Headquarters Army of Tennessee, April 28, 1865, *Official Records*, ser. 1, vol. 47, pt. 3, 851; Lieutenant General Alexander P. Stewart to Lieutenant Colonel Archer Anderson, April 29, 1865, *Official Records*, ser. 1, vol. 47, pt. 3, 853 (quotation); M. B. McMicken to Major Norman W. Smith, April 29, 1865, *Official Records*, ser. 1, vol. 47, pt. 3, 855; Anderson to Stewart, April 30, 1865, *Official Records*, ser. 1, vol. 47, pt. 3, 857; Lieutenant General Stephen D. Lee to Lieutenant Colonel A. Anderson, April 30, 1865, *Official Records*, ser. 1, vol. 47, pt. 3, 857; General Orders No. 21, May 1, 1865,

Official Records, ser. 1, vol. 47, pt. 3, 858–59; General Orders No. 23, May 2, 1865, *Official Records,* ser. 1, vol. 47, pt. 3, 864; Special Orders No. —, May 2, 1865, *Official Records,* ser. 1, vol. 47, pt. 3, 865.

71. Lee to Johnston, May 7, 1865, *Official Records,* ser. 1, vol. 47, pt. 3, 873; Green to Johnston, May 7, 1865, *Official Records,* ser. 1, vol. 47, pt. 3, 873; Johnston to Major General Lovell, May 5, 1865, *Official Records,* ser. 1, vol. 47, pt. 3, 872; Lee to Anderson, April 30, 1865, *Official Records,* ser. 1, vol. 47, pt. 3, 857 (quotations).

72. S. M. Gross Journal, April 16–May 2, 1865, South Caroliniana Library, University of South Carolina, Columbia (hereafter cited as USC); Porter, "The Life of John C. Porter," 37, Hill College; W. A. Johnson, "Closing Days with Johnston," *National Tribune,* June 5, 1902; John F. Wheaton, *Reminiscences of the Chatham Artillery During the War 1861–1865. Read at Armory Hall, March 21st, 1887* (Savannah, GA: Press of the Morning News, 1887), 31, 33; B. P. Gallaway, *Ragged Rebel: A Common Soldier in Parsons's Texas Cavalry, 1861–1865* (Austin: University of Texas Press, 1988), 130; John Herbert Roper, ed., *Repairing the "March of Mars": The Civil War Diaries of John Samuel Apperson, Hospital Steward in the Stonewall Brigade, 1861–1865* (Macon, GA: Mercer University Press, 2001), 614; Clark, *Under the Stars and Bars,* 199–200; Howard O. Hendricks, "Imperiled City: The Movements of the Union and Confederate Armies Toward Greensboro in the Closing Days of the Civil War in North Carolina," (MA thesis, University of North Carolina, Greensboro, 1987), 161.

73. Major W. E. Moore to Major Isaac Scherck, May 5, 1865, *Official Records,* ser. 1, vol. 47, pt. 3, 872. For additional information on initial routes of the Army of Tennessee, see multiple entries in *Official Records,* ser. 1, vol. 47, pt. 3, 865, 868, 870–72, and ser. 1, vol. 49, pt. 2, 793.

74. Pitcock and Gurley, eds., *I Acted from Principle,* 306 (quotation); Billingsley, ed., "'Such Is War,'" 183–91; Porter, "The Life of John C. Porter," 37, Hill College; Frank Mixson, *Reminiscences of a Private* (Columbia, SC: State Company, 1910), 125; Cate, ed., *Two Soldiers,* 210–11; Campbell H. Brown, ed., *The Reminiscences of Sergeant Newton Cannon, from Holograph Material Provided by His Grandson, Samuel M. Fleming, Jr.* (Franklin, TN: Carter House Association, 1963), 68; Moore, ed., "Diary of Maj. Kinloch Falconer," 408; Wiley, ed., *This Infernal War,* 448; Ridley, *Battles and Sketches,* 482; Nicholson, *Stories from Dixie,* 210–11; Mullen, "Last Days of Johnston's Army," 111; Daniel Branson Coltrane, *The Memoirs of Daniel Branson Coltrane, Co. I, 63rd Reg. N. C. Cavalry, CSA* (Raleigh, NC: Edwards & Broughton, 1956), 44; Graber, *The Life Record of H. W. Graber,* 248–49, 256–57; Massey, ed., *Memoirs of Captain J. M. Bailey,* 106–9; Ada Christine Lightsey, *The Veteran's Story* (Meridian, MS: Meridian News, 1899), 44–45.

For additional examples of soldiers who chose indirect and therefore longer routes of travel, see Henry F. Wilson Diary, April 12–June 17, 1865, ADAH; Gallagher, ed., *Fighting for the Confederacy,* 545–52; Jim Turner, "Jim Turner, Co. G, 6th Texas Infantry, CSA, From 1861–1865," *Texana* 12, no. 2 (1974): 177–78; Davis, ed., *Diary of a Confederate Soldier,* 168–69.

3. REBELS AND REBELS: WHEN JOHNNY REB CAME MARCHING HOME

1. W. E. Preston, "History of the 33rd Alabama," 71, Alabama Department of Archives and History, Montgomery (hereafter cited as ADAH); Robert Amos Jarman, "The History of Company K, 27th Mississippi Infantry," entry dated May 2, 1890, Robert Amos Jarman Papers, Mississippi Department of Archives and History, Jackson (hereafter cited as MDAH); Francis H. Nash Diary, May

3–7, 1865, Dolph Briscoe Center for American History, University of Texas, Austin (hereafter cited as DBCAH); Robert G. Shaver, "Recollections and Reminiscences of the last days of the Confederate Trans-Mississippi Department, Marshall, Texas," 7–12, Robert G. Shaver Papers, Arkansas History Commission, Little Rock (hereafter cited as AHC); Archer Anderson to Lieutenant General S. D. Lee, May 2, 1865, in United States War Department, *The War of the Rebellion: A Compilation of the Official Records of the Union and Confederate Armies,* 128 vols. (hereafter cited as *Official Records*), (Washington, DC: Government Printing Office, 1880–1901), ser. 1, vol. 47, pt. 3, 865; Major W. E. Moore to Major Isaac Scherck, May 5, 1865, *Official Records,* ser. 1, vol. 47, pt. 3, 872; Thomas L. Connelly, *Autumn of Glory: The Army of Tennessee, 1862–1865* (Baton Rouge: Louisiana State University Press, 1971), 534–35.

For published wartime accounts, see Michael E. Banasik, ed., *Serving with Honor: The Diary of Captain Eathan Allen Pinnell, Eight Missouri Infantry (Confederate)* (Iowa City: Camp Pope Bookshop, 1999), 228–31; Roger S. Durham, ed., *The Blues in Gray: The Civil War Journal of William Daniel Dixon and the Republican Blues Daybook* (Knoxville: University of Tennessee Press, 2000), 282–85; Mary Elizabeth Sanders, ed., *Diary in Gray: Civil War Letters and Diary of Jared Young Sanders II* (Baton Rouge: Louisiana Genealogical & Historical Society, 1994), 95; J. Luke Austin, ed., *General John Bratton: Sumter to Appomattox in Letters to His Wife* (Sewanee, TN: Proctor's Hall Press, 2003), 268.

For published postwar accounts, see Walter Alexander Montgomery, *The Days of Old and the Years That Are Past* (Charlottesville, VA: Michie, 1939), 63; Henry Lane Stone, *"Morgan's Men": A Narrative of Personal Experiences* (Louisville, KY: Brandt & Fowler, 1919), 21–22; John F. Wheaton, *Reminiscences of the Chatham Artillery During the War 1861–1865. Read at Armory Hall, March 21st, 1887* (Savannah, GA: Press of the Morning News, 1887), 31–33; Elbert Decatur Willett, *History of Company B (Originally Pickens Planters), 40th Alabama Regiment, Confederate States Army, 1862 to 1865* (Anniston, AL: Norwood, 1902), 89; Johnson Hagood, *Memoirs of the War of Secession* (Columbia, SC: State Company, 1910), 372–73; D. Augustus Dickert, *History of Kershaw's Brigade, with Complete Roll of Companies, Biographical Sketches, Incidents, Anecdotes, etc.* (Newberry, SC: Elbert H. Aull, 1899), 531; J. H. Curry, *History of Company B, 40th Alabama Regiment, Confederate States Army, 1862 to 1865* (Anniston, AL: Norwood, 1902), 89; D. H. Hamilton, *History of Company M, First Texas Volunteer Infantry, Hood's Brigade, Longstreet's Corps, Army of the Confederate States of America* (Waco, TX: W. M. Morrison, 1962), 69–71; Winchester Hall, *The Story of the 26th Louisiana Infantry in the Service of the Confederate States* (n.p., 1890), 137; George Washington Finley Harper, *Sketch of the Fifty-Eighth Regiment (Infantry) North Carolina Troops* (Lenoir, NC: n.p., 1901), 18–19; John Milton Hubbard, *Notes of a Private* (Memphis: E. H. Clarke & Brother, 1909), 179–80; James T. Lambright, *History of the Liberty Independent Troop During the Civil War, 1862–1865* (Brunswick, GA: Press of Glover Brothers, 1910), pages unnumbered; Henry D. Jamison and Marguerite J. McTigue, eds., *Letters and Recollections of a Confederate Soldier* (Nashville, TN: H. D. Jamison, 1964), 184–85; Charles C. Jones Jr., *Historical Sketch of the Chatham Artillery during the Confederate Struggle for Independence* (Albany, NY: Joel Munsell, 1867), 222–24; W. J. McMurray, *History of the Twentieth Tennessee Regiment Volunteer Infantry, CSA* (Nashville, TN: Publication Committee, 1904), 359; J. B. Miller, *The Watauga Boys in the Great Civil War* (n.p., 1885), 13–14; Frank Mixson, *Reminiscences of a Private* (Columbia, SC: State Company, 1910), 123–24; George Dallas Mosgrove, *Kentucky Cavaliers in Dixie; or The Reminiscences of a Confederate Cavalryman* (Louisville, KY: Carrier-Journal Job

Printing, 1895), 263; Natalie Jenkins Bond and Osmun Latrobe Coward, eds., *The South Carolinians: Colonel Asbury Coward's Memoirs* (New York: Vintage Press, 1968), 180–82; Norman D. Brown, ed., *One of Cleburne's Command: The Civil War Reminiscences and Diary of Captain Samuel T. Foster, Granbury's Texas Brigade, CSA* (Austin: University of Texas Press, 1980), 173; Douglas John Cater, *As It Was: Reminiscences of a Soldier of the Third Texas Cavalry and the Nineteenth Louisiana Infantry* (Austin, TX: State House Press, 1990), 213–17.

2. Shaver, "Recollections and Reminiscences," 8–12, AHC; Banasik, ed., *Serving with Honor,* 228–31; McMurray, *History of the Twentieth Tennessee,* 359.

3. William S. Haggard Diary, April 10–May 5, 1865, Special Collections Research Center, University of Kentucky Libraries, Lexington (hereafter cited as UKY); Henry F. Wilson Diary, April 12, May 1, 1865, ADAH; John C. Porter, "The Life of John C. Porter and Sketch of His Experiences in the Civil War," 37, Simpson History Complex, Hill College, Hillsboro, Texas (hereafter cited as Hill College); W. J. Andrews, *Sketch of Company K, 23rd South Carolina Volunteers in the Civil War from 1862–1865* (Richmond, VA: Whittet and Shepperson Printers, n.d.), 28–29; Davis Bitton, ed., *The Reminiscences and Civil War Letters of Levi Lamoni Wight; Life in a Mormon Splinter Colony on the Texas Frontier* (Salt Lake City: University of Utah Press, 1970), 39; Wirt Armistead Cate, ed., *Two Soldiers: The Campaign Diaries of Thomas J. Key, C.S.A., December 7, 1863–May 17, 1865, and Robert J. Campbell, U.S.A., January 1, 1864–July 21, 1864* (Chapel Hill: University of North Carolina Press, 1938), 206–16; John Frank Edwards, *Army Life of Frank Edwards, Confederate Veteran, Army of Northern Virginia, 1861–1865* (La Grange, GA: n.p., 1911), 69, 78, 83; Robert G. Evans, ed., *The 16th Mississippi Infantry: Civil War Letters and Reminiscences* (Jackson: University Press of Mississippi, 2002), 307; William A. Fletcher, *Rebel Private Front and Rear: Memoirs of a Confederate Soldier* (New York: Dutton, 1995), 200, 206; Arthur P. Ford, *Life in the Confederate Army: Being the Experiences of a Private Soldier in the Confederate Army* (New York: Neale Publishing, 1905), 65; G. Ward Hubbs, ed., *Voices from Company D: Diaries by the Greensboro Guards, Fifth Alabama Infantry Regiment, Army of Northern Virginia* (Blacksburg, VA: Wilson, 2006), 387; James M. McCaffrey, ed., *Only a Private: A Texan Remembers the Civil War: The Memoirs of William J. Oliphant* (Houston: Halcyon Press, 2004), 88; Franklin Alexander Montgomery, *Reminiscences of a Mississippian in Peace and War, by Frank A. Montgomery, Lieutenant-Colonel First Mississippi Cavalry* (Cincinnati, OH: Robert Clarke Co. Press, 1901), 255–59; James Nicholson, *Stories of Dixie* (New York: American Books, 1915), 235–41; William Miller Owen, *In Camp and Battle with the Washington Artillery of New Orleans: A Narrative of Events during the Late Civil War from Bull Run to Appomattox and Spanish Fort* (Boston: Ticknor, 1885), 393.

4. James Marten, *Sing Not War: The Lives of Union and Confederate Veterans in Gilded Age America* (Chapel Hill: University of North Carolina Press, 2011), 40–44.

5. Joseph B. Polley, Hood's Texas Brigade: Its Marches, Its Battles, Its Achievements (New York: Neale Publishing, 1910), 279; Mixson, Reminiscences of a Private, 123–24.

6. Ted R. Worley, ed., *The War Memoirs of Captain John W. Lavender, CSA* (Pine Bluff, AR: Southern Press, 1956), 136–39; David E. Johnston, *The Story of a Confederate Boy in the Civil War* (Portland, OR: Glass & Prudhomme, 1914), 344–47; James Edward Whitehorne Diary, April 10–16, 1865, Southern Historical Collection, Wilson Library, University of North Carolina, Chapel Hill (hereafter cited as SHC); Henry Brockman Journal, June 14–24, 1865, AHC; Henry George, *History of the 3rd, 7th, 8th, and 12th Kentucky, CSA* (Louisville, KY: C. T. Dearing Printing, 1911), 144–45;

Polley, *Hood's Texas* Brigade, 279; Thomas Benton Reed, *A Private in Gray* (Camden, AR: T. B. Reed, 1905), 116–17; Daniel E. Sutherland, ed., *Reminiscences of a Private: William E. Bevens of the First Arkansas Infantry, CSA* (Fayetteville: University of Arkansas Press, 1992), 237–43; Montgomery, *Days of Old*, 63; Dickert, *History of Kershaw's Brigade*, 531; Cater, *As It Was*, 216–17; Chris M. Calkins, *The Final Bivouac: The Surrender Parade at Appomattox and the Disbanding of the Armies, April 10–May 20, 1865* (Lynchburg, VA: M. E. Howard, 1988), 46; T. P. Devereux, "The Homeward March after Stacking Arms at Appomattox," in *Recollections and Reminiscences, 1861–1865* (vol. 1) (South Carolina Division, United Daughters of the Confederacy, 1990), 253.

7. Marcus Bearden Dewitt Diary, May 15 (quotation), 1865, Civil War Collection, Tennessee State Library and Archives, Nashville (hereafter cited as TSLA); John Will Dyer, *Reminiscences; or, Four Years in the Confederate Army* (Evansville, IN: Keller Printing and Publishing, 1898), 294–95; Bond and Coward, eds., *The South Carolinians*, 180; Thomas D. Cockerell and Michael B. Ballard, eds., *A Mississippi Rebel in the Army of Northern Virginia: The Civil War Memoirs of Private David Holt* (Baton Rouge: Louisiana State University Press, 1995), 341; R. Hugh Simmons, "The 12th Louisiana Infantry in North Carolina, January–April, 1865," *Louisiana History* 36, no. 1 (1995): 104.

8. Porter, "The Life of John C. Porter," 37–38, Hill College; Joseph I. Waring, ed., "The Diary of William G. Hinson During the War of Secession," (pt. 2) *South Carolina Historical Magazine* 75 (April 1974): 119; Kenneth Wiley, ed., *Norfolk Blues: The Civil War Diary of the Norfolk Light Artillery Blues* (Shippensburg, PA: Burd Street Press, 1997), 226–27; Austin, ed., *General John Bratton*, 268; Bond and Coward, eds., *The South Carolinians*, 184; Mixson, *Reminiscences of a Private*, 123–24; Polley, *Hood's Texas Brigade*, 279; Robert M. Dunkerly, *The Confederate Surrender at Greensboro: The Final Days of the Army of Tennessee, April 1865* (Jefferson, NC: McFarland, 2013), 154; Noah Andre Trudeau, *Out of the Storm: The End of the Civil War, April–June, 1865* (Boston: Little, Brown, 1994), 382–83; George B. Guild, *A Brief Narrative of the Fourth Tennessee Cavalry Regiment, Wheeler's Corps, Army of Tennessee* (Nashville, TN: n.p., 1913), 151–52.

9. Hagood, *Memoirs of the War of Secession,* 373; Ada Christine Lightsey, *The Veteran's Story* (Meridian, MS: Meridian News, 1899), 45; Bromfield L. Ridley, *Battles and Sketches of the Army of Tennessee* (Mexico, MO: Missouri Printing and Publishing, 1906), 466; Mixson, *Reminiscences of a Private*, 125; R. M. Collins, *Chapters from the Unwritten History of the War Between the States; or, the Incidents in the Life of a Confederate Soldier* (St. Louis: Nixon-Jones Printing, 1893), 302 (quotation).

10. In addition to the sources cited in notes 1–8 above, hundreds of other accounts by veterans describe group travel. See *Tennessee Civil War Veteran Questionnaires* (5 vols.) (Easley, SC: Southern Historical Press, 1985) (hereafter cited as *TCWVQ*).

11. Thomas Herndon Civil War Diary and Journal, April 21–23, 29, May 10, 1865, Civil War Document Collection, United States Army Heritage and Education Center, Carlisle, Pennsylvania (hereafter cited as USAHEC); Charles Bickem Fields Diary, April 12, 13, 15, 1865, Virginia Historical Society, Richmond (hereafter cited as VHS); Marcus Bearden Dewitt Diary, May 3, 5–10, 12, 1865, Civil War Collection, TSLA; Robert A. Turner Diary, April 13, 1865, and subsequent undated entries, South Caroliniana Library, University of South Carolina, Columbia (hereafter cited as USC); Samuel Lewis Moore, "Autobiography of Samuel Lewis Moore," 14–15, Civil War Document Collection, USAHEC; William S. Haggard Diary, April 25, May 1, 1865, UKY; Thomas Benton Alexander Diary, May 7, 17, 1865, Hesburgh Libraries, Special Collections, University of Notre Dame, Notre Dame, Indiana (hereafter cited as UND); Maddie Lou Teague Crow, ed., *The Diary of a Confederate Soldier:*

John Washington Inzer (Huntsville, AL: Strode Publishers, 1977), 132–55; Royce Gordon Shingleton, ed., "South from Appomattox: The Diary of Abner R. Cox," *South Carolina Historical Magazine* 75, no. 4 (October 1974): 241; Edward Crenshaw, "Diary of Captain Edward Crenshaw of the Confederate States Army," *Alabama Historical Quarterly* 2, no. 4 (Winter 1940): 472, 474, 476; Frederick W. Moore, ed., "Diary of Maj. Kinloch Falconer," *Confederate Veteran Magazine* 9 (October 1901): 450–53; Richard A. Baumgartner, ed., *Blood and Sacrifice: The Civil War Journal of a Confederate Soldier* (Huntington, WV: Blue Acorn Press, 1994), 214–19; Cate, ed., *Two Soldiers,* 206–8; Joseph T. Durkin, ed., *John Dooley: Confederate Soldier. His War Journal* (Washington, DC: Georgetown University Press, 1945), 182–87, 191, 202–3; Thomas W. Cutrer, ed., *Longstreet's Aide: The Civil War Letters of Major Thomas J. Goree* (Charlottesville: University of Virginia Press, 1995), 145–46; A. D. Kirwan, ed., *Johnny Green of the Orphan Brigade: The Journal of a Confederate Soldier* (Louisville: University of Kentucky Press, 1956), 197–201; Archie P. McDonald, ed., *Make Me a Map of the Valley: The Civil War Journal of Stonewall Jackson's Topographer* (Dallas: Southern Methodist University Press, 1973), 266; George M. Neese, *Three Years in the Confederate Horse Artillery* (Dayton, OH: Press of the Morningside Bookshop, 1983), 359–60; W. F. Pendleton, *Confederate Diary of W. F. Pendleton, January to April 1865* (Bryn Athyn, PA: n.p., 1957), 17–18, 20–21; Wiley, ed., *Norfolk Blues,* 226–27; Henry Steele Commager, ed., *The Blue and the Gray: The Story of the Civil War as Told by Its Participants* (2 vols.) (New York: Bobbs-Merrill, 1950), vol. 2, 1145–47; Ridley, *Battles and Sketches,* 467, 470, 477. Ridley's work is part diary and part memoir.

For published postwar accounts, see Henry William Graber, *The Life Record of H. W. Graber, a Terry Texas Ranger, 1861–1865: Sixty-two Years in Texas* (H. W. Graber, 1916), 246, 253, 254, 256–57, 259–60; W. A. Russell, "Tragic Adventures as the War Closed," *Confederate Veteran Magazine* 22 (February 1914): 403; R. S. Bevier, *A History of the First and Second Missouri Confederate Brigades, 1861–1865, and from Wakarusa to Appomattox* (St. Louis: Bryan, Brand, 1879), 470; Edwards, *Army Life of Frank Edwards,* 83–84; Ford, *Life in the Confederate Army,* 64, 68–70; Johnston, *Story of a Confederate Boy,* 346; Hamilton, *History of Company M,* 69–70; Jim Turner, "Jim Turner, Co. G, 6th Texas Infantry, CSA, From 1861–1865," *Texana* 12, no. 2 (1974): 177–78; Carlton McCarthy, *Detailed Minutiae of Soldier Life in the Army of Northern Virginia, 1861–1865* (Richmond: Carlton McCarthy, 1894), 167–68, 171–74; J. M. Miller, *Recollections of a Pine Knot in the Lost Cause* (Greenwood, MS: Commonwealth Publishing, 1910), 24; Mixson, *Reminiscences of a Private,* 125, 128; Montgomery, *Reminiscences of a Mississippian,* 251; Montgomery, *Days of Old,* 64–65; Nicholson, *Stories of Dixie,* 207, 211–14; Owen, *In Camp and Battle with the Washington Artillery,* 393, 394; Devereux, "The Homeward March after Stacking Arms at Appomattox," 253–55.

12. Henry Felix Wilson Diary, April 12 (first quotation), 16 (second quotation), 17, May 4, 9, 1865, ADAH.

13. Spencer Glasgow Welch, *A Confederate Surgeon's Letters to His Wife* (New York: Neale Publishing, 1911), 117–20; William D. Alexander Diary, April 12, 19, 1865, SHC; Shingleton, ed., "South from Appomattox," 243; Harry C. Townsend, "Townsend's Diary—January–May, 1865; From Petersburg to Appomattox, Thence to North Carolina to Join Johnston's Army," *Southern Historical Society Papers* 34 (1906): 112; Durkin, ed., *John Dooley,* 202; Ford, *Life in the Confederate Army,* 69–70; Devereux, "The Homeward March after Stacking Arms at Appomattox," 253 (quotation).

14. Graber, *The Life Record of H. W. Graber,* 246; Lightsey, *The Veteran's Story,* 45; Moore, "Autobiography of Samuel Lewis Moore," 15 (quotation).

15. Patricia J. Bennett, ed., "Curtis R. Burke's Civil War Journal," (pt. 4) *Indiana Magazine of History* (June 1971): 162; Turner, "Jim Turner, Co. G, 6th Texas Infantry," 178; Andrews, *Sketch of Company K*, 29; Jamison and McTigue, eds., *Letters and Recollections of a Confederate Soldier*, 184–85; William H. Runge, ed., *Four Years in the Confederate Artillery: The Diary of Private Henry Robinson Berkeley* (Richmond: Virginia Historical Society, 1991), 144–45; Mosgrove, *Kentucky Cavaliers in Dixie*, 264–65; Joseph McClure, "A Wounded Texan's Trip Home on Crutches," *Confederate Veteran Magazine* 17 (April 1909): 162–63.

16. Bradley R. Clampitt, *Occupied Vicksburg* (Baton Rouge: Louisiana State University Press, 2016), 205; McCaffrey, ed., *Only a Private*, 89.

17. Reid Mitchell, *Civil War Soldiers* (New York: Viking Press, 1988), 201; James J. Broomall, *Private Confederacies: The Emotional Worlds of Southern Men as Citizens and Soldiers* (Chapel Hill: University of North Carolina Press, 2019), 106–7; Nathaniel Cheairs Hughes Jr., ed., *The Civil War Memoir of Phillip Daingerfield Stephenson, D. D.* (Conway: University of Central Arkansas Press, 1995), 380 (quotation).

18. Collins, *Chapters from the Unwritten History of the War Between the States*, 317–20; Newberry (SC), *Tri-Weekly Herald*, May 16, 1865; Augusta (GA) *Chronicle & Sentinel*, May 10, 1865; Marshall *Texas Republican*, June 2, 1865; Alfred Roman, *Military Operations of General Beauregard, in the War Between the States, 1861 to 1865* (New York: Harper & Brothers, 1884), 411–15; Marten, *Sing Not War*, 46.

19. James Robert McMichael Diary, June 19, 22, 1865, SHC; Thomas Herndon Civil War Diary and Journal, May 10, 1865, Civil War Document Collection, USAHEC; Roman, *Military Operations of General Beauregard*, 411–15; Owen, *In Camp and Battle with the Washington Artillery*, 395; Townsend, "Townsend's Diary," 127; Charles Crosland, *Reminiscences of the Sixties* (Columbia, SC: State Company, 1910), 52; Graber, *The Life Record of H. W. Graber*, 258–60; Marten, *Sing Not War*, 38–39, 45–46.

20. Thomas Benton Alexander Diary, May 15–17, 1865, UND; Louis H. Manarin, ed., "The Civil War Diary of Rufus James Woolwine," *Virginia Magazine of History and Biography* 71 (1963): 447; Brown, ed., *One of Cleburne's Command*, 185; McDonald, ed., *Make Me a Map of the Valley*, 267; William C. Davis, ed., *Diary of a Confederate Soldier: John S. Jackman of the Orphan Brigade* (Columbia: University of South Carolina Press, 1990), 168–69.

21. Miller, *Recollections of a Pine Knot*, 24; Nicholson, *Stories of Dixie*, 222–23 (quotations); John Taylor Wood Diary, May 1, 1865, SHC; George Alexander Martin Diary, May 12, 1865, VHS; James M. Mullen, "Last Days of Johnston's Army, a Comrade's Experience With General L. S. Baker's Command at Weldon, N. C., During the Fifteen Days Preceding Johnston's Surrender at Greensboro, N. C.," *Southern Historical Society Papers* 18 (1890): 108; Montgomery, *Days of Old*, 67; Alfred Tyler Fielder, *The Civil War Diaries of Capt. Alfred Tyler Fielder, 12th Tennessee Regiment Infantry, Company B, 1861–1865* (Louisville, KY: Ann York Franklin, 1996), 232; Campbell H. Brown, ed., *The Reminiscences of Sergeant Newton Cannon, from Holograph Material Provided by His Grandson, Samuel M. Fleming, Jr.* (Franklin, TN: Carter House Association, 1963), 66–67; Charles D. Spurlin, ed., *The Civil War Diary of Charles A. Leuschner* (Austin, TX: Eakin Press, 1992), 54; Cate, ed., *Two Soldiers*, 206–8; Howard O. Hendricks, "Imperiled City: The Movements of the Union and Confederate Armies Toward Greensboro in the Closing Days of the Civil War in North Carolina" (MA thesis, University of North Carolina, Greensboro, 1987), 161; *TCWVQ*, vol. 1, 176; *TCWVQ*, vol. 2, 591.

22. Lavender R. Ray Diary, April 29, 1865, Lavender R. Ray Papers, Georgia Archives, Morrow (hereafter cited as Georgia Archives); William S. Haggard Diary, April 25, 1865, UKY; Thomas Benton Alexander Diary, May 10, 15–17, 1865, UND; William Clyde Billingsley, ed., "'Such Is War': The Confederate Memoirs of Newton Asbury Keen" (pt. 4), *Texas Military History* 7 (Fall 1968): 190–91; James Troy Massey, ed., *Memoirs of Captain J. M. Bailey* (James Troy Massey, 1994), 108; Hamilton, *History of Company M*, 69–70; Ridley, *Battles and Sketches*, 470; Wiley, ed., *Norfolk Blues*, 226; Devereux, "The Homeward March after Stacking Arms at Appomattox," 253–54; McClure, "A Wounded Texan's Trip Home on Crutches," 163; Moore, ed., "Diary of Maj. Kinloch Falconer," 409; Shingleton, ed., "South from Appomattox: The Diary of Abner R. Cox," 241; Graber, *The Life Record of H. W. Graber*, 256–57; Mosgrove, *Kentucky Cavaliers in Dixie*, 264–65; Nicholson, *Stories of Dixie*, 211–14.

23. Devereux, "The Homeward March after Stacking Arms at Appomattox," 253–54.

24. Porter, "The Life of John C. Porter," 38, Hill College.

25. Porter, "The Life of John C. Porter," 38.

26. George Alexander Martin Diary, April 21, 1865, VHS; Marcus Bearden Dewitt Diary, May 5–6, 1865, Civil War Collection, TSLA; William S. Haggard Diary, May 1, 1865, UKY.

27. James Edward Whitehorne Diary, April 13, 1865, SHC; Cutrer, ed., *Longstreet's Aide*, 146 (first quotation); Brown, ed., *The Reminiscences of Sergeant Newton Cannon*, 66, 67 (second quotation).

28. Avington Wayne Simpson Diary, May 23, 1865, SHC; James Edward Whitehorne Diary, April 14, 16, 1865, SHC; Crenshaw, "Diary of Captain Edward Crenshaw of the Confederate States Army," 478, 479; McClure, "A Wounded Texan's Trip Home on Crutches," 163; James L. Nichols, ed., "Reminiscing from 1865 to 1865; An Ex-'Confed,' H. P. Morrow," *East Texas Historical Journal* 9 (March 1971): 15; Ford, *Life in the Confederate Army*, 68; Johnston, *The Story of a Confederate Boy in the Civil War*, 347; Lightsey, *The Veteran's Story*, 47; Massey, ed., *Memoirs of Captain J. M. Bailey*, 108–9; Devereux, "The Homeward March after Stacking Arms at Appomattox," 254.

29. Edwards, *Army Life of Frank Edwards*, 84–85.

30. Clampitt, *Occupied Vicksburg*, 70–71.

31. Susan Williams Benson, ed., *Berry Benson's Civil War Book: Memoirs of a Confederate Scout and Sharpshooter* (Athens: University of Georgia Press, 1962), 202–3; McCarthy, *Detailed Minutiae of Soldier Life*, 171–72; Nichols, ed., "Reminiscing from 1865 to 1865," 14; Owen, *In Camp and Battle with the Washington Artillery*, 393; Kirwan, ed., *Johnny Green of the Orphan Brigade*, 198–201; Crenshaw, "Diary of Captain Edward Crenshaw of the Confederate States Army," 467 (quotations).

32. Montgomery, *Days of Old*, 66–67.

33. Kirwan, ed., *Johnny Green of the Orphan Brigade*, 198–201.

34. Kirwan, ed., *Johnny Green of the Orphan Brigade*, 201.

35. Porter, "The Life of John C. Porter," 38, Hill College; Spurlin, ed., *The Civil War Diary of Charles A. Leuschner*, 53–54; Collins, *Chapters from the Unwritten History of the War Between the States*, 317–20; Massey, ed., *Memoirs of Captain J. M. Bailey*, 108; Roman, *Military Operations of General Beauregard*, 411–12; John C. Breckinridge, "A Rebel Leader's Flight," *Civil War Times Illustrated* 6, no. 3 (June 1967): 5.

36. McCaffrey, ed., *Only a Private*, 90.

37. Graber, *The Life Record of H. W. Graber*, 249; Nichols, ed., "Reminiscing from 1865 to 1865," 14.

38. Turner, "Jim Turner, Co. G, 6th Texas Infantry," 177; Mixson, *Reminiscences of a Private*, 125; McCaffrey, ed., *Only a Private*, 156; Nicholson, *Stories of Dixie*, 207; Calkins, *The Final Bivouac*, 46;

Trudeau, *Out of the Storm*, 382–83; Joseph T. Glatthaar, *General Lee's Army: From Victory to Collapse* (New York: Free Press, 2008), 471.

39. James Edward Whitehorne Diary, April 13, 1865, SHC; William S. Haggard Diary, April 26, 1865, UKY (quotation); Wiley, ed., *Norfolk Blues*, 226; Nicholson, *Stories of Dixie*, 207; Valerius C. Giles, *Rags and Hope: The Recollections of Val. C. Giles, Four Years with Hood's Brigade, Fourth Texas Infantry, 1861–1865* (New York: Coward-McCann, 1961), 278.

40. Unknown Confederate Soldier Diary, May 23, 1865, AHC; John Taylor Wood Diary, April 11, 16, 1865, SHC; Montgomery, *Days of Old*, 66; Crenshaw, "Diary of Captain Edward Crenshaw of the Confederate States Army," 477; Graber, *The Life Record of H. W. Graber*, 249.

41. Moore, ed., "Diary of Maj. Kinloch Falconer," 408–10, 451 (quotations). The editor of Falconer's diary incorrectly located the officer's home of Bridgeville, Alabama, in Mississippi.

42. Unknown Confederate Soldier Diary, May 25, 1865, AHC (quotation); Henry F. Wilson Diary, May 8, 1865, ADAH; Shaver, "Recollections and Reminiscences," 6–7, AHC; Durkin, ed., *John Dooley*, 188; Edwards, *Army Life of Frank Edwards*, 79–80; Ford, *Life in the Confederate Army*, 68–69; Calkins, *The Final Bivouac*, 49.

43. Durkin, ed., *John Dooley*, 182, 183 (quotation), 184–87; United States Bureau of the Census, Eighth U.S. Census, 1860, Schedule 1 (Free Inhabitants).

44. Lavender R. Ray Diary, April 6, 29, 1865, Lavender R. Ray Papers, Georgia Archives; Thomas Herndon Civil War Diary and Journal, April 29, 1865 (quotation), Civil War Document Collection, USAHEC; Ridley, *Battles and Sketches*, 467, 477.

45. Cockerell and Ballard, eds., *A Mississippi Rebel in the Army of Northern Virginia*, 337 (first quotation); John Taylor Wood Diary, May 16, 1865, SHC; Daniel Branson Coltrane, *The Memoirs of Daniel Branson Coltrane, Co. I, 63rd Reg. N. C. Cavalry, CSA* (Raleigh: Edwards & Broughton, 1956), 42; Ford, *Life in the Confederate Army*, 68–69.

46. Wiley, ed., *Norfolk Blues*, 226.

47. Unknown Confederate Soldier Diary, May 24, 1865, AHC (quotations); Devereux, "The Homeward March after Stacking Arms at Appomattox," 253.

48. Marcus Bearden Dewitt Diary, May 10, 12, 1865, Civil War Collection, TSLA; William S. Haggard Diary, May 1, 1865, UKY; Massey, ed., *Memoirs of Captain J. M. Bailey*, 108; Mixson, *Reminiscences of a Private*, 127; Andrews, *Sketch of Company K*, 29; Joe Ashley and Lavon Ashley, eds., *Oh for Dixie! The Civil War Record and Diary of Capt. William V. Davis, 30th Mississippi Infantry, CSA* (Colorado Springs, CO: Standing Pine Press, 2001), 135; Baumgartner, ed., *Blood and Sacrifice*, 216; W. A. Callaway, "Reminiscences of War at the Close," *Confederate Veteran Magazine* 17 (October 1909): 504; Cate, ed., *Two Soldiers*, 209–10; Richard B. McCaslin, ed., *A Soldier's Letters to Charming Nellie, by J. B. Polley of Hood's Texas Brigade* (Knoxville: University of Tennessee Press, 2008), 176–84; Sutherland, ed., *Reminiscences of a Private*, 239.

49. Montgomery, *Reminiscences*, 258; Cate, ed., *Two Soldiers*, 215–16. Soldiers did not always *expect* free rail travel, but countless sources cited throughout this study support the conclusion that soldiers almost universally believed that railroads *should* transport them without charge.

50. Cate, ed., *Two Soldiers*, 206 (quotation), 209–10; McCarthy, *Detailed Minutiae of Soldier Life*, 168; Cutrer, ed., *Longstreet's Aide*, 151; Waring, ed., "The Diary of William G. Hinson During the War of Secession," 120; James W. Brown Diary, May 6, 1865, James W. Brown Papers, Georgia Archives; Moore, ed., "Diary of Maj. Kinloch Falconer," 408–9, 450; Mixson, *Reminiscences of a Private*,

125–27; Roman, *Military Operations of General Beauregard*, 411; Brown, ed., *The Reminiscences of Sergeant Newton Cannon*, 65; Wiley, ed., *Norfolk Blues*, 226; Breckinridge, "A Rebel Leader's Flight," 8; Hendricks, "Imperiled City," 163.

51. Moore, ed., "Diary of Maj. Kinloch Falconer," 408–9 (first quotation), 450 (second quotation); James W. Brown Diary, May 6, 1865, James W. Brown Papers, Georgia Archives (third quotation); United States Bureau of the Census, Eighth U.S. Census, 1860, Schedule 1 (Free Inhabitants).

52. Wiley, ed., *Norfolk Blues*, 226; Roman, *Military Operations of General Beauregard*, 411.

53. Cate, ed., *Two Soldiers*, 206–10; Mixson, *Reminiscences of a Private*, 125–29.

54. Brian Matthew Jordan, *Marching Home: Union Veterans and Their Unending Civil War* (New York: Liveright Publishing, 2014), 34–39; Marshall *Texas Republican*, June 2, 1865 (quotation).

55. Marten, *Sing Not War*, 18–21 (quotation 18); Jordan, *Marching Home*, 36–39 (quotation 39), 47, 226n54; Paul A. Cimbala, *Veterans North and South: The Transition from Soldier to Civilian after the American Civil War* (Santa Barbara, CA: Praeger, 2015), 20–25, 36–38.

56. Marten, *Sing Not War*, 18–21 (quotation 20).

57. B. P. Gallaway, *The Ragged Rebel: A Common Soldier in W. H. Parsons' Texas Cavalry, 1861–1865* (Austin: University of Texas Press, 1988), 131; Graber, *The Life Record of H. W. Graber*, 258–60; John E. Stegeman, *These Men She Gave: The Civil War Diary of Athens, Georgia* (Athens: University of Georgia Press, 1964), 141–42; Larry M. Logue, *To Appomattox and Beyond: The Civil War Soldier in War and Peace* (Chicago: Ivan R. Dee, 1996), 103.

58. Edwards, *Army Life of Frank Edwards*, 77; I. G. Bradwell, "Making Our Way Home from Appomattox," *Confederate Veteran Magazine* 29 (March 1921): 103 (quotation).

59. William S. Haggard Diary, April–July, 1865 entries, UKY; Brown, ed., *One of Cleburne's Command*, 196–97; Hughes, ed., *The Civil War Memoir of Phillip Daingerfield Stephenson*, 372; *TCWVQ*, vol. 1, 285 (first quotation); *TCWVQ*, vol. 2, 760, 771, 867 (second quotation); *TCWVQ*, vol. 3, 932 (third quotation), 1099–1100, 1302; Cimbala, *Veterans North and South*, 17.

For more on general conditions that confronted Confederate soldiers who returned to East Tennessee, see Noel C. Fisher, *War at Every Door: Partisan Politics and Guerrilla Violence in East Tennessee, 1860–1869* (Chapel Hill: University of North Carolina Press, 1997), 154–71; W. Todd Groce, *Mountain Rebels: East Tennessee Confederates and the Civil War, 1860–1870* (Knoxville: University of Tennessee Press, 1999), 127–51; Stephen V. Ash, *A Year in the South: Four Lives in 1865* (New York: Palgrave Macmillan, 2002), 171–96.

60. Mixson, *Reminiscences of a Private*, 127 (quotations); Kirwan, ed., *Johnny Green of the Orphan Brigade*, 197.

61. Brian Craig Miller, "Manhood," in Aaron Sheehan-Dean, ed., *A Companion to the U.S. Civil War* (2 vols.) (Chichester, West Sussex, UK: John Wiley & Sons, Ltd., 2014), vol. 2, 795–810; Lee-Ann Whites, *The Civil War as a Crisis in Gender: Augusta, Georgia, 1860–1890* (New York: Palgrave Macmillan, 2005), 134.

62. *TCWVQ*, vol. 4, 1375–76.

63. Michael L. Bradley, *This Astounding Close: The Road to Bennett Place* (Chapel Hill: University of North Carolina Press, 2000), 240, 242; Willene B. Clark, ed., *Valleys of the Shadow: The Memoir of Confederate Captain Reuben G. Clark, Company I, 59th Tennessee Mounted Infantry* (Knoxville: University of Tennessee Press, 1994), 69–70; Clampitt, "The Breakup: The Collapse of the Confederate Trans-Mississippi Army in Texas, 1865," *Southwestern Historical Quarterly* 108 (April 2005): 528–30; Shaver, "Recollections and Reminiscences," 4–8, AHC; Matthew Jack Davis, "A Long Jour-

ney Home," *Civil War Times Illustrated* 36, no. 2 (May 1997): 50–54; Thilbert H. Pearce, ed., *Diary of Captain Henry A. Chambers* (Wendell, NC: Broadfoot's Bookmark, 1983), 264–65; *TCWVQ*, vol. 1, 318; *TCWVQ*, vol. 2, 657, 765.

64. Thomas Benton Alexander Diary, April 9–May 10, 1865, UND; Brown, ed., *One of Cleburne's Command*, 196–97; Neese, *Three Years in the Confederate Horse Artillery*, 359–60; Welch, *A Confederate Surgeon's Letters to His Wife*, 117–20; Graber, *The Life Record of H. W. Graber*, 256–57.

65. Richard Lowe, ed., *A Texas Cavalry Officer's Civil War: The Diary and Letters of James C. Bates* (Baton Rouge: Louisiana State University Press, 1999), 333–34; Pearce, ed., *Diary of Captain Henry A. Chambers*, 264–65; Slann L. C. Simmons, ed., "Diary of Abram W. Clement, 1865," *South Carolina Historical Magazine* 59 (1958): 78–83; Martin Brett, *Experiences of a Georgia Boy in the Army of Northern Virginia* (Gainesville, GA: Magnolia Press, 1988), 35–36; Welch, *A Confederate Surgeon's Letters to His Wife*, 117–20; Robert H. Dacus, *Reminiscences of Company "H," First Arkansas Mounted Rifles* (Dardanelle, AR: Post-Despatch Printing, 1897), 27–29; Simmons, "The 12th Louisiana Infantry in North Carolina, January–April, 1865," 106; *TCWVQ*, vol. 2, 771; *TCWVQ*, vol. 4, 1741; *TCWVQ*, vol. 5, 2101; Chattahoochee Valley Historical Society, ed., *War Was the Place: A Centennial Collection of Confederate Soldiers' Letters* (Chambers County, AL: Chattahoochee Valley Historical Society, 1961), 115–17.

66. *TCWVQ*, vol. 2, 605; *TCWVQ*, vol. 4, 1555; Mosgrove, *Kentucky Cavaliers in Dixie*, 265 (quotation); William S. Haggard Diary, May 5–July 15, 1865 entries, UKY; Francis H. Nash Diary, May 13, 16, 1865, DBCAH; Porter, "The Life of John C. Porter," 37–38, Hill College; Welch, *A Confederate Surgeon's Letters to His Wife*, 117–20; Benson, ed., *Berry Benson's Civil War Book*, 202–3; J. P. Austin, *The Blue and the Gray, Sketches of a Portion of the Unwritten History of the Great American Civil War* (Atlanta: Franklin Printing and Publishing, 1899), 170; Hubert L. Ferguson, ed., "Letters of John W. Duncan, Captain Confederate States of America," *Arkansas Historical Quarterly* 9 (1960): 311; John Overton Casler, *Four Years in the Stonewall Brigade* (Guthrie, OK: State Capital Printing, 1903), 288.

67. Ferguson, ed., "Letters of John W. Duncan," 298, 310–12; Dewitt Diary, May 3–19, 1865, Civil War Collection, TSLA; Lambright, *History of the Liberty Independent Troop*, pages unnumbered; John Milton Hoge, *A Journal by John Milton Hoge, 1862–5: Containing Some of the Most Particular Incidents That Occurred During His Enlistment as a Soldier in the Confederate Army* (Cincinnati, OH: M. H. Bruce, 1961), 43; *TCWVQ*, vol. 1, 349–50; *TCWVQ*, vol. 2, 467, 826; *TCWVQ*, vol. 3, 1075; Sam Davis Elliott, *Soldier of Tennessee: General Alexander P. Stewart and the Civil War in the West* (Baton Rouge: Louisiana State University Press, 2004), 272.

68. Quoted in Cimbala, *Veterans North and South*, 13.

69. *TCWVQ*, vol. 2, 631 (first quotation); Lowe, ed., *A Texas Cavalry Officer's Civil War*, 330–33, 334 (second quotation).

70. Eric J. Leed, *No Man's Land: Combat & Identity in World War I* (London: Cambridge University Press, 1979), 32–33; Thomas W. Cutrer, *Theater of a Separate War: The Civil War West of the Mississippi River* (Chapel Hill: University of North Carolina Press, 2017), 440–41; Andrew Rolle, *The Lost Cause: The Confederate Exodus to Mexico* (Norman: University of Oklahoma Press, 1965), 3–10; Breckinridge, "A Rebel Leader's Flight," 4–10; *TCWVQ*, vol. 1, 257 (second quotation), 262 (first quotation); Cimbala, *Veterans North and South*, 81–82.

71. William B. Holberton, *Homeward Bound: The Demobilization of Union and Confederate Armies, 1865-1866* (Mechanicsburg, PA: Stackpole Books, 2001), 122; Constantine A. Hege Letters, June 19, 29 (quotation), 1865, Lewis Leigh Collection, USAHEC.

72. Avington Wayne Simpson Diary, May 9–August 9, 1865, UNC; United States Bureau of the Census, Ninth U.S. Census, 1870.

73. Kirwan, ed., *Johnny Green of the Orphan Brigade*, 197–207.

4. EVERY REBEL FOR HIMSELF: THE LAWLESS SUMMER OF 1865

1. *Tennessee Civil War Veteran Questionnaires* (Easley, SC: Southern Historical Press, 1985), 4, 1682 (hereafter cited as *TCWVQ*).

2. John Taylor Wood Diary, May 6 (first quotation), 1865, John Taylor Wood Papers, Southern Historical Collection, University of North Carolina, Chapel Hill (hereafter cited as SHC); Camden (SC) *Tri-Weekly Journal*, June 5, 1865; Newberry (SC) *Tri-Weekly Herald*, May 16, 1865; Augusta (GA) *Chronicle & Sentinel*, May 10, 1865; Sam Davis Elliott, ed., *Doctor Quintard, Chaplain CSA and Second Bishop of Tennessee* (Baton Rouge: Louisiana State University Press, 2003), 257 (second quotation); George Cary Eggleston, *A Rebel's Recollections* (New York: Hurd and Houghton, 1874), 246–47; Thad Holt Jr., ed., *Miss Waring's Journal: 1863 and 1865, Being the Diary of Miss Mary Waring of Mobile, During the Final Days of the War Between the States* (Chicago: Wyvern Press of S. F. E., 1964), 15; A. V. Winkler, *The Confederate Capital and Hood's Texas Brigade* (Austin, TX: Eugene Von Boeckmann, 1894), 250–53; Jon Herbert Roper, ed., *Repairing the "March of Mars": The Civil War Diaries of John Samuel Apperson, Hospital Steward in the Stonewall Brigade, 1861–1865* (Macon, GA: Mercer University Press, 2001), 610; W. Stanley Hoole, ed., "Admiral on Horseback: The Diary of Brigadier General Raphael Semmes, February–May, 1865," *Alabama Review* 28 (April 1975): 140; Chris M. Calkins, *The Final Bivouac: The Surrender Parade at Appomattox and the Disbanding of the Armies, April 10–May 20, 1865* (Lynchburg, VA: M. E. Howard, 1988), 54.

3. Valerius C. Giles, *Rags and Hope: The Recollections of Val C. Giles, Four Years with Hood's Brigade, Fourth Texas Infantry, 1861–1865* (New York: Coward-McCann, 1961), 278.

4. Winkler, *The Confederate Capital*, 250–53; Cornelius M. Buckley, ed., *A Frenchman, a Chaplain, a Rebel: The War Letters of Pere Louis-Hippolyte Gache, S. J.* (Chicago: Loyola University Press, 1981), 220–21; Oscar Weisiger to Q. M. Ward, May 25, 1865, Oscar Weisiger Letter, Virginia Military Institute, Lexington (hereafter cited as VMI); Edward Crenshaw, "Diary of Captain Edward Crenshaw of the Confederate States Army," *Alabama Historical Quarterly* 2 (Winter 1940): 465; John Withers and Anita Withers, *The Civil War Through the Eyes of Lt. Col. John Withers and His Wife, Anita Dwyer Withers* (Bakersfield, CA: Diamond Press, 2011), 193–94; Walter Sullivan, ed., *The War the Women Lived: Female Voices from the Confederate South* (Nashville, TN: J. S. Sanders, 1995), 266–72; Newberry (South Carolina) *Tri-Weekly Herald*, May 16, 1865; Edward Schenck Miers, ed., *A Rebel War Clerk's Diary* (New York: Sagamor Press, 1958), 526–35; George C. Underwood, *History of the Twenty-Sixth Regiment of the North Carolina Troops in the Great War, 1861–1865* (Goldsboro, NC: Nash Bros., 1901), 90; Roper, ed., *Repairing the "March of Mars,"* 610.

5. Winkler, *The Confederate Capital*, 252 (first quotation); George Alexander Martin Diary, April 2, 1865, Virginia Historical Society, Richmond (hereafter cited as VHS); Howard Malcolm Walthall Reminiscences, 41–42 (second quotation), Civil War Document Collection, United States Army Heritage and Education Center, Carlisle, Pennsylvania (hereafter cited as USAHEC).

6. Joseph I. Waring, ed., "The Diary of William G. Hinson During the War of Secession" (pt. 2), *South Carolina Historical Magazine* 75 (April 1974): 118.

7. Joseph T. Durkin, ed., *John Dooley: Confederate Soldier, His War Journal* (Washington, DC: Georgetown University Press, 1945), 177–80; Crenshaw, "Diary of Captain Edward Crenshaw," 465–66.

8. Royce Gordon Shingleton, ed., "South from Appomattox: The Diary of Abner R. Cox," *South Carolina Historical Magazine* 75 (October 1974): 242; Frank Mixson, *Reminiscences of a Private* (Columbia, SC: State Company, 1910), 125–27; Crenshaw, "Diary of Captain Edward Crenshaw," 467–68; James J. Broomall, *Private Confederacies: The Emotional Worlds of Southern Men as Citizens and Soldiers* (Chapel Hill: University of North Carolina Press, 2019), 98.

9. George Alexander Martin Diary, April 9, 1865, VHS; William Nelson Pendleton to United States Quartermaster, April 21, 1865, William Nelson Pendleton Papers, SHC; Shingleton, ed., "South from Appomattox," 241; Sullivan, ed., *The War the Women Lived*, 283–91; Calkins, *The Final Bivouac*, 54; *TCWVQ*, vol. 5, 1958; Broomall, *Private Confederacies*, 99.

10. Eggleston, *A Rebel's Recollections*, 246–47.

11. Eggleston, *A Rebel's Recollections*, 247–51; Archie P. McDonald, ed., *Make Me a Map of the Valley: The Civil War Journal of Stonewall Jackson's Topographer* (Dallas: Southern Methodist University Press, 1973), 266.

12. Durkin, ed., *John Dooley*, 194–95.

13. Hoole, ed., "Admiral on Horseback," 140 (quotation); George Alexander Martin Diary, April 18, 1865, VHS; Unknown Confederate Soldier Diary, May 23, 1865, Arkansas Historical Commission, Little Rock (hereafter cited as AHC); Harry C. Townshend, "Townshend's Diary—January–May 1865: From Petersburg to Appomattox, Thence to North Carolina to Join Johnston's Army," *Southern Historical Society Papers* 34 (1906): 118; Charles Crosland, *Reminiscences of the Sixties* (Columbia, SC: State Company, 1910), 51–52; William A. Fletcher, *Rebel Private Front and Rear: Memoirs of a Confederate Soldier* (New York: Dutton, 1995), 191, 196; Henry William Graber, *The Life Record of H. W. Graber, a Terry Texas Ranger, 1861–1865: Sixty-two Years in Texas* (H. W. Graber, 1916), 248–50; Arthur P. Ford, *Life in the Confederate Army: Being the Experiences of a Private Soldier in the Confederate Army* (New York: Neale Publishing, 1905), 66; Michael L. Bradley, *This Astounding Close: The Road to Bennett Place* (Chapel Hill: University of North Carolina Press, 2000), 200–201; Robert M. Dunkerly, *The Confederate Surrender at Greensboro: The Final Days of the Army of Tennessee, April 1865* (Jefferson, NC: McFarland, 2014), 164–78; Augusta (Ga.) *Chronicle & Sentinel*, April 19, 1865; Joseph E. Johnston, *Narrative of Military Operations Directed During the Late War Between the States* (Bloomington: Indiana University Press, 1959), 417–18; Broomall, *Private Confederacies*, 100–101.

14. W. A. Johnson, "Closing Days with Johnston" (pt. 2), *National Tribune*, June 5, 1901; Durkin, ed., *John Dooley*, 203; Johnston, *Narrative of Military Operations*, 417–18; Crenshaw, "Diary of Captain Edward Crenshaw," 467; John H. Reagan, *Memoirs: With Special Reference to Secession and the Civil War* (Austin, TX: Pemberton Press, 1968), 200; Howard O. Hendricks, "Imperiled City: The Movements of the Union and Confederate Armies Toward Greensboro in the Closing Days of the Civil War in North Carolina" (MA thesis, University of North Carolina, Greensboro, 1987), 160, 161; Bradley, *This Astounding Close*, 240, 245–46; Dunkerly, *The Confederate Surrender at Greensboro*, 176–78.

15. Crenshaw, "Diary of Captain Edward Crenshaw," 467–69; Bradley, *This Astounding Close*, 240; Dunkerly, *The Confederate Surrender at Greensboro*, 176–78.

16. Special Field Orders No. 45, April 29, 1865, in United States War Department, *The War of the Rebellion: A Compilation of the Official Records of the Union and Confederate Armies*, 128 vols.

(hereafter cited as *Official Records*), (Washington, DC: Government Printing Office, 1880–1901), ser. 1, vol. 47, pt. 3, 351; Archer Anderson to Brigadier General Kennedy, May 2, 1865, *Official Records,* ser. 1, vol. 47, pt. 3, 351; Durkin, ed., *John Dooley,* 203; Crenshaw, "Diary of Captain Edward Crenshaw," 467–69; Reagan, *Memoirs,* 200; Bradley, *This Astounding Close,* 240, 245–46.

17. Durkin, ed., *John Dooley,* 203–4.

18. Durkin, ed., *John Dooley,* 203–4.

19. John Taylor Wood Diary, April 21, 1865, John Taylor Wood Papers, SHC; Crenshaw, "Diary of Captain Edward Crenshaw," 467; Mixson, *Reminiscences of a Private,* 126–27; Durkin, ed., *John Dooley,* 195; John F. Wheaton, *Reminiscences of the Chatham Artillery During the War 1861–1865. Read at Armory Hall, March 21st, 1887* (Savannah, GA: Press of the Morning News, 1887), 31–32; Bradley, *This Astounding Close,* 243.

20. Townshend, "Townshend's Diary," 124 (first quotation), 125; James Morris Morgan, *Recollections of a Rebel Reefer* (Boston: Houghton Mifflin, 1917), 231 (second quotation), 232; Graber, *The Life Record of H. W. Graber,* 250–51.

21. Daniel Elliott Huger Smith, ed., *Mason Smith Family Letters, 1860–1868* (Columbia: University of South Carolina Press, 1950), 201–2, 208, 209–13; Norman D. Brown, ed., *One of Cleburne's Command: The Civil War Reminiscences and Diary of Captain Samuel T. Foster, Granbury's Texas Brigade, CSA* (Austin: University of Texas Press, 1980), 180; T. P. Devereux, "The Homeward March after Stacking Arms at Appomattox," in *Recollections and Reminiscences, 1861–1865* (South Carolina Division, United Daughters of the Confederacy, 1990), 1, 254–55; Anderson (SC) *Intelligencer,* June 29, 1865; Frederick W. Moore, ed., "Diary of Maj. Kinloch Falconer," *Confederate Veteran Magazine* 9 (September 1901): 409.

22. *TCWVQ,* vol. 3, 1291; James M. McCaffrey, ed., *Only a Private: A Texan Remembers the Civil War: The Memoirs of William J. Oliphant* (Houston: Halcyon Press, 2004), 90; Wirt Armistead Cate, ed., *Two Soldiers: The Campaign Diaries of Thomas J. Key, C.S.A., December 7, 1863–May 17, 1865, and Robert J. Campbell, U.S.A., January 1, 1864–July 21, 1864* (Chapel Hill: University of North Carolina Press, 1938), 209 (quotation); Marcus Bearden Dewitt Diary, May 15, 1865, Civil War Collection, Tennessee State Library and Archives, Nashville (hereafter cited as TSLA).

23. Elliott, ed., *Doctor Quintard,* 255–57; William Marvel, *Andersonville: The Last Depot* (Chapel Hill: University of North Carolina Press, 1994), 239–40; Sam Jones to P. E. Love, R. H. Hardaway, and A. Dekle, May 8, 1865, *Official Records,* ser. 1, vol. 47, pt. 3, 874 (quotation).

24. Thomas Herndon Civil War Diary and Journal, May 2, 1865, Civil War Document Collection, USAHEC; I. G. Bradwell, "Making Our Way Home from Appomattox," *Confederate Veteran Magazine* 29 (March 1921): 102–3; Durkin, ed., *John Dooley,* 197; Smith, ed., *Mason Smith Family Letters,* 204–5; Augusta (GA) *Chronicle & Sentinel,* May 10, 1865; LeeAnn Whites, *The Civil War as a Crisis in Gender: Augusta, Georgia, 1860–1890* (Athens: University of Georgia Press, 1995), 127–28.

25. Kenneth Coleman, ed., *Athens, 1861–1865: As Seen Through the Letters in the University of Georgia Libraries* (Athens: University of Georgia Press, 1969), 116–17.

26. George Alexander Martin Diary, May 4, 1865 (first quotation), VHS; William C. Davis, ed., *Diary of a Confederate Soldier: John S. Jackman of the Orphan Brigade* (Columbia: University of South Carolina Press, 1990), 167 (second and third quotations).

27. Eliza Frances Andrews, *The War-time Journal of a Georgia Girl, 1864–1865* (New York: D. Appleton, 1908), 193 (quotation); E. Upton to Major General Wilson, May 3, 1865, *Official Records,* ser. 1, vol. 49, pt. 2, 587.

28. John Will Dyer, *Reminiscences; or, Four Years in the Confederate Army* (Evansville, IN: Keller Printing and Publishing, 1898), 294–95; Cate, ed., *Two Soldiers*, 206–9; E. Upton to Major General Wilson, May 3, 1865, *Official Records*, ser. 1, vol. 49, pt. 2, 587; B. B. Eggleston to Brevet Major General Upton, May 5, 1865, *Official Records*, ser. 1, vol. 49, pt. 2, 618–19; E. F. Winslow to Major General Wilson, May 5, 1865, *Official Records*, ser. 1, vol. 49, pt. 2, 619 (quotation).

29. Major General Sam Jones to Governor Allison, May 9, 1865, *Official Records*, ser. 1, vol. 47, pt. 3, 875; Circular, May 5, 1865, *Official Records*, ser. 1, vol. 49, pt. 2, 620; *TCWVQ*, vol. 4, 1330; *TCWVQ*, vol. 5, 2173; Meridian (MS) *Daily Clarion*, May 7, 1865.

30. Davis Tillson to Maj. G. M. Bascom, May 5, 1865, *Official Records*, ser. 1, vol. 49, pt. 2, 622–23 (quotation); Meridian (MS) *Daily Clarion*, May 7, 1865.

31. A. D. Kirwan, ed., *Johnny Green of the Orphan Brigade: The Journal of a Confederate Soldier* (Louisville: University of Kentucky Press, 1956), 199–201; Graber, *The Life Record of H. W. Graber*, 252–56; Holt, ed., *Miss Waring's Journal*, 15–16; Chattachoochee Valley Historical Society, ed., *War Was the Place: A Centennial Collection of Confederate Soldiers' Letters* (Chambers County, AL: Chattachoochee Valley Historical Society, 1961), 123; Grady McWhiney, Warner O. Moore Jr., and Robert F. Pace, eds., *Fear God and Walk Humbly: The Agricultural Journal of James Mallory, 1843–1877* (Tuscaloosa: University of Alabama Press, 1997), 349–50.

32. Bradley R. Clampitt, "The Breakup: The Collapse of the Confederate Trans-Mississippi Army in Texas, 1865," *Southwestern Historical Quarterly* 108 (April 2005): 498–534; Unknown Confederate Soldier Diary, May 10, 23, 25, 1865, AHC (quotation); James Troy Massey, ed., *Memoirs of Captain J. M. Bailey* (James Troy Massey, 1994), 107–8; Robert L. Kerby, *Kirby Smith's Confederacy: The Trans-Mississippi South, 1863–1865* (New York: Columbia University Press, 1972), 422–23.

33. Isaac Asbury Clarke Letter Book, June 15, 22, July 4, 8, 1865, Isaac Asbury Clarke Papers, AHC.

34. Isaac Asbury Clarke Letter Book, June 15, 1865, AHC.

35. Isaac Asbury Clarke Letter Book, June 15, 1865, AHC.

36. D. H. Cooper to Capt. T. M. Scott, May 17, 1865, *Official Records*, ser. 1, vol. 48, pt. 2, 1310–12, 1311 (first quotation); Cooper to Brig. Gen. H. E. McCulloch, May 18, 1865, *Official Records*, ser. 1, vol. 48, pt. 2, 1312–13; Cooper to Capt. T. M. Scott, June 26, 1865, *Official Records*, ser. 1, vol. 48, pt. 2, 1324 (second quotation).

37. J. L. Brent to Lieut. L. L. Conrad, May 5, 1865, *Official Records*, ser. 1, vol. 48, pt. 2, 1294–95; Brent to Col. R. L. Capers, May 11, 1865, *Official Records*, ser. 1, vol. 48, pt. 2, 1299; Brent to Capers, May 13, 1865, *Official Records*, ser. 1, vol. 48, pt. 2, 1301; D. F. Boyd to Col. L. A. Bringier, May 17, 1865, *Official Records*, ser. 1, vol. 48, pt. 2, 1310 (quotations); John D. Winters, *The Civil War in Louisiana* (Baton Rouge: Louisiana State University Press, 1963), 425.

38. William G. Vincent to Captain Sam Flower, May 19, 1865, *Official Records*, ser. 1, vol. 48, pt. 2, 1313; D. F. Boyd to Col. L. A. Bringier, *Official Records*, ser. 1, vol. 48, pt. 2, 1314 (quotation).

39. Winters, *The Civil War in Louisiana*, 423–25; Cynthia Dehaven Pitcock and Bill J. Gurley, eds., *I Acted from Principle: The Civil War Diary of Dr. William M. McPheeters, Confederate Surgeon in the Trans-Mississippi* (Fayetteville: University of Arkansas Press, 2002), 306–7.

40. Winchester Hall, *The Story of the 26th Louisiana Infantry in the Service of the Confederate States* (n. p., 1890), 136; Arthur W. Bergeron Jr., ed., *The Civil War Reminiscences of Major Silas T. Grisamore, CSA* (Baton Rouge: Louisiana State University Press, 1993), 181–82, 181n113 (quotation); Winters, *The Civil War in Louisiana*, 424; John Kelly Damico, "Confederate Soldiers Take Matters

into Their Own Hands: The End of the Civil War in North Louisiana," *Louisiana History* 39, no. 2 (1998): 202.

41. Hall, *Story of the 26th Louisiana*, 136 (quotation); Bergeron, ed., *The Civil War Reminiscences of Major Silas T. Grisamore*, 181–83.

42. General Orders No. 28, May 18, 1865, *Official Records*, ser. 1, vol. 48, pt. 2, 1312; Clampitt, "The Breakup," 499–500; Winters, *The Civil War in Louisiana*, 423–25; John Kelly Damico, "Confederate Soldiers Take Matters into Their Own Hands," 202; Richard Harrison Diary, April 26, 29 (quotation), 1865, AHC; Henry Brockman Journal, May 19, 21, 1865, AHC; Thomas W. Cutrer and T. Michael Parrish, eds., *Brothers in Gray: The Civil War Letters of the Pierson Family* (Baton Rouge: Louisiana State University Press, 1997), 256–60; W. H. Tunnard, *A Southern Record: The History of the Third Regiment Louisiana Infantry* (Dayton, OH: Morningside Bookshop, 1866), 335–37.

43. Henry Brockman Journal, May 21, 1865, AHC; Michael E. Banasik, ed., *Serving with Honor: The Diary of Captain Eathan Allen Pinnell, Eighth Missouri Infantry* (Confederate) (Iowa City: Camp Pope Bookshop, 1999), 223–27; Winters, *The Civil War in Louisiana*, 423–25; Sarah Anne Dorsey, ed., *Recollections of Henry Watkins Allen, Brigadier General Confederate States Army, ex-Governor of Louisiana* (New York: M. Doolady, 1866), 294–95; Tunnard, *A Southern Record*, 337 (first quotation), 338 (second quotation).

44. Henry Brockman Journal, May 22–June 6, 1865, AHC; J. H. P. Baker Civil War Diary, June 10, 1865, State Historical Society of Missouri, Springfield (hereafter cited as SHSM); Banasik, ed., *Serving with Honor*, 225–28; Damico, "Confederate Soldiers Take Matters into Their Own Hands," 202–3; William Robertson Boggs, *Military Reminiscences of General William R. Boggs, CSA* (Durham, NC: Seeman Printery, 1913), 85.

45. Henry Brockman Journal, June 3, 1865, AHC; Charles D. Spurlin, ed., *The Civil War Diary of Charles A. Leuschner* (Austin, TX: Eakin Press, 1992), 53–54; Clampitt, "The Breakup," 499–534.

46. Report of Major General William T. Sherman, May 9, 1865, *Official Records*, ser. 1, vol. 47, pt. 1, p. 32; Brigadier General George L. Andrew to Commissary General of Prisoners, Washington, DC, August 15, 1865, *Official Records*, ser. 2, vol. 8, p. 717; Major General John Pope to Lieutenant General Edmund Kirby Smith, April 19, 1865, *Official Records*, ser. 1, vol. 48, pt. 1, pp. 186–87; Major General John Pope to Lieutenant Colonel J. T. Sprague, April 19, 1865, *Official Records*, ser. 1, vol. 48, pt. 1, pp. 187–88; Report of Sprague, April 19, 1865, *Official Records*, ser. 1, vol. 48, pt. 1, pp. 188–89; Kirby Smith to Pope, May 9, 1865, *Official Records*, ser. 1, vol. 48, pt. 1, p. 189 (first quotation); Kirby Smith to governors, May 9, 1865, *Official Records*, ser. 1, vol. 48, pt. 1, pp. 189–90; Governors to Kirby Smith, May 13, 1865, *Official Records*, ser. 1, vol. 48, pt. 1, pp. 190–91; Kirby Smith to Sprague, May 15 and 30, 1865, *Official Records*, ser. 1, vol. 48, pt. 1, pp. 191–94; Report of C. S. Bell, May 11, 1865, *Official Records*, ser. 1, vol. 48, pt. 2, pp. 398–403; Kirby Smith to Jefferson Davis, March 7, 1865, *Official Records*, ser. 1, vol. 48, pt. 1, pp. 1411–12; General Orders No. 28, Headquarters of the Trans-Mississippi Department, May 18, 1865, *Official Records*, ser. 1, vol. 48, pt. 2, p. 1312; Kerby, *Kirby Smith's Confederacy*, 415–20; Clampitt, "The Breakup," 499–534.

47. Magruder to Kirby Smith, May 16, 1865, *Official Records*, ser. 1, vol. 48, pt. 2, p. 1308; Elizabeth Silverthorne, *Ashbel Smith of Texas: Pioneer, Patriot, Statesman, 1805–1886* (College Station: Texas A & M University Press, 1982), 167; Ashbel Smith to Captain E. P. Turner, May 15, 1865, Military Order Book, Ashbel Smith Papers, DBCAH; Cotham, *Battle on the Bay*, 178; John F. Smith to Cousin, May 19, 1865, John F. Smith Letters, Dolph Briscoe Center for American History, University of Texas, Austin (hereafter cited as DBCAH).

48. Magruder and General John G. Walker to Kirby Smith, May 16, 1865, *Official Records*, ser. 1, vol. 48. pt. 2, pp. 1308–9 (quotation); Clampitt, "The Breakup," 501–9.

49. General Orders No. 48, Headquarters of the Trans-Mississippi Department, May 18, 1865, *Official Records*, ser. 1, vol. 48, pt. 2, p. 1312; Magruder and General John G. Walker to Kirby Smith, May 16, 1865, *Official Records*, ser. 1, vol. 48, pt. 2, pp. 1308–9; Brigadier General James Slaughter to Magruder, May 19, 1865, *Official Records*, ser. 1, vol. 48, pt. 2, 1313–14; Goyne, ed., *Lone Star and Double Eagle*, 174; William Job Hale to Sue, May 21, 1865, Hale Letters, DBCAH; Enrique D'Hamel, *The Adventures of a Tenderfoot* (Waco: W. M. Morrison, 1965), 21; Heartsill, *Fourteen Hundred Ninety-one Days*, 244–45; Joseph Palmer Blessington, *The Campaigns of Walker's Texas Division* (1875; reprint, Austin: State House Press, 1994), 307; John Q. Anderson, ed., *Campaigning with Parsons' Texas Cavalry Brigade CSA* (Hillsboro, TX: Hill Junior College Press, 1967), 159; B. P. Gallaway, *Ragged Rebel: A Common Soldier in Parsons' Texas Cavalry, 1861–1865* (Austin: University of Texas Press, 1988), 130; M. Jane Johansson, *Peculiar Honor: A History of the 28th Texas Cavalry, 1862–1865* (Fayetteville: University of Arkansas Press, 1998), 136; Boesel, *Big Guns of Fayette*, 69; Walton, *Epitome of My Life*, 93; Debray, *History of Debray's Rgiment*, 25; Stephen B. Oates, *Confederate Cavalry West of the River* (Austin: University of Texas Press, 1961), 160; Kerby, *Kirby Smith's Confederacy*, 423; Clampitt, "The Breakup," 509–27.

50. Assistant Adjutant General E. P. Turner to Ashbel Smith, May 21, 1865, *Official Records*, ser. 1, vol. 48, pt. 2, pp. 1316–17; Silverthorne, *Ashbel Smith*, 168; Smith to General Gordon Granger, June 23, 1865, Ashbel Smith Papers, DBCAH; Charlotte (NC) *Western Democrat*, June 13, 1865.

51. H. A. Wallace, "Reminiscences of the Last Vestiges of a Lost Cause," (quotation), H. A. Wallace Recollections, DBCAH; Galveston *Daily News*, June 7, 1865; *Flake's Bulletin* (Galveston), June 4, 1865; Smith to Granger, June 23, 1865, Ashbel Smith Papers, DBCAH; Clampitt, "The Breakup," 512–13.

52. David G. McComb, *Galveston: A History* (Austin: University of Texas Press, 1986), 81 (quotation); Graber, *The Life Record of H. W. Graber*, 258–59; Clampitt, "The Breakup," 513.

53. Paula Mitchell Marks, ed., *When Will the Weary War Be Over? The Civil War Letters of the Maverick Family of San Antonio* (Dallas: Book Club of Texas, 2008), 229–30; Houston *Tri-weekly Telegraph*, May 24, 31, 1865; Mamie Yeary, ed., *Reminiscences of the Boys in Gray, 1861–1865* (Dallas: Smith and Lamar, M. E. Church, South, 1912), 595; Goyne, ed., *Lone Star and Double Eagle*, 174; Clampitt, "The Breakup," 513–14.

54. H. A. Wallace, "Reminiscences of the Last Vestiges of a Lost Cause," DBCAH; Craven to A. Smith, May 24, 1865, A. Smith Papers, DBCAH; Houston *Tri-weekly Telegraph*, May 24, 31, 1865; Marks, ed., *When Will the Weary War Be Over?*, 230 (quotation); X. B. Debray, *A Sketch of the History of Debray's 26th Regiment of Texas Cavalry* (Waco, TX: Waco Village Press, 1961), 25; Ronald B. Jager, "Houston, Texas, Fights the Civil War," *Texana* 11, no. 1 (1973): 47; William W. White, "The Disintegration of an Army: Confederate Forces in Texas, April–June, 1865," *East Texas Historical Journal* 26, no. 2 (1988): 44–45; Clampitt, "The Breakup," 514–15.

55. H. A. Wallace, "Reminiscences of the Last Vestiges of a Lost Cause," DBCAH; Craven to A. Smith, May 24, 1865, A. Smith Papers, DBCAH; Houston *Tri-weekly Telegraph*, May 24, 31, 1865; Bellville (TX) *Countryman*, June 6, 1865 (quotation); Debray, *A Sketch of the History of Debray's 26th Regiment*, 25; Clampitt, "The Breakup," 514–15.

56. Marks, ed., *When Will the Weary War Be Over?*, 231–33.

57. John C. Porter, "The Life of John C. Porter and Sketch of His Experiences in the Civil War," 37, Simpson History Complex, Hill College, Hillsboro, Texas (hereafter cited as Hill College); Wil-

liam N. Still, ed., *Odyssey in Gray: A Diary of Confederate Service, 1863–1865* (Richmond: Virginia State Library, 1979), 308–16, 309 (quotations); John Q. Anderson, ed., *Campaigning with Parsons' Texas Cavalry Brigade, CSA* (Hillsboro, TX: Hill Junior College Press, 1967), 160; Clampitt, "The Breakup," 515–16.

58. Dallas *Herald*, June 15, 1865; Houston *Tri-weekly Telegraph*, May 31, June 14, 19, 1865; Kerby, *Kirby Smith's Confederacy*, 423; Clampitt, "The Breakup," 516–17.

59. La Grange (TX) *Patriot*, May 6, 20, 1865; Houston *Tri-weekly Telegraph*, June 7, 1865; Clampitt, "The Breakup," 517.

60. La Grange (TX) *Patriot*, June 3, 1865 (quotations); Houston *Tri-weekly Telegraph*, June 3, 7, 1865; Clampitt, "The Breakup," 517.

61. Bellville (TX) *Countryman*, June 19, 17, 1865; Galveston *Daily News*, May 30, 1865; Clampitt, "The Breakup," 517–18.

62. Goyne, ed., *Lone Star and Double Eagle*, 172 (quotation); Houston *Tri-weekly Telegraph*, June 5, 1865; Still, ed., *Odyssey in Gray*, 317–12; D'Hamel, *Adventures of a Tenderfoot*, 21–22; Kerby, *Kirby Smith's Confederacy*, 428; Clampitt, "The Breakup," 518–19.

63. Amelia Barr, *All the Days of My Life: An Autobiography* (New York: D. Appleton, 1913), 249–50 (first quotation); Frank Brown, "Annals of Travis County," chapter 24, pp. 14–16 (second quotation), 22–28, DBCAH; Houston *Tri-weekly Telegraph*, May 30, June 16, 1865; Report of George R. Freeman to General Gordon Granger, George R. Freeman Papers, DBCAH; Kerby, *Kirby Smith's Confederacy*, 429; Clampitt, "The Breakup," 519–21.

64. Houston *Tri-weekly Telegraph*, June 16, 1865; Matamoros *Daily Ranchero*, May 31, 1865; D'Hamel, *Adventures of a Tenderfoot*, 21; Thomas North, *Five Years in Texas; or, What You Did Not Hear During the War from January 1861 to January 1866* (Cincinnati, OH: Elm Street Publishing, 1871), 183; Clampitt, "The Breakup," 521–22.

65. Clampitt, "The Breakup," 522–27.

66. Vicki Betts, *Smith County, Texas, in the Civil War* (Tyler, TX: Smith County Historical Society, 1978), 77–78; William A. Albaugh III, *Tyler, Texas, C. C. A.* (Harrisburg, PA: Stackpole, 1958), 205–8; Clampitt, "The Breakup," 522–24; Gabriel Hill Letters, May 22, 24, 26, 1865, AHC.

67. John Q. Anderson, ed., *Brokenburn: The Journal of Kate Stone, 1861–1868* (Baton Rouge: Louisiana State University Press, 1955), 345–46.

68. Robert G. Shaver, "Recollections and Reminiscences of the Last Days of the Confederate Trans-Mississippi Department, Marshall, Texas," 4–5, Robert G. Shaver Papers, AHC.

69. General Orders No. 27, April 18, 1865, *Official Records*, ser. 1, vol. 48, pt. 2, 1282; Richard I. Stone Diary, April 27, 1865, DBCAH; Randolph B. Campbell, *A Southern Community in Crisis: Harrison County, Texas, 1850–1880* (Austin: Texas State Historical Association, 1983), 218–19; Clampitt, "The Breakup," 524–25.

70. Marshall *Texas Republican*, May 26, June 2, 1865; Max Lale, "The Military Occupation of Marshall, Texas, by the 8th Illinois Volunteer Infantry U.S.A., 1865," *Military History of Texas and the Southwest* 13, no. 3 (1976): 41–42; Clampitt, "The Breakup," 525–26.

71. J. H. P. Baker Diary, April 11–June 6, May 25 (quotation), 1865, SHSM; Clarksville (TX) *Standard*, June 10, 1865; Kerby, *Kirby Smith's Confederacy*, 423; Clampitt, "The Breakup," 526–27.

72. Joseph Howard Parks, *General Edmund Kirby Smith, CSA* (Baton Rouge: Louisiana State University Press, 1954), 473–75; Kerby, *Kirby Smith's Confederacy*, 425; Clarksville (TX) *Standard*,

June 17, 1865; Clampitt, "The Breakup," 511–12, 527–28; John N. Edwards, *Shelby and His Men: or, The War in the West* (Cincinnati, OH: Miama Printing and Publishing, 1867), 535 (quotation).

73. Kirby Smith to Col. John T. Sprague, May 30, 1865, *Official Records*, ser. 1, vol. 48, pt. 1, 193–94 (quotation); Terms of Surrender of Confederate Trans-Mississippi Army, May 26, June 2, 1865, *Official Records*, ser. 1, vol. 48, pt. 2, 600–601; Clampitt, "The Breakup," 528.

74. Sheridan to Brevet Major General Rawlins, June 12, 1865, *Official Records*, ser. 1, vol. 48, pt. 2, p. 858 (quotation); Report of Sheridan, May 29, 1865–November 14, 1866, Operations in Texas and on the Rio Grande, *Official Records*, ser. 1, vol. 48, pt. 1, 297–98; Clampitt, "The Breakup," 532–33.

75. Frank Brown, "Annals of Travis County," chapter 24, p. 17, DBCAH; Houston *Tri-weekly Telegraph*, May 24, 31, June 3, 1865; Marks, ed., *When Will the Weary War Be Over?*, 230; Magruder to Kirby Smith, May 16, 1865, *Official Records*, ser. 1, vol. 48, pt. 2, 1309 (quotation); E. P. Turner to Col. A. Smith, May 21, 1865, *Official Records*, ser. 1, vol. 48, pt. 2, 1316–17; Kerby, *Kirby Smith's Confederacy*, 425; Clampitt, "The Breakup," 510–16, 528–29.

76. Houston *Tri-Weekly Telegraph*, June 14, 19, 1865; Clarksville (TX) *Standard*, June 10, 1865; Brown, "Annals of Travis County," chapter 24, p. 22, DBCAH; Lale, "Military Occupation of Marshall," 42; Clampitt, "The Breakup," 513–31.

77. Clampitt, "The Breakup," 520–21, 523, 525, 531; Freeman Report, George R. Freeman Papers, DBCAH; Brown, "Annals of Travis County," chapter 24, pp. 22–26, DBCAH; Edwards, *Shelby and His Men*, 534–37; Daniel O' Flaherty, *General Jo Shelby, Undefeated Rebel* (Chapel Hill: University of North Carolina Press, 1954), 235, 238; Edwin Adams Davis, *Fallen Guidon: The Saga of General Jo Shelby's March to Mexico* (College Station: Texas A&M University Press, 1995), 33, 40–43.

78. Clarksville (TX) *Standard*, June 10, 1865 (quotation); Clampitt, "The Breakup," 529–30.

79. Henry Brockman Journal, May 21, 1865, AHC; Robert G. Shaver, "Recollections and Reminiscences of the Last Days of the Confederate Trans-Mississippi Department, Marshall, Texas," 7, Robert G. Shaver Papers, AHC; Cutrer and Parrish, eds., *Brothers in Gray*, 260; Banasik, ed., *Serving with Honor*, 225–28; Massey, ed., *Memoirs of Captain J. M. Bailey*, 106; Tunnard, *A Southern Record*, 337; Winters, *The Civil War in Louisiana*, 424.

80. Cooper to Brigadier General H. E. McCulloch, May 18, 1865, *Official Records*, ser. 1, vol. 48, pt. 2, 1312–13.

81. W. A. Johnson, "Closing Days with Johnston" (pt. 2), *National Tribune*, June 5, 1901; Crenshaw, "Diary of Captain Edward Crenshaw," 468–69; Holt, ed., *Miss Waring's Journal*, 15; Eggleston, *A Rebel's Recollections*, 250–52; Charles C. Jones Jr., *Historical Sketch of the Chatham Artillery during the Confederate Struggle for Independence* (Albany, NY: Joel Munsell, 1867), 223; Alfred Tyler Fielder, *The Civil War Diaries of Capt. Alfred Tyler Fielder, 12th Tennessee Regiment Infantry, Company B, 1861–1865* (Louisville, KY: Ann York Franklin, 1996), 227; Dunkerly, *The Confederate Surrender at Greensboro*, 174; William B. Holberton, *Homeward Bound: The Demobilization of the Union and Confederate Armies, 1865–1866* (Mechanicsburg, PA: Stackpole Books, 2001), 20–21; Willene B. Clark, ed., *Valleys of the Shadow: The Memoir of Confederate Captain Reuben G. Clark, Company I, 59th Tennessee Mounted Infantry* (Knoxville: University of Tennessee Press, 1994), 109–10; Broomall, *Private Confederacies*, 103–5.

82. Marks, ed., *When Will the Weary War Be Over?*, 232 (first quotation); Eggleston, *A Rebel's Recollections*, 248 (second quotation).

83. Buckley, ed., *A Frenchman, a Chaplain, a Rebel*, 220–21 (quotation); Special Orders No. 45,

April 29, 1865, *Official Records*, ser. 1, vol. 47, pt. 3, 351; Archer Anderson to Brigadier General Kennedy, May 2, 1865, *Official Records*, ser. 1, vol. 47, pt. 3, 866; Sam Jones to Love, Hardaway, and Dekle, May 8, 1865, *Official Records*, ser. 1, vol. 47, pt. 3, 874; Johnson to Whipple, May 9, 1865, *Official Records*, ser. 1, vol. 49, pt. 2, 688; Andrews, *The War-time Journal of a Georgia Girl*, 213; Boggs, *Military Reminiscences*, 85; Winters, *Civil War in Louisiana*, 427–28; Damico, "Confederate Soldiers Take Matters into Their Own Hands," 203.

84. Report of Major General Philip H. Sheridan, May 29, 1865–November 14, 1866, *Official Records*, ser. 1, vol. 48, pt. 1, 297–303; Clampitt, "The Breakup," 531.

85. Report of Major General Philip H. Sheridan, May 29, 1865–November 14, 1866, *Official Records*, ser. 1, vol. 48, pt. 1, 297–303; Lale, "Military Occupation of Marshall," 42; Clampitt, "The Breakup," 531.

86. General Orders No. 4, Headquarters District of Texas, June 19, 1865, *Official Records*, ser. 1, vol. 48, pt. 2, 929 (quotation); Clampitt, "The Breakup," 531–32.

87. Special Orders No. 2, Headquarters District of Texas, June 22, 1865, *Official Records*, ser. 1, vol. 2, pt. 2, 969; David J. Eddleman Collection, University of North Texas Archives, Willis Library, Denton; General Orders No. 5, Headquarters Military Division of the Southwest, June 30, 1865, *Official Records*, ser. 1, vol. 48, pt. 2, 1031–32; Sheridan to Lieutenant General U. S. Grant, July 1, 1865, *Official Records*, ser. 1, vol. 48, pt. 2, 1035–36; Clampitt, "The Breakup," 532.

88. Cate, ed., *Two Soldiers*, 206–8.

89. James Nicholson, *Stories from Dixie* (New York: American Books, 1915), 227 (first quotation); Campbell H. Brown, ed., *The Reminiscences of Sergeant Newton Cannon, from Holograph Material Provided by His Grandson, Samuel M. Fleming Jr.* (Franklin, TN: Carter House Association, 1963), 65 (second quotation).

For additional wartime discussions of soldier theft, looting, etc., see Unknown Confederate Soldier Diary, May 23, 1865, AHC; William Nelson Pendleton to United States Quartermaster, April 21, 1865, William Nelson Pendleton Papers, SHC; James Edward Whitehorne Diary, April 13, 1865, SHC; Smith, ed., *Mason Smith Family Letters*, 208; Shingleton, ed., "South from Appomattox," 241–43; Moore, ed., "Diary of Maj. Kinloch Falconer," 409.

For additional postwar discussions of soldier theft, looting, etc., see H. W. Barclay Reminiscences, unnumbered pages, DBCAH; Graber, *The Life Record of H. W. Graber*, 250–51; Johnston, *Narrative of Military Operations*, 417–18; Massey, ed., *Memoirs of Captain J. M. Bailey*, 103–5; Mixson, *Reminiscences of a Private*, 125–27; Devereux, "The Homeward March after Stacking Arms at Appomattox," 253–55; Jeffrey D. Stocker, ed., *From Huntsville to Appomattox: R. T. Coles's History of the 4th Regiment, Alabama Volunteer Infantry, CSA, Army of Northern Virginia* (Knoxville: University of Tennessee Press, 1997), 192; Matthew Jack Davis, "A Long Journey Home," *Civil War Times Illustrated* 36, no. 2 (May 1997): 51–52; Hall, *Story of the 26th Louisiana*, 136; Thomas Benton Reed, *A Private in Gray* (Camden, AR: T. B. Reed, 1905), 116–17; Daniel Branson Coltrane, *The Memoirs of Daniel Branson Coltrane, Co. I, 63rd Reg. N. C. Cavalry, CSA* (Raleigh, NC: Edwards & Broughton, 1956), 44; Dyer, *Reminiscences*, 296; Dorsey, ed., *Recollections of Henry Watkins Allen*, 295; Ford, *Life in the Confederate Army*, 66–67; Brown, ed., *One of Cleburne's Command*, 180; Elliott, ed., *Doctor Quintard*, 255–57. (*One of Cleburne's Command* and *Doctor Quintard* both draw upon wartime diaries and postwar memoirs.)

90. Coltrane, *The Memoirs of Daniel Branson Coltrane*, 44; Andrews, *The War-time Journal of a Georgia Girl*, 225 (quotations).

91. Massey, ed., *Memoirs of Captain J. M. Bailey*, 103–4; Daniel E. Sutherland, ed., *Reminiscences*

of a Private: William E. Bevens of the First Arkansas Infantry, CSA (Fayetteville: University of Arkansas Press, 1992), 247 (quotation).

92. Rex Pope, "British Demobilization after the Second World War," *Journal of Contemporary History* 30, no. 1 (January 1995): 65–81, 71 (quotation); John F. Shortal, "20th-Century Demobilization Lessons," *Military Review 78, no.* 5 (September–November 1998): 66–71; R. Alton Lee, "The Army 'Mutiny' of 1946," *Journal of American History* 53 (December 1966): 555–71; Daniel Eugene Garcia, "Class and Brass: Demobilization, Working Class Politics, and American Foreign Policy between World War and Cold War," *Diplomatic History* 34, no. 40 (2010): 681–98; W. Butler, "'The British Soldier Is No Bolshevik': The British Army, Discipline, and the Demobilization Strikes of 1919," *20th Century British History* 30, no. 3 (September 2001): 321–46; Eric J. Leed, *No Man's Land: Combat & Identity in World War I* (London: Cambridge University Press, 1979), 201–4. For broader coverage of American demobilization in different eras, see John C. Sparrow, *History of Personnel Demobilization in the United States Army* (Washington, DC: Department of the Army, 1952).

93. Edith Abbott, "The Civil War and the Crime Wave of 1865–1870," *Social Science Review* 51 (March 1977): 71–93.

94. Abbott, "The Civil War and the Crime Wave of 1865–1870," 71–72.

95. Leed, *No Man's Land,* 37, 194 (first quotation), 200 (second quotation).

96. Joan E. Cashin, *War Stuff: The Struggle for Human and Environmental Resources in the American Civil War* (Cambridge, UK: Cambridge University Press, 2018), 155–71; Caroline E. Janney, "Free to Go Where We Liked: The Army of Northern Virginia After Appomattox," *Journal of the Civil War Era* 9 (March 2019): 4–28.

97. Dorsey, ed., *Recollections of Henry Watkins Allen,* 295; Hall, *Story of the 26th Louisiana,* 136; Shingleton, ed., "South from Appomattox," 243; Reed, *A Private in Gray,* 116–17.

98. Joseph T. Glatthaar, *General Lee's Army: From Victory to Collapse* (New York: Free Press, 2008), 471; Massey, ed., *Memoirs of Captain J. M. Bailey,* 104–6; Stocker, ed., *From Huntsville to Appomattox,* 192; Davis, "A Long Journey Home," 51–52.

99. Ford, *Life in the Confederate Army,* 66–67; Mixson, *Reminiscences of a Private,* 126–27; Douglas Hale, *The Third Texas Cavalry in the Civil War* (Norman: University of Oklahoma Press, 1993), 274.

100. William Nelson Pendleton to United States Quartermaster, April 21, 1865, William Nelson Pendleton Papers, SHC; Graber, *The Life Record of H. W. Graber,* 252; H. W. Barclay Reminiscences, unnumbered pages, DBCAH.

101. Johnston, *Narrative of Military Operations,* 417–18; Johnston to Lovell, May 5, 1865, *Official Records,* ser. 1, vol. 47, pt. 3, 872; Dyer, *Reminiscences,* 296 (first quotation); Andrews, *The War-time Journal of a Georgia Girl,* 193; Massey, ed., *Memoirs of Captain J. M. Bailey,* 104–6; Sam Jones to Love, Hardaway, and Dekle, May 8, 1865, *Official Records,* ser. 1, vol. 47, pt. 3, 874; Hall, *Story of the 26th Louisiana,* 136; Crenshaw, "Diary of Captain Edward Crenshaw," 467–69; Lale, "Military Occupation of Marshall," 41–42; Anderson, ed., *Brokenburn,* 346 (second quotation); Clampitt, "The Breakup," 524, 525.

102. Anderson, ed., *Brokenburn,* 346, 348; Clampitt, "The Breakup," 524; Marks, ed., *When Will the Weary War Be Over?,* 230.

103. Clarksville (TX) *Standard,* June 10, 1865.

104. Paul A. Gilje, *The Road to Mobocracy: Popular Disorder in New York City, 1763-1834* (Chapel Hill: University of North Carolina Press, 1987), 51–52, 71 (quotation), 77, 90–91.

105. Clampitt, "The Breakup," 533–34; Dorsey, ed., *Recollections of Henry Watkins Allen,* 294–95 (quotation); Damico, "Confederate Soldiers Take Matters into Their Own Hands," 203.

106. Coltrane, *The Memoirs of Daniel Branson Coltrane,* 44–46.

107. Ford, *Life in the Confederate Army,* 66; Massey, ed., *Memoirs of Captain J. M. Bailey,* 104–6, 106 (quotation).

108. John Frank Edwards, *Army Life of Frank Edwards, Confederate Veteran, Army of Northern Virginia, 1861–1865* (La Grange, GA: 1911), 67–69, 83; William S. Haggard Diary, May 1, 1865, Special Collections Research Center, University of Kentucky Libraries, Lexington; William T. Alderson, ed., "The Civil War Diary of Captain James Litton Cooper, September 30, 1861, to January 1865," *Tennessee Historical Quarterly* 15 (June 1956): 173; Moore, ed., "Diary of Maj. Kinloch Falconer," 408; Jack Sullivan, ed., "'The Dark Clouds of War': The Civil War Diary of John Zimmerman of Alexandria. Part II The Journey Toward Appomattox," *The Alexandria Chronicle* (Fall 2014): 12–13; Brown, ed., *One of Cleburne's Command,* 185–86; Cate, ed., *Two Soldiers,* 215–16; Douglas John Cater, *As It Was: Reminiscences of a Soldier of the Third Texas Cavalry and the Nineteenth Louisiana Infantry* (Austin: State House Press, 1990); Robert G. Evans, ed., *The 16th Mississippi Infantry: Civil War Letters and Reminiscences* (Jackson: University Press of Mississippi, 2002), 308; Kenneth Wiley, ed., *Norfolk Blues: The Civil War Diary of the Norfolk Light Artillery Blues* (Shippensburg, PA: Burd Street Press, 1997), 225.

5. REBELS REUNITED: HOMECOMING, REBIRTH, AND REDEMPTION

1. Adam Fulkerson to wife, May 7, 1865, Adam Fulkerson Civil War Letters, Virginia Military Institute Archives, Lexington (hereafter cited as VMI).

2. George Alexander Martin Diary, April 21, 1865, Virginia Historical Society, Richmond (hereafter cited as VHS) (first quotation); Kent Masterson Brown, ed., *One of Morgan's Men: Memoirs of Lieutenant John M. Porter of the Ninth Kentucky Cavalry* (Lexington: University of Kentucky Press, 2011), 202 (second quotation); Valerius C. Giles, *Rags and Hope: The Recollections of Val. C. Giles, Four Years with Hood's Brigade, Fourth Texas Infantry, 1861–1865* (New York: Coward-McCann, 1961), 280 (third quotation); B. P. Gallaway, *Ragged Rebel: A Common Soldier in Parsons's Texas Cavalry, 1861–1865* (Austin: University of Texas Press, 1988), 131.

3. W. A. McClendon, *Recollections of War Times: By an Old Veteran While Under Stonewall Jackson and Lieutenant General James Longstreet: How I Got In, and How I Got Out* (Montgomery, AL: Paragon Press, 1909), 235; Mrs. Mary Mosely Pratt, "A Confederate Soldier's Return," in *Recollections and Reminiscences, 1861–1865* (South Carolina Division, United Daughters of the Confederacy, 1990), vol. 10, 52–53; John Will Dyer, *Reminiscences; or, Four Years in the Confederate Army* (Evansville, IN: Keller Printing and Publishing, 1898), 311.

4. Harry Hall, *A Johnny Reb Band from Salem: The Pride of Tarheelia* (Raleigh: North Carolina Confederate Centennial Commission, 1963), 108.

5. Giles, *Rags and Hope,* 279; Thomas D. Cockrell and Michael B. Ballard, eds., *A Mississippi Rebel in the Army of Northern Virginia: The Civil War Memoirs of Private David Holt* (Baton Rouge: Louisiana State University Press, 1995), 332–42; John Frank Edwards, *Army Life of Frank Edwards, Confederate Veteran, Army of Northern Virginia, 1861–1865* (La Grange, GA: 1911), 85; William N.

Still, ed., *Odyssey in Gray: A Diary of Confederate Service, 1863–1865* (Richmond: Virginia State Library, 1979), 325; John H. Lewis, *Recollections from 1860 to 1865* (Washington, DC: Peake Publishers, 1895), 91; James Marten, *Sing Not War: The Lives of Union and Confederate Veterans in Gilded Age America* (Chapel Hill: University of North Carolina Press, 2011), 45.

6. D. H. Hamilton, *History of Company M, First Texas Volunteer Infantry, Hood's Brigade, Longstreet's Corps, Army of the Confederate States of America* (Waco, TX: W. M. Morrison, 1962), 76 (quotation); Henry T. Bahnson, "The Last Days of the War," *North Carolina Booklet* 2, no. 12 (April 1903): 21; Still, ed., *Odyssey in Gray*, 325; Franklin Alexander Montgomery, *Reminiscences of a Mississippian in Peace and War, by Frank A. Montgomery, Lieutenant-Colonel First Mississippi Cavalry* (Cincinnati, OH: Robert Clarke Press, 1901), 259; Lewis, *Recollections from 1860 to 1865*, 91.

7. Samuel Lewis Moore Autobiography, 1–7, 15 (quotations), Civil War Document Collection, United States Army Heritage and Education Center, Carlisle, Pennsylvania (hereafter cited as USAHEC).

8. Edwards, *Army Life of Frank Edwards*, 85.

9. Austin V. Dobbins, ed., *Grandfather's Journal: Company B, Sixteenth Mississippi Infantry Volunteers, Harris' Brigade, Mahone's Division, Hill's Corps, A. N. V. May 27, 1861–July 15, 1865* (Dayton, OH: Morningside House, 1988), 251–52; Campbell H. Brown, ed., *The Reminiscences of Sergeant Newton Cannon, from Holograph Material Provided by His Grandson, Samuel M. Fleming, Jr.* (Franklin, TN: Carter House Association, 1963), 68; Daniel E. Sutherland, ed., *Reminiscences of a Private: William E. Bevens of the First Arkansas Infantry, CSA* (Fayetteville: University of Arkansas Press, 1992), 249; Arthur N. Skinner and James L. Skinner, eds., *The Death of a Confederate: Selections from the Letters of the Archibald Smith Family of Roswell, Georgia, 1864–1956* (Athens: University of Georgia Press, 1996), 280–89; John H. King, *Three Hundred Days in a Yankee Prison: Reminiscences of War Life, Captivity, Imprisonment at Camp Chase* (Atlanta: James P. Daves, 1904), 102; Joshua Hilary Hudson, *Sketches and Reminiscences* (Columbia, SC: State Company, 1903), 27–28; Cockrell and Ballard, eds., *A Mississippi Rebel in the Army of Northern Virginia*, 341.

10. War Record of John Oliver Andrews, 7, Civil War Document Collection, USAHEC (quotation); Edwards, *Army Life of Frank Edwards*, 85.

11. Martin Whitlock, "A Confederate Soldier Returns After the War to Hear His Funeral Preached," in *Recollections and Reminiscences, 1861–1865*, vol. 1, 270; Bahnson, "The Last Days of the War," 21 (quotations).

12. Edwards, *Army Life of Frank Edwards*, 85; Dyer, *Reminiscences*, 310; James Edward Whitehorne Diary, April 6, 1865, Southern Historical Collection, Wilson Library, University of North Carolina, Chapel Hill (hereafter cited as SHC); Robert Harley Mackintosh Jr., ed., *Dear Martha: The Confederate War Letters of a South Carolina Soldier, Alexander Faulkner Fewell* (Columbia, SC: Mackintosh, 1976), 130.

13. George M. Neese, *Three Years in the Confederate Horse Artillery* (Dayton, OH: Press of the Morningside Bookshop, 1983), 361–62.

14. Norman D. Brown, ed., *One of Cleburne's Command: The Civil War Reminiscences and Diary of Captain Samuel T. Foster, Granbury's Texas Brigade, CSA* (Austin: University of Texas Press, 1980), 186 (quotations); Howard Malcolm Walthall Reminiscences, 44–45, Civil War Document Collection, USAHEC; Gary W. Gallagher, ed., *Fighting for the Confederacy: The Personal Recollections of Edward Porter Alexander* (Chapel Hill: University of North Carolina Press, 1980), 552; Henry F.

Wilson Diary, June 17, 1865, Alabama Department of Archives and History, Montgomery (hereafter cited as ADAH); Thomas Jefferson Talley LaMotte Diary, April 24, 1865, South Caroliniana Library, University of South Carolina, Columbia; Alfred Tyler Fielder, *The Civil War Diaries of Capt. Alfred Tyler Fielder, 12th Tennessee Regiment Infantry, Company B, 1861–1865* (Louisville, KY: Ann York Franklin, 1996), 234–35; W. A. Russell, "Tragic Adventures as the War Closed," *Confederate Veteran Magazine* 22 (February 1914): 403; Jack Sullivan, ed., "'The Dark Clouds of War': The Civil War Diary of John Zimmerman of Alexandria. Part II The Journey Toward Appomattox," *The Alexandria Chronicle* (Fall 2014): 12–13; Hambleton Tapp, ed., "A Sketch of the Early Life and Service in the Confederate Army of Dr. John A. Lewis of Georgetown, Ky.," *Register of the Kentucky Historical Society* 75 (April 1977): 138–39; Ephraim McDowell Anderson, *Memoirs: Historical and Personal, Including the Campaigns of the First Missouri Brigade* (St. Louis: Times Printing, 1868), 414; John Overton Casler, *Four Years in the Stonewall Brigade* (Guthrie, OK: State Capital Printing, 1903), 289; Wirt Armistead Cate, ed., *Two Soldiers: The Campaign Diaries of Thomas J. Key, C.S.A., December 7, 1863–May 17, 1865, and Robert J. Campbell, U.S.A., January 1, 1864–July 21, 1864* (Chapel Hill: University of North Carolina Press, 1938), 216–17; Douglas John Cater, *As It Was: Reminiscences of a Soldier of the Third Texas Cavalry and the Nineteenth Louisiana Infantry* (Austin, TX: State House Press, 1990), 218; Nathaniel Cheairs Hughes Jr., ed., *The Civil War Memoir of Phillip Daingerfield Stephenson, D. D.* (Conway: University of Central Arkansas Press, 1995), 371; King, *Three Hundred Days in a Yankee Prison*, 99–100; A. D. Kirwan, ed., *Johnny Green of the Orphan Brigade: The Journal of a Confederate Soldier* (Louisville: University of Kentucky Press, 1956), 207; Ada Christine Lightsey, *The Veteran's Story* (Meridian, MS: Meridian News, 1899), 47; Archie P. McDonald, ed., *Make Me a Map of the Valley: The Civil War Journal of Stonewall Jackson's Topographer* (Dallas: Southern Methodist University Press, 1973), 267; T. P. Devereux, "The Homeward March After Stacking Arms at Appomattox," in *Recollections and Reminiscences, 1861–1865*, vol. 1, 255; G. Moxley Sorrel, *Recollections of a Confederate Staff Officer* (New York: Neale Publishing, 1905), 291.

15. James W. Brown Diary, May 9, 1865 (quotation), Georgia Archives, Morrow (hereafter cited as Georgia Archives); William H. Runge, ed., *Four Years in the Confederate Artillery: The Diary of Private Henry Robinson Berkeley* (Richmond: Virginia Historical Society, 1991), 145.

16. Henry F. Wilson Diary, June 17, 1865 (quotation), ADAH; Hughes, ed., *The Civil War Memoir of Phillip Daingerfield Stephenson*, 382–83; Russell, "Tragic Adventures as the War Closed," 403; Casler, *Four Years in the Stonewall Brigade*, 289; Cater, *As It Was*, 218; Kirwan, ed., *Johnny Green of the Orphan Brigade*, 207; *Tennessee Civil War Veteran Questionnaires* (5 vols.) (Easley, SC: Southern Historical Press, 1985) (hereafter cited as *TCWVQ*), vol. 5, 1824.

17. King, *Three Hundred Days in a Yankee Prison*, 99–102.

18. Russell, "Tragic Adventures as the War Closed," 403.

19. Hughes, ed., *The Civil War Memoir of Phillip Daingerfield Stephenson*, 382–83.

20. Maddie Lou Teague Crow, ed., *The Diary of a Confederate Soldier: John Washington Inzer* (Huntsville, AL: Strode Publishers, 1977), 151 (first quotation); James M. McCaffrey, ed., *Only a Private: A Texan Remembers the Civil War: The Memoirs of William J. Oliphant* (Houston: Halcyon Press, 2004), 91 (second quotation); McClendon, *Recollections of War Times*, 235; Sutherland, ed., *Reminiscences of a Private*, 251 (third quotation); Edwards, *Army Life of Frank Edwards*, 85.

21. Cater, *As It Was*, 218 (first quotation); R. S. Bevier, *A History of the First and Second Missouri Confederate Brigades, 1861–1865, and from Wakarusa to Appomattox* (St. Louis: Bryan, Brand, 1879),

472 (second quotation); Dyer, *Reminiscences,* 310 (third quotation); Runge, ed., *Four Years in the Confederate Artillery,* 145; Edwards, *Army Life of Frank Edwards,* 84–85; James Nicholson, *Stories of Dixie* (New York: American Books, 1915), 238–39; Brown, ed., *The Reminiscences of Sergeant Newton Cannon,* 68; Bromfield L. Ridley, *Battles and Sketches of the Army of Tennessee* (Mexico: Missouri Printing and Publishing, 1906), 483–84; King, *Three Hundred Days in a Yankee Prison,* 101; Pratt, "A Confederate Soldier's Return," 52–53.

22. Runge, ed., *Four Years in the Confederate Artillery,* 145.

23. George Alexander Martin Diary, May 20, 1865, VHS; Thomas Herndon, "Civil War Diary and Journal of Capt. Thomas Herndon," Civil War Document Collection, USAHEC (see addendum after diary); Fielder, *The Civil War Diaries of Capt. Alfred Tyler Fielder,* 235–36; Edward Crenshaw, "Diary of Captain Edward Crenshaw of the Confederate States Army," *Alabama Historical Quarterly* 2 (Winter 1940): 479–80; Edwards, *Army Life of Frank Edwards,* 85 (quotation); Dyer, *Reminiscences,* 309–11; Brown, ed., *The Reminiscences of Sergeant Newton Cannon,* 68–69; Sutherland, ed., *Reminiscences of a Private,* 249–51.

24. William S. Haggard Diary, May 5–July17, 1865, Special Collections Research Center, University of Kentucky Libraries, Lexington (hereafter cited as UK).

25. Lightsey, *The Veteran's Story,* 47 (quotation); Russell, "Tragic Adventures as the War Closed," 403; Cater, *As It Was,* 218; Drew Gilpin Faust, *This Republic of Suffering: Death and the American Civil War* (New York: Random House, 2008), 5, 24–26, 48–49; Aaron Sheehan-Dean, *Why Confederates Fought: Family and Nation in Civil War Virginia* (Chapel Hill: University of North Carolina Press, 2007), 83–85.

26. Joseph I. Waring, ed., The Diary of William G. Hinson During the War of Secession" (pt. 2) *South Carolina Historical Magazine* 75 (April 1974): 120.

27. John Q. Anderson, ed., *Brokenburn: The Journal of Kate Stone, 1861–1868* (Baton Rouge: Louisiana State University Press, 1955), 346.

28. H. W. Barclay Reminiscences, unnumbered pages, Dolph Briscoe Center for American History, University of Texas, Austin (hereafter cited as DBCAH); Dyer, *Reminiscences,* 311; James Troy Massey,ed., *Memoirs of Captain J. M. Bailey* (James Troy Massey, 1994), 109; William M. Cash and Lucy Somerville Howorth, eds., *My Dear Nellie: The Civil War Letters of William L. Nugent to Eleanor Smith Nugent* (Jackson: University Press of Mississippi, 1977), 237; W. A. Callaway, "Reminiscences of War at the Close," *Confederate Veteran Magazine* 17, no. 10 (October 1909): 504–5; Casler, *Four Years in the Stonewall Brigade,* 289; Frank Mixson, *Reminiscences of a Private* (Columbia, SC: State Company, 1910), 129–30; Lewis, *Recollections from 1860 to 1865,* 91; A. W. Sparks, *The War Between the States as I Saw It. Reminiscent, Historical and Personal* (Tyler, TX: Lee & Burnett Printers, 1901), 289–90; George B. Guild, *A Brief Narrative of the Fourth Tennessee Cavalry Regiment, Wheeler's Corps, Army of Tennessee* (Nashville, TN: n. p., 1913), 152; Noah Andre Trudeau, *Out of the Storm: The End of the Civil War, April–June, 1865* (Boston: Little, Brown, 1994), 382–83.

29. Bell I. Wiley, ed., *Four Years on the Firing Line* (Jackson, TN: McCowat-Mercer Press, 1963), 240 (quotation); Henry F. Wilson Diary, June 17, 1865, ADAH; Lafayette McLaws to Emily, May 25, 1865, Lafayette McLaws Papers, SHC; Mixson, *Reminiscences of a Private,* 129–30; Nicholson, *Stories of Dixie,* 240–41; Neese, *Three Years in the Confederate Horse Artillery,* 361–62; James H. Wood, *The War: "Stonewall" Jackson, His Campaigns, and Battles, the Regiment as I Saw Them* (Cumberland, MD: Eddy Press Corp., 1910), 179–80.

30. Eric T. Dean, *Shook Over Hell: Post-Traumatic Stress, Vietnam, and the Civil War* (Cambridge, MA: Harvard University Press, 1999), 100–114, 135–44; Paul A. Cimbala, *Veterans North and South: The Transition from Soldier to Civilian after the American Civil War* (Santa Barbara, CA: Praeger, 2015), xv–xviii; Brian Matthew Jordan, *Marching Home: Union Veterans and Their Unending Civil War* (New York: W. W. Norton, 2014), 39, 69–70, 127–28; Sarah Handley-Cousins, "Speaking for Themselves: Disabled Veterans and Civil War Medical Photography," in Brian Matthew Jordan and Evan C. Rothera, eds., *The War Went On: Reconsidering the Lives of Civil War Veterans* (Baton Rouge: Louisiana State University Press, 2020), 101–17; Diane Miller Sommerville, "'A Burden Too Heavy to Bear': War Trauma, Suicide, and Confederate Soldiers," *Civil War History* 59 (December 2013): 453–91; Marten, *Sing Not War,* 47–48; Dixon Wecter, "The Veteran Wins Through," in Larry M. Logue and Michael Barton, eds., *The Civil War Veteran: A Historical Reader* (New York: Oxford University Press, 2007), 83–91.

31. Sommerville, "A Burden Too Heavy to Bear," 453–91; Brian Craig Miller, *Empty Sleeves: Amputation in the Civil War South* (Athens; University of Georgia Press, 2015), see esp. chapters 2 and 3; Jeffrey W. McClurken, *Take Care of the Living: Reconstructing Confederate Veteran Families in Virginia* (Charlottesville: University of Virginia Press, 2009), see esp. chapters 2, 5, and 6; R. B. Rosenburg, *Living Monuments: Confederate Soldiers' Homes in the New South* (Chapel Hill: University of North Carolina Press, 1993), 13–18; Christopher Lyle McIlwain, *Alabama 1865: From Civil War to Uncivil Peace* (Tuscaloosa: University of Alabama Press, 2016), 126.

32. Montgomery, *Reminiscences of a Mississippian,* 260 (quotation); George Alexander Martin Diary, May 19–20, 1865, VHS; R. F. Bunting Papers, April 7, 1865, DBCAH; Henry McCall Holmes, *Diary of Henry McCall Holmes, Army of Tennessee, Assistant Surgeon, Florida Troops, and Related Letters, Documents, etc.* (State College, MS, 1968), 35; Michael Golay, *A Ruined Land: The End of the Civil War* (New York: John Wiley & Sons, 1999), 216–18.

33. McDonald, ed., *Make Me a Map of the Valley,* 267 (quotation); Bessie to Dear Father, April 3, 1865, Drury Lacy Papers, SHC; John Sergeant Wise, *The End of an Era* (Boston: Houghton, Mifflin, 1899), 459–60; Patricia J. Bennett, ed., "Curtis R. Burke's Civil War Journal" (pt. 4), *Indiana Magazine of History* (June 1971), 168; Festus P. Summers, ed., *A Borderland Confederate* (Pittsburgh, PA: University of Pittsburgh Press, 1962), 106–7; William T. Alderson, ed., "The Civil War Reminiscences of John Johnston, 1861–1865" (pt. 6), *Tennessee Historical Quarterly* 14 (June 1955): 174–75; Cimbala, *Veterans North and South,* 53, 59–60; James Marten, "Fatherhood in the Confederacy: Southern Soldiers and Their Children," *Journal of Southern History* 63 (May 1997): 290.

34. J. W. Ford., ed., *The Hour of Our Nation's Agony: The Civil War Letters of Lt. William Cowper Nelson of Mississippi* (Knoxville: University of Tennessee Press, 2007), 181–83; John Oliver Andrews War Record, Civil War Document Collection, USAHEC, 7 (quotation); Nicholson, *Stories of Dixie,* 240–41.

35. Warren J. Alston Diary, poem after last entry, Georgia Archives (quotation); Charles D. Spurlin, ed., *The Civil War Diary of Charles A. Leuschner* (Austin, TX: Eakin Press, 1992), 54; G. Ward Hubbs, ed., *Voices from Company D: Diaries by the Greensboro Guards, Fifth Alabama Infantry Regiment, Army of Northern Virginia* (Blacksburg, VA: Wilson, 2006), 388; Bobbie Swearingen Smith, ed., *A Palmetto Boy: Civil War–Era Diaries and Letters of James Adams Tillman* (Columbia: University of South Carolina Press, 2010), 151; John Rozier, ed., *Granite Farm Letters: Correspondence of Edgeworth and Sallie Byrd* (Athens: University of Georgia Press, 1988), 249; Mauriel

Philips Joslyn, ed., *Charlotte's Boys: Civil War Letters of the Branch Family of Savannah* (Berryville, VA: Rockbridge Publishing, 1996), 302; Nathaniel Cheairs Hughes Jr., ed., *Liddell's Record; St. John Richardson Liddell, Brigadier General, CSA, Staff Officer and Brigadier Commander, Army of Tennessee* (Dayton, OH: Morningside Press, 1985), 198–200; Hughes, ed., *The Civil War Memoir of Phillip Daingerfield Stephenson*, 386–87; Wise, *The End of an Era*, 461–62; Runge, ed., *Four Years in the Confederate Artillery*, 144; Crenshaw, "Diary of Captain Edward Crenshaw," 479.

36. Carl Schurz, "Report on the Condition of the South," 39th Congress, Senate Ex. Doc. 1st Session, No. 2, 1865, 42–43.

37. Schurz, "Report on the Condition of the South," 42–43.

38. Stephen V. Ash, *When the Yankees Came: Conflict and Chaos in the Occupied South, 1861–1865* (Chapel Hill: University of North Carolina Press, 1995), 229–35; Cimbala, *Veterans North and South*, 15–16; Gary W. Gallagher, *The Confederate War: How Popular Will, Nationalism, and Military Strategy Could Not Stave Off Defeat* (Cambridge, MA: Harvard University Press, 1997), 158–63; Thomas W. Cutrer, *Theater of a Separate War: The Civil War West of the Mississippi River, 1861–1865* (Chapel Hill: University of North Carolina Press, 2018), 441; Bradley R. Clampitt, ed., *The Civil War and Reconstruction in Indian Territory* (Lincoln: University of Nebraska Press, 2015), 9, 13–15, 78–80, 160–64; William C. Davis, *The Orphan Brigade: The Kentucky Confederates Who Couldn't Go Home* (Garden City, NY: Doubleday, 1980), 260–61; Jason Philips, *Diehard Rebels: The Confederate Culture of Invincibility* (Athens: University of Georgia Press, 2007), 180–81.

39. Jordan, *Marching Home*, 16–17; Cimbala, *Veterans North and South*, 15–16; Joan E. Cashin, *War Stuff: The Struggle for Human and Environmental Resources in the American Civil War* (Cambridge, UK: Cambridge University Press, 2018), 104–7.

40. Henry F. Wilson Diary, May 5, 12, 20, 1865, ADAH; Unknown Confederate Soldier Diary, May 1865 entries, Arkansas Historical Commission, Little Rock (hereafter cited as AHC); Gabriel H. Hill Letters, May 24, 1865, AHC; Thomas Herndon, "Civil War Diary and Journal of Capt. Thomas Herndon," May 5, 1865, Civil War Document Collection, USAHEC; Howard Malcolm Walthall Reminiscences, 43–44, Civil War Document Collection, USAHEC; John Bateman Rushing Autobiography, 12–13, Civil War Document Collection, USAHEC; George W. Waldrip Reminiscences, 42–45, Civil War Document Collection, USAHEC; Bessie to Dear Father, April 3, 1865, Drury Lacy Papers, SHC; George Alexander Martin Diary, May 20, 1865, VHS; William Alexander Smith, *The Anson Guards: Company C Fourteenth Regiment North Carolina Volunteers, 1861–1865* (Charlotte, NC: Stone Publishing, 1914), 309; George Jefferson Hundley, "Beginning and the Ending: Reminiscences of the First and Last Days of the War, by Gen. George Hundley," *Southern Historical Society Papers* 23 (1895): 313; John E. Stegeman, *These Men She Gave: The Civil War Diary of Athens, Georgia* (Athens: University of Georgia Press, 1964), 141–42; Mary Elizabeth Sanders, ed., *Diary in Gray: Civil War Letters and Diary of Jared Young Sanders II* (Baton Rouge: Louisiana Genealogical & Historical Society, 1994), 96–98; Samuel G. French, *Two Wars: An Autobiography* (Nashville, TN: Confederate Veteran, 1901), 310–12; Charles Crosland, *Reminiscences of the Sixties* (Columbia, SC: State Company, 1910), 51–52; Sparks, *The War Between the States*, 289–90; Hughes, ed., *Liddell's Record*, 199; *TCWVQ*, vol. 4, 1683.

41. Anderson, ed., *Brokenburn*, 359.

42. James E. Whitehorne Diary, April 9, 1865 (first quotation), SHC; Thomas Benton Reed, *A Private in Gray* (Camden, AR: T. B. Reed, 1905), 117 (second quotation).

43. B. E. Miller to Watkins, May 19, 1866, Civil War Soldiers' Letters, ADAH; Lavender Ray Diary, May 3, 1865, Lavender Ray Papers, Georgia Archives; Walter Alexander Montgomery, *The Days of Old and Years That Are Past* (Charlottesville, VA: Michie, 1939), 47.

44. Davis Bitton, ed., *The Reminiscences and Civil War Letters of Levi Lamoni Wight; Life in a Mormon Splinter Colony on the Texas Frontier* (Salt Lake City: University of Utah Press, 1970), 41–42; Lavender Ray Diary, May 5, 1865, Lavender Ray Papers, Georgia Archives; Phil Gottschalk, *In Deadly Earnest: The History of the First Missouri Brigade, CSA* (Columbia: Missouri River Press, 1991), 526–27; Blakey, Arch Frederic, Ann Smith Lainhart, and Winston Bryant Stephens Jr., eds., *Rose Cottage Chronicles: Civil War Letters of the Bryant-Stephens Families of North Florida* (Gainesville: University of Florida Press, 1998), 366–67; Natalie Jenkins Bond and Osmun Latrobe Coward, eds., *The South Carolinians: Colonel Asbury Coward's Memoirs* (New York: Vantage Press, 1968), 186; Henry Clay Dickinson, *Diary of Henry Clay Dickinson, CSA, Morris Island, 1864–1865* (Denver, CO: Press of Williamson-Haffner, n.d.), 187; Gary W. Gallagher, ed., *Fighting for the Confederacy: The Personal Recollections of Edward Porter Alexander* (Chapel Hill: University of North Carolina Press, 1980), 545, 549; James Watson Morton, *The Artillery of Nathan Bedford Forrest's Cavalry* (Nashville, TN: Publishing House of the M. E. Church, South, 1909), 316; William Miller Owen, *In Camp and Battle with the Washington Artillery of New Orleans: A Narrative of Events during the Late Civil War from Bull Run to Appomattox and Spanish Fort* (Boston: Ticknor, 1885), 391; Cynthia Dehaven Pitcock and Bill J. Gurley, eds., *I Acted from Principle: The Civil War Diary of Dr. William M. McPheeters, Confederate Surgeon in the Trans-Mississippi* (Fayetteville: University of Arkansas Press, 2002), 291–92; Daniel Elliott Huger Smith, ed., *Mason Smith Family Letters, 1860–1868* (Columbia: University of South Carolina Press, 1950), 204; William N. Still, ed., *Odyssey in Gray: A Diary of Confederate Service, 1863–1865* (Richmond: Virginia State Library, 1979), 325; Bell I. Wiley, ed., *This Infernal War: The Confederate Letters of Edwin H. Fay* (Austin: University of Texas Press, 1958), 441–42, 447–48; John B. Gordon, *Reminiscences of the Civil War* (New York: Charles Scribner's Sons, 1904), 348; Sanders, ed., *Diary in Gray*, 96; Hughes, ed., *Liddell's Record*, 201; Hughes, ed., *The Civil War Memoir of Phillip Daingerfield Stephenson*, 378, 386; Montgomery, *Reminiscences of a Mississippian*, 260–61; Kurt Hackemer, "Civil War Veteran Colonies on the Western Frontier," in Jordan and Roberts, eds., *The War Went On*, 61–80.

45. Philip Hickey Morgan Letter, June 16, 1865, Louisiana and Lower Mississippi Valley Collections, Hill Memorial Library, Louisiana State University, Baton Rouge; R. S. Bevier, *A History of the First and Second Missouri Confederate Brigades, 1861–1865, and from Wakarusa to Appomattox* (St. Louis: Bryan, Brand, 1879), 472–77; Francis W. Dawson, *Reminiscences of Confederate Service, 1861–1865* (Charleston, SC: News and Courier Book Presses, 1882), 210–12; H. Grady Howell Jr., *Going to Meet the Yankees: A History of the "Bloody Sixth" Mississippi Infantry, CSA* (Jackson, MS: Chickasaw Bayou Press, 1981), 270; McIlwain, *Alabama 1865*, 143; Cimbala, *Veterans North and South*, 81–82.

46. Montgomery, *Reminiscences of a Mississippian*, 261 (quotation); Sanders, ed., *Diary in Gray*, 96; Bond and Coward, eds., *The South Carolinians*, 186; Still, ed., *Odyssey in Gray*, 325; William Clyde Billingsley, ed., "'Such Is War': The Confederate Memoirs of Newton Asbury Keen" (pt. 4), *Texas Military History* (Fall 1968): 184–86; Larry M. Logue, *To Appomattox and Beyond: The Civil War Soldier in War and Peace* (Chicago: Ivan R. Dee, 1995), 104–5.

47. Bond and Coward, eds., *The South Carolinians*, 186.

48. James I. Robertson Jr., ed., *Soldier of Southwestern Virginia: The Civil War Letters of Captain John Preston Sheffey* (Baton Rouge: Louisiana State University Press, 2004), 229; James E. Green

Diary, April 26, 1865, SHC; George Alexander Martin Diary, May 19–20, 1865, VHS; B. E. Miller to Watkins, May 19, 1866, Civil War Soldiers' Letters, ADAH; Thomas Herndon, Reminiscences, in "Civil War Diary and Journal of Capt. Thomas Herndon," 19, Civil War Document Collection, USAHEC; John Bateman Rushing Autobiography, 13, Civil War Document Collection, USAHEC; Preston Lafayette Ledford, *Reminiscences of the Civil War, 1861–1865* (Thomasville, NC: News Printing House, 1909), 88–89; McHenry Howard, *Recollections of a Maryland Confederate Soldier and Staff Officer under Johnston, Jackson, and Lee* (Dayton, OH: Morningside Bookshop, 1975), 404–5; Richard Taylor, *Destruction and Reconstruction: Personal Experiences of the Late War* (New York: D. Appleton, 1879), 228–29; Walter H. Taylor, *General Lee. His Campaigns in Virginia, 1861–1865 with Personal Reminiscences* (Norfolk, VA: Nusbaum Book and News, 1906), 298; Hughes, ed., *Liddell's Record*, 197–98; Gottschalk, *In Deadly Earnest*, 526–27; Sanders, ed., *Diary in Gray,* 96–97; Cimbala, *Veterans North and South,* 71–74.

49. Robertson, ed., *Soldier of Southwestern Virginia,* 229.

50. Martin Van Kees Diary, April–July 1865 entries, Mississippi Department of Archives and History, Jackson (hereafter cited as MDAH); James E. Green Diary, April–July 1865 entries, SHC; Avington Wayne Simpson Diary, April–August 1865 entries, SHC; Charles Bickem Fields Diary, April 1865 entries, VHS; William S. Haggard Diary, May–July 1865 entries, UK; War Record of John Oliver Andrews, 7, Civil War Document Collection, USAHEC; Gallaway, *Ragged Rebel,* 131; Wood, *The War,* 180; Hughes, ed., *Liddell's Record,* 200; Jeffrey D. Stocker, ed., *From Huntsville to Appomattox: R. T. Coles's History of the 4th Alabama Volunteer Infantry, CSA, Army of Northern Virginia* (Knoxville: University of Tennessee Press, 1996), 303n5; Anderson, ed., *Brokenburn,* 346–48; Smith, ed., *Mason Smith Family Letters,* 214–31; J. Luke Austin, ed., *General John Bratton: Sumter to Appomattox in Letters to His Wife* (Sewanee, TN: Proctor's Hall Press, 2003), 268–72; Wiley, ed., *Four Years on the Firing Line,* 241–49, 254; Bitton, ed., *The Reminiscences and Civil War Letters of Levi Lamoni Wight,* 41–42; Crenshaw, "Diary of Captain Edward Crenshaw," 482.

51. John Waldrop Diary, April 18–May 31, 1865, Richard Woolfolk Waldrop Papers, SHC; Bennett, ed., "Curtis R. Burke's Civil War Journal," 168; Summers, ed., *A Borderland Confederate,* 107–18; Lawrence L. Hewitt, Thomas Edwin Schott, and Marc Kunis, eds., *To Succeed or Perish: The Diaries of Sergeant Edmund Trent Eggleston, 1st Mississippi Light Artillery Regiment, CSA* (Knoxville: University of Tennessee Press, 2015), xix, 77–78; Thomas Herndon, Reminiscences, in "Civil War Diary and Journal of Capt. Thomas Herndon," 19, Civil War Document Collection, USAHEC; Howard Malcolm Walthall Reminiscences, 43–44, Civil War Document Collection, USAHEC; Diary of Unknown Confederate Soldier, May 4–11, 1865, William G. B. Morris Papers, Civil War Times Illustrated Collection, USAHEC; Oscar Weisiger Letter, May 25, 1865, VMI; Alderson, ed., "The Civil War Reminiscences of John Johnston," 174–75; Wise, *The End of an Era,* 458–62; Skinner and Skinner, eds., *The Death of a Confederate,* 181, 188; Thomas McGuire, *McGuire Papers: Containing Major Thomas McGuire's Civil War Letters; and Patriotic Documents and Other Letters from 1854 to the Turn of the Twentieth Century* (Tusquahoma, LA: Daughters of the American Revolution, 1966), 47–54; Thomas W. Cutrer, ed., "'Bully for Flournoy's Regiment, We Are Some Pumkins, You'll Bet': The Civil War Letters of Virgil Sullivan Rabb, Captain, Company I Sixteenth Texas Infantry, CSA" (pt. 2), *Military History of the Southwest* 20 (Spring 1990): 95.

52. Reed, *A Private in Gray,* 117 (quotation), 118; Cater, *As It Was,* 222; Bessie to Dear Father, April 3, 1865, Drury Lacy Papers, SHC; Hubert L. Ferguson, ed., "Letters of John W. Duncan, Captain Confederate States of America," *Arkansas Historical Quarterly* 9 (1960): 311–12; Willene B.

Clark, ed., *Valleys of the Shadow: The Memoir of Confederate Captain Reuben G. Clark, Company I, 59th Tennessee Mounted Infantry* (Knoxville: University of Tennessee Press, 1994), 75–76; Nat S. Turner III, ed., *A Southern Soldier's Letters Home: The Civil War Letters of Samuel A. Burney, Cobb's Georgia Legion, Army of Northern Virginia* (Macon, GA: Mercer University Press, 2002), 294; Jane Bonner Peacock, ed., "A Wartime Story: The Davidson Letters 1862–1865," *Atlanta Historical Bulletin* 20, no. 1 (1975): 112–16.

53. James E. Whitehorne Diary, April 13, 14, 16, 22, 1865, SHC; Compiled Records Showing Service of Military Units in Confederate Organizations, Record Group 109, War Department Collection of Confederate Records, National Archives, Washington, DC.

54. Glenn Linden and Virginia Linden, eds., *Disunion, War, Defeat, and Recovery in Alabama: The Journal of Augustus Benners, 1850–1885* (Macon, GA: Mercer University Press, 2007), 138–39.

55. Smith, *The Anson Guards*, 309 (quotation); George Cary Eggleston, *A Rebel's Recollections* (New York: Hurd and Houghton, 1874), 258–60; Hughes, ed., *The Civil War Memoir of Phillip Daingerfield Stephenson*, 374–75; Grady McWhiney, Warner O. Moore Jr., and Robert F. Pace, eds., *Fear God and Walk Humbly: The Agricultural Journal of James Mallory, 1843–1877* (Tuscaloosa: University of Alabama Press, 1997), 350–51.

56. James Robert McMichael Diary, June 24, 1865, SHC (first and second quotations); Hundley, "Beginning and the Ending," 313 (third quotation); Frederick W. Moore, ed., "Diary of Major Kinloch Falconer," *Confederate Veteran Magazine* 9 (October1901): 451; Carlton McCarthy, *Detailed Minutiae of Soldier Life in the Army of Northern Virginia, 1861–1865* (Richmond: Carlton McCarthy, 1894), 183–84; Wiley, ed., *Four Years on the Firing Line*, 240–41; Richard H. Adams Jr. to Lottie Putnam Adams, July 2, 23, 1865, Richard H. Adams Jr. Correspondence, VMI; Callaway, "Reminiscences of War at the Close," 505; Hamilton, *History of Company M*, 77; McWhiney, Moore, and Pace, eds., *Fear God and Walk Humbly*, 350–51; J. E. Robuck, *My Own Personal Experience and Observation as a Soldier in the Confederate Army During the Civil War, 1861–1865, also During Reconstruction* (Birmingham, AL: Leslie Printing and Publishing, 1911), 71–72; Edward Younger, ed., *Inside the Confederate Government: The Diary of Robert Garlick Hill Kean, Head of the Bureau of War* (New York: Oxford University Press, 1997), 209.

57. Joseph T. Durkin, ed., *John Dooley: Confederate Soldier. His War Journal* (Washington: Georgetown University Press, 1945), 207 (first quotation); Moore, ed., "Diary of Major Kinloch Falconer," 451 (second quotation); Robuck, *My Own Personal Experience*, 74; King, *Three Hundred Days in a Yankee Prison*, 100–114.

58. Durkin, ed., *John Dooley*, 205 (quotation); Still, ed., *Odyssey in Gray*, 324; Cater, *As It Was*, 215; Sparks, *The War Between the States*, 290; Luther Wesley Hopkins, *From Bull Run to Appomattox, a Boy's View, by Luther W. Hopkins of Genl. J. E. B. Stuart's cavalry, 6th Virginia regiment* (Baltimore: Press of Fleet-McGinley, 1908), 204–5; Eggleston, *A Rebel's Recollections*, 254–60; E. Eric Emerson and Karen Stokes, eds., *Faith, Valor, Devotion: The Civil War Letters of William Porcher Dubose* (Columbia: University of South Carolina Press, 2010), 329.

59. Cater, *As It Was*, 215 (quotation); Cate, ed., *Two Soldiers*, 215–16; Hopkins, *From Bull Run to Appomattox*, 203–5; Eggleston, *A Rebel's Recollections*, 257–58.

60. Hopkins, *From Bull Run to Appomattox*, 203–5.

61. David A. Welker, ed., *A Keystone Rebel: The Civil War Diary of Joseph Garey Hudson's Battery, Mississippi Volunteers* (Gettysburg: Thomas Publications, 1997), 103 (quotation); Reed, *A Pri-*

vate in Gray, 117; William Campbell Preston Breckenridge, *"The Ex-Confederate, and What He Has Done in Peace." An Address Delivered Before the Association of the Army of Northern Virginia, at the Meeting Held in Richmond, Va., October 26, 1892* (Richmond: J. L. Hill Printing, 1892), 6.

62. Charles Reagan Wilson, *Baptized in Blood: The Religion of the Lost Cause, 1865–1920* (Athens: University of Georgia Press, 1980), 107–8; George C. Rable, *God's Almost Chosen Peoples: A Religious History of the American Civil War* (Chapel Hill: University of North Carolina Press, 2010), 393–93; Leon F. Litwack, *Been in the Storm So Long: The Aftermath of Slavery* (New York: Alfred A. Knopf, 1979), 23–26, 122, 170, 218, 464–70.

63. Unknown Confederate Soldier Diary, May 6, 1865, AHC.

64. Gordon, *Reminiscences of the Civil War,* 448 (quotation); Hughes, ed., *The Civil War Memoir of Phillip Daingerfield Stephenson,* 374–76; Younger, ed., *Inside the Confederate Government,* 208–11; Wiley, ed., *Four Years on the Firing Line,* 240–41; Cimbala, *Veterans North and South,* 16.

65. Sanders, ed., *Diary in Gray,* 96, 97 (quotation); Hughes, ed., *The Civil War Memoir of Phillip Daingerfield Stephenson,* 374–76; Carroll Jones, ed., *Captain Lenoir's Diary: Tom Lenoir and His Civil War Company from Western North Carolina* (Wilmington, NC: Winoca Press, 2010), 232; Thomas Felix Hickerson, *Echoes of Happy Valley: Letters and Diaries, Family Life in the South; Civil War History* (Chapel Hill, NC: Bulls Head Bookshop, 1962), 103–4.

66. Montgomery, *Reminiscences of a Mississippian,* 260; Cater, *As It Was,* 221–22; Hickerson, *Echoes of Happy Valley,* 103–4; Younger, ed., *Inside the Confederate Government,* 208–9.

67. Richard H. Adams Jr. to Lottie Putnam Adams, July 2, 23, 1865, Richard H. Adams Jr. Correspondence, VMI; Fannie E. Taylor Dickinson Diary, April 17, 1865, VHS; Mrs. Pendleton to sister and brother, May 26, 1865, William Nelson Pendleton Papers, SHC; DeWitt Boyd Stone, ed., *Wandering to Glory: Confederate Veterans Remember Evans's Brigade* (Columbia: University of South Carolina Press, 2002), 246; Jones, ed., *Captain Lenoir's Diary,* 232–33; Cater, *As It Was,* 221–22; Hickerson, *Echoes of Happy Valley,* 103–4; Brown, ed., *The Reminiscences of Sergeant Newton Cannon,* 70, 72; French, *Two Wars,* 321–22; Blakey, Lainhart, and Stephens, eds., *Rose Cottage Chronicles,* 365–66; Linden and Linden, eds., *Disunion, War, Defeat, and Recovery in Alabama,* 138–43; Callaway, "Reminiscences of War at the Close," 505.

68. Lafayette McLaws to Emily, May 25, 1865, Lafayette McLaws Papers, SHC; James Griffin to J. S. Bryant, June 21, 1865, James Griffin Letters, Civil War Times Illustrated Collection, USAHEC; Mixson, *Reminiscences of a Private,* 130; Crenshaw, "Diary of Captain Edward Crenshaw," 480–81; French, *Two Wars,* 321–22.

69. Richard H. Adams Jr. to Lottie Putnam Adams, July 2, 1865, Richard H. Adams Jr. Correspondence, VMI; Mackintosh Jr., ed., *Dear Martha,* 195; Jones, ed., *Captain Lenoir's Diary,* 232–33; Brown, ed., *The Reminiscences of Sergeant Newton Cannon,* 72; French, *Two Wars,* 321–22; Blakey, Lainhart, and Stephens, eds., *Rose Cottage Chronicles,* 365–66; Linden and Linden, eds., *Disunion, War, Defeat, and Recovery in Alabama,* 139–43; Cater, *As It Was,* 221–22; Hickerson, *Echoes of Happy Valley,* 103–4; Montgomery, *Reminiscences of a Mississippian,* 260; Eggleston, *A Rebel's Recollections,* 259–60; Crenshaw, "Diary of Captain Edward Crenshaw," 480–81; Callaway, "Reminiscences of War at the Close," 505; Stone, ed., *Wandering to Glory,* 246.

70. United States Bureau of the Census, Eighth U.S. Census, 1860, Schedule 1 (Free Inhabitants); United States Bureau of the Census, Eighth U.S. Census, 1860, Schedule 2 (Slave Inhabitants); Compiled Records Showing Service of Military Units in Confederate Organizations, Record Group 109,

War Department Collection of Confederate Records, National Archives, Washington, DC; Patricia A. Kaufmann, "An Aristocratic Planter Goes to War," *La Posta* (Third Quarter, 2014): 27–28; Judith N. McArthur and Orville Vernon Burton, eds., *A Gentleman and an Officer: A Military and Social History of James B. Griffin's Civil War* (New York: Oxford University Press, 1996).

71. James Griffin to J. S. Bryant, June 21, 1865, James Griffin Letters, Civil War Times Illustrated Collection, USAHEC.

72. James Griffin to J. S. Bryant, June 21, 1865.

73. Brown, ed., *The Reminiscences of Sergeant Newton Cannon,* 70–75; Wiley, ed., *Four Years on the Firing Line,* 240–41; Richard H. Adams Jr. to Lottie Putnam Adams, July 2, 23, 1865, Richard H. Adams Jr. Correspondence, VMI; Fannie E. Taylor Dickinson Diary, April 17, 1865, VHS; Carl Schurz, "Report on the Condition of the South," 39th Congress, Senate Ex. Doc. 1st Session, No. 2, 1865; John Richard Dennett, *The South As It Is: 1865–66* (New York: Viking Press, 1965); Cater, *As It Was,* 219–22.

74. Arthur P. Ford, *Life in the Confederate Army: Being the Experiences of a Private Soldier in the Confederate Army* (New York: Neale Publishing, 1905), 71.

75. Logue, *To Appomattox and Beyond,* 105; W. R. Houghton and Mitchell Bennett Houghton, *Two Boys in the Civil War and After* (Montgomery, AL: Paragon Press, 1912), 54–56, 96–99, 153–56, 176–78, 193–94, 197–98, 210–11; R. M. Collins, *Chapters from the Unwritten History of the War Between the States; or, the Incidents in the Life of a Confederate Soldier* (St. Louis: Nixon-Jones Printing, 1893), 303–7; Crow, ed., *Diary of a Confederate Soldier,* 152–54; Jones, ed., *Captain Lenoir's Diary,* 231; Anderson, *Memoirs: Historical and Personal,* 405–8; Bitton, ed., *Reminiscences of Levi Lamoni Wight,* 42; Blakey, Lainhart, and Stephens, eds., *Rose Cottage Chronicles,* 367; Brown, ed., *One of Cleburne's Command,* 174; Robuck, *My Own Experience,* 74–97; French, *Two Wars,* 312, 327, 328–51; Gordon, *Reminiscences of the Civil War,* 457; King, *Three Hundred Days in a Yankee Prison,* 100–114; Ledford, *Reminiscences of the Civil War,* 89–104; Montgomery, *Reminiscences of a Mississippian,* 262–99; Sparks, *The War Between the States,* 289–92; Augustus Pitt Adamson, *Brief History of the Thirtieth Georgia Regiment* (Griffin, GA: Mills Printing, 1912), 139–40; J. P. Austin, *The Blue and the Gray, Sketches of a Portion of the Unwritten History of the Great American Civil War* (Atlanta: Franklin Printing and Publishing, 1899), see several chapters on Reconstruction era; Thornton Bowman, *Reminiscences of an ex-Confederate Soldier; or, Forty Years on Crutches* (Austin, TX: Gammel-Statesman, 1904), 58; Edward M. Boykin, *The Falling Flag. Evacuation of Richmond, Retreat, and Surrender at Appomattox, by An Officer of the Rear-Guard* (New York: E. J. Hale & Son, 1874), 66–67; John William Carroll, *Autobiography and Reminiscences* (Henderson, TN: n. p., 1898), 42–46; James Dinkins, *1861 to 1865, by an Old Johnnie, Personal Recollections and Experiences in the Confederate Army* (Cincinnati, OH: Robert Clarke, 1897), 270–80; Hamilton, *History of Company M,* 76–77; David E. Johnston, *The Story of a Confederate Boy in the Civil War* (Portland, OR: Glass & Prudhomme, 1914), 347–48, 361; Edward Young McMorries, *History of the First Regiment Alabama Volunteer Infantry, CSA* (Montgomery, AL: Brown Printing, 1904), 94; George T. Todd, *Sketch of History: The First Texas Regiment, Hood's Brigade, Army of Northern Virginia* (Tyler, TX: Lee & Burnett, Printers, 1901), 27; W. H. Morgan, *Personal Reminiscences of the War, 1861–5* (Lynchburg, VA: J. P. Bell, 1911), 270.

76. Unknown Confederate Soldier Diary, May 14, 1865, AHC (first quotation); John Q. Anderson, ed., *Campaigning with Parsons' Texas Cavalry Brigade, CSA* (Hillsboro, TX: Hill Junior College

Press, 1967), 159 (second quotation); William Sylvester Dillon Diary, May 27, June 25, 1865, Georgia Archives; Bennett, ed., "Curtis R. Burke's Civil War Journal," 167–68; Vicki Betts, ed., "The Civil War Letters of Elbridge Littlejohn," *Chronicles of Smith County, Texas* 18 (Summer 1979): 37; J. W. Yale to daughter, May 17, 1865, J. W. Yale Letters, Civil War Miscellany, DBCAH; William Nelson Pendleton Letters, June 5, 1865, SHC; Gordon, *Reminiscences of the Civil War,* 447–48; Logue, *To Appomattox and Beyond,* 103–5.

77. Betts, ed., "The Civil War Letters of Elbridge Littlejohn," 37 (quotation); Dolly Sumner Lunt Diary, April 29, 1865, in *Confederate Reminiscences and Letters* (14 vols.) (Atlanta: Georgia Division of UDC, 1995), vol. 5; Eliza F. Andrews, *The War-Time Journal of a Georgia Girl, 1864–1865* (New York: D. Appleton, 1908), 198; Philips, *Diehard Rebels,* 178–79.

78. Meridian (MS) *Daily Clarion,* May 7, 1865; Cater, *As It Was,* 219 (quotation); William Nelson Pendleton Letters, June 12, 14, July 10, 16, 18, August 2, 28, 1865, SHC; Pitcock and Gurley, eds., *I Acted from Principle,* 307; Thomas North, *Five Years in Texas; or, What You Did Not Hear During the War from January 1861 to January 1866* (Cincinnati, OH: Elm Street Printing, 1871), 187–88.

79. William Nelson Pendleton Letters, May 26, June 27, 1865, SHC; George Lee Robertson to sister, May 8, 1865, George Lee Robertson Papers, DBCAH; Bradley R. Clampitt, "'Not Intended to Dispossess Females': Southern Women and Civil War Amnesty," *Civil War History* 56 (December 2010): 325–49; Clampitt, "Two Degrees of Rebellion: Amnesty and Texans after the Civil War," *Civil War History* 52 (September 2006): 255–58.

80. Bond and Coward, eds., *The South Carolinians,* 186 (quotation); Adam Fulkerson to wife, May 7, 1865, Adam Fulkerson Civil War Letters, VMI; Welker, ed., *A Keystone Rebel,* 102–3; Clark, ed., *Valleys of the Shadow,* 73–74; Turner, ed., *A Southern Soldier's Letters Home,* 293–94; Younger, ed., *Inside the Confederate Government,* 211–12; Betts, ed., "The Civil War Letters of Elbridge Littlejohn," 37; William B. Styple, ed., *Writing and Fighting the Confederate War: The Letters of Peter Wellington Alexander, Confederate War Correspondent* (Kearny, NJ: Belle Grove Publishing, 2002), 267–68.

81. Bradley R. Clampitt, *Occupied Vicksburg* (Baton Rouge: Louisiana State University Press, 2016), 43, 78–79, 81–84, 86–91, 137–38, 168–211; Ash, *When the Yankees Came,* 38–75.

82. Carroll, *Autobiography and Reminiscences,* 42–46 (quotation 45–46); John Bateman Rushing Autobiography, 12, Civil War Document Collection, USAHEC; Thomas Herndon Reminiscences, 19, in "Civil War Diary and Journal of Capt. Thomas Herndon," Civil War Document Collection, USAHEC; Broomall, *Private Confederacies,* 7, 102–6; I. G. Bradwell, "Making Our Way Home from Appomattox," *Confederate Veteran Magazine* 29 (March 1921): 103.

83. William Blair, *Virginia's Private War: Feeding Body and Soul in the Confederacy, 1861–1865* (New York: Oxford University Press, 1998), 134–36; George C. Rable, *But There Was No Peace: The Role of Violence in the Politics of Reconstruction* (Athens: University of Georgia Press, 2007), 1–15; Broomall, *Private Confederacies,* 102, 107.

84. William Sylvester Dillon Diary, June 11, 1865 (first quotation), Georgia Archives; Tapp, ed., "A Sketch of the Early Life and Service in the Confederate Army of Dr. John A. Lewis," 139 (second quotation); Fielder, *The Civil War Diaries of Capt. Alfred Tyler Fielder,* 235; Wood, *The War,* 180–81; Edwards, *Army Life of Frank Edwards,* 89; Bahnson, "The Last Days of the War," 22; William A. Fletcher, *Rebel Private Front and Rear: Memoirs of a Confederate Soldier* (New York: Dutton, 1995), 212; Kenneth A. Hafendorfer, ed., *Civil War Journal of William L. Trask, Confederate Sailor and Soldier* (Louisville, KY: KH Press, 2003), 193; James M. Mullen, "Last Days of Johnston's Army, a Comrade's

Experience With General L. S. Baker's Command at Weldon, N. C., During the Fifteen Days Preceding Johnston's Surrender at Greensboro, NC," *Southern Historical Society Papers* 18 (1890): 111–12.

85. George Alexander Martin Diary, May 20, 1865, VHS; Kenneth Wiley, ed., *Norfolk Blues: The Civil War Diary of the Norfolk Light Artillery Blues* (Shippensburg, PA: Burd Street Press, 1997), 230; John C. Oeffinger, ed., *A Soldier's General: The Civil War Letters of Major General Lafayette McLaws* (Chapel Hill: University of North Carolina Press, 2002), 273–74; John H. Worsham, *One of Jackson's Foot Cavalry: His Experience and What He Saw During the War 1861–1865* (New York: Neale Publishing, 1912), 293; William C. Davis and Meredith L. Swentor, eds., *Bluegrass Confederate: The Headquarters Diary of Edward O. Guerrant* (Baton Rouge: Louisiana State University Press, 1999), 688; J. Peter W. Houck, ed., *Confederate Surgeon: The Personal Recollections of E. A. Craighill* (Lynchburg, VA: H. E. Howard, 1989), 85; Roger S. Durham, ed., *The Blues in Gray: The Civil War Journal of William Daniel Dixon and the Republican Blues Daybook* (Knoxville: University of Tennessee Press, 2000), 288; Hughes, ed., *The Civil War Memoir of Phillip Daingerfield Stephenson*, 380; Stocker, ed., *From Huntsville to Appomattox*, 196; Clampitt, *Occupied Vicksburg*, 205; Aaron Sheehan-Dean, *Why Confederates Fought: Family and Nation in Civil War Virginia* (Chapel Hill: University of North Carolina Press, 2007), 190–92; *TCWVQ*, vol. 2, 672; Marten, *Sing Not War*, 43–44; Broomall, *Private Confederacies*, 106–7. On the importance of material culture to Confederate veterans, see Peter S. Carmichael, "The Trophies of Victory and the Relics of Defeat: Returning Home in the Spring of 1865," in Joan E. Cashin, ed., *War Matters: Material Culture in the Civil War Era* (Chapel Hill: University of North Carolina Press, 2018), 198–221.

86. Cimbala, *Veterans North and South*, 120–24; James Marten, "Civil War Veterans," in Aaron Sheehan-Dean, ed., *A Companion to the U.S. Civil War* (2 vols.) (Chichester, West Sussex, UK: John Wiley & Sons, 2014), vol. 1, 613–16. See also Edward L. Ayers, *The Promise of the New South: Life after Reconstruction* (New York: Oxford University Press, 1992), and Gaines M. Foster, *Ghosts of the Confederacy: Defeat, the Lost Cause, and the Emergence of the New South, 1865–1913* (New York: Oxford University Press, 1987).

87. Broomall, *Private Confederacies*, 10–11, 94 (first quotation), 109, 120 (second quotation).

88. Wilson, *Baptized in Blood*, 1–15; Foster, *Ghosts of the Confederacy*, 3–21; Rable, *God's Almost Chosen Peoples*, 473–74n4 (quotation).

89. John Waldrop Diary, July 4, 1865, Richard Woolfolk Waldrop Papers, SHC (first quotation); Cater, *As It Was*, xxiv (second quotation); William Nelson Pendleton Letters, June 5, 7, 12, 1865, SHC; Margaret Crozier Ramsey Diary, April 29, 1865, SHC; Moore, ed., "Diary of Major Kinloch Falconer," 451–52.

90. William Nelson Pendleton Letters, June 5, 9, 10, 12 (quotations), July 10, 16, 18, August 2, 28, 1865, William Nelson Pendleton Papers, SHC; Gayle Ann Brown, Confederate Surrenders in Indian Territory," *Journal of the West* 12, no. 3 (1973): 459–60; Junius L. Hempstead to Major DeWitt C. Craun, September 2, 1865, Junius L. Hempstead Collection, VMI; Welker, ed., *A Keystone Rebel*, 102–3; Dinkins, *1861 to 1865*, 260–63; Boykin, *The Falling Flag*, 66; Thomas J. Marshall Diary, in *Recollections and Reminiscences, 1861–1865*, vol. 8; Clark, ed., *Valleys of the Shadow*, 73–74; Gregory A. Coco, *The Civil War Infantryman: In Camp, on the March, and in Battle* (Gettysburg, PA: Thomas Publications, 1996), 149–50; Clampitt, *Occupied Vicksburg*, 168–211.

91. Brian Craig Miller, "Manhood," in Sheehan-Dean, ed., *A Companion to the U.S. Civil War*, 795–810; John Pettegrew, "The Soldier's Faith: Turn-of-the-Century Memory of the Civil War and

the Emergence of Modern American Nationalism," *Journal of Contemporary History* 31 (1996): 49–73; Adam Fairclough, "'Scalawags,' Southern Honor, and the Lost Cause: Explaining the Fatal Encounter of James H. Cosgrove and Edward L. Pierson," *Journal of Southern History* 77 (November 2011): 799–826. For contrasting views on the notion of surrendering to external definitions of manhood, see Nina Silber, *Gender and the Sectional Crisis* (Chapel Hill: University of North Carolina Press, 2008), and LeeAnn Whites, *The Civil War as a Crisis in Gender: Augusta, Georgia, 1860–1890* (Athens: University of Georgia Press, 1995).

92. Adam Fulkerson to wife, May 7, 1865, Adam Fulkerson Civil War Letters, VMI.

BIBLIOGRAPHY

PRIMARY SOURCES

Manuscript Collections

Alabama Department of Archives and History, Montgomery
    Austill, Hurrieosco. Memoir and Diary
    Battle, Cullen A. Manuscript
    Bliss, Robert Lewis. Papers
    Brown, Edward Norphlet. Letters
    Civil War Soldiers' Letters, 1858–1909
        Hardman Family Letters
        Miller, B. E. Letters
    Espy, Sarah Rousseau. Diary
    Glover, Benjamin. Letters
    Lyons, Mark. Letters
    Meadows, R. B. "Experiences and Recollections of R. B. Meadows"
    Preston, W. E. "History of the 33rd Alabama"
    Wilson, Henry F. Diary

Arkansas History Commission, Little Rock
    Bracey, John Murrell. Papers
    Brockman, Henry. Journal
    Clarke, Isaac Asbury. Papers
    Daniel, Burdet L. Papers
    Harrison, Richard. Diary
    Hill, Gabriel H. Letters
    Jones, Joseph H. Papers

Shaver, Robert G. Papers
Unknown Confederate Soldier Diary

Dolph Briscoe Center for American History, University of Texas, Austin
Barclay, H. W. Reminiscences
Brown, Frank. "Annals of Travis County"
Brown, John M. Reminiscences
Bunting, R. F. Papers
Cavaness, I. F. Diary
Civil War Miscellany, 1855–1894
    J. W. Yale from Texas 1865
Davidson, James D. Letters
Freeman, George R. Papers
Hale, William Job. Letters
Nash, Francis H. Diary
Oldham, Williamson. "Last Days of the Confederacy"
Ray, David M. Papers
Robertson, George Lee. Papers
Smith, Ashbel. Papers
Smith, John F. Papers
Spaight, Ashley Wood. Papers
Stone, Richard I. Diaries
Wallace, H. A. Recollections

Georgia Archives, Morrow, Georgia
Alston, Warren J. Diary
Andrews, John Oliver. Memoirs
Barton, James Lewis. Diary
Brown, James W. Diary
Coalson, Charles C. Diary
Dillon, William Sylvester. Diary
McCorkle, Hezekia. Diary
Poe, John C. Papers
Ray, Lavender R. Papers
Telford, R. C. Diary

Hesburgh Libraries, Special Collections, University of Notre Dame, Notre Dame, Indiana
Alexander, Thomas Benton. Diary
Murphy, George H. Diary

Hoole Special Collections Library, University of Alabama, Tuscaloosa
    Fulton, William. Letter
    Roycroft, A. C. Papers

Louisiana and Lower Mississippi Valley Collections, Hill Memorial Library,
Louisiana State University, Baton Rouge
    Anonymous Letters, 1864–1865
    Ellis, E. John and C. W. Family Papers
    Ellis, William H. Papers
    Frierson, Jacob Alison. Correspondence
    Hyatt, Arthur W. Papers
    Leet, Edwin. Letters
    Morgan, Philip Hickey. Letter
    Renwick, W. P. and Joseph. Papers

Mississippi Department of Archives and History, Jackson
    Bigger, J. A. Manuscript
    Carey, Cora E. Watson. Papers
    Civil War Miscellaneous Collection
    Elder, William D. Papers
    Hill, William H. Diary. (John C. Rietti Papers)
    Hughstone, Sanford Venable. Letters
    Jarman, Robert Amos. Papers
    Jones, Archibald K. Papers
    Kees, Martin Van Buren. Diary
    McCollum, Duncan. Diary
    Palmer, James. Civil War Diary
    Porter, Albert Quincy. Diary

Mitchell Memorial Library, Special Collections, Mississippi State University, Starkville
    Rice, Nannie Herndon. Family Papers

Newberry Library, Chicago, Illinois
    Irvine, James Bennington. Diary

Simpson History Complex, Hill College, Hillsboro, Texas
    Jefferies, Evan Shelby. Civil War Letters. 16th Mississippi Infantry File
    Porter, John C. "The Life of John C. Porter and Sketch of His Experiences in the
        Civil War"

South Carolina Historical Society, Charleston
    Simons, Alfred Drayton. Diary

South Caroliniana Library, University of South Carolina, Columbia
    Gross, S. M. Journal
    LaMotte, Thomas Jefferson Talley. Papers
    Turner, Robert A. Diary

Southern Historical Collection, Wilson Library, University of North Carolina,
Chapel Hill
    Alexander, William D. Diary
    Finley, George Washington Harper. Papers
    Green, James E. Diary
    Grimes, Bryan. Papers
    Haskell, Alexander C. Papers
    Hutson, Charles Woodward. Papers
    Jones Family. Papers
    Joyner Family. Papers
    Lacy, Drury. Papers
    McLaws, Lafayette. Papers
    McMichael, James Robert. Diary
    Pendleton, William Nelson. Papers
    Ramsey, Margaret B. Crozier. Diary
    Simpson, Avington Wayne. Papers
    Sims, William H. Diary
    Thurman, John and Sallie Ecklin. Papers
    Waldrop, Richard W. Papers
    Wallace, James T. Diary
    Whitehorne, J. E. Diary
    Wood, John Taylor. Papers

Special Collections Research Center, University of Kentucky Libraries, Lexington
    Haggard, William S. Diary

State Historical Society of Missouri, Springfield
    Baker, J. H. P. Civil War Diary
    Coale, Stephen D. Letters
    Hoskin, William N. Civil War Diary
    Rhoades, Marcus Morton. Diary

Tennessee State Library and Archives, Nashville
 Cartmell, Robert H. Papers
 Civil War Collection
  Dewitt, Marcus Bearden. Diary
  Pollard, William Mebane. Diary
  Porter, Nimrod. Diary
  Sloan, William E. Diary
  Sullivan, Thomas L. Account Book

United States Army Heritage and Education Center, Carlisle, Pennsylvania
 Burke, Curtis R. Papers
 Civil War Document Collection
  Andrews, John Oliver. War Record
  Barineau, Ann. "Memoir of Reverend Ben H. Bounds of Greenville, Texas"
  Featherston, Winfield Scott. Manuscript
  Herndon, Captain Thomas. "Civil War Diary and Journal of Capt. Thomas Herndon"
  Manson, Joseph Richard. "A Spiritual Diary"
  Moore, Samuel Lewis. Autobiography
  Ruffin, Joel. Letter
  Rushing, John Bateman. Autobiography
  Smith, Miles Vance. "Reminiscences of the Civil War"
  Waldrip, George W. Reminiscences
  Walthall, Howard Malcolm. Reminiscences
 Civil War Times Illustrated Collection
  Griffin, James. Letters
 Leigh, Lewis, Jr. Collection
  Hege, Constantine A. Letters
 Morris, William G. B. Papers
 Patterson, Josiah. Papers

University of North Texas Archives, Willis Library, Denton
 Eddleman, David J. Collection

Virginia Historical Society, Richmond
 Cole, David Lawson. Diary
 Cook, Lelian M. Diary
 Cooke, Giles Buckner. Diary
 Cox, E. L. Diary

Dickinson, Fannie E. Taylor. Diary
Fields, Charles Bickem. Diary
Jones, Thomas Catesby. Reminiscences
Martin, George Alexander. Diary
Turrentine, James Alexander. Diary
Vincent, John Bell. Bennington Diary

Virginia Military Institute, Lexington
Adams, Richard H., Jr. Correspondence
Boyd, Robert A. Diary
Civil War Broadside, General Orders No. 1, U.S. Army Occupation of Lexington,
    Virginia, July 5, 1865
Fulkerson, Adam. Civil War Letters
Harden, James. Correspondence
Hempstead, Junius L. Collection
Munford, Thomas T. Civil War Letters
Vincent, John Bell. Diary
Weisiger, Oscar. Letter

Government Documents

Schurz, Carl. "Report on the Condition of the South." 39th Congress, Senate Ex. Doc. 1st
    Session. No. 2.
*The Statutes at Large of the Confederate States of America, Passed at the Fourth Session of
    the First Congress, 1863–4.* Richmond: R. M. Smith, 1864.
United States Bureau of the Census. Eighth Census of the United States, 1860. Schedule
    1 (Free Inhabitants).
United States Department of Commerce. *Distance Between U.S. Ports.* Washington, DC:
    Government Printing Office, 2013.
United States Navy Department. *Official Records of the Union and Confederate Navies in
    the War of the Rebellion.* Washington, DC: Government Printing Office, 1932.
United States War Department. Compiled Records Showing Service of Military Units in
    Confederate Organizations. Record Group 109. National Archives, Washington, DC
United States War Department. *The War of the Rebellion: A Compilation of the Official
    Records of the Union and Confederate Armies.* 128 vols. Washington, DC: Govern-
    ment Printing Office, 1880–1901.

Newspapers

Anderson *Intelligencer* (SC)
Augusta *Chronicle & Sentinel* (GA)
Belleville *Countryman* (TX)
Camden *Tri-Weekly Journal* (SC)
Charlotte *Western Democrat* (NC)
Chattanooga *Daily Rebel* (Selma, AL)
Clarksville *Standard* (TX)
Columbia *Phoenix* (SC)
Dallas *Herald* (TX)
Flake's Bulletin (Galveston, TX)
Galveston *Daily News* (TX)
Greensborough *Patriot* (NC)
Houston *Tri-weekly Telegraph* (TX)
La Grange *Patriot* (TX)
Marshall *Texas Republican (TX)*
Matamoros *Daily Ranchero* (Mexico)
Meridian *Daily Clarion* (MS)
Nashville *Daily Union* (TN)
National Tribune (Washington, DC)
Newberry *Tri-Weekly Herald* (SC)
New Orleans *Times (LA)*
New York *Herald (NY)*
Raleigh *Daily Confederate* (NC)
Shreveport *Semi-Weekly News* (LA)

Books

Adamson, Augustus Pitt. *Brief History of the Thirtieth Georgia Regiment.* Griffin, GA: Mills, 1912.

Anderson, Ephraim McDowell. *Memoirs: Historical and Personal, Including the Campaigns of the First Missouri Brigade.* St. Louis: Times Printing, 1868.

Anderson, John Q., ed. *Brokenburn: The Journal of Kate Stone, 1861–1868.* Baton Rouge: Louisiana State University Press, 1955.

———, ed. *Campaigning with Parsons' Texas Cavalry Brigade, CSA.* Hillsboro, TX: Hill Junior College Press, 1967.

Andrews, Eliza F. *The War-Time Journal of a Georgia Girl, 1864–1865.* New York: D. Appleton, 1908.

Andrews, Sidney. *The South Since the War: As Shown by Fourteen Weeks of Travel and Observation in Georgia and the Carolinas*. Boston: Ticknor and Fields, 1866.

Andrews, W. H. *Diary of W. H. Andrews, 1st Sergt., Co. M., 1st Georgia Regulars, From February, 1861, to May 2, 1865*. Atlanta: n. p., 1891.

Andrews, W. J. *Sketch of Company K, 23rd South Carolina Volunteers, in the Civil War from 1862–1865*. Richmond: Whittet and Shepperson, n.d.

Ashley, Joe, and Lavon Ashley, eds. *Oh for Dixie! The Civil War Record and Diary of Capt. William V. Davis, 30th Mississippi Infantry, CSA*. Colorado Springs: Standing Pine, 2001.

Austin, J. Luke, ed. *General John Bratton: Sumter to Appomattox in Letters to His Wife*. Sewanee, TN: Proctor's Hall, 2003.

Austin, J. P. *The Blue and the Gray: Sketches of a Portion of the Unwritten History of the Great American Civil War*. Atlanta: Franklin, 1899.

Bailey, Anne J., ed. *In the Saddle with the Texans: Day-by-Day with Parsons's Cavalry Brigade, 1862–1865*. Abilene, TX: McWhiney Foundation Press, 2003.

Baird, W. Davis, ed. *A Creek Warrior for the Confederacy: The Autobiography of Chief G. W. Grayson*. Norman: University of Oklahoma Press, 1988.

Banasik, Michael E., ed. *Serving with Honor: The Diary of Captain Eathan Allen Pinnell, Eighth Missouri Infantry (Confederate)*. Iowa City: Camp Pope Bookshop, 1999.

Barr, Amelia. *All the Days of My Life: An Autobiography*. New York: D. Appleton, 1913.

Barrett, John G., ed. *Yankee Rebel: The Civil War Journal of Edmund DeWitt Patterson*. Knoxville: University of Tennessee Press, 2004.

Barron, S. B. *Lone Star Defenders: A Chronicle of the Third Texas Cavalry, Ross' Brigade*. New York: Neale, 1908.

Baumgartner, Richard A., ed. *Blood and Sacrifice: The Civil War Journal of a Confederate Soldier*. Huntington, WV: Blue Acorn, 1994.

Bearss, Edwin C., ed. *A Louisiana Confederate: Diary of Felix Pierre Poche*. Natchitoches: Louisiana Studies Institute, Northwestern State University, 1972.

Benson, Susan Williams, ed. *Berry Benson's Civil War Book: Memoirs of a Confederate Scout and Sharpshooter*. Athens: University of Georgia Press, 1962.

Bergeron, Arthur W., Jr. *The Civil War Reminiscences of Major Silas T. Grisamore, CSA*. Baton Rouge: Louisiana State University Press, 1993.

Berry, Thomas F. *Four Years with Morgan and Forrest*. Oklahoma City: Harlow-Ratliff, 1914.

Bettersworth, John K., ed. *Mississippi in the Confederacy: As They Saw It*. Baton Rouge: Louisiana State University Press, 1961.

Betts, Alexander Davis. *Experience of a Confederate Chaplain, 1861–1864*. Greenville, SC: W. A. Betts, 1901.

Bevier, R. S. *A History of the First and Second Missouri Confederate Brigades, 1861–1865, and from Wakarusa to Appomattox*. St. Louis: Bryan, Brand, 1879.

Bitton, Davis, ed. *The Reminiscences and Civil War Letters of Levi Lamoni Wight: Life in a Mormon Splinter Colony on the Texas Frontier.* Salt Lake City: University of Utah Press, 1970.

Blackford, Susan Leigh. *Letters from Lee's Army.* New York: Charles Scribner's Sons, 1947.

Blakey, Arch Frederic, Ann Smith Lainhart, and Winston Bryant Stephens Jr., eds. *Rose Cottage Chronicles: Civil War Letters of the Bryant-Stephens Families of North Florida.* Gainesville: University of Florida Press, 1998.

Blessington, Joseph P. *The Campaigns of Walker's Texas Division.* New York: Lange, Little & Co., 1875.

Boggs, William Robertson. *Military Reminiscences of General William R. Boggs, CSA.* Durham, NC: The Seeman Printery, 1913.

Bond, Natalie Jenkins, and Osmun Latrobe Coward, eds. *The South Carolinians: Colonel Asbury Coward's Memoirs.* New York: Vantage Press, 1968.

Bowman, Thornton. *Reminiscences of an Ex-Confederate Soldier: Or, Forty Years on Crutches.* Austin: Gammel-Statesman, 1904.

Boykin, Edward M. *The Falling Flag: Evacuation of Richmond, Retreat and Surrender at Appomattox, by An Officer of the Rear-Guard.* New York: E. J. Hale, 1874.

Breckenridge, William Campbell Preston. *"The Ex-Confederate, and What He Has Done in Peace": An Address Delivered Before the Association of the Army of Northern Virginia, at the Meeting Held in Richmond, Va., October 26, 1892.* Richmond: J. L. Hill, 1892.

Brett, Martin. *Experiences of a Georgia Boy in the Army of Northern Virginia, 1861–1865.* Gainesville, GA: Magnolia Press, 1988.

Brinsfield, John Wesley, Jr., ed. *The Spirit Divided: Memoirs of Civil War Chaplains, the Confederacy.* Macon, GA: Mercer University Press, 2006.

Brooke, George M., Jr., ed. *Ironclads and Big Guns of the Confederacy: The Journal and Letters of John M. Brooke.* Columbia: University of South Carolina Press, 2002.

Brooks, Ulysses R. *Butler and His Cavalry in the War of Secession, 1861–1865.* Columbia, SC: The State Company, 1909.

Brown, Campbell H., ed. *The Reminiscences of Sergeant Newton Cannon, from Holograph Material Provided by His Grandson, Samuel M. Fleming, Jr.* Franklin, TN: Carter House Association, 1963.

Brown, Kent Masterson, ed. *One of Morgan's Men: Memoirs of Lieutenant John M. Porter of the Ninth Kentucky Cavalry.* Lexington: University of Kentucky Press, 2011.

Brown, Norman D., ed. *One of Cleburne's Command: The Civil War Reminiscences and Diary of Captain Samuel T. Foster, Granbury's Texas Brigade, CSA.* Austin: University of Texas Press, 1980.

Brown, Shepherd Spencer Norville, ed. *War Years, CSA: 12th Mississippi Regiment, Major S. H. Giles, Q. M., Original Letters, 1860–1865.* Hillsboro, TX: Hill College Press, 1998.

Buckley, Cornelius M., ed. *A Frenchman, a Chaplain, a Rebel: The War Letters of Pere Louis-Hippolyte Gache, S. J.* Chicago: Loyola University Press, 1981.

Cabaniss, Jim R., ed. *Civil War Journal and Letters of Washington Ives, 4th Fla. CSA.* Tallahassee, FL: Jim Cabaniss, 1987.

Caldwell, J. F. J. *The History of a Brigade of South Carolinians, Known First as "Gregg's" and Subsequently as "McGowan's Brigade."* Philadelphia: King and Baird, 1866.

Campbell, John Archibald. *Reminiscences and Documents Relating to the Civil War During the Year 1865.* Baltimore: John Murphy, 1887.

Campbell, R. Thomas, ed. *Southern Service on Land & Sea: The Wartime Journal of Robert Watson, CSA/CSN.* Knoxville: University of Tennessee Press, 2002.

Cannon, J. P. *Bloody Banners and Barefoot Boys: A History of the 27th Regiment Alabama Infantry, CSA: the Civil War Memoirs and Diaries of J. P. Cannon, M. D.* Shippensburg, PA: Burd Street Press, 1997.

Carroll, John William. *Autobiography and Reminiscences.* Henderson, TN: n. p., 1898.

Carter, Howell. *A Cavalryman's Reminiscences of the Civil War.* New Orleans: American Printing, 1900.

Casler, John Overton. *Four Years in the Stonewall Brigade.* Guthrie, OK: State Capital Printing, 1903.

Cash, William M., and Lucy Somerville Howorth, eds. *My Dear Nellie: The Civil War Letters of William L. Nugent to Eleanor Smith Nugent.* Jackson: University Press of Mississippi, 1977.

Cate, Wirt Armistead, ed. *Two Soldiers: The Campaign Diaries of Thomas J. Key, C.S.A., December 7, 1863–May 17, 1865, and Robert J. Campbell, U.S.A., January 1, 1864–July 21, 1864.* Chapel Hill: University of North Carolina Press, 1938.

Cater, Douglas John. *As It Was: Reminiscences of a Soldier of the Third Texas Cavalry and the Nineteenth Louisiana Infantry.* Austin, TX: State House Press, 1990.

Chamberlain, Joshua Lawrence. *The Passing of the Armies: An Account of the Final Campaign of the Army of the Potomac, Based Upon the Personal Reminiscences of the Fifth Army Corps.* New York: G. P. Putnam, 1915.

Chapman, Sarah Bahnson, ed. *Bright and Gloomy Days: The Civil War Correspondence of Captain Charles Frederic Bahnson, a Moravian Confederate.* Knoxville: University of Tennessee Press, 2003.

Chattahoochee Valley Historical Society, ed. *War Was the Place: A Centennial Collection of Confederate Soldiers' Letters.* Chambers County, AL: Chattahoochee Valley Historical Society, 1961.

Clark, Walter Augustus. *Under the Stars and Bars; or, Memories of Four Years Service with the Oglethorpes, of Augusta, Georgia.* Augusta, GA: Chronicle Printing, 1900.

Clark, Willene B., ed. *Valleys of the Shadow: The Memoir of Confederate Captain Reuben G. Clark, Company I, 59th Tennessee Mounted Infantry.* Knoxville: University of Tennessee Press, 1994.

Cockrell, Thomas D., and Michael B. Ballard, eds. *A Mississippi Rebel in the Army of Northern Virginia: The Civil War Memoirs of Private David Holt*. Baton Rouge: Louisiana State University Press, 1995.

Coleman, Kenneth, ed. *Athens, 1861–1865: As Seen Through the Letters in the University of Georgia Libraries*. Athens: University of Georgia Press, 1969.

Collins, R. M. *Chapters from the Unwritten History of the War Between the States; or, the Incidents in the Life of a Confederate Soldier*. St. Louis, MO: Nixon-Jones Printing, 1893.

Coltrane, Daniel Branson. *The Memoirs of Daniel Branson Coltrane, Co. I, 63rd Reg. N. C. Cavalry, CSA*. Raleigh, NC: Edwards & Broughton, 1956.

Commager, Henry Steele. *The Blue and the Gray: The Story of the Civil War as Told by Its Participants*. New York: Bobbs-Merrill, 1950.

Confederate Reminiscences and Letters. 14 vols. Atlanta: Georgia Division of the United Daughters of the Confederacy, 1995.

Copley, John M. *A Sketch of the Battle of Franklin; with Reminiscences of Camp Douglas*. Austin, TX: Eugene von Boeckmann, 1893.

Corson, William Clark, and Blake W. Corson Jr., eds., *My Dear Jennie: A Collection of Love Letters from a Confederate Soldier to his Fiancée During the Period 1861–1865*. Madison, WI: B. W. Corson, 1982.

Crosland, Charles. *Reminiscences of the Sixties*. Columbia, SC: The State Company, 1910.

Crow, Maddie Lou Teague, ed. *The Diary of a Confederate Soldier: John Washington Inzer*. Huntsville, AL: Strode Publishers, 1977.

Curry, J. H. *History of Company B, 40th Alabama Regiment, Confederate States Army, 1862 to 1865*. Anniston, AL: Norwood, 1902.

Cutrer, Thomas W., ed. *Longstreet's Aide: The Civil War Letters of Major Thomas J. Goree*. Charlottesville: University of Virginia Press, 1995.

———, ed. *'Our Trust is in the God of Battles': The Civil War Letters of Robert Franklin Bunting, Chaplain, Terry's Texas Rangers, CSA*. Knoxville: University of Tennessee Press, 2006.

Cutrer, Thomas W., and T. Michael Parrish, eds. *Brothers in Gray: The Civil War Letters of the Pierson Family*. Baton Rouge: Louisiana State University Press, 1997.

Cuttino, George Peddy, ed. *Saddle Bag and Spinning Wheel: Being the Civil War Letters of George W. Peddy, M. D., Surgeon, 56th Georgia Volunteers Regiment, CSA, and His Wife Kate Featherston Peddy*. Macon, GA: Mercer University Press, 1981.

Dacus, Robert H. *Reminiscences of Company "H," First Arkansas Mounted Rifles*. Dardanelle, AR: Post-Dispatch Printing, 1897.

Daniel, F. E. *Recollections of a Rebel Surgeon (and other sketches); or in the Doctor's Sappy Days*. Chicago: Clinic Publishing, 1901.

Davis, William C., ed. *Diary of a Confederate Soldier: John S. Jackman of the Orphan Brigade*. Columbia: University of South Carolina Press, 1990.

Davis, William C., and Meredith L. Swentor, eds. *Bluegrass Confederate: The Headquarters Diary of Edward O. Guerrant.* Baton Rouge: Louisiana State University Press, 1999.

Davison, Nora Fontaine M., *Cullings from the Confederacy.* Washington, DC: Rufus H. Darby, 1903.

Dawson, Francis W. *Reminiscences of Confederate Service, 1861–1865.* Charleston, SC: News and Courier Book Presses, 1882.

Dayton, Ruth Woods, ed. *The Diary of a Confederate Soldier: James E. Hall.* Lewisburg, WV: n.p., 1961.

Debray, X. B. *A Sketch of the History of Debray's 26th Regiment of Texas Cavalry.* Waco, TX: Waco Village Press, 1961.

Dennett, John Richard, *The South As It Is, 1865–1866.* New York: Viking, 1965.

D'Hamel, Enrique. *The Adventures of a Tenderfoot: History of the 2nd Regiment Mounted Rifles and Company G, 33 Regiment and Captain Coopwood's Spy Company and 2nd Texas in Texas and New Mexico.* Waco, TX: W. M. Morrison, 1965.

Dickert, D. Augustus. *History of Kershaw's Brigade, with Complete Roll of Companies, Biographical Sketches, Incidents, Anecdotes, etc.* Newberry, SC: Elbert H. Aull, 1899.

Dickinson, Henry Clay. *Diary of Henry Dickinson, CSA, Morris Island, 1864–1865.* Denver, Co.: Press of the Williamson-Haffner Co., n.d.

Dinkins, James. *1861 to 1865, by an Old Johnnie, Personal Recollections and Experiences in the Confederate Army.* Cincinnati, OH: Robert Clarke, 1897.

Dobbins, Austin V., ed. *Grandfather's Journal: Company B, Sixteenth Mississippi Infantry Volunteers, Harris' Brigade, Mahone's Division, Hill's Corps, A. N. V. May 27, 1861–July 15, 1865.* Dayton, OH: Morningside House, 1988.

Dorsey, Sarah Anne, ed. *Recollections of Henry Watkins Allen, Brigadier General Confederate States Army, ex-Governor of Louisiana.* New York: M. Doolady, 1866.

Dunlop, William S. *Lee's Sharpshooters; or the Forefront of Battle.* Little Rock, AR: Tunnan & Pittard, 1899.

Durham, Roger S., ed. *The Blues in Gray: The Civil War Journal of William Daniel Dixon and the Republican Blues Daybook.* Knoxville: University of Tennessee Press, 2000.

Durkin, Joseph T., ed. *Confederate Chaplain: A War Journal of Rev. James B. Sheeran, CSA.* Milwaukee, WI: Bruce, 1960.

———, ed. *John Dooley: Confederate Soldier. His War Journal.* Washington, DC: Georgetown University Press, 1945.

Dyer, John Will. *Reminiscences; or, Four Years in the Confederate Army.* Evansville, IN: Keller Printing, 1898.

Early, Jubal A. *A Memoir of the Last Year of the War for Independence in the Confederate States of America Containing an Account of His Commands in the Years 1864 and 1865.* Toronto, ON: Lovell & Gibson, 1866.

Edwards, John Frank. *Army Life of Frank Edwards, Confederate Veteran, Army of Northern Virginia, 1861–1865.* La Grange, GA: F. Edwards, 1911.

Edwards, John N. *Shelby and His Men; or, The War in the West.* Cincinnati, OH: Miami Printing,1867.

Eggleston, George Cary. *A Rebel's Recollections.* New York: Hurd and Houghton, 1874.

Elliott, Sam Davis, ed. *Doctor Quintard, Chaplain CSA, and Second Bishop of Tennessee.* Baton Rouge: Louisiana State University Press, 2003.

Emerson, W. Eric, and Karen Stokes, eds. *Faith, Valor, Devotion: The Civil War Letters of William Porcher DuBose.* Columbia: University of South Carolina Press, 2010.

Evans, Clement A., ed. *Confederate Military History.* 12 vols. Atlanta: Confederate Publishing, 1899.

Evans, Robert G., ed. *The 16th Mississippi Infantry: Civil War Letters and Reminiscences.* Jackson: University Press of Mississippi, 2002.

Fielder, Alfred Tyler. *The Civil War Diaries of Capt. Alfred Tyler Fielder, 12th Tennessee Regiment Infantry, Company B, 1861–1865.* Louisville, KY: Ann York Franklin, 1996.

Fletcher, William A. *Rebel Private Front and Rear: Memoirs of a Confederate Soldier.* New York: Dutton, 1995.

Folmar, John Kent, ed. *From that Terrible Field: Civil War Letters of James M. Williams, Twenty-First Alabama Infantry Volunteers.* Tuscaloosa: University of Alabama Press, 1981.

Ford, Arthur P. *Life in the Confederate Army: Being the Experiences of a Private Soldier in the Confederate Army.* New York: Neale, 1905.

Ford, J. W., ed. *The Hour of Our Nation's Agony: The Civil War Letters of Lt. William Cowper Nelson of Mississippi.* Knoxville: University of Tennessee Press, 2007.

Fort, John Porter. *John Porter Fort, A Memorial and Personal Reminiscences.* New York: Knickerbocker, 1918.

French, Samuel G. *Two Wars: An Autobiography.* Nashville: Confederate Veteran, 1901.

Gallagher, Gary W., ed. *Fighting for the Confederacy: The Personal Recollections of Edward Porter Alexander.* Chapel Hill: University of North Carolina Press, 1980.

Garber, Pat, ed. *Heart Like a River: The Story of Confederate Soldier Sergeant-Major Newsom Edward Jenkins' Years in the American Civil War, 1861–1865, as Recorded in His Diary, Letters, and Other Sources.* Lynchburg, VA: Schroeder Publications, 2011.

George, Henry. *History of the 3d, 7th, 8th, and 12th Kentucky, CSA.* Louisville, KY: C. T. Dearing, 1911.

Gibbons, Alfred R. *Recollections of an Old Confederate Soldier.* Shelbyville, MO: Herald, 1931.

Giesecke, Julius. *Giesecke's Civil War Diary: The Story of Company G of the Fourth Regiment of the First Texas Cavalry Brigade of the Army of the Confederate States of America (1861–1865).* Manor, TX: Patrick Historical Research, 1999.

Giles, Valerius C. *Rags and Hope: The Recollections of Val. C. Giles, Four Years with Hood's Brigade, Fourth Texas Infantry, 1861–1865.* New York: Coward-McCann, 1961.

Gordon, John B. *Reminiscences of the Civil War.* New York: Charles Scribner's Sons, 1904.

Govan, Gilbert E., and James W. Livingood, eds. *The Haskell Memoirs: John Cheves Haskell*. New York: G. P. Putnam, 1960.

Goyne, Minetta Altgelt, ed. *Lone Star and Double Eagle: Civil War Letters of a German Family*. Fort Worth: Texas Christian University Press, 1982.

Graber, Henry William. *The Life Record of H. W. Graber, a Terry Texas Ranger, 1861–1865: Sixty-two Years in Texas*. n. p.: H. W. Graber, 1916.

Green, Jennette, ed. *The Civil War Through the Eyes of Lt. Col. John Withers and His Wife, Anita Dwyer Withers: American Civil War Diaries of a Confederate Army Officer and His Wife, a Woman in Civil War History*. Bakersfield, CA: Diamond Press, 2011.

Green, Wharton J. *Recollections and Reflections: An Autobiography of Half a Century and More*. Raleigh, NC: Edwards and Broughton, 1906.

Grimes, Bryan. *Extract of Letters of Major-General Grimes to His Wife, Written While In Active Service in the Army of Northern Virginia, Together with Some Personal Recollections of the War*. Raleigh: Alfred Williams, 1884.

Guild, George B. *A Brief Narrative of the Fourth Tennessee Cavalry Regiment, Wheeler's Corps, Army of Tennessee*. Nashville: n.p., 1913.

Hafendorfer, Kenneth A., ed. *Civil War Journal of William L. Trask, Confederate Sailor and Soldier*. Louisville, KY: KH Press, 2003.

Hagood, Johnson. *Memoirs of the War of Secession*. Columbia, SC: The State Company, 1910.

Hall, Winchester. *The Story of the 26th Louisiana Infantry in the Service of the Confederate States*. n.p., 1890.

Hamilton, D. H. *History of Company M, First Texas Volunteer Infantry, Hood's Brigade, Longstreet's Corps, Army of the Confederate States of America*. Waco, TX: W. M. Morrison, 1962.

Hancock, Richard R. *Hancock's Diary: or, A History of the Second Tennessee Cavalry, with Sketches of First and Seventh Battalions*. Nashville: Brandon Printing, 1887.

Harper, George Washington Finley. *Sketch of the Fifty-Eighth Regiment (Infantry) North Carolina Troops*. Lenoir, NC: n.p., 1901.

Harwell, Richard Barksdale, ed. *Kate: The Journal of a Confederate Nurse*. Baton Rouge: Louisiana State University Press, 1959.

Head, Thomas Anthony. *Campaigns and Battles of the Sixteenth Regiment, Tennessee Volunteers, In The War Between the States*. Nashville: Cumberland Presbyterian Publishing, 1885.

Hewitt, Lawrence L., Thomas Edwin Schott, and Marc Kunis, eds. *To Succeed or Perish: The Diaries of Sergeant Edmund Trent Eggleston, 1st Mississippi Light Artillery Regiment, CSA*. Knoxville: University of Tennessee Press, 2015.

Hickerson, Thomas Felix. *Echoes of Happy Valley: Letters and Diaries, Family Life in the South; Civil War History*. Chapel Hill, NC: Bulls Head Bookshop, 1962.

Hinsdale, John Wetmore. *History of the Seventy-Second Regiment of the North Carolina Troops in the War Between the States, 1861–1865.* Goldsboro, NC: Nash Brothers, 1901.

Hoge, John Milton. *A Journal by John Milton Hoge, 1862–5: Containing Some of the Most Particular Incidents that Occurred During His Enlistment as a Soldier in the Confederate Army.* Cincinnati, OH: M. H. Bruce, 1961.

Holmes, Henry McCall. *Diary of Henry McCall Holmes, Army of Tennessee, Assistant Surgeon, Florida Troops, with Related Letters, Documents, etc.* State College, MS: n.p., 1968.

Holt, Thad, Jr., ed. *Miss Waring's Journal: 1863 and 1865, Being the Diary of Miss Mary Waring of Mobile, During the Final Days of the War Between the States.* Chicago: Wyvern Press of S. F. E., 1964.

Hood, John Bell. *Advance and Retreat: Personal Experiences in the United States and Confederate States Armies.* Bloomington: Indiana University Press, 1959.

Hopkins, Luther Wesley. *From Bull Run to Appomattox, a boy's view, by Luther W. Hopkins of Genl. J. E. B. Stuart's cavalry, 6th Virginia regiment.* Baltimore: Press of Fleet-McGinley, 1908.

Houck, J. Peter W., ed. *Confederate Surgeon: The Personal Recollections of E. A. Craighill.* Lynchburg, VA: H. E. Howard, 1989.

Houghton, Mitchell Bennett. *From the Beginning Until Now.* Montgomery, AL: M. B. Houghton, 1914.

Houghton, W. R., and Mitchell Bennett Houghton. *Two Boys in the Civil War and After.* Montgomery, AL: Paragon, 1912.

Howard, McHenry. *Recollections of a Maryland Confederate Soldier and Staff Officer Under Johnston, Jackson, and Lee.* Dayton, OH: Morningside Bookshop, 1975.

Hubbard, John Milton. *Notes of a Private.* Memphis, TN: E. H. Clarke & Brother, 1909.

Hubbs, G. Ward, ed. *Voices from Company D: Diaries by the Greensboro Guards, Fifth Alabama Infantry Regiment, Army of Northern Virginia.* Athens: University of Georgia Press, 2003.

Huddle, Randal, and James F. Wilson, eds. *Civil War Diary of Benjamin Jacob Huddle, Company B, 29th Virginia Infantry.* Blacksburg, VA: Wilson, 2006.

Hudson, Joshua Hilary. *Sketches and Reminiscences.* Columbia, SC: State Company, 1903.

Hudson, Weldon I., ed. *The Civil War Diary of William Spencer Hudson.* St. Louis: Micro-Records Publishing, 1973.

Hughes, Nathaniel Cheairs, Jr., ed. *The Civil War Memoir of Phillip Daingerfield Stephenson, D. D.* Conway: University of Central Arkansas Press, 1995.

——, ed. *Liddell's Record; St. John Richardson Liddell, Brigadier General, CSA, Staff Officer and Brigadier Commander, Army of Tennessee.* Dayton, OH: Morningside Press, 1985.

Ingram, George W., and Martha F. Ingram. *Civil War Letters of George W. and Martha F. Ingram, 1864–1865.* College Station: Texas A&M University Press, 1973.

Jamison, Henry D., and Marguerite J. McTigue, eds. *Letters and Recollections of a Confederate Soldier, 1860–1865.* Nashville: H. D. Jamison, 1964.

Johnston, David E. *The Story of a Confederate Boy in the Civil War.* Portland, OR: Glass & Prudhomme, 1914.

Johnston, Joseph E. *Narrative of Military Operations Directed During the Late War Between the States.* Bloomington: Indiana University Press, 1959.

Joiner, Gary D., Marilyn S. Joiner, and Clifton D. Cardin, eds. *No Pardons to Ask, nor Apologies to Make: The Journal of William Henry King, Gray's 28th Louisiana Infantry Regiment.* Knoxville: University of Tennessee Press, 2006.

Jones, Carroll, ed. *Captain Lenoir's Diary: Tom Lenoir and his Civil War Company from Western North Carolina.* Wilmington, NC: Winoca, 2010.

Jones, Charles C., Jr. *Historical Sketch of the Chatham Artillery during the Confederate Struggle for Independence.* Albany, NY: Joel Munsell, 1867.

Jones, J. Keith, ed. *The Boys of Diamond Hill: the Lives and Civil War Letters of the Boyd Family of Abbeville County, South Carolina.* Jefferson, NC: McFarland, 2011.

Jones, Terry L., ed. *Campbell Brown's Civil War: With Ewell and the Army of Northern Virginia.* Baton Rouge: Louisiana State University Press, 2001.

Jones, Thomas G. *The Last Days of the Army of Northern Virginia: An Address Delivered by Gov. Thos. G. Jones before the Virginia Division of the Association of the Army of Northern Virginia at the Annual Meeting.* Richmond, VA: n.p., 1893.

Joslyn, Mauriel Phillips, ed. *Charlotte's Boys: Civil War Letters of the Branch Family of Savannah.* Berryville, VA: Rockbridge, 1996.

Keener, Lawson Jefferson. *Letters from Lawson Jefferson Keener Written During His Confederate Service to Alcesta (Allie) Benson Carter.* Longview, TX: Mrs. Rogers Lacy, 1963.

Kennaway, John S. *On Sherman's Track: The South After the War.* London: Seeley, Jackson, and Halliday, 1868.

Kerr, Homer L., ed. *Fighting with Ross' Texas Cavalry Brigade, CSA: Diary of Lieut. George L. Griscom, Adjutant, 9th Texas Cavalry Regiment.* Hillsboro, TX: Hill Junior College Press, 1976.

King, John H. *Three Hundred Days in a Yankee Prison: Reminiscences of War Life, Captivity, Imprisonment at Camp Chase Ohio.* Atlanta: James P. Daves, 1904.

Kirwan, A. D., ed. *Johnny Green of the Orphan Brigade: The Journal of a Confederate Soldier.* Louisville: University of Kentucky Press, 1956.

Lale, Max S., ed. *The Civil War Letters of David R. Garrett, Detailing the Adventures of the 6th Texas Cavalry, 1861–1865.* Marshall, TX: Port Caddo Press, 1964.

Lambright, James T. *History of the Liberty Independent Troop During Civil War, 1862–1865.* Brunswick, GA: Press of Glover Brothers, 1910.

Ledford, Preston Lafayette. *Reminiscences of the Civil War, 1861–1865.* Thomasville, NC: News Printing House, 1909.

Lemke, W. J., ed. *The Journals of James A. Walden*. Fayetteville, AR: Washington County Historical Society, 1954.

———, ed. *The War-time Letters of Captain T. C. Dupree, CSA, 1864–1865*. Fayetteville, Ar.: Washington County Historical Society, 1953.

Leon, Louis. *Diary of a Tar-Heel Confederate Soldier*. Charlotte, NC: Stone, 1913.

Lewis, John H. *Recollections from 1860 to 1865*. Washington, DC: Peake, 1895.

Lightsey, Ada Christine. *The Veteran's Story*. Meridian, MS: Meridian News, 1899.

Linden, Glenn, and Virginia Linden, eds. *Disunion, War, Defeat, and Recovery in Alabama: The Journal of Augustus Benners, 1850–1885*. Macon, GA: Mercer University Press, 2007.

Longstreet, James I. *From Manassas to Appomattox: Memoirs of the Civil War in America*. Philadelphia: J. B. Lippincott, 1896.

Loughery, Augusta M. *War and Reconstruction Times in Texas: 1861–1865*. 2nd edition; Austin: Von-Boeckmann Jones, 1914.

Lowe, Jeffrey C., and Sam Hodges, eds. *Letters to Amanda: The Civil War Letters of Marion Hill Fitzpatrick, Army of Northern Virginia*. Macon, GA: Mercer University Press, 1998.

Lowe, Richard, ed. *A Texas Cavalry Officer's Civil War: The Diary and Letters of James C. Bates*. Baton Rouge: Louisiana State University Press, 1999.

Lubbock, Francis R. *Six Decades in Texas*. Austin: Ben C. Jones,1900.

Mackintosh, Robert Harley, Jr., ed. *Dear Martha: The Confederate War Letters of a South Carolina Soldier, Alexander Faulkner Fewell*. Columbia, SC: Mackintosh, 1976.

Malone, Thomas H. *Memoir of Thomas H. Malone*. Nashville: Baird-Ward, 1928.

Marks, Paula Mitchell, ed. *When Will the Weary War Be Over? The Civil War Letters of the Maverick Family of San Antonio*. Dallas: The Book Club of Texas, 2008.

Massey, James Troy, ed. *Memoirs of Captain J. M. Bailey*. James Troy Massey, 1994.

Mathis, Ray, ed. *In the Land of the Living: Wartime Letters by Confederates from the Chattahoochee Valley of Alabama and Georgia*. Troy, AL: Troy State University Press, 1981.

McArthur, Judith N., and Vernon Burton, eds. *A Gentleman and an Officer: A Military and Social History of James B. Griffin's Civil War*. London: Oxford University Press, 1996.

McCaffrey, James M., ed. *Only a Private: A Texan Remembers the Civil War: The Memoirs of William J. Oliphant*. Houston: Halcyon, 2004.

McCarthy, Carlton. *Detailed Minutiae of Soldier Life in the Army of Northern Virginia, 1861–1865*. Richmond: Carlton McCarthy, 1894.

McCaslin, Richard B., ed. *A Soldier's Letters to Charming Nellie, by J. B. Polley of Hood's Texas Brigade*. Knoxville: University of Tennessee Press, 2008.

McClendon, W. A. *Recollections of War Times: By an Old Veteran While Under Stonewall Jackson and Lieutenant General James Longstreet : How I Got In, and How I Got Out*. Montgomery, AL: Paragon, 1909.

McClure, Judy Watson, ed. *Confederate from East Texas: The Civil War Letters of James Monroe Watson.* Quanah, TX: Nortex, 1976.

McCollum, Duncan. *The Diary of Captain Duncan McCollum, Co. A, 4th Mississippi Cavalry, 1865.* San Bernardino, CA: Duncan McCollum, 1964.

McDonald, Archie P., ed. *Make Me a Map of the Valley: The Civil War Journal of Stonewall Jackson's Topographer.* Dallas: Southern Methodist University Press, 1973.

McGuire, Thomas. *McGuire Papers, Containing Major Thomas McGuire's Civil War Letters; and Patriotic Documents and Other Letters from 1854 to the Turn of the Twentieth Century.* Tusquahoma, LA: Daughters of the American Revolution, 1966.

McKim, Randolph H. *A Soldier's Recollections.* New York: Longmans, Green, 1910.

McMorries, Edward Young. *History of the First Regiment Alabama Volunteer Infantry, CSA.* Montgomery, AL: Brown, 1904.

McMurray, W. J. *History of the Twentieth Tennessee Regiment Volunteer Infantry, CSA.* Nashville: The Publication Committee, 1904.

McSwain, Eleanor D., ed. *Crumbling Defenses: or the Memoirs and Reminiscences of John Logan Black, Colonel CSA.* Macon, GA: J. W. Burke, 1960.

McWhiney, Grady, Warner O. Moore Jr., and Robert F. Pace, eds. *Fear God and Walk Humbly: The Agricultural Journal of James Mallory, 1843–1877.* Tuscaloosa: University of Alabama Press, 1997.

Miers, Earl Schenck, ed. *A Rebel War Clerk's Diary.* New York: Sagamor, 1958.

Miller, J. B., *The Watauga Boys in the Great Civil War.* N.p., 1885.

Miller, J. M. *Recollections of A Pine Knot in the Lost Cause.* Greenwood, MS: Commonwealth, 1900.

Mitchell, Adele H., ed. *The Letters of John S. Mosby.* N.p.: Stuart-Mosby Historical Society, 1986.

Mixson, Frank. *Reminiscences of a Private.* Columbia, South Carolina: The State Company, 1910.

Montgomery, Franklin Alexander. *Reminiscences of a Mississippian in Peace and War, by Frank A. Montgomery, Lieutenant-Colonel First Mississippi Cavalry.* Cincinnati, OH: Robert Clarke, 1901.

Montgomery, Walter Alexander. *The Days of Old and the Years that are Past.* Charlottesville, VA: Michie, 1939.

Moore, Edward A. *The Story of a Cannoneer Under Stonewall Jackson.* Lynchburg, VA: J. P. Bell, 1910.

Morgan, James Morris. *Recollections of a Rebel Reefer.* Boston: Houghton Mifflin, 1917.

Morgan, W. H., *Personal Reminiscences of the War 1861–5.* Lynchburg, VA: J. P. Bell, 1911.

Morrison, James L., Jr., ed. *The Memoirs of Henry Heth.* Westport, CT: Greenwood, 1974.

Morton, James Watson. *The Artillery of Nathan Bedford Forrest's Cavalry.* Nashville: Publishing House of the M. E. Church, South, 1909.

Mosgrove, George Dallas. *Kentucky Cavaliers in Dixie; or The Reminiscences of a Confederate Cavalryman.* Louisville, KY: *Carrier-Journal* Job Printing, 1895.

Nanzig, Thomas P., ed. *The Civil War Memoirs of a Virginia Cavalryman: Lt. Robert T. Hubard, Jr.* Tuscaloosa: University of Alabama Press, 2007.

Neese, George M., *Three Years in the Confederate Horse Artillery.* New York: Neale, 1911.

Nicholson, James. *Stories of Dixie.* New York: American Books, 1915.

North, Thomas. *Five Years in Texas; or, What You Did Not Hear During the War from January 1861 to January 1866.* Cincinnati, OH: Elm Street Printing, 1871.

Oates, Dan, ed. *Hanging Rock Rebel: Lt. John Blue's War in West Virginia and the Shenandoah Valley.* Shippensburg, PA: Burd Street Press, 1994.

Oates, William C. *The War between the Union and Confederacy and Its Lost Opportunities.* New York: Neale, 1905.

Oeffinger, John C., ed. *A Soldier's General: The Civil War Letters of Major General Lafayette McLaws.* Chapel Hill: University of North Carolina Press, 2002.

Owen, William Miller. *In Camp and Battle with the Washington Artillery of New Orleans: A Narrative of Events during the Late Civil War from Bull Run to Appomattox and Spanish Fort.* Boston: Ticknor, 1885.

———. *A Soldier's Story of the War, Including the Marches and Battles of the Washington Artillery and of Other Louisiana Troops.* New Orleans: Clark & Hofeline, 1874.

Pate, James P., ed. *When This Evil War is Over: The Correspondence of the Francis Family, 1860–1865.* Tuscaloosa: University of Alabama Press, 2006.

Pearce, Thilbert H., ed. *Diary of Captain Henry A. Chambers.* Wendell, NC: Broadfoot's Bookmark, 1983.

Pendleton, W. F. *Confederate Diary of Captain W. F. Pendleton, January to April 1865.* Bryn Athyn, PA: privately printed, 1957.

Pfanz, Donald C., ed. *The Letters of General Richard S. Ewell: Stonewall's Successor.* Knoxville: University of Tennessee Press, 2012.

Pickens, Samuel. *Civil War Diary of Samuel Pickens, Company "D," 5th Alabama Regiment, July 27, 1862–June 17, 1865.* N.p.

Pickett, George E. *The Heart of a Soldier, as Revealed in the Intimate Letters of Genl. George E. Pickett, CSA.* New York: Seth Moyle, 1913.

Pierson, William Whatley, Jr., ed. *Whipt 'em Every Time: The Diary of Bartlett Yancey Malone, Co. H, 6th N. C. Regiment.* Jackson, TN: McCowat-Mercer Press, 1960.

Pitcock, Cynthia Dehaven, and Bill J. Gurley, eds. *I Acted from Principle: The Civil War Diary of Dr. William M. McPheeters, Confederate Surgeon in the Trans-Mississippi.* Fayetteville: University of Arkansas Press, 2002.

Polley, Joseph B. *Hood's Texas Brigade: Its Marches, Its Battles, Its Achievements.* New York: Neale, 1910.

Reagan, John H. *Memoirs: With Special Reference to Secession and the Civil War.* Austin: Pemberton, 1968.

Recollections and Reminiscences, 1861–1865. 12 vols. West Columbia: South Carolina Division, United Daughters of the Confederacy, 1990.

Reed, Thomas Benton. *A Private in Gray.* Camden, AR: T. B. Reed, 1905.

Reid, Whitelaw. *After the War: A Southern Tour May 1865, to May 1, 1866.* New York: Moore, Wilstach, & Baldwin, 1866.

Ridley, Bromfield L. *Battles and Sketches of the Army of Tennessee.* Mexico, MO: Missouri Printing, 1906.

Robertson, James I., ed. *Soldier of Southwestern Virginia: The Civil War Letters of Captain John Preston Sheffey.* Baton Rouge: Louisiana State University Press, 2004.

Robuck, J. E. *My Own Personal Experience and Observation as a Soldier in the Confederate Army During the Civil War, 1861–1865, also During Reconstruction.* Birmingham, AL: Leslie Printing, 1911.

Roman, Alfred. *Military Operations of General Beauregard, in the War Between the States, 1861 to 1865.* 2 vols. New York: Harper & Brothers, 1884.

Roper, John Herbert, ed. *Repairing the "March of Mars": The Civil War Diaries of John Samuel Apperson, Hospital Steward in the Stonewall Brigade, 1861–1865.* Macon, GA: Mercer University Press, 2001.

Rosenburg, R. B., ed. *"For the Sake of My Country": The Diary of Colonel W. W. Ward, Ninth Tennessee Cavalry, Morgan's Brigade, CSA.* Murfreesboro, TN: Southern Heritage, 1992.

Rozier, John, ed. *Granite Farm Letters: Correspondence of Edgeworth and Sallie Byrd.* Athens: University of Georgia Press, 1988.

Runge, William H., ed. *Four Years in the Confederate Artillery: The Diary of Private Henry Robinson Berkeley.* Richmond: Virginia Historical Society, 1991.

Russell, Charles Wells, ed. *The Memoirs of Colonel John S. Mosby* (Boston: Little Brown, 1917).

Sams, Anita B., ed. *With Unabated Trust: Major Henry McDaniel's Love Letters from Confederate Battlefields as Treasured in Hester McDaniel's Bonnet Box.* Monroe, GA: Historical Society of Walton County, 1977.

Sanders, Mary Elizabeth, ed. *Diary in Gray: Civil War Letters and Diary of Jared Young Sanders II.* Baton Rouge: Louisiana Genealogical & Historical Society, 1994.

Schiller, Herbert M., ed. *A Captain's War: The Letters and Diaries of William H. S. Burgwyn, 1861–1865.* Shippensburg, PA: White Mane, 1994.

Schofield, John M. *Forty-Six Years in the Army.* New York: Century, 1897.

Shaver, Lewellyn A. *A History of the Sixtieth Alabama Regiment, Gracie's Alabama Brigade.* Montgomery: Barrett & Brown, 1867.

Shelton, Perry Wayne, comp., and Shelly Morrison, ed. *Personal Letters of General Lawrence Sullivan Ross, with Other Letters.* Austin: Shelly and Richard Morrison, 1994.

Shotwell, Randolph Abbott. *The Papers of Randolph Abbott Shotwell.* Raleigh: North Carolina Historical Commission, 1931.

Silver, James W., ed. *The Confederate Soldier.* 1902. Reprint, Memphis, TN: Memphis State University Press, 1973.

Simmons, R. Hugh. *The Story of the 12th Louisiana Infantry in the Final Campaign in North Carolina with the Confederate Army of Tennessee, January to April, 1865.* N.p.: 1993.

Simpson, Harold B., ed. *The Bugle Softly Blows: The Confederate Diary of Benjamin M. Seaton.* Waco, TX: Texian Press, 1965.

Simpson, Kenrick, ed. *Worthy of Record: The Civil War and Reconstruction Diaries of Columbus Lafayette Turner.* Raleigh: North Carolina Office of Archives and History, 2008.

Skinner, Arthur N., and James L. Skinner, eds. *The Death of a Confederate: Selections from the Letters of the Archibald Smith Family of Roswell, Georgia, 1864–1956.* Athens: University of Georgia Press, 1996.

Sloan, John Alexander. *Reminiscences of the Guilford Grays, Co. B, 27th NC Regiment.* Washington, DC: R. O. Polkinhorn, 1883.

Smith, Bobbie Swearingen, ed. *A Palmetto Boy: Civil War–Era Diaries and Letters of James Adams Tillman.* Columbia: University of South Carolina Press, 2010.

Smith, Daniel Elliott Huger, ed. *Mason Smith Family Letters, 1860–1868.* Columbia: University of South Carolina Press, 1950.

Smith, William Alexander. *The Anson Guards: Company C Fourteenth Regiment North Carolina Volunteers, 1861–1865.* Charlotte, NC: Stone Publishing Co., 1914.

Snell, William R., ed. *Myra Inman: A Diary of the Civil War in East Tennessee.* Macon, GA: Mercer University Press, 2000.

Sorrel, G. Moxley. *Recollections of a Confederate Staff Officer.* New York: Neale, 1905.

Sparks, A. W. *The War Between the States as I Saw It. Reminiscent, Historical and Personal.* Tyler, TX: Lee & Burnett, 1901.

Spurlin, Charles D., ed. *The Civil War Diary of Charles A. Leuschner.* Austin, TX: Eakin, 1992.

Stegeman, John E. *These Men She Gave: Civil War Diary of Athens, Georgia.* Athens: University of Georgia Press, 1964.

Stephens, Robert Grier, Jr., ed. *Intrepid Warrior: Clement Anselm Evans.* Dayton, OH: Morningside, 1992.

Stiles, Robert. *Four Years Under Marse Robert, by Robert Stiles, Major of Artillery in the Army of Northern Virginia.* New York: Neale, 1903.

Still, William N., ed. *Odyssey in Gray: A Diary of Confederate Service, 1863–1865.* Richmond: Virginia State Library, 1979.

Stocker, Jeffrey D., ed. *From Huntsville to Appomattox: R. T. Coles's History of the 4th Regiment, Alabama Volunteer Infantry, CSA, Army of Northern Virginia.* Knoxville: University of Tennessee Press, 1996.

Stone, DeWitt Boyd, ed. *Wandering to Glory: Confederate Veterans Remember Evans's Brigade.* Columbia: University of South Carolina Press, 2002.

Stone, Henry Lane. *"Morgan's Men": A Narrative of Personal Experiences.* Louisville, KY: Brandt & Fowler, 1919.

Styple, William B., ed. *Writing and Fighting the Confederate War: The Letters of Peter Wellington Alexander, Confederate War Correspondent.* Kearny, NJ: Belle Grove, 2002.

Sullivan, Walter, ed. *The War the Women Lived: Female Voices from the Confederate South.* Nashville: J. S. Sanders, 1995.

Summers, Festus P., ed. *A Borderland Confederate.* Pittsburgh, PA: University of Pittsburgh Press, 1962.

Sutherland, Daniel E., ed. *Reminiscences of a Private: William E. Bevens of the First Arkansas Infantry, CSA.* Fayetteville: University of Arkansas Press, 1992.

Tarpley, Robert Branch. *The Tarpley Diary, 1861–1865.* Clarksville, TN: Clarksville–Montgomery County Historical Museum, 1985.

Taylor, Jay F., ed. *Reluctant Rebel: The Secret Diary of Robert Patrick, 1861–1865.* Baton Rouge: Louisiana State University Press, 1959.

Taylor, Richard. *Destruction and Reconstruction: Personal Experiences of the Late War.* New York: D. Appleton, 1879.

Taylor, Walter H. *General Lee. His Campaigns in Virginia 1861–1865 with Personal Reminiscences.* Norfolk, VA: Nusbaum Book and News, 1906.

Tennessee Civil War Veterans Questionnaires. Easley, SC: Southern Historical Press, 1985.

Thomas, Henry Walter. *History of the Doles-Cook Brigade, Army of Northern Virginia, CSA* Atlanta: Franklin, 1903.

Thompson, William T., Jr. *Family Letters by Dr. John T. Claiborne, April 1864–April 1865.* Petersburg, VA: n.p., 1961.

Todd, George T. *Sketch of History: The First Texas Regiment, Hood's Brigade, Army of Northern Virginia.* Tyler, TX: Lee & Burnett, 1901.

Tower, R. Lockwood, ed. *Lee's Adjutant: The Wartime Letters of Colonel Walter Herron Taylor, 1862–1865.* Columbia: University of South Carolina Press, 1995.

Trammell, Camilla Davis, ed. *Seven Pines: Its Occupants and Their Letters, 1825–1872.* Houston: Distributed by Southern Methodist University Press, 1986.

Trowbridge, John T. *The South: A Tour of Its Battlefields and Ruined Cities, A Journey through the Desolated States, and Talks with the People, 1867.* Macon, GA: Mercer University Press, 2006.

Tunnard, W. H. *A Southern Record: The History of the Third Regiment Louisiana Infantry.* Dayton, OH: Morningside Bookshop, 1866.

Turner, James K., ed. *My Dear Emma: War Letters of Col. James K. Edmondson, 1861–1865.* Verona, VA: McClure, 1978.

Turner, Nat S., III, ed. *A Southern Soldier's Letters Home: The Civil War Letters of Samuel A. Burney, Cobb's Georgia Legion, Army of Northern Virginia.* Macon, GA: Mercer University Press, 2002.

Turner, Norman Vincent, ed. *The March from Greensboro, North Carolina to Georgia: (May 3, 1865–May 19, 1865) as Kept by Private Thaddeus Madison Rahn Company I, 47th Georgia Regiment Volunteer Infantry.* Springfield, GA: Turner, 2002.

Underwood, George C. *History of the Twenty-Sixth Regiment of the North Carolina Troops in the Great War, 1861–1865.* Goldsboro, NC: Nash Bros., 1901.

Walker, Cornelius Irvine. *Rolls and Historical Sketch of the Tenth Regiment, South Carolina Volunteers, In the Army of the Confederate States.* Charleston: Walker, Evans, & Cogswell, 1881.

Walton, William Martin. *An Epitome of My Life: Civil War Reminiscences of Major Buck Walton.* Austin, TX: Waterloo Press, 1965.

Watkins, Samuel R. *"Co. Aytch": A Side Show of the Big Show.* New York: Collier, 1962.

Welch, Spencer Glasgow. *A Confederate Surgeon's Letters to His Wife.* New York: Neale, 1911.

Welker, David A., ed. *A Keystone Rebel: The Civil War Diary of Joseph Garey Hudson's Battery, Mississippi Volunteers.* Gettysburg: Thomas Publications, 1997.

Wheaton, John F. *Reminiscences of the Chatham Artillery During the War 1861–1865. Read at Armory Hall, March 21st, 1887.* Savannah, GA: Press of the Morning News, 1887.

Wiggins, Sarah Woolfolk, ed. *The Journals of Josiah Gorgas, 1857–1878.* Tuscaloosa: University of Alabama Press, 1995.

Wiley, Bell I., ed. *Fourteen Hundred Ninety-one Days in the Confederate Army.* 1876. Reprint, Jackson, TN: McCowat-Mercer, 1954.

———, ed. *Four Years on the Firing Line.* Jackson, TN: McCowat-Mercer, 1963.

———, ed. *This Infernal War: The Confederate Letters of Edwin H. Fay.* Austin: University of Texas Press, 1958.

Wiley, Kenneth, ed. *Norfolk Blues: The Civil War Diary of the Norfolk Light Artillery Blues.* Shippensburg, PA: Burd Street, 1997.

Willett, Elbert Decatur. *History of Company B (Originally Pickens Planters), 40th Alabama Regiment, Confederate States Army, 1862 to 1865.* Anniston, AL: Norwood, 1902.

Williams, Edward B., ed. *Rebel Brothers: The Civil War Letters of the Truehearts.* College Station: Texas A&M University Press, 1995.

Wilson, William Lyne. *A Borderland Confederate.* Pittsburgh, PA: University of Pittsburgh Press, 1962.

Winkler, A. V. *The Confederate Capital and Hood's Texas Brigade.* Austin, TX: Eugene Von Boeckmann, 1894.

Wise, John Sergeant. *The End of an Era.* Boston: Houghton Mifflin, 1899.

Withers, John, and Anita Dwyer Withers, *The Civil War through the Eyes of Lt. Col. John Withers and His Wife, Anita Dwyer Withers.* Bakersfield, CA: Diamond, 2011.

Wood, James H. *The War: "Stonewall" Jackson, His Campaigns, and Battles, the Regiment as I Saw Them.* Cumberland, MD: Eddy, 1910.

Worley, Ted R., ed. *The War Memoirs of Captain John W. Lavender, CSA*. Pine Bluff, AR: Southern Press, 1956.

Worsham, John H. *One of Jackson's Foot Cavalry*. New York: Neale, 1912.

Worsham, W. J. *The Old Nineteenth Tennessee Regiment, CSA, June 1861–April 1865*. Knoxville: Press of Paragon, 1902.

Wyeth, John Allen. *With Sabre and Scalpel: The Autobiography of a Soldier and Surgeon*. New York: Harper, 1914.

Wynne, Lewis N., and Robert A. Taylor, eds., *This War So Horrible: The Civil War Diary of Hiram Smith Williams*. Tuscaloosa: University of Alabama Press, 1993.

Yeary, Mamie, ed. *Reminiscences of the Boys in Gray, 1861–1865*. Dallas: Smith and Lamar, M. E. Church, South, 1912.

Young, John Preston. *The Seventh Tennessee Cavalry (Confederate), A History*. Nashville: Publishing House of the Methodist Episcopal Church, South, 1890.

Younger, Edward, ed. *Inside the Confederate Government: The Diary of Robert Garlick Hill Kean, Head of the Bureau of War*. New York: Oxford University Press, 1957.

Zuber, William Physick. *My Eighty Years in Texas*. Austin: University of Texas Press, 1971.

Articles

Alderson, William T., ed. "The Civil War Diary of Captain James Litton Cooper, September 30, 1861, to January 1865." *Tennessee Historical Quarterly* 15 (June 1956): 141–73.

———, ed. "The Civil War Reminiscences of John Johnston, 1861–1865" (pt. 6). *Tennessee Historical Quarterly* 14 (June 1955): 142–75.

Bahlmann, William E. "Down in the Ranks." *Journal of the Greenbrier Historical Society* 2, no. 2 (October 1979): 41–93.

Bahnson, Henry T. "The Last Days of the War." *North Carolina Booklet* 2, no. 12 (April 1903): 3–22.

Bailey, Russell B., ed. "Reminiscences of the Civil War by T. J. Walker." *Confederate Chronicles of Tennessee* 1 (1986): 37–74.

Bennett, Patricia J., ed. "Curtis R. Burke's Civil War Journal." (Pt. 4) *Indiana Magazine of History* 67 (June 1971): 129–70.

Betts, Vicki, ed. "The Civil War Letters of Elbridge Littlejohn." *Chronicles of Smith County, Texas* 18 (Summer 1979): 11–50.

Billingsley, William Clyde, ed. "'Such is War': The Confederate Memoirs of Newton Asbury Keen." (Pt. 4) *Texas Military History* 7 (Fall 1968): 176–94.

Bradwell, I. G. "Making Our Way Home from Appomattox." *Confederate Veteran Magazine* 29 (March 1921): 102–3.

Breckinridge, John C. "A Rebel Leader's Flight." *Civil War Times Illustrated* 6, no. 3 (June 1967): 4–10.

Breckinridge, William Campbell Preston. "The ex-Confederate and What He Has Done in Peace." *Southern Historical Society Papers* 20 (1892): 225–38.

Callaway, W. A. "Reminiscences of War at the Close." *Confederate Veteran Magazine* 17 (October 1909): 504–5.

Cawthon, John A., ed. "Letters of a North Louisiana Private to His Wife, 1862–1865." *Mississippi Valley Historical Review* 30 (1944): 533–50.

Crenshaw, Edward. "Diary of Captain Edward Crenshaw of the Confederate States Army." *Alabama Historical Quarterly* 2 (Winter 1940): 465–82.

Cutrer, Thomas W., ed. "'Bully for Flournoy's Regiment, We Are Some Pumkins, You'll Bet': The Civil War Letters of Virgil Sullivan Rabb, Captain, Company I Sixteenth Texas Infantry, CSA." (Pt. 2) *Military History of the Southwest* 20 (Spring 1990): 61–96.

Davis, Matthew Jack. "A Long Journey Home." *Civil War Times Illustrated* 36, no. 2 (May 1997): 14–16, 50–52, 54–55.

Duncan, J. S., ed. "Alexander Cameron in the Louisiana Campaign, 1863–1865." (Pt. 2) *Military History of Texas and the Southwest* 13, no. 1 (1976): 37–57.

Fordney, Chris, ed. "Letters From the Heart." *Civil War Times Illustrated* 34 (September/October 1995): 28, 73–82.

Fortin, Maurice S., ed. "Colonel Hilary A. Herbert's 'History of the Eighth Alabama Volunteer Regiment, CSA.'" *Alabama Historical Quarterly* 39 (1977): 5–321.

Ferguson, Hubert L., ed. "Letters of John W. Duncan, Captain Confederate States of America." *Arkansas Historical Quarterly* 9 (1960): 298–312.

Gregorie, Anne King, ed. "Diary of Captain Joseph Julius Wescoat, 1863–1865." (Pt. 2) *South Carolina Historical Magazine* 59 (April 1958): 11–23, 84–95.

Harrison, Jon, ed. "The Confederate Letters of John Simmons." *Chronicles of Smith County, Texas* 14 (Summer 1975): 25–57.

Harrison, Lowell H., ed. "The Diary of an 'Average' Confederate Soldier." *Tennessee Historical Quarterly* 29 (Fall 1970): 256–71.

Hoole, W. Stanley, ed. "Admiral on Horseback: The Diary of Brigadier General Raphael Semmes, February–May, 1865." *Alabama Review* 28 (April 1975): 129–50.

Hundley, George Jefferson. "Beginning and the Ending, Reminiscences of the First and Last Days of the War, by Gen. George Hundley." *Southern Historical Society Papers* 23 (1895): 294–313.

Manarin, Louis H., ed. "The Civil War Diary of Rufus James Woolwine." *Virginia Magazine of History and Biography* 71 (1963): 416–48.

McClure, Joseph. "A Wounded Texan's Trip Home on Crutches." *Confederate Veteran Magazine* 17 (April 1909): 162–63.

McNeilly, John S. "A Mississippi Brigade in the Last Days of the Confederacy." *Publications of the Mississippi Historical Society* 7 (1903): 33–55.

Mitchell, George. "Memories of Surrender and Journey Home." *Confederate Veteran Magazine* 17 (April 1909): 172.

Montgomery, Walter A. "Appomattox and the Return Home." *North Carolina Regiments, 1861–1865* 5 (1938): 1–13.

Moore, Frederick W., ed. "Diary of Maj. Kinloch Falconer." *Confederate Veteran Magazine* 9 (September 1901): 408–10; (October 1901): 450–53.

Mullen, James M. "Last Days of Johnston's Army, a Comrade's Experience With General L. S. Baker's Command at Weldon, N. C., During the Fifteen Days Preceding Johnston's Surrender at Greensboro, N. C." *Southern Historical Society Papers* 18 (1890). 97–113.

Nichols, James L., ed. "Reminiscing From 1861 to 1865; An 'Ex-Confed,' H. P. Morrow." *East Texas Historical Journal* 9 (March 1971): 5–19.

Oram, Richard W., ed. "Harpers Ferry to the Fall of Richmond: Letters of Colonel John De Hart Ross, CSA, 1861–1865." *West Virginia History* 45 (1984): 159–74.

Park, Robert E. "Diary of Captain Robert E. Park, Twelfth Alabama Regiment." *Southern Historical Society Papers* 3 (January–June 1887): 244–54.

Peacock, Jane Bonner, ed. "A Wartime Story: The Davidson Letters 1862–1865." *Atlanta Historical Bulletin* 20 no. 1 (1975): 8–121.

Pitcock, Cynthia Dehaven, and Bill J. Gurley, eds. "'I Acted Out of Principle': William Marcellus McPheeters, Confederate Surgeon." *Missouri Historical Review* 89 (July 1995): 384–405.

Reed, Wallace P. "Last Forlorn Hope of the Confederacy." *Southern Historical Society Papers* (1902): 117–21.

Russell, W. A. "Tragic Adventures as the War Closed." *Confederate Veteran Magazine* 22 (February 1914): 401–3.

Shingleton, Royce Gordon, ed. "South from Appomattox: The Diary of Abner R. Cox." *South Carolina Historical Magazine* 75, no. 4 (October 1974): 238–44.

———, ed. "'With Loyalty and Honor as a Patriot': Recollections of a Confederate Soldier." *Alabama Historical Quarterly* 33 (Fall/Winter 1971): 240–63.

Simmons, Slann L. C., ed. "Diary of Abram W. Clement, 1865." *South Carolina Historical Magazine* 59 (1958): 78–83.

Sterkx, H. E., ed. "Autobiography and Letters of Joel Murphree of Troy, Alabama, 1864–1865." *Alabama Historical Quarterly* 19 (Spring 1957): 170–208.

Still, William N., ed. "The Civil War Letters of Robert Tarleton." *Alabama Historical Quarterly* 32 (Spring and Summer 1970): 51–80.

Sullivan, Jack, ed. "'The Dark Clouds of War': The Civil War Diary of John Zimmerman of Alexandria. Part II The Journey Toward Appomattox." *The Alexandria Chronicle* (Fall 2014): 1–14.

Tapp, Hambleton, ed. "A Sketch of the Early Life and Service in the Confederate Army of Dr. John A. Lewis of Georgetown, Ky." *Register of the Kentucky Historical Society* 75 (April 1977): 121–40.

Townsend, Harry C. "Townsend's Diary—January–May 1865; From Petersburg to Appomattox, Thence to North Carolina to Join Johnston's Army." *Southern Historical Society Papers* 34 (1906): 99–127.

Turner, Jim. "Jim Turner, Co. G, 6th Texas Infantry, CSA, From 1861–1865." *Texana* 12, no. 2 (1974): 149–78.

Waring, Joseph I., ed. "The Diary of William G. Hinson During the War of Secession." (Pt. 2) *South Carolina Historical Magazine* 75 (April 1974): 111–20.

Williams, Charles G., ed. "A Saline Guard: The Civil War Letters of Col. William Ayers Crawford, CSA, 1861–1865." *Arkansas Historical Quarterly* 31 (Winter 1972): 328–55 (Pt. 1); 32 (Spring 1973): 71–93 (Pt. 2).

SECONDARY SOURCES

Books

Albaugh, William A., III. *Tyler, Texas, CSA.* Harrisburg, PA: Stackpole, 1958.

Andrew, Rod, Jr. *Wade Hampton: Confederate Warrior to Southern Redeemer.* Chapel Hill: University of North Carolina Press, 2008.

Andrews, J. Cutler. *The South Reports the Civil War.* Princeton, NJ: Princeton University Press, 1970.

Ash, Stephen V. *A Massacre in Memphis: The Race Riot that Shook the Nation One Year After the Civil War.* New York: Hill and Wang, 2013.

———. *Middle Tennessee Society Transformed, 1860–1870.* Baton Rouge: Louisiana State University Press, 1988.

———. *When the Yankees Came: Conflict and Chaos in the Occupied South, 1861–1865.* Chapel Hill: University of North Carolina Press, 1995.

———. *A Year in the South: Four Lives in 1865.* New York: Palgrave Macmillan, 2002.

Ashcraft, Alan C. *Civil War Texas: A Resume History.* Austin: Texas Civil War Centennial Commission, 1962.

Ayers, Edward L. *The Promise of the New South: Life after Reconstruction.* New York: Oxford University Press, 1992.

Ballard, Michael B. *A Long Shadow: Jefferson Davis and the Final Days of the Confederacy.* Jackson: University Press of Mississippi, 1986.

Benner, Judith Ann. *Sul Ross: Soldier, Statesman, Educator.* College Station: Texas A&M University Press, 1983.

Berry, Stephen W., II. *All That Makes a Man: Love and Ambition in the Civil War South.* New York: Oxford University Press, 2003.

Betts, Vicki. *Smith County, Texas, in the Civil War*. Tyler, TX: Smith County Historical Society, 1978.

Black, Robert C. *The Railroads of the Confederacy*. Chapel Hill: University of North Carolina Press, 1998.

Blair, William. *Virginia's Private War: Feeding Body and Soul in the Confederacy, 1861–1865*. New York: Oxford University Press, 1998.

Blight, David W. *Race and Reunion: The Civil War in Memory*. Cambridge, MA: Harvard University Press, 2001.

Boatner, Mark M., *The Civil War Dictionary*. New York: D. McKay, 1959.

Boethal, Paul C. *The Big Guns of Fayette*. Austin: Von-Boeckmann-Jones, 1965.

Bradley, Michael L. *This Astounding Close: The Road to Bennett Place*. Chapel Hill: University of North Carolina Press, 2000.

Broomall, James J. *Private Confederacies: The Emotional Worlds of Southern Men as Citizens and Soldiers*. Chapel Hill: University of North Carolina Press, 2019.

Calkins, Chris M. *The Final Bivouac: The Surrender Parade at Appomattox and the Disbanding of the Armies, April 10–May 20, 1865*. Lynchburg, VA: M. E. Howard, 1988.

Campbell, Randolph B. *A Southern Community in Crisis: Harrison County, Texas, 1850–1880*. Austin: Texas State Historical Association, 1983.

Cantrell, Mark Lea, and Mac Harris, eds. *Kepis and Turkey Calls: An Anthology of the War between the States in Indian Territory*. Oklahoma City: Western Heritage, 1982.

Carpenter, Bonnie. *Old Mountain City: An Early Settlement in Hayes County*. San Antonio: Naylor, 1970.

Casdorph, Paul D. *Prince John Magruder: His Life and Campaigns*. New York: John Wiley and Sons, 1996.

Cashin, Joan E., ed. *War Matters: Material Culture in the Civil War Era*. Chapel Hill: University of North Carolina Press, 2018.

———. *War Stuff: The Struggle for Human and Environmental Resources in the American Civil War*. Cambridge, UK: Cambridge University Press, 2018.

Cimbala, Paul A. *Veterans North and South: The Transition from Soldier to Civilian after the American Civil War*. Santa Barbara, CA: Praeger, 2015.

Clampitt, Bradley R., ed. *The Civil War and Reconstruction in Indian Territory*. Lincoln: University of Nebraska Press, 2015.

———. *The Confederate Heartland: Military and Civilian Morale in the Western Confederacy*. Baton Rouge: Louisiana State University Press, 2011.

———. *Occupied Vicksburg*. Baton Rouge: Louisiana State University Press, 2016.

Clark, James L. *Last Train South: The Flight of the Confederate Government from Richmond*. Jefferson, NC: McFarland, 1999.

Clark, John E. *Railroads in the Civil War: The Impact of Management on Victory and Defeat*. Baton Rouge: Louisiana State University Press, 2008.

Coco, Gregory A. *The Civil War Infantryman: In Camp, on the March, and in Battle*. Gettysburg, PA: Thomas Publications, 1996.

Connelly, Thomas L. *Autumn of Glory: The Army of Tennessee, 1862–1865*. Baton Rouge: Louisiana State University Press, 1971.

Coski, John M. *Capital Navy: The Men, Ships, and Operations of the James River Squadron*. New York: Savas Beatie, 2005.

Cotham, Edward T. *Battle on the Bay: The Civil War Struggles for Galveston*. Austin: University of Texas Press, 1998.

Cutrer, Thomas W. *Theater of a Separate War: The Civil War West of the Mississippi River, 1861–1865*. Chapel Hill: University of North Carolina Press, 2018.

Daniel, Larry J. *Soldiering in the Army of Tennessee: A Portrait of Life in a Confederate Army*. Chapel Hill: University of North Carolina Press, 2003.

Davis, Burke. *The Long Surrender*. New York: Open Road Integrated Media, 2016.

Davis, Edwin Adams. *Fallen Guidon: The Saga of General Jo Shelby's March to Mexico*. College Station: Texas A&M University Press, 1995.

Davis, William C. *An Honorable Defeat: The Last Days of the Confederate Government*. New York: Harcourt, 2001.

———. *The Orphan Brigade: The Kentucky Confederates Who Couldn't Go Home*. Garden City, New York: Doubleday, 1980.

Dean, Eric T. *Shook Over Hell: Post-Traumatic Stress, Vietnam, and the Civil War*. Cambridge, MA: Harvard University Press, 1999.

Dunkerly, Robert M. *The Confederate Surrender at Greensboro: The Final Days of the Army of Tennessee, April 1865*. Jefferson, NC: McFarland, 2013.

———. *To the Bitter End: Appomattox, Bennett Place, and the Surrenders of the Confederacy*. El Dorado Hills, CA: Savas Beatie, 2015.

Elliott, Sam Davis. *Soldier of Tennessee: General Alexander P. Stewart and the Civil War in the West*. Baton Rouge: Louisiana State University Press, 2004.

Fisher, Noel C. *War at Every Door: Partisan Politics and Guerilla Violence in East Tennessee, 1860–1869*. Chapel Hill: University of North Carolina Press, 1997.

Foote, Lorien. *The Gentlemen and the Roughs: Manhood, Honor, and Violence in the Union Army*. New York: New York University Press, 2010.

Forbes, William H. *Hauling Brass: Capt. Croft's Flying Battery, Columbus, Georgia*. Dayton, OH: Morningside House, 1993.

Foster, Gaines M. *Ghosts of the Confederacy: Defeat, the Lost Cause, and the Emergence of the New South, 1865–1913*. New York: Oxford University Press, 1987.

Gallagher, Gary. *The Confederate War: How Popular Will, Nationalism, and Military Strategy Could Not Stave Off Defeat*. Cambridge, MA: Harvard University Press, 1997.

Gallaway, B. P. *Ragged Rebel: A Common Soldier in Parsons's Texas Cavalry, 1861–1865*. Austin: University of Texas Press, 1988.

Gannon, Barbara A. *The Won Cause: Black and White Comradeship in the Grand Army of the Republic.* Chapel Hill; University of North Carolina Press, 2011.

Gile, Paul A. *The Road to Mobocracy: Popular Disorder in New York City, 1763–1834.* Chapel Hill: University of North Carolina Press, 1987.

Glaatthar, Joseph T. *General Lee's Army: From Victory to Collapse.* New York: Free Press, 2009.

———. *The March to the Sea and Beyond: Sherman's Troops in the Savannah and Carolinas Campaign.* New York: New York University Press, 1985.

Golay, Michael. *A Ruined Land: The End of the Civil War.* New York: John Wiley & Sons, 1999.

Gottschalk, Phil. *In Deadly Earnest: The History of the First Missouri Brigade, CSA.* Columbia: Missouri River Press, 1991.

Grimsley, Mark, and Brooks D. Simpson, eds. *The Collapse of the Confederacy.* Lincoln: University of Nebraska Press, 2001.

Groce, W. Todd. *Mountain Rebels: East Tennessee Confederates and the Civil War, 1860–1870.* Knoxville: University of Tennessee Press, 1999.

Hale, Douglas. *The Third Texas Cavalry in the Civil War.* Norman: University of Oklahoma Press, 1993.

Hall, Harry A. *A Johnny Reb Band from Salem: The Pride of Tarheelia.* Raleigh: North Carolina Confederate Centennial Commission, 1963.

Hess, Earl J. *The Union Soldier in Battle: Enduring the Ordeal of Combat.* Lawrence: University Press of Kansas, 1997.

Hodes, Martha. *Mourning Lincoln.* New Haven, Ct.: Yale University Press, 2015.

Holberton, William B. *Homeward Bound: The Demobilization of the Union and Confederate Armies, 1865–1866.* Mechanicsburg, PA: Stackpole, 2001.

Horn, Stanley F. *The Army of Tennessee: A Military History.* Indianapolis: Bobbs-Merrill, 1941.

Howell, H. Grady, Jr. *Going to Meet the Yankees: A History of the "Bloody Sixth" Mississippi Infantry, CSA.* Jackson, MS: Chickasaw Bayou Press, 1981.

———. *To Live and Die in Dixie: A History of the Third Mississippi Infantry, CSA.* Jackson, MS: Chickasaw Bayou Press, 1991.

Hughes, Nathaniel Cheairs. *Bentonville: The Final Battle of Sherman and Johnston.* Chapel Hill: University of North Carolina Press, 2006.

Hunt, Jeffrey William. *The Last Battle of the Civil War: Palmetto Ranch.* Austin: University of Texas Press, 2002.

Jamieson, Perry D. *Spring 1865: The Closing Campaigns of the Civil War.* Lincoln: University of Nebraska Press, 2015.

Janney, Caroline E., ed. *Petersburg to Appomattox: The End of the War in Virginia.* Chapel Hill: University of North Carolina Press, 2018.

————. *Remembering the Civil War: Reunion and the Limits of Reconciliation.* Chapel Hill: University of North Carolina Press, 2013.

Johansson, M. Jane. *Peculiar Honor: A History of the 28th Texas Cavalry, 1862–1865.* Fayetteville: University of Arkansas Press, 1998.

Jordan, Brian Matthew. *Marching Home: Union Veterans and Their Unending Civil War.* New York: W. W. Norton, 2014.

Jordan, Brian Matthew and Evan C. Rothera, eds. *The War Went On: Reconsidering the Lives of Civil War Veterans.* Baton Rouge: Louisiana State University Press, 2020.

Kentucky's Civil War, 1861–1865. Clay County, KY: Back Home in Kentucky, Inc., 2005.

Laboda, Lawrence R. *From Selma to Appomattox: The History of the Jeff Davis Artillery.* Shippensburg, PA: White Mane, 1994.

Lash, Jeffrey N. *Destroyer of the Iron Horse: General Joseph E. Johnston and Confederate Rail Transport, 1861–1865.* Kent, Ohio: Kent State University Press, 1991.

Leed, Eric J. *No Man's Land: Combat & Identity in World War I.* London: Cambridge University Press, 1979.

Linderman, Gerald. *Embattled Courage: The Experience of Combat in the American Civil War.* New York: Free Press, 1987.

Litwack, Leon F. *Been in the Storm So Long: The Aftermath of Slavery.* New York: Alfred A. Knopf, 1979.

Logue, Larry M. *To Appomattox and Beyond: The Civil War Soldier in War and Peace.* Chicago: Ivan R. Dee, 1996.

Logue, Larry M. and Michael Barton, eds. *The Civil War Veteran: A Historical Reader.* New York: New York University Press, 2007.

Losson, Christopher. *Tennessee's Forgotten Warriors: Frank Cheatham and His Confederate Division.* Knoxville: University of Tennessee Press, 1989.

Marten, James. *Sing Not War: The Lives of Union and Confederate Veterans in Gilded Age America.* Chapel Hill: University of North Carolina Press, 2011.

Marvel, William A. *Andersonville: The Last Depot.* Chapel Hill: University of North Carolina Press, 1994.

————. *Lee's Last Retreat: The Flight to Appomattox.* Chapel Hill: University of North Carolina Press, 2002.

————. *A Place Called Appomattox.* Chapel Hill: University of North Carolina Press, 2002.

McCaffrey, James M. *This Band of Heroes: Granbury's Texas Brigade, CSA.* Austin: Eakin, 1985.

McClurken, Jeffrey W. *Take Care of the Living: Reconstructing Confederate Veteran Families in Virginia.* Charlottesville: University of Virginia Press, 2009.

McComb, David G. *Galveston: A History.* Austin: University of Texas Press, 1986.

McIlwain, Christopher Lyle. *Alabama 1865: From Civil War to Uncivil Peace.* Tuscaloosa: University of Alabama Press, 2016.

McPherson, James M. *For Cause and Comrades: Why Men Fought in the Civil War.* New York: Oxford University Press, 1997.

Mitchell, Reid. *Civil War Soldiers.* New York: Viking, 1988.

———. *The Vacant Chair: The Northern Soldier Leaves Home.* New York: Oxford University Press, 1993.

Neff, Robert O. *Tennessee's Battered Brigadier: The Life of General Joseph B. Palmer CSA.* Franklin, TN: Hillsboro, 2000.

Noe, Kenneth W. *Reluctant Rebels: The Confederates Who Joined the Army after 1861.* Chapel Hill: University of North Carolina Press, 2010.

Oates, Stephen B. *Confederate Cavalry West of the River.* Austin: University of Texas Press, 1961.

O'Flaherty, Daniel. *General Jo Shelby, Undefeated Rebel.* Chapel Hill: University of North Carolina Press, 1954.

Parks, Joseph Howard. *General Edmund Kirby Smith, CSA.* Baton Rouge: Louisiana State University Press, 1954.

Pfanz, Donald C. *Richard S. Ewell: A Soldier's Life.* Chapel Hill: University of North Carolina Press, 2000.

Phillips, Jason. *Diehard Rebels: The Confederate Culture of Invincibility.* Athens: University of Georgia Press, 2007.

Rable, George C. *But There Was No Peace: The Role of Violence in the Politics of Reconstruction.* Athens: University of Georgia Press, 2007.

———. *Civil Wars: Women and the Crisis of Southern Nationalism.* Urbana: University of Illinois Press, 1991.

———. *God's Almost Chosen Peoples: A Religious History of the American Civil War.* Chapel Hill: University of North Carolina Press, 2010.

Radley, Kenneth. *Rebel Watchdog: The Confederate States Army Provost Guard.* Baton Rouge: Louisiana State University Press, 1989.

Ramsdell, Charles W. *Reconstruction in Texas.* New York: Columbia University Press, 1910.

Rolle, Andrew F. *The Lost Cause: The Confederate Exodus to Mexico.* Norman: University of Oklahoma Press, 1965.

Rosenburg, R. B. *Living Monuments: Confederate Soldiers' Homes in the New South.* Chapel Hill: University of North Carolina Press, 1993.

Sheehan-Dean, Aaron, ed. *A Companion to the U.S. Civil War.* 2 vols. Chichester, West Sussex, UK: John Wiley & Sons, 2014.

———, ed. *The View from the Ground: Experiences of Civil War Soldiers.* Lexington: University of Kentucky Press, 2007.

———. *Why Confederates Fought: Family and Nation in Civil War Virginia.* Chapel Hill: University of North Carolina Press, 2007.

Silkenat, David. *Moments of Despair: Suicide, Divorce, and Debt in Civil War Era North Carolina.* Chapel Hill: University of North Carolina Press, 2011.

Silverthorne, Elizabeth. *Ashbel Smith of Texas: Pioneer, Patriot, Statesman, 1805–1886.* College Station: Texas A&M University Press, 1982.

Sparrow, John C. *History of Personnel Demobilization in the United States Army.* Washington, DC: Department of the Army, 1952.

Sternhell, Yael A. *Routes of War: The World of Movement in the Confederate South.* Cambridge, MA: Harvard University Press, 2012.

Trudeau, Noah Andre. *Out of the Storm: The End of the Civil War, April–June, 1865.* Boston: Little, Brown, 1994.

Tucker, Phillip Thomas. *The Final Fury: Palmito Ranch, the Last Battle of the Civil War.* Mechanicsburg, PA: Stackpole, 2001.

Ural, Susannah J. *Hood's Texas Brigade: The Soldiers and Families of the Confederacy's Most Celebrated Unit.* Baton Rouge: Louisiana State University Press, 2017.

Varon, Elizabeth. *Appomattox: Victory, Defeat, and Freedom at the End of the Civil War.* New York: Oxford University Press, 2014.

Wallace, Ernest. *Texas in Turmoil: The Saga of Texas, 1849–1875.* Austin: Steck-Vaughan, 1965.

Wecter, Dixon, *When Johnny Comes Marching Home.* Cambridge, MA: Houghton Mifflin, 1944.

Weddle, Robert S. *Plow-Horse Cavalry: The Caney Creek Boys of the 34th Texas.* Austin: Madrona Press, 1974.

Wheelan, Joseph. *The Last Full Measure: The Final Days of the Civil War.* Boston: Da Capo, 2016.

Wiley, Bell I. *The Life of Johnny Reb: The Common Soldier of the Confederacy.* Baton Rouge: Louisiana State University Press, 1984.

Williams, T. Harry. *P. G. T. Beauregard: Napoleon in Gray.* Baton Rouge: Louisiana State University Press, 1955.

Wilson, Charles Reagan. *Baptized in Blood: The Religion of the Lost Cause, 1865–1920.* Athens: University of Georgia Press, 1980.

Wingfield, Marshall. *General A. P. Stewart: His Life and Letters.* Memphis: West Tennessee Historical Society, 1954.

Winik, Jay. *April 1865.* New York: Harper Collins, 2010.

Winters, John D. *The Civil War in Louisiana.* Baton Rouge: Louisiana State University Press, 1963.

Womack, Bob. *Call Forth the Mighty Men.* Bessemer, AL: Colonial Press, 1987.

Wyatt-Brown, Bertram. *The Shaping of Southern Culture: Honor, Grace, and War, 1760s–1880s.* Chapel Hill: University of North Carolina Press, 2000.

———. *Southern Honor: Ethics and Behavior in the Old South.* New York: Oxford University Press, 1982.

Articles

Abbott, Edith. "The Civil War and the Crime Wave of 1865–1870." *Social Service Review* 51 (March 1977): 71–93.

Ashcraft, Allan C. "Confederate Indian Territory Conditions in 1865." *Chronicles of Oklahoma* 42 (Winter 1964–1965): 421–28.

Brown, Gayle Ann. "Confederate Surrenders in Indian Territory." *Journal of the West* 12, no. 3 (1973): 455–61.

Clampitt, Bradley R. "The Breakup: The Collapse of the Confederate Trans-Mississippi Army in Texas, 1865." *Southwestern Historical Quarterly* 108 (April 2005): 498–534.

———. "'An Indian Shall Not Spill an Indian's Blood': The Confederate-Indian Conference at Camp Napoleon, Indian Territory, 1865." *Chronicles of Oklahoma* 83 (Spring 2005): 34–53.

———. "'Not Intended to Dispossess Females': Southern Women and Civil War Amnesty" *Civil War History* 56 (December 2010): 325–49.

———. "Two Degrees of Rebellion: Amnesty and Texans after the Civil War." *Civil War History* 52 (September 2006): 255–81.

Damico, John Kelly. "Confederate Soldiers Take Matters into Their Own Hands: The End of the Civil War in North Louisiana." *Louisiana History* 39, no. 2 (1998): 189–205.

Davis, William C. "John C. Breckinridge." *Civil War Times Illustrated* 6, no. 3 (June 1967): 11–18.

Fairclough, Adam. "'Scalawags,' Southern Honor, and the Lost Cause: Explaining the Fatal Encounter of James H. Cosgrove and Edward L. Pierson." *Journal of Southern History* 77 (November 2011): 799–826.

Frank, Stephen. "'Rendering Aid and Comfort': Images of Fatherhood in the Letters of Civil War Soldiers from Massachusetts and Michigan." *Journal of Social History* 26 (Fall 1992): 5–32.

Janney, Caroline E. "Free to Go Where We Liked: The Army of Northern Virginia After Appomattox." *Journal of the Civil War Era* 9 (March 2019): 4–28.

Jewell, James Robbins, ed. "Last Days of the War with Confederacy's Boy General: Captain Theodore Garnett with Roberts's North Carolina Cavalry Brigade to Appomattox." *North Carolina Historical Review* 81, no. 1 (January 2004): 73–96.

Kaufman, Patricia A. "An Aristocratic Planter Goes to War." *La Posta* (Third Quarter, 2014): 27–30.

Lale, Max. "The Military Occupation of Marshall, Texas, by the 8th Illinois Volunteer Infantry U. S. A., 1865." *Military History of Texas and the Southwest* 13, no. 3 (1976): 39–47.

Marten, James. "Fatherhood in the Confederacy: Southern Soldiers and Their Children." *Journal of Southern History* 63 (May 1997): 269–92.

Oates, Stephen B. "Texas Under the Secessionists." *Southwestern Historical Quarterly* 67 (October 1963): 167–212.

Pettegrew, John. "The Soldier's Faith: Turn-of-the-Century Memory of the Civil War and the Emergence of Modern American Nationalism." *Journal of Contemporary History* 31 (1996): 49–73.

Sheehan-Dean, Aaron. "The Long Civil War: A Historiography of the Consequences of the Civil War." *Virginia Magazine of History and Biography* 119 (January 2011): 106–53.

Simmons, R. Hugh. "The 12th Louisiana Infantry in North Carolina, January–April, 1865." *Louisiana History* 36, no. 1 (1995): 77–108.

Sommerville, Diane Miller. "'A Burden Too Heavy to Bear': War Trauma, Suicide, and Confederate Soldiers." *Civil War History* 59 (December 2013): 453–91.

Tarbell, Ida M. "Disbanding the Confederate Army" (1901; reprint, *Civil War Times Illustrated* 6, no. 9 (January 1968): 10–19).

Thomas, Emory M. "Rebel Nationalism: E. H. Cushing and the Confederate Experience." *Southwestern Historical Quarterly* 73 (January 1970): 343–55.

White, William W. "The Disintegration of an Army: Confederate Forces in Texas, April–June, 1865." *East Texas Historical Journal* 26, no. 2 (1988): 40–47.

Wooster, Ralph A., and Robert Wooster, "'Rarin' for a Fight': Texans in the Confederate Army." *Southwestern Historical Quarterly* 84 (April 1981): 387–426.

Thesis

Hendricks, Howard O. "Imperiled City: The Movements of the Union and Confederate Armies Toward Greensboro in the Closing Days of the Civil War in North Carolina." (MA thesis, University of North Carolina, Greensboro, 1987).

INDEX